Hospitality Management Strategies

Hospitality Management Strategies

Ronald A. Nykiel, Ph.D., CHA, CHE

PEARSON
Prentice Hall

Prentice Hall
Upper Saddle River, NJ 07458

Library of Congress Cataloging-in-Publication Data

Nykiel, Ronald A.
   Hospitality management strategies / Ronald A. Nykiel.
      p. cm.
   Includes bibliographical references and index.
   ISBN 0-13-061876-4
   1. Hospitality industry—Management. 2. Hospitality industry—Management—Case
studies. I. Title.
   TX911.3.M27N95 2005
   647.94'068—dc22

2003069009

Executive Editor: Vernon R. Anthony
Associate Editor: Marion Gottlieb
Executive Assistant: Nancy Kesterson
Editorial Assistant: Beth Dyke
Director of Manufacturing and Production: Bruce Johnson
Managing Editor: Mary Carnis
Production Liaison: Adele M. Kupchik
Creative Director: Cheryl Asherman
Manufacturing Manager: Ilene Sanford
Manufacturing Buyer: Cathleen Petersen
Production Editor: Linda Zuk, WordCrafters

Senior Marketing Manager: Ryan DeGrote
Senior Marketing Coordinator: Elizabeth Farrell
Marketing Assistant: Les Roberts
Composition: Pine Tree Composition, Inc.
Full-Service Project Management: WordCrafters Editorial Services, Inc.
Cover Designer: Ruta Fiorino
Cover Image: Marc Carter, Getty Images/ Stone/Allstock
Printer/Binder: R.R. Donnelley & Sons Co.
Cover Printer: Phoenix Color Corp.

Pearson Education LTD.
Pearson Education Singapore, Pte. Ltd
Pearson Education, Canada, Ltd
Pearson Education–Japan

Pearson Education Australia PTY, Limited
Pearson Education North Asia Ltd
Pearson Educación de Mexico, S.A. de C.V.
Pearson Education Malaysia, Pte. Ltd

10 9 8 7 6 5 4 3
ISBN 0-13-061876-4

Brief Contents

v

Contents

Access this book's Companion Website at: http://www.prenhall.com/nykiel

PART 4   The Functional Strategies of Human Resources, Technology, and Purchasing   237

Chapter 10   Human Resource Management Strategies   239

Chapter 11   Technology Management and Applications   257

Chapter 12   Purchasing Concepts   272

List of Cases

Preface

Just as the hospitality industry has evolved from individually owned and developed enterprises to public global corporations, management strategies have also changed. While we still see the entrepreneur launching new brands and service concepts, success is being measured by revenue per available customer and earnings per share. The industry and management strategies remain dynamic. Macro trends such as labor availability, new technologies, economic ups and downs, terrorism, security, and globalization—to name a few—are having and will continue to have substantial impact on management strategies.

This book provides a perspective on how and why management strategies are changing. It examines the external and internal driving forces behind the changes. Focal points include strategy selection, positioning, and business development techniques and options. Further, major managerial strategy areas are viewed through select case examples that exemplify the strategy application. The book also provides insight into the strategic planning process and emerging organizational and operating concepts.

The text discusses managerial strategies and concepts in six parts, beginning with Part 1, Understanding Strategy, Forces, Selection, and Positioning. Part 2 delineates the Growth Strategies of Development, Financial Options, and Brand Strategy. Part 3 focuses on the Offensive (Revenue Development) Strategies of Marketing, Sales, and Customer Retention. Part 4 provides a look at the Functional Managerial Strategies of Human Resources, Technology, and Purchasing. Part 5 presents the Defensive (Business Preservation) Strategies of Risk Management, Crisis Management, and Communications. Finally, Part 6 focuses on the Implementation of Strategic Planning, Organizational and Operational Concepts, and Leadership.

This book provides a global perspective of the hospitality industry. It focuses on disciplines and concepts that impact and have applicability to all sectors of the industry. Through the many examples, cases, and illustrations, key managerial strategies are delineated for brands, customer service, communications, crisis management, ethics, finance, human resources, leadership, marketing, purchasing, operations, risk management, security, organizational concepts, sales, and technology. Each of these disciplines and concepts is viewed with industry sector examples. Sectors include: attractions, clubs, food service, gaming, lodging, meetings and conventions, and almost all travel and tourism-related segments.

Each chapter begins with a set of objectives for the chapter and concludes with a summation and list of key terms and concepts. Also, discussion questions and case examples are presented. Throughout the text you will see boxes highlighting ethics and technology. Virtually every management function and activity will continue to undergo change as a result of technology. Likewise, irrespective of the discipline, managerial strategies and actions are subject to ethical considerations. The highlights point out applications, considerations, developments, and potential future directions related to each chapter topic. Finally, a comprehensive glossary provides clear definitions of the many acronyms and industry-related terms.

Acknowledgments

I would like to thank the following individuals: Dr. Jim Myers, author of *Marketing Structure Analysis;* and Peter F. Drucker, Professor of Marketing emeritus at the Claremont Graduate School, for sharing his knowledge on market positioning and brand preference. Thank you, Dr. Robert Buzzell, former Sebastian S. Kresge Professor of Marketing at the Harvard University Graduate School of Business, for helping me remain academically active in the field. To Eric Orkin, sincere thanks for the healthy discussions on pricing and managing revenue. My special appreciation goes to Bill Marriott, Chairman of the Marriott Corporation; the late Kemmons Wilson, Founder of Holiday Inns and the Wilson Companies; Mike Rose, Chairman of Gaylord Entertainment and former Chairman of the Promus Companies; Juergen Bartels, President of Meridien Hotels and Resorts; Bill Hulett, former President of Stouffer Hotels and Resorts; and Jim Biggar, former Chairman and CEO of Nestlé Enterprises, Inc., for the opportunities they provided me and the knowledge I gained from exposure to their leadership.

A special thanks to the great associations that serve the many sectors of the industry and have provided wonderful learning opportunities through their educational programs and conference agendas. Thank you, American Hotel & Lodging Association, the National Restaurant Association, the International Hotel and Restaurant Association, the Travel Industry Association of America, and UCLA Extension Program for their outstanding conferences.

I would like to thank the many industry friends, acquaintances, and leaders whom I have been fortunate to encounter during the past 30 years in the industry. Your entrepreneurial ideas, examples of leadership, and accomplishments have contributed greatly to the shaping of the industry and the evolution of the concepts in this book.

A debt of gratitude goes to the following reviewers, who provided helpful insights and suggestions for improvement of the manuscript: Kevin Cooper, Cal Poly San Luis Obispo; Chris Roberts, University of Massachusetts; and Jinlin Zhao, Florida International University.

A special acknowledgment to my father for sharing with me his 40 years of managerial wisdom during his career at Colgate-Palmolive Company; to my son Ron, for keeping me technologically up to date; and to my wife Karen, for listening to both my good and bad ideas during my managerial career.

Finally, a special thanks to Trish, my secretary, and Pete, my research assistant, for all their patience and help during this endeavor.

Discover the Supplements Accompanying This Book

THE PRENTICE HALL VIRTUAL LEARNING ENVIRONMENT

Technology is a constantly growing and changing aspect of our field that is creating a need for content and resources. To address this emerging need, Prentice Hall has developed an online learning environment for students and professors alike to support *Hospitality Management Strategies*.

Our goal is to build on and enhance what the textbook already offers by featuring a variety of meaningful resources.

FOR THE PROFESSOR—

The Instructor's Manual is available in two formats:

1. Print
2. Online through the www. prenhall.com website—password protected

The Instructor's Manual provides chapter overviews, teaching sugestions, learning assessment file, transparency masters, glossary of key terms and concepts, and a suggested instructor syllabus.

FOR THE STUDENT—

A Student Companion Website, accessed at www.prenhall.com/nykiel, contains self-evaluation questions, key terms and definitions, and PowerPoint slides for each chapter.

About the Author

Author, business executive, lecturer, professor, and founder are all appropriate descriptions for Dr. Ronald A. Nykiel. He began his business career with IBM in the Human Resources department. With Xerox and Marriott Corporation he held managerial positions in market research and strategic and operational planning. He has been a senior officer of Holiday Corporation, serving in a development and strategic planning capacity. As a senior officer of Ramada Incorporated, Nestlé, Stouffer Hotel Company, and Grand Met's Pearle Incorporated, Dr. Nykiel was responsible for all brand management and marketing functions worldwide.

Dr. Nykiel has served on the boards of associations, corporations, public television, and universities. He has consulted with two United States Presidential Commissions, various other federal and state entities, and numerous corporations. He founded World Institute Associates, a global business strategy and marketing consulting firm, and he serves as its chairman.

Dr. Nykiel has addressed many corporate and association groups and has lectured at the Harvard Graduate School of Business and other prestigious universities on such subjects as corporate strategy, marketing, consumer behavior, brand management, service excellence, and executive development. He is recognized as an international authority in the field of hospitality, travel and tourism, and marketing, and is the author of twelve books in the hospitality and marketing areas on business strategy, marketing, consumer behavior, and service excellence. He has appeared on national television and radio and has contributed to a variety of journals, magazines, and other publications.

Dr. Nykiel received his Bachelor of Arts degree in Liberal Arts from the State University of New York, his Master of Arts degree in Spanish from the Pennsylvania State University, and his Ph.D. in Management and Administration from Walden University. He also holds the Certified Hotel Administrator (CHA) and Certified Hospitality Educator (CHE) designation from the Educational Institute of the American Hotel and Lodging Association. Dr. Nykiel is currently the Conrad N. Hilton Distinguished Chair in Hotel and Restaurant Management at the Conrad N. Hilton College at the University of Houston, Chairman of the Hospitality Industry Hall of Honor, and publisher of the *Hospitality Business Review*.

PART 1

Understanding Strategy, Forces, Selection, and Positioning

Part 1 consists of the first three chapters of the text and focuses upon understanding the strategies and forces that influence hospitality management strategies. It views the historic development of the industry and the strategic forces behind that development. In Chapter 1 this review includes the identification of significant events, concepts, and individual entrepreneurs who shaped the hospitality industry through managerial and developmental concepts.

This part looks into both the "external" forces that had a major impact on the industry and related managerial strategies and the "internal" forces that drove managerial strategy. Chapter 2 delineates these macro forces, relating each to specific industry and segment developments.

In Chapter 3, a delineation of strategy selection and positioning options are covered with specific examples of approaches to hospitality industry management strategies.

Each chapter in Part 1 concludes with applicable case examples and related discussion questions. These case examples include companies and brands from the major sectors of the hospitality industry.

Chapter 1

Hospitality Management Strategies in Perspective

CHAPTER OBJECTIVES

- To identify the major sectors of the hospitality industry
- To provide an understanding of the dynamics and evolution of the industry
- To describe management strategies that played a major role in the development of the industry
- To identify selected focal points of management strategies

The hospitality industry remains extremely dynamic. The industry is one in which many different management strategies have fostered change. Product and brand segmentation, franchising, real estate investment trusts, and new product concepts are but a few of the strategic driving forces that cause this industry to be so dynamic. Furthermore, it is an industry that was, and is to a great extent today, driven by entrepreneurs, changes in legislation, and the dynamics of the marketplace. These marketplace dynamics include a changing population mix, the globalization of travel, multiculturalism, and a plethora of psychographic trends.[1] All of these forces have contributed to an industry that keeps redefining itself with new concepts, new segments, and new ideas.

A concise definition for an industry that has experienced rapid development and continual change is virtually impossible. Moreover, definitions of the hospitality industry are often limited by the unique viewpoints of sectors within the industry. A hotelier might see the industry defined as rooms with food and beverage. A restaurateur might picture the industry as a quality dining experience with the focus on menu offerings and good service. An airline executive might believe that providing travel to people for business or pleasure defines the industry best. All of these viewpoints fit under a wider perspective that defines the hospitality industry in terms of products and services offered to consumers away from home. As shown in Figure 1-1, the industry, in its broadest perspective, encompasses travel, lodging, food service, clubs, gaming, attractions, entertainment, and recreation.

This chapter also provides a historic perspective on the growth of brands, concepts of development, and other key strategies that have helped shape what we know as today's hospitality industry. Many of these management strategies, such as franchising, brand development, and frequency programs, have propelled growth for the major sectors of the industry.

TECHNOLOGY

Throughout the history of the hospitality industry, technological invention has propelled change. Electricity, telex, telephones, television, trains, automobiles, airplanes, air conditioning, and refrigeration are but a few of the inventions of technology to change the hospitality industry during its development era.

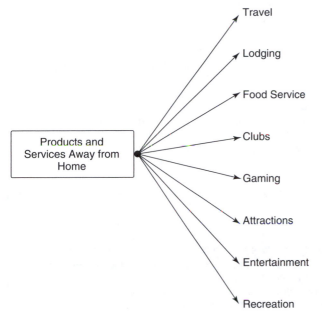

Figure 1–1   Sectors of the Hospitality Industry
Source: R. A. Nykiel, *Marketing in the Hospitality Industry,* (East Lansing, MI: Educational Institute of the American Hotel and Lodging Association, 1997): 4.

A HISTORICAL PERSPECTIVE—THE GROWTH OF THE INDUSTRY

Restaurants with white tablecloths, hotels with grand ballrooms, business executives pampered by their favorite airlines with personalized matches and reserved seats—these are traditional and, to some extent, obsolete images of the hospitality industry. Today, more than just the personalized matches are gone. New images of the industry abound, created by the way airlines, hotels, and foodservice establishments have developed and marketed products and services to meet the changing needs of consumers. Figure 1-2 briefly identifies some milestones of industry development prompted by the changing needs of consumers.

Historically, the consumer's perception of the industry centered on full-service independent hotels, business travelers, and the "glory" of travel. Conrad Hilton changed the image that consumers had of the lodging industry by creating one of the first powerful hotel brands. The chain of hotels and the name "Hilton" positioned the concept of a brand (Hilton) to be synonymous with the word "hotel" in the minds of consumers across the country and eventually across the globe.

New concepts in lodging evolved as other great entrepreneurs conceived new products and services. Kemmons Wilson founded what would become the world's largest single lodging chain, Holiday Inn. In the 1950s, Holiday Inn developed a lodging product that met the needs of a rapidly growing consumer segment—the interstate auto traveler. The adventure of the family vacation replaced the traditional image of the glory of travel. Across the market, the brand name "Holiday Inn" became synonymous with the word "motel." The

1800s	Private rooms become the norm in hotels.
1859	The first hotel elevator is installed in New York's Fifth Avenue Hotel.
1860–1900	The Manhattan cocktail is invented.
	The Tremont House in Boston becomes the first hotel to have indoor plumbing, free soap, and guestroom doors with locks.
	The Waiters and Bartenders National Union is formed.
1900	The American Hotel Association is formed.
1920s	More new hotels are built than during any other 10-year period before or since, resulting in a record low occupancy rate of 51% in 1933.
1929	The first airport hotel opens in Oakland, California.
1935	Howard Johnson initiates the first hospitality industry franchise.
1940	The first hotel management contract is signed by InterContinental Hotels.
1946	The hotel industry experiences its highest occupancy rate ever—95%.
1950s	Holiday Inn's roadside properties begin the era of the motel.
1960s	Market segmentation and product segmentation begin in earnest in the hotel industry.
	Motor hotels and roadside inns develop along the interstate highway system.
1970s	Spectacular design and architecture (exemplified by the Hyatt Regency Hotel in Atlanta) establish a new era of the hotel.
1980s	Major developments in computers, telecommunications, and other technological areas result in sophisticated reservation systems.
	Industry deregulation arrives.
	Full product segmentation occurs in lodging with brands ranging from economy/budget lines to full-service hotels, all-suite properties, resorts, and mega-hotels.
1990s	Travel-related companies emerge as multi-billion-dollar forces in lodging, foodservice, air transportation, and travel-related businesses.
	Travel purchasing systems emerge and purchasing consortiums develop into service companies.
2000s	Consumer-driven technology results in paperless airline tickets, keyless doors, and at-home purchasing and delivery systems.
	Supersonic mass passenger aircraft coupled with computer-directed ground transport usher in a new age of travel.

Figure 1–2   Some Milestones of Industry Development

continued success of Holiday Inn Worldwide can be attributed to its ability to change its product and associated levels of service to reach many market segments and fulfill many different consumer segment needs.

The hospitality industry grew rapidly due to the genius and hard work of other founders who built great hospitality companies. J. Willard and Alice Marriott developed foodservice concepts (such as the Hot Shoppes Cafeteria and in-flight catering) that met the needs of particular market segments. Their son, Bill Marriott, continued their work in the hotel and food business and made the Marriott brand recognized around the world.

These pioneers and entrepreneurs also established their future company's code of ethics and managerial climate/work environment through their work and behavioral examples.

New food concepts became globally recognized brands as companies targeted the ever-changing needs of consumers. McDonald's, Kentucky Fried Chicken (KFC), and other companies went beyond being just food concepts; they became delivery systems as well that specifically addressed the needs of consumers.

Today, Hilton and Marriott are multi-billion-dollar companies and are very different from what they were even just 20 years ago. For that matter, most of the growth firms in the hospitality industry today are very different from what they were 10 years or even 5 years ago. Their products and services evolved from consumers' needs, their creativity resulted in new forms of businesses, and their profits from sales of products and services have grown substantially.

BRAND NAMES EMERGE

Just as the lodging and foodservice sectors of the industry saw their founders' names become household words representing globally recognized brands, other sectors of the industry saw this happen as well. The name "Walt Disney" became a brand in the entertainment and attractions sectors, and the name "Curt Carlson" became associated with the travel management and services sectors of hospitality. These individuals conceived products and services that turned into brands that not only fulfilled the needs of consumers but also stimulated others to develop more industry products and services and more brands.[2]

Millions of consumers around the globe developed sets of expectations associated with the logos and the signage of hospitality brands. The same development and growth of brands held true for airlines (American, Delta, United, etc.) and car rental firms (Avis, Hertz, etc.). Consumers responded to products and services that met their needs, and management quickly developed the brand names associated with those products and services. Brand strategies emerged along with new segmentations and product development.

As products and services developed by the industry emerged, so did new marketing, finance, and operating strategies evolve. As the firms grew, they had to refocus their managerial strategies from pure growth to include multiple service-level perspectives and to frequently segment targeted products and services. Management had to develop strategies related to both internal and external constituencies. As shown in Figure 1-3, the focal points of manage-

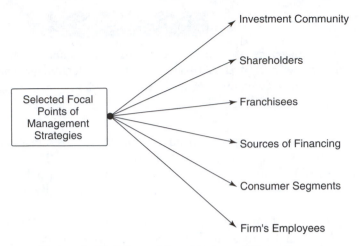

Figure 1–3   Selected Focal Points of Management

ment strategies today include a much wider scope, including everything from employees to sources of financing to public opinion.

Today, management strategies involve traditional growth strategies, operational strategies, and also external managerial strategies required of a sophisticated, large, and complex industry—the hospitality industry. In the next chapter we take a closer look at these external and internal driving forces.

CHAPTER REVIEW

People, events, inventions, business development concepts, and changes in the law all helped shape today's hospitality industry. Entrepreneurial management and driving forces shaped the growth of the industry. Today, managerial focus must address a more complex environment where corporate audiences and related pressures play a substantially greater role. Management strategies must take into consideration the internal complexities of running and growing the business as well as the external constituencies, trends, and competition. The hospitality industry remains a growth industry where new ideas and concepts are embraced and readily duplicated. It is also an industry whose focus has turned to performance with increasing public (shareholder) interest.

KEY CONCEPTS/TERMS

Brand   Strategy

DISCUSSION QUESTIONS

1. In viewing the various sectors of the hospitality industry (e.g., airlines, attractions, car rental, cruise lines), what do you believe are the greatest driving forces or factors that contributed to that sector's growth?
2. How important do you believe the individual entrepreneurs were in building the brands they founded?
3. Why have some sectors of the hospitality industry consolidated faster than others (e.g., airlines versus food service)?
4. Do you feel the emphasis on financial performance has helped or hurt the development of brands in the industry?

ENDNOTES

1. R. A. Nykiel, "Meeting the Challenges in the Next Millennium," *Hospitality Business Review* 2, no. 2 (Spring 1999): 28–32.
2. R. A. Nykiel, *Marketing in the Hospitality Industry,* 3rd ed. (East Lansing, MI: Educational Institute of the American Hotel and Lodging Association, 1997): 4.

CASE 1

Harland Sanders—Kentucky Fried Chicken/KFC

In this chapter we stated that it was the entrepreneurial spirit and individual drive that were behind many business successes. We often think of entrepreneurs as young, aggressive individuals. This case example is about an entrepreneur who blossomed into one of the world's most successful franchisees at the time most people retire.

Colonel Harland Sanders, born September 9, 1890, began actively franchising his chicken business at the age of 65. Now, the Kentucky Fried Chicken business he started has grown to be one of the largest retail foodservice systems in the world. And Colonel Sanders, a quick-service restaurant pioneer, has become a symbol of entrepreneurial spirit. In fact, today KFC serves over two billion chicken dinners and operates in more than 82 countries.

When the Colonel was 6, his father died. His mother was forced to go to work, and young Harland had to take care of his 3-year-old brother and baby sister. This meant doing much of the family cooking. By the age of 7, he was master of a score of regional dishes.

At age 10, he got his first job working on a nearby farm for $2 a month. When he was 12, his mother remarried and he left his home near Henryville, Indiana, for a job on a more distant farm. He held a series of jobs over the next few years, first as a 15-year-old streetcar conductor, and then as a 16-year-old private, soldiering for 6 months in Cuba.

After that he was a railroad fireman, studied law by correspondence, practiced in justice-of-the-peace courts, sold insurance, operated an Ohio River steamboat ferry, sold tires, and operated service stations. When he was 40, the Colonel began cooking for hungry travelers who stopped at his service station in Corbin, Kentucky. He didn't have a restaurant then, but served folks on his own dining table in the living quarters of his service station.

As more people started coming just for food, he moved across the street to a motel and restaurant that seated 142 people. Over the next 9 years, he perfected his secret blend of 11 herbs and spices and the basic cooking technique that is still used today.

Sanders' fame grew. Governor Ruby Laffoon made him a Kentucky Colonel in 1935 in recognition of his contributions to the state's cuisine. And in 1939, his establishment was first listed in Duncan Hines' "Adventures in Good Eating."

In the early 1950s a new interstate highway was planned to bypass the town of Corbin. Seeing an end to his business, the Colonel auctioned off his operations. After paying his bills, he was reduced to living on his $105 Social Security checks.

Confident of the quality of his fried chicken, the Colonel devoted himself to the chicken franchising business that he started in 1952. He traveled across the country by car from restaurant to restaurant, cooking batches of chicken for restaurant owners and their employees. If the reaction was favorable, he entered into a handshake agreement on a deal that stipulated a payment to him of a nickel for each chicken the restaurant sold. By 1964, Colonel Sanders had more than 600 franchised outlets for his chicken in the United States and Canada. That year, he sold his interest in the U.S. company for $2 million to a group of investors including John Y. Brown, Jr., who later was governor of Kentucky from 1980 to 1984. The Colonel remained a public spokesman for the company. In 1976, an independent survey ranked the Colonel as the world's second most recognized celebrity.

Until he was fatally stricken with leukemia in 1980 at the age of 90, the Colonel traveled 250,000 miles a year visiting the KFC empire he founded.

Kentucky Fried Chicken became a subsidiary of R.J. Reynolds Industries, Inc. (now RJR Nabisco, Inc.), when Heublein, Inc., was acquired by Reynolds in 1982. KFC was acquired in October 1986 from RJR Nabisco by PepsiCo, Inc., for approximately $840 million.

In January 1997, PepsiCo announced the spin-off of its quick-service restaurants—KFC, Taco Bell, and Pizza Hut—into an independent restaurant company. TRICON Global Restaurants, Inc., is the world's largest restaurant system, with nearly 30,000 KFC, Pizza Hut, and Taco Bell restaurants in more than 100 countries and territories.* In 2002, TRICON changed its stock symbol to YUM and began referring to its holdings as Yum! Brands.

Today, KFC and the Colonel's image are found across the landscape of America and many parts of the world. Colonel Sanders' accomplishments provide examples of entrepreneurship, concept development franchising, and brand development.

Case Discussion Questions

1. What impact did the interstate highway system have on KFCs as well as the growth of other chains?
2. Why do most successful hospitality industry executives travel extensively?

*Courtesy of the Public Affairs Department, KFC Corporation, Louisville, KY.

CASE 2

Juan Trippe—Pan American Airways

As stated in this chapter, people, events, inventions, and new ideas were some of the driving forces behind the successful examples in the hospitality industry. Unfortunately, these same driving forces often are the cause of the eventual failure of a hospitality industry company. The case of Pan Am and Juan Trippe illustrates that impact of driving forces.

Juan Trippe exemplifies an entrepreneur who was self taught. He made mistakes like most entrepreneurs do, but was ultimately very successful.

Trippe, founder of Pan American Airways, needed to understand the problems that pilots in the fledgling airline industry ran into as they flew across the country. So he went straight to the airmen and asked them.

As Robert Daley wrote in his biography *An American Saga: Juan Trippe and His Pan Am Empire,** "Day after day, Trippe waited at the dirt airfield in New Brunswick, N.J., to watch the airmail planes come in from the other side of the continent, and when they landed he quizzed the pilots about their problems. There was much to learn, and he was learning all of it as fast as he could."

Trippe (1899–1981) learned to fly when he was just 18 years old, but it wasn't the romance of the air that interested him. It was the prospect of airplanes as a business.

Trippe enlisted as an aviator in the Navy during World War I, but the war ended before he saw action. He returned to Yale where he showed the kind of entrepreneurial initiative that was to be a hallmark of his life. Among his achievements was founding a student magazine, the *Yale Graphic*. "He was not then, and never became, a literary man. He was learning how to run a business and how to meet a payroll."

Summer vacations were similarly used to good advantage. He worked for an investment bank and soaked up information that would stand him in good stead. "He learned how companies were organized, how funds were raised, what it meant to operate in margin."

Backed by investors, Trippe purchased seven surplus Navy planes and organized Long Island Airways, the first of several airlines he ran in this highly volatile industry. He believed in doing things the right way. "Most young men of Trippe's time—or any time—might not have bothered to organize a formal company just to sell airplane rides, for this took time and work, and it cost money in legal fees," noted Daley.

Trippe tried to think at least one step ahead of everyone else. His planes had room for only the pilot and a single passenger. If he could get another passenger in the plane, Trippe reasoned, he could double his profits. After study-

*C. Schleir. "Trippe was a Long-Haul Man," *Investors Business Daily* (July 10, 2002): A4.

ing the situation, he was able to make changes that allowed him to double his passenger capacity. A new business was born—flying rich couples to popular resorts: the Hamptons, Newport, and Atlantic City.

That wasn't enough for Trippe. He continued to prepare for the future, going to the public library and studying the history of railroading. He wanted to know the laws that governed the railroads, and their costs. He wanted to find out how great a premium customers would pay if an airline could offer greater speeds. That was a visionary guess at the time, when air travel was still slow and limited to daylight hours in good weather.

Trippe believed he'd win at the negotiating table if he lasted longer than the other negotiator. Talks with him frequently dragged on—with Trippe repeating points. In negotiations with Richard and Kenneth Bevier that led to the creation of the modern Pan Am, Trippe kept at it even though a deadline for an airmail contract was fast approaching. Both parties risked losing it all because they wanted to be the surviving partners in the merger. The Beviers blinked first.

Still, to make the merger work, Trippe had to deliver mail from Key West, Florida, to Havana, Cuba, in a week. The problem was there was no working airport in Key West. So he hammered one out of the swamp—it was less an airport than two intersecting dirt roads—and it appeared his victory was assured.

Unfortunately, rains washed out the "airport" two days before the airmail flight was scheduled to depart. All appeared lost. But Trippe was convinced there's more than one way to complete a mission. If a land-based plane couldn't be used, why not try a seaplane? Finally one was found in Miami. However, the pilot was about to depart for Haiti and wasn't interested in changing his flight plan. But Trippe's offer of a $250 fee—an enormous sum in those days—persuaded him. The airmail contract was preserved and a $25,000 performance bond saved.

Trippe knew that in a cutting-edge industry, equipment "became obsolete very, very fast." Some competitors purchased more planes than they needed and ran them sparingly so they wouldn't wear out as quickly. Trippe purchased fewer planes but ran them as hard as possible—and then bought more advanced planes as they became available.

Trippe knew what planes Pan Am needed. He made sure manufacturers had suitable aircraft ready when he needed them. As *Time* magazine noted, "Trippe always rode shotgun with any new airplane (Pan Am) ordered." He insisted aircraft be modified to his specifications, and was instrumental in the development and design of aircraft ranging from the Sikorsky S-42 to the Boeing 747.

He believed you could capture more routes with honey than vinegar. "Trippe wanted friends, not enemies," Daley wrote. When Trippe went into a new territory, he wanted the established transportation systems—usually the shipping lines—on his side.

Trippe refused to give in to adversity. By 1938, Pan Am was the world's largest airline. But profit wasn't rolling in the way the board of directors felt it should be. So Trippe lost his chief executive title to Sonny Whitney, who tried to run the airline as best he could. Other executives in that situation would have resigned and left the company to its fate, but not Trippe. He took a demotion and stayed at Pan Am. Within 9 months he was asked to resume his duties as CEO.

Trippe believed in giving his employees responsibility and letting them run with it. Once they proved themselves, he trusted their judgment. For example, after the end of World War II, Trippe had faith in the future of Pan Am's subsidiary airline in China. His man there, Bill Bond, was convinced the communists would take over, wiping out Pan Am's investment. Against his instincts, Trippe deferred to Bond—who sold most of the subsidiary and was ultimately proved correct.

Trippe was the first proponent of mass travel in an industry that at the time catered largely to the luxury market. He was willing to put his muscle behind his beliefs. In 1945, he created the first tourist-class fares to Europe, defying the International Air Transport Association (IATA) which set fares.

As noted in *Time*, at one point Britain closed its airports to Pan Am flights with tourist seats, forcing the planes to land in Ireland. Trippe then offered $75 fares between New York and San Juan, Puerto Rico. Eventually he wore IATA down, and tourist-class fares became standard in the industry.*

When Trippe retired from Pan Am in 1968, the airline served 85 nations on six continents.

Pan Am struggled throughout the latter decades of the 20th century. Just as events helped propel the airline's reputation and development, other external events would lead to Pan Am's demise. Three major external events or factors combined to eventually sink Pan Am. These included a general economic downturn, spiraling operating costs (the price of jet fuel), and the Pan Am 103 disaster. This latter terror incident and related fear of international travel were perhaps the final straw for this great airline, as shortly thereafter Pan Am became bankrupt due to declining revenues and increased costs.

Case Discussion Questions

1. External events both helped and hurt many hospitality businesses and brands. Name a few successes or failures and see if you can identify any external events that contributed to the success/failure of the hospitality business.

2. Juan Trippe's success was partially due to his belief in developing technology related to the aircraft business. Discuss other sectors of the hospitality industry and how developing technology influenced their respective success or failure.

Ibid., A4.

Chapter 2

External and Internal Driving Forces

CHAPTER OBJECTIVES

- Explain the historical foundations of corporate strategies.
- Describe how internal and external forces helped shape corporate strategies.
- Describe the forces likely to have a significant impact on the hospitality industry in the 21st century.

Understanding management strategies in the hospitality industry today requires an insight into both internal (within the industry itself) and external (socio-demographic and psychographic) factors affecting these strategies. During the 20th century many external trends and internal industry occurrences helped shape strategies. In the 21st century, new driving forces are influencing the hospitality corporations' overall management strategies.

A HISTORICAL PERSPECTIVE—THE EVOLUTION OF MANAGEMENT STRATEGIES

A brief historical review is essential to understanding the evolution of most corporate strategies in the hospitality industry. Historically, the hotel was a lodging property that served the person traveling to urban centers. In the 1950s, one of the first alternative corporate strategies to hotels was the invention of a new roadside lodging property—the "motel"—by Kemmons Wilson, which he called Holiday Inn. Thus, two major product segments emerged in the hospitality industry: the hotel, a downtown product, and the motel, a highway or roadside product. One was geared for business travelers; the other was aimed at the family market. With this development came the beginning of large-scale market segmentation in the hospitality industry.

In the early decades of the 20th century, Marriott, Howard Johnson, and other companies grew from root beer stands, ice cream shops, and coffee shops into legitimate foodservice companies. The evolutionary strategy that took J. Willard Marriott from one simple, small food establishment into the full gamut of foodservice facilities continued until it manifested itself in the next logical service to travelers—providing beds. This became the multiple product strategy: providing multiple services with integrated, generally related products to consumers.

As these early hospitality entrepreneurs began to succeed, demand for their concepts outstripped their resources for expansion. The answer for bringing more of their products and services to the market was quickly found in another pioneering corporate strategy called franchising, an expansionary strategy. The phenomenal growth of Holiday Inn best exemplifies franchising in its heyday. One need only look at other franchising companies within the hospitality industry such as McDonald's, Burger King, and Wendy's to see how successful franchising is as a strategy for growth.

These basic market segmentation, multiple product, and expansionary strategies nurtured growth in the hospitality industry throughout the 20th century. These three strategies are the foundation of today's corporate strategies. Internally driven forces and externally driven forces made these strategies dynamic rather than static.

Internally Driven Forces

The early strategies of today's hospitality corporations were internally driven. Simply stated, it was the driving force of entrepreneurs, the desire to see their businesses grow, and the new ideas that were the principal corporate strategies. This occurred during a time—the 1950s and 1960s—in which quantitative units and growth rates were the only buzzwords known in hospitality companies. In fact, not until the early 1970s did "strategic planning" even become a part of the vocabulary of hospitality corporations. This internal strategic drive resulted in further market and product segmentation. It took on different meanings for different companies. For Holiday Inn it meant locations that were at logical stopping points along the highway. Later, for Hilton and others, it meant entering the marketplace with an "inn" product and expanding this product through franchising. For the hospitality industry as a whole, it meant the birth and development of what would one day be known as the age of brand proliferation in the 1980s. Ramada Inn, Quality Inn, Sheraton Inn, and Hilton Inn emerged, along with larger companies such as Sheraton, Hilton, and InterContinental.

It is evident that a dual strategic thrust existed—internally driven product diversification and externally demanded market segmentation. However, in the 1950s and early 1960s the motivator or cause was internal, and growth in the number of units was the game.

Externally Driven Forces

Long before John Naisbitt wrote or even conceived of *Megatrends*, major external forces were in place that would have a lasting impact on the strategies of corporations in the hospitality industry. These external forces were large enough to influence and shape corporate strategy as it related to markets, products, quality, levels of services, pricing strategies, and so on. Those who stayed in step with these trends would become the industry leaders and growth companies of the 1980s. Key external forces can be succinctly listed:

- Population trends (growth, mix, and movement)
- Growth of affluence (wealth, discretionary income, etc.)
- Emergence of classes (low, middle, upper-middle, upper)
- Development of transportation systems (interstates, airports, "hub" airports, etc.)

- Tiering and qualitative segmentation of values, tastes, and psychographics
- Internationalism of commerce; global perspective versus national isolationism

What is significant is not the importance of each of these external forces, but the fact that components of each (a wealthier America, an older population, the emergence of "yuppies," etc.) were strong enough to cause everything from today's supply of luxury accommodations to a surge in the budget motel segment to low-priced air carriers. In the late 1980s and early 1990s, the hospitality industry lived up to its label as a dynamic industry. The savings and loan crisis, real estate devaluations, the falling away of weak companies, and constant changes of ownership, not just of properties, but of entire chains, were prevalent throughout the last decades of the 20th century. Airline deregulation, the emergence of gaming and attractions, and huge growth in new foodservice concepts propelled the industry into a global force.

TECHNOLOGY

As we view the driving forces of this century, it is likely that the macro force called technology will most dramatically impact virtually every sector and area of the hospitality industry.

CORPORATE HOSPITALITY MANAGEMENT STRATEGIES

As you have read, there is no single overriding factor that determines a hospitality corporation's strategies. Rather, multiple internally and externally driven forces combine with a company's historic roots to determine its strategies today. There are as many ways to categorize strategies as there are corporate strategists in the industry. The perspective presented in this section is based on participation in planning processes within several of the companies used as examples and on 35 years of study and observation of other corporations in the industry.[1]

Strategy 1: Horizontal Expansion

The hospitality industry encompasses food and beverage, lodging, and travel-related services. Therefore, horizontal expansion simply means expanding from one line of hospitality product or service—for example, food—to another—

for example, lodging. For instance, Carlson Companies, Inc., now encompasses many hospitality services: food, lodging, cruise ships, travel-related services, and so on. Hilton now offers multiple lodging brands. Other chains comprise restaurants, resorts, and gaming and casino operations.

Strategy 2: Geographic Expansion

At first, hospitality companies developed within a relatively small radius of their origin. For example, Marriott was known primarily as a Washington, D.C.–area company until the late 1970s. But its rapid growth in lodging west of the Mississippi helped it develop into a national brand in the 1980s. Holiday Inn was a midsouthern company, Ramada a southwestern company, La Quinta a Texas company. A combination of factors—market growth opportunities, sales of franchises, and the unit-growth mentality of the 1960s and 1970s—caused many local and regional hospitality firms to emerge with national, and ultimately international, status. The same is true of the restaurant sector and brands such as Denny's, Wendy's, and Burger King. For airlines, mergers and route system expansions created regional and then national carriers. Southern, Mohawk, Northeast, and Hughes Airwest all were absorbed into larger carriers, while others such as Eastern and Western disappeared as brands.

Strategy 3: Product Hybridization

Perhaps because of Holiday Inn's phenomenal growth and the entry of other motel developers into the marketplace, it wasn't long before traditional high-rise hotel companies began developing and franchising low-rise "inns." Hilton Inn and Sheraton Inn are two examples of product hybrids (variations on base products) that developed in the late 1960s and early 1970s. Product hybrids also were natural strategies for companies that began as motels; soon there were high-rise motels called Holiday Inn, Ramada Inn, and Marriott Inn. Motel product hybrids continued to appear as high-rise (in urban markets) and midrise (in other markets) facilities, offering more services than had the traditional motel.

Strategy 4: Specialization

Just as Holiday Inn began with the idea of offering families affordable accommodations, other entrants into the marketplace began as specialists categorized by price or service level. For example, Motel 6, Days Inn, and La Quinta began with a specialized product offering limited facilities—essentially guest-rooms only. In the food segment of the industry came fast-food establishments, salad bars, pizza parlors, specialty restaurants, steak houses, and seafood eateries. Specialization also went upscale in both pricing and services offered. Today there are all-suite brands (Embassy Suites), luxury-only hotel chains (Four Seasons), and extended stay products (Extended Stay America). Interestingly enough, some of these specialized products and services were the result of what is one of the most commented-upon corporate strategies, product "tiering."

Strategy 5: Product Tiering

Product tiering was an initial corporate response to growth limitations and the aging of corporations' prevalent products. The limitations of growth could have resulted from market saturation or could have occurred when the actual economics of the original concept no longer worked or were not as lucrative as an alternative approach. Ramada developed a three-tiered approach in the early 1980s: Ramada Inn, Ramada Hotel, and Ramada Renaissance Hotel. Each of these product tiers reflected different pricing, different levels of service, and operational variations. Holiday Inn, Holiday Inn Hotel, and Holiday Inn Crowne Plaza represented Holiday Inn's original product tiering. Other companies soon followed with various forms of product tiering, manifested in an up-the-scale movement from inn to hotel to luxury hotel. Product tiering also influenced companies such as Marriott, which de-emphasized inns and franchising and opted to go in other directions with hotels and mega-hotels (1,000 rooms or more) called Marriott Marquis. Marriott Marquis was followed by a low-rise lodging product, Courtyards by Marriott, and extended stay and all-suite products. Radisson, Choice Hotels International, Hyatt, and other lodging chains all developed types of facilities with varying levels of services, amenities, and pricing structures. This was simply the lodging industry's response to the mega-forces of population growth and demographic, economic, and psychographic segmentation. Product tiering was rampant in the industry by the early 1980s and continued to expand in the 1990s. In the food-service sector, variations of product tiering also took place. Burger King and McDonald's could be found within other larger establishments, such as Wal-Mart, or in the form of a small storefront or even kiosk-type operation. Air carriers acquired, affiliated with, or began regional airlines. Rental car companies developed limited facilities for more remote or lower-volume locations.

Strategy 6: Product Branding

Product branding is one of the more recent corporate strategies. This is a result in part of the proliferation of tiering and the subsequent consumer and franchisee confusion it caused. The confusion was the result of a considerable amount of product relabeling mixed in with some genuine product tiering. An establishment looked like a motel and smelled like a motel but had another name (e.g., low-rise Doubletree Hotel). As a result of this confusion and of an even stronger force or marketplace dynamic known as consumer awareness, product branding emerged. Ironically, this occurred as the hospitality industry, one of the world's oldest industries, was just entering the era of brand identification. The focus of product branding is to clearly define what a product or service is, in terms of level and quality of service, location, price, and other key consumer-oriented factors such as the psychographic appeal of "prestige" or "thrift" and of course benefit provided and need met.

There are a number of clear examples of today's product branding. To understand these, one might think of a hospitality corporation as analogous to General Motors. For example, Holiday Inn followed the General Motors product branding concept of offering multiple brands, such as Crowne Plaza, Holiday Inn, and Holiday Inn Express—everything from a Chevrolet to a Cadillac. Marriott adopted a similar strategy, with Marriott Hotel, Marriott Resort, Marriott Marquis, Courtyards by Marriott, and Fairfield Inn. Other companies have elected to develop what might be analogous to the Porsche or Ferrari concept—one product of high quality, one brand, no variations. Examples of hospitality corporations with one-brand strategies include Four Seasons, Ritz-Carlton, and Westin, to name a few. These brands may change ownership, but their labels and names depict a very specific product positioning.

Strategy 7: Nonfranchising

Usually firms that wish to keep greater control over the quality, ownership, and management of their properties do not franchise. Often these firms are strong enough financially that franchising is not necessary. Examples of lodging chains that do not franchise are few (e.g., Four Seasons, Westin, and Ritz-Carlton).

Strategy 8: Franchising

Franchising companies are more prevalent in the hospitality industry than are nonfranchising companies. Holiday Inn, Radisson, and Choice Hotels International are examples of lodging firms that are large franchisors. McDonald's, Burger King, Wendy's, KFC, and Dunkin' Donuts are examples of leading franchisors in the fast-food area. Today it is possible to purchase a franchise for virtually everything from a travel agency to a destination resort.

Strategy 9: Brand Collection

During the late 1980s and 1990s "brand collectors" emerged. These were companies primarily driven by investors who took advantage of the relatively low prices needed to acquire chains or brands that had growth potential through global franchising. Companies such as Hospitality Franchise Systems—now

Cendant (owner of the Howard Johnson, Ramada, and Days Inn brands) and Choice Hotels International (owner of Quality Inn, Comfort Inn, and Comfort Suites brands) are now among the largest brand collectors in the industry.

Strategy 10: Management Contracts

Another byproduct of the lodging industry sort-out of the late 1980s and early 1990s was the growth of large "management contract" companies. These are firms that specialize in managing hotels and motels for owners such as banks, insurance companies, trusts, pension funds, partnerships, or individuals. Examples include both independent management companies such as Interstate and chain-affiliated management companies such as Marriott International.

Strategy 11: Vertical and Horizontal Integration

Vertical and horizontal integration are corporate strategies that involve a hospitality company in more than one component of the hospitality business. One example is Carlson Companies. Carlson is the parent of multiple levels of hotel brands and foodservice concepts, and its line of hospitality products includes the world's second largest travel agency group and a cruise ship company, among others. Unlike the period before 1980, when integration in the hospitality industry meant firm-owned hotels and restaurants or an airline and a hotel chain, deregulation has provided hospitality companies the opportunity to gain a competitive edge by owning or investing in multiple components of the industry.

Strategy 12: Singleness

Some hospitality firms have chosen to develop just one product or service, forgoing product segmentation, tiering, and vertical and horizontal integration strategies. Four Seasons, for example, has opted for a single product of all first-class hotels with total ownership, equity participation, and management control.

Strategy 13: Value-Related Product and Services

Residence Inn and Embassy Suites exemplify lodging concepts developed to respond to specific value and psychographic trends among consumers. As the consumer continues to express new product and service demands, corporations will identify and satisfy these demands with appropriate and timely product and service strategies. Other examples of value-related products and services include the variety of credit cards such as rebate cards, mileage/point redemption cards, affinity cards, and the variety of air travel options, such as all-first-class, low-price carriers, and contracted travel.

Strategy 14: Global Positioning

The oceans, political ideologies, and other traditional trade barriers were not seen as insurmountable hurdles for the hospitality industry. Holiday Inn, Radisson, Marriott, Cendant, Best Western, Accor, Choice Hotels, Hertz, Avis, American Airlines, United, McDonald's, Burger King, and others have products throughout the world. The signs of fast-food chains can be seen in most international cities and airports. As the brands originating in the United States expanded globally, foreign brands also entered the U.S. market—Le Meridien, Trusthouse Forte, Sofitel, Nikko, Swissotels, British Airways, Japan Airlines, and others. Investment reasons, risk levels, growth strategies, and reasons for expansion all vary by corporation and by market. These are influenced by many different social, economic, and political trends and events. These corporations' perspectives are as varied as the products, services, and markets they serve.

Strategy Implications

The once relatively simple family-driven foodservice businesses or single-branded lodging concepts that made up the hospitality industry in the first two-thirds of the 20th century have given way to much more complex business concepts and multiple branding. Some businesses with family origins grew enormously, such as Marriott, while others were acquired or merged, such as Stouffer (whose hotels and resorts now bear the Renaissance brand). Global ownership of physical assets, brand switching, short-term management contracts, changes of ownership, brand collection, global brand expansion through franchising and joint ventures, and vertical integration are all changing the dynamics of the industry and accelerating its pace of change.

To consumers, the hospitality industry gets more confusing as their favorite hotel switches brands, changes management, or is replaced with a new concept or product. For industry management, it's more challenging to bring in new customers and retain existing customers because of internally driven industry dynamics. But there is yet more challenge for today's hospitality management, in the form of new externally driven forces or trends to which managers must respond. Let's briefly look at some of the key strategic trends that also will impact the hospitality industry in the future and the implications of these trends.

STRATEGIC ASSESSMENT

Earlier in the chapter a number of key internal and external forces were listed that shaped the hospitality industry during the 20th century. As we look to the future there are forces that are likely to have a significant impact on both the industry and management strategies throughout the 21st century.[2] They are:

- Globalization/cultural diversity
- Technology

- Behavioral pendulums
- Consolidation
- Vertical and horizontal integration
- Branding

Globalization

The marketplace is becoming increasingly global. As business investment and business and related travel flow across every region of the globe, multinational and cultural positioning will be essential to attract market share in the hospitality industry. Linkages and networks to major origin markets—the geographical areas where large numbers of travelers come from—will be necessary for a hospitality company to remain competitive in the world marketplace. As new businesses and business investment flow to new regions, leisure travel will also develop in these regions. Economic growth in Asia, the Pacific Basin, Latin America, and China will provide impetus to a more diverse travel market. Understanding these regions and knowing how to relate on a multinational and culturally diverse basis will be essential for managerial success.

Technology

Integrating the latest technologies into a company's business practices is an all-encompassing survival strategy. Management must keep pace with technological developments not only to remain competitive but—more importantly—to meet the changing needs of consumers. New technologies that reduce costs and provide consumer conveniences receive and will continue to receive the highest priority. Implementing these technologies will attract consumers and gain market share. In addition, as globalization accelerates, being "plugged in" to the right global distribution systems will be a competitive advantage. Providing the latest technology in guest conveniences, security, and safety are and will be key advantages as well. The implications and stakes are immense in the technology area. Technology that facilitates the purchase process, allows for efficient operations, and meets the consumers' needs will be the focal point for management that wishes to achieve a competitive advantage.

ETHICS

Globalization and technology have eradicated borders in international relations and business. Managerial practitioners in the hospitality industry must adhere to their code of ethics wherever they do business.

Behavioral Pendulums

The prolonged recession of the late 1980s, the economic uncertainties of the early 1990s and the early 2000s, forced career changes, and new ways of doing business, combined with the resultant human psychological consequence of stress, have caused deep behavioral changes in consumers that are likely to remain, not only in North America, but wherever in the world economic or political turmoil occurs. Unless we enter into a new age of global wealth, the overriding concept of "value" will remain with us throughout our lives. Value in good economic times will weigh more heavily toward quality; in times of economic uncertainty, value will be price oriented. More important, in today's highly demanding world, value is now being driven more and more by the concept of convenience or ease of purchase. Management strategies that are in tune with the prevailing definition of value will likely be the more successful.

Consolidation

Whether through mergers and acquisitions or through affiliations and agreements, consolidating with other companies may prove essential for a hospitality company's survival. Establishing a marketing relationship with the components of the industry that can help you either distribute your product/service or provide you with brand presence is a necessity. The big companies are likely to get bigger and the specialized organizations are likely to get better. Whether a company is big or specialized, it will rely more on its booking sources, suppliers (of customers, etc.), and preferred consumers (key corporate accounts). The farther the reach, the more likely the ability to attract market share from the growing international feeder markets—those economically emerging areas that are now beginning to generate more travelers. The bottom line is that "critical mass" will be advantageous—that is, the larger you are, the more clout you will have in the marketplace. Most all sectors of the hospitality industry are rapidly consolidating.

Vertical and Horizontal Integration

Vertical and horizontal integration takes on a new meaning in the 21st century. Survival is more and more closely connected to agreements, coalitions, mergers, joint ventures, acquisitions, and expanded distribution channels. This is driven not just by economies of scale but, more importantly, by the consumer's expectations of "single-source conveniences." More and more consumers prefer one-stop shopping or one call or one online service to handle all of their air, hotel, and car rental arrangements, rather than making three separate trips/calls. Survival will necessitate developing the right affiliations with other suppliers within the travel industry, "stretching" marketing presence through extensive co-ops (joint marketing or service offerings with travel partners). Strategies that are rapidly gaining management's attention include those related to:

- Security
- Outsourcing
- Purchasing co-ops
- New organizational concepts—team management
- Cluster management
- Increased automation
- Functional consolidations and cross-functional management

Branding

Branding has become increasingly important as consumers seek to sort through the plethora of new market entrants around the globe. Brands that are clearly identified, have distinct positioning, and are consistent in multiple global markets will emerge as the winners. Developing a global brand image with universal appeal may well be another key to successful managerial strategy.

THE NEW PARADIGM

Under the new paradigm, management strategy takes on new meaning. "Urgency" and "critical" are replaced with "immediacy" and "act now." Customers will expect immediate action. Loyalty is replaced with "You've got one chance to keep me as a customer." Brand loyalty will be won by performance—this time and every time. Competitiveness now means providing what is most convenient and best for the customer. Today and throughout the 21st century, management must be proactive and react immediately to survive. Fundamental change must occur on demand. Understanding multifunctional concepts and technological applications and selecting the correct ones will be critical to winning. There will be little room for mistakes or defects, and few second chances. Individual managerial superstars will be replaced by all-star teams (and teamwork) whose focus will shift from being "just good enough to win" to "continually improving so as to never lose." Most important of all, the ability to change, to adapt to the new, and to understand the diverse will form the basis for success.[3]

Up to this point, we have provided a historical perspective of the evolution of management strategy and the dynamic environment in which the industry developed. In the next chapter we will begin to focus on the management concepts of strategy selection and positioning.

CHAPTER REVIEW

Fourteen different strategies were presented in this chapter, which help provide an understanding of the way the industry and sectors of the industry have evolved. Product segmentation driven by consumer needs and growth has led to a large variety of products and services in nearly all hospitality industry sectors. Growth has been driven by developmental strategies such as franchising, management contracts, changes in tax laws, and external forces. Geographic expansion within one region of a country has evolved into global expansion. Single brands in one sector have evolved into conglomerates with multiple brands serving multiple sectors and markets. And macro trends/forces will continue to influence management strategies. Globalization, increased cultural diversity, and technology will continue to provide even more challenge to management in the years ahead. Along with these challenges will come new and improved management strategies and ideas to achieve performance objectives. Concepts such as outsourcing, co-ops in purchasing and marketing, and new organizational concepts will all play a role in managerial strategy today and in the future.

KEY CONCEPTS/TERMS

Franchising

Management contract

Outsourcing

Product branding

Product hybrid

Product tiering

Vertical and horizontal integration

DISCUSSION QUESTIONS

1. What external forces or trends do you believe will have the greatest influence on the hospitality market in the 21st century?

2. Do you believe franchising will continue as a major growth technique in the years ahead?

3. What are the benefits of consolidation?

4. Does the consumer win or lose in an industry that consolidates?

5. Has product segmentation led to consumer confusion in the lodging and foodservice sectors of the hospitality industry?

6. What role do you see "brands" playing in the gaming and cruise sectors of the hospitality industry?

ENDNOTES

1. R. A. Nykiel, *Marketing in the Hospitality Industry*, 3rd ed. (East Lansing, MI: Educational Institute of the American Hotel and Motel Association, 1997): 227–281.

2. R. A. Nykiel, "Meeting the Challenges in the Next Millennium," *Hospitality Business Review* 2, no. 2 (Spring 1999): 28–32.

3. Ibid.

CASE 1

Hyatt Corporation—A Variation of the Singleness Strategy through Product Type/Identification and Market Segment Positioning*

In this chapter we discussed both corporate hospitality management strategies and the internal and external driving forces that helped shape today's hospitality industry. In its own way Hyatt Corporation had a dramatic impact on shaping the "look" of the hotel and resort product in today's hospitality industry. Working with renowned architect John Portman, Hyatt placed its Regency brand on the first major modern "atrium" hotel with the opening of the Hyatt Regency in Atlanta. With its spectacular atrium design and revolving rooftop restaurant and lounge, this hotel would not only start the atrium hotel and resort design trend but also establish a new position and image for Hyatt.

Hyatt Corporation opened its first hotel on September 27, 1957. Today, the company operates over 200 hotels throughout the world. At the time of this writing, Hyatt has two subordinate companies: Hyatt Hotels and Resorts and Hyatt International. Hyatt International operates over 60 hotels and 20 resorts in 37 countries, while Hyatt Hotels and Resorts operates over 120 hotels and resorts in the United States, Canada, and the Caribbean. Hyatt specializes in luxury hotels with meeting facilities and special services catering to the business traveler. There are three brand names under Hyatt operation: Hyatt Regency, Grand Hyatt, and Park Hyatt. Each maintains the general level of quality and service associated with the Hyatt brand with slight variations.

Hyatt Regency hotels are Hyatt's core brand of hotels, with a contemporary image recognizable by the brand's distinguished atrium architectural design. Hyatt Regency hotels are located in metropolitan areas, targeting the business traveler. Most Hyatt Regency hotels are typical business transit hotels. Major competitors are Hilton and Marriott.

Hyatt Regency hotels are positioned to serve the individual upscale business traveler market segment with full services, lodging, and amenities. Most Hyatt Regency hotels have medium-sized meeting facilities.

Grand Hyatt hotels serve major business destinations that attract major conventions and meetings as well as business and leisure travelers. Major competitors are Hilton, Marriott, and Westin. The hotels include features such as state-of-the-art technology, business centers, leisure amenities, and banquet and conference facilities. Grand Hyatt hotels are positioned to serve meetings and conventions as a primary target market and secondarily business and leisure individual travelers.

Park Hyatt hotels are smaller luxury hotels designed to cater to the discriminating individual traveler seeking the privacy, personalized service, and amenities of a small boutique hotel. Park Hyatt hotels, with other deluxe

---

*Information derived from www.hyatt.com/corporate/index.jhtml.

hotels such as Ritz-Carlton and Four Seasons, are located in major cities and popular upscale resort destinations.

Hyatt's hotel brands as represented in Figure 1 are positioned with slight differences in price, levels of service, and targeted market segments. The image and perception of each type of Hyatt brand is upscale and consistent. Hyatt's Gold Passport Program (frequency program) is honored by all three Hyatt brands and contributes to their success by building repeat business. Hyatt believes this multiple positioning/branding strengthens its appeal and the link to its frequency program helps capture the individual and group segments. Hyatt's quality and service levels, as well as pricing strategies, support the concept of a varied singleness strategy for the overall brand.

In summary, beginning with the Hyatt Regency Atlanta three decades ago, Hyatt's growth strategy has focused on the upscale market with "product" as a key differentiator. Prior to this development, Hyatt had a mixed product line ranging from West Coast motels to some less-spectacular full-service hotels. By selecting the "singleness" strategy, deleting the lower-end product and concentrating on design leadership in the upper-level segment, Hyatt built a very strong and consistent brand in the hospitality industry.

Case Discussion Questions

1. What are the advantages of a singleness strategy such as Hyatt's?
2. How does the physical product's external and internal perception influence a brand's positioning?

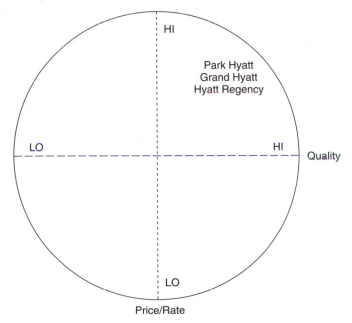

Figure 1   Hyatt Positioning Map

CASE 2

Sonic Drive-In—External Forces Revive the Concept*

Sometimes a business gets a whole new lease on life and is invigorated by unforeseen external driving forces. Three major external driving forces had a dramatic impact on Sonic Drive-In and caused a reinvigoration of the growth process.

A brief history of Sonic Drive-In will help provide an understanding of the concept and business. In 1953, Troy Smith, the founder of Sonic, was living in Shawnee, Oklahoma. Troy's dream was to own his own business. In fact, he had already tried his hand at running a restaurant . . . twice.

Troy's first venture was a tiny diner with 12 stools and 4 booths called the Cottage Cafe. It was barely large enough to make a living for his wife and two children. He sold it and bought a bigger place. Troy's Panful of Chicken was so successful that Troy tried opening more of them. Unfortunately, the fried chicken concept didn't fly in early 1950s Oklahoma, and Troy's Panful of Chicken quietly faded away. What didn't fade was Troy's desire to own a restaurant. His ultimate dream was to run a fancy steakhouse in Shawnee. And, for a while, he did.

The lot where Troy's steakhouse sat also had a rootbeer stand. Troy meant to tear it down to add more parking for the steakhouse. Until he got around to it, he figured the rootbeer stand could make him a little extra pocket change. In a twist of fate, the humble Top Hat Drive-In, as the rootbeer stand was called, proved to be more profitable and outlasted the steakhouse.

The Top Hat was like other rootbeer stands of the era. It was a cash business, serving easily prepared hamburgers and hot dogs cooked to order. Customers would park on the lot and order at the walk-up window. They could eat at a picnic table or in their cars. The Top Hat was moderately successful.

Ever the entrepreneur, Troy continued to look for ways to improve the business. Yet he could not have predicted that his improvements would earn him a place in American fast-food history.

While traveling in Louisiana, Troy saw homemade intercom speakers at a hamburger stand that let customers order right from their cars. A light bulb went on in Troy's head. He contacted the innovator in Louisiana and asked him to make an intercom for the Top Hat. Troy hired some local electronics wizards, whom he called the "jukebox boys," to install the speaker system at his drive-in. He also added a canopy for cars to park under and hired servers to deliver food directly to customers' cars. "Carhops," as the servers were called, was a moniker from the early days of drive-in restaurants, when servers jumped onto the running boards of early-day automobiles driving onto the lot and directed them to their parking spots. Troy Smith now had the prototype of the future Sonic. The first week after the new intercom was installed, the Top

*Information derived from www.sonicdrivein.com.

Hat took in three times as much revenue as before the changes. It was 1954. The first Chevrolet Corvettes were rolling off the assembly line.

Space-age technology and "carhops" had come to Oklahoma.

Over in Woodward, Oklahoma, Charlie Pappe was managing the local Safeway supermarket. He wanted to get out of the grocery business and start his own restaurant.

While visiting friends in Shawnee, Charlie stopped by the Top Hat for dinner. Charlie had never met Troy Smith, but he was so impressed with the whole concept and operation that he went in and introduced himself. Charlie opened the second Top Hat Drive-In in May 1956 in Woodward. Top Hat Drive-Ins were a big hit with both customers and businessmen. By 1958, there were Top Hat Drive-Ins in Enid and Stillwater, Oklahoma, as well. Although more entrepreneurs wanted in on their success, only four Top Hats were ever opened.

Troy and Charlie would have kept the Top Hat name, but lawyers informed them that it was copyrighted. So they opened up the dictionary and started searching for a new name. Echoing a common theme of those days, Top Hat's slogan had been "Service with the Speed of Sound." Indeed, the post-war world was changing fast. The country had seen the dawn of the Atomic Era and the beginnings of the Jet Age and the Space Race. When Troy and Charlie ran across "sonic," meaning "speed of sound," they knew they had the perfect name. The Stillwater Top Hat Drive-In became the first Sonic Drive-In and still serves hot dogs, rootbeer, and Frozen Favorites® desserts on the same site.

The new name sparked more requests from aspiring Sonic operators. One of the reasons Troy Smith believes Sonic has been so successful through the years is that the drive-in operators are also part owners, something he thinks makes a terrific difference.

The first Sonic franchise ever sold came with the first formal Sonic franchise agreement. The one-and-a-half page, double-spaced franchise contract was drafted by Shawnee lawyer O. K. Winterringer (who also happened to be Troy's landlord). The royalty fee of one penny per bag was based on the number of Sonic sandwich bags sold through Cardinal Paper, one of Sonic's early vendors. With each new franchisee, Troy would call Winterringer and another one-and-a-half page, double-spaced contract based on the penny-a-bag royalty was drafted. Troy and Charlie helped new partners with the layout, site selection, and operation of their Sonic Drive-Ins.

In the early days, there was no national advertising and there were no territorial rights. If two prospects wanted the same town, Winterringer and Troy would talk to them and convince one to go somewhere else.

Charlie Pappe unexpectedly died of a heart attack in 1967 at the age of 54. Troy Smith was left alone to run the burgeoning, 14-year-old company and its 41 Sonic Drive-Ins. Troy invited two franchisees to take over running Sonic Supply, the supply and distribution division of Sonic. In the next 6 years, the trio built an additional 124 Sonics in a core group of states including Oklahoma, Texas, and Kansas.

In 1973, a group of 10 key, principal franchise owners restructured the company into Sonic Systems of America, later changing the name to Sonic Corp. They became the officers and board of directors and purchased the Sonic name, slogan, trademark, logos, and supply company from Troy. They also offered each store operator the option to buy 1,250 shares of stock at $1 per share.

Sonic was now owned by its franchisees. Due to the number of shares offered, Sonic also became an over-the-counter, publicly traded company. There were now 165 Sonics in the chain.

In a period of tremendous growth, more than 800 Sonics opened between 1973 and 1978. By early 1975, Sonic Drive-Ins were in 13 southern and southwestern states. O. K. Winterringer established the Sonic School to formally train new managers. The public saw the first Sonic television advertising in 1977.

Interest in Sonic skyrocketed, but then the oil embargo of the early 1970s (major external driving force) and record inflation later in the decade took a big bite out of business. Profits fell 21 percent during 1978 and 1979. Despite the downturn, January 1980 saw the first Sonic National Convention. This demonstrated to franchise owners that company management was determined to weather the storm and increase cooperation between Sonic and its franchisees. Plans were unveiled for more evenly paced growth.

Unfortunately, the 1980 annual report showed sales and operating revenues down more than $5 million, with a net operating loss of $300,000. In response, Sonic consolidated store operations and development and closed 28 low-volume, company-owned drive-ins. Sonic was down, but not out. The key element to Sonic's comeback was its traditional franchise policy of owner-operators.

In 1984, Sonic was more like a collection of independent stores than a cohesive business entity. Nearly 1,000 Sonics operated in 19 states, yet there was no national advertising program or national purchasing cooperative. This was the same year that Cliff Hudson joined the Sonic legal department. He was instrumental in making several major changes in the company before eventually becoming president and CEO in 1995.

Hudson was on a team that led Sonic's management in a successful leveraged buyout from its franchisee shareholders for $10 million in May 1986. He also spearheaded two pivotal changes in the company. The first of these was taking Sonic public in March 1991 and initiating a secondary stock offering in 1995 that raised enough cash to pay off the company's debt and add to its working capital. Second, franchises in 17 key markets began purchasing together, giving significant cost savings to franchisees and consistency and quality to customers. Advertising also increased to 1 percent of sales.

By 2000, Sonic's media spending approached $64 million, and during the same fiscal year, total system-wide restaurant sales exceeded $1.7 billion with an estimated market value of more than $600 million.

In 1994 and 1995, customers, franchisees, suppliers, and drive-in managers were invited to join a series of Dream Team meetings to discuss what Sonic was doing right and what Sonic could improve.

The meetings spawned Sonic 2000, a new multilayered strategy to further unify the company in terms of a consistent menu, brand identity, products, packaging, and service. As a result, the new "retro-future" Sonic logo was introduced, and the entire system adopted a consistent new look and menu, including a section dedicated to Fountain and Frozen Favorites. The strategy resulted in Sonic's continued success. The chain is expanding, brand awareness has increased, and franchises are enjoying accelerated growth. Chain operations are now better unified for greater cost efficiencies.

Today, Sonic leads the fast-food industry in real sales growth, with higher same-store sales each year since 1987. As of February, 2002 there were 2,432 Sonic Drive-Ins in 30 states, making it the nation's largest drive-in chain.

The country and the fast-food business have changed a great deal since Troy Smith installed the first intercom system at the Top Hat Drive-In. Food fads have come and gone, but Sonic has differentiated itself through its business model, unique menu items, and, of course, friendly "Service with the Speed of Sound℠." Sonic has also benefited from a number of external driving forces, which have supported that growth.

It has been said that no one loves their automobiles more than North Americans. Combine that love of the car with the growth of the Baby Boom generation and you have one strong external driving force (no pun intended) that supports the basic concept offered by Sonic, a drive-in fast-food establishment.

We also see that in the early 2000s there was a shift back toward family values. This swing of the pendulum provided a second external driving force that supported the Sonic concept—the family eating together at a drive-in fast-food restaurant. You could also add to this the return of teenage "cruising" as yet another support for the Sonic concept.

The third external driving force was the after-effects of the tragedy of September 11, 2001, and the ongoing terrorism threats. This event caused more families and individuals to stay closer to home as well as drive versus fly. In fact, in 2002 summer auto travel by families as well as business travel by car accelerated substantially, while airline passenger counts declined or remained flat. For Sonic this meant a strong external driving force favoring its business concept.

These external forces combined with a number of internal forces and strategic management decisions have proven to be essential ingredients to Sonic's success. Sonic's strong growth and continued earnings success is attributed to five factors: (1) a multilayered growth strategy, (2) a highly differentiated concept, (3) an accelerated expansion program, (4) strong sales trends, and (5) solid financial performance.

Multilayered Growth Strategy

Sonic pursues a multilayered growth strategy to achieve targeted annual gains in earnings per share in the range of 18 to 20 percent. The following steps help diversify growth potential and strengthen profitability:

- Expanding the chain through the addition of both company-owned and franchised drive-ins

- Boosting brand awareness with steadily increasing media expenditures and new product news (which drives same-store sales and average unit volumes)
- Steadily growing franchise income due to accelerated franchise development and the company's unique ascending royalty rate
- Unifying chain operations for greater cost efficiencies

Highly Differentiated Concept

As the nation's largest chain of drive-in restaurants, Sonic is distinguished as the most highly differentiated quick-service brand through:

- A streamlined service delivery system
- Personalized carhop service that's fast, convenient, and a lot more friendly than the typical drive-through
- A unique menu with a variety of high-quality, made-to-order sandwiches and specialty items

Accelerated Expansion Program

Sonic subscribes to a lower-risk, higher-return development strategy that relies heavily on growth in the franchise side of the business. Recent program benchmarks include:

- A record 157 new franchise-owned drive-in openings during fiscal 2001
- A record total of 191 new drive-in openings (company- and franchisee-owned) during fiscal 2001—a significantly faster expansion than the range of 170 to 176 new drive-in openings annually over the past 3 years
- 190 new drive-in openings during fiscal 2002

Strong Sales Trends

Sonic enjoys one of the strongest growth records in the restaurant industry, having posted more than 15 consecutive years of higher sales on a same-store basis. New product news and product innovations, along with higher media spending, continue to drive top-line gains. In fiscal 2001:

- System-wide sales reached $2.0 billion, increasing 11 percent during the year and doubling from the $1.0 billion mark set just 4 years earlier

- System-wide same-store sales increased 1.8 percent, with gains accelerating to 4.8 percent and 4.9 percent in the third and fourth quarters of the year
- System average unit volumes advanced 2.5 percent
- Total revenues rose 18 percent

Solid Financial Performance

Sonic's multilayered growth strategy continues to drive a strong bottom-line performance:

- Revenues increased at a compound annual rate of 17 percent during the 5-year period that ended in August 2001.
- Net income per share during the same period rose at a compound annual rate of 21 percent.
- Return on stockholders' equity increased for 5 consecutive years, reaching almost 22 percent in fiscal 2001.

Sonic Drive-Ins are often viewed as a reflection of the nostalgic past (1950s and 1960s), but are also now viewed as meeting the needs of today's current market. It can be said they will likely meet the needs of the future marketplace as America's love of the automobile and desire for convenient food form some very strong external driving forces moving to support the Sonic Drive-In concept.

Case Discussion Questions

1. "Retro" trends (reflections of past eras) are sometimes linked to hospitality brands like Sonic. Select one such hospitality brand and discuss the benefits and/or pitfalls of a retro positioning strategy.
2. What future external driving forces do you see impacting the hospitality industry?

Chapter 3

Strategy Selection and Positioning

CHAPTER OBJECTIVES

- To identify strategy selection options available to hospitality-related businesses
- To delineate hospitality business positioning options
- To discuss the rationale behind management decisions related to both strategy selection and positioning options

When Kemmons Wilson, founder of Holiday Inn, decided to build motels along interstate highways, he was selecting a number of strategies. First, he identified a market—families who traveled by car. He also identified a location or geographic strategy and a product positioning strategy (moderately priced motels). When Southwest Airlines decided to offer low-cost air service with no first-class seating or fares, they too had selected a market and product positioning strategy. Both Holiday Inn and Southwest Airlines also had a brand strategy and growth strategy. As we begin this chapter, we will look at strategy selection options and then look at execution of these options through positioning strategies and examples.

STRATEGY SELECTION

In the hospitality industry there are numerous strategy areas and options. These include:

- Brand strategies (product or service)
- Business development strategies
- Financial strategies
- Marketing strategies
- Operational strategies

In addition to these areas, the nature of the hospitality industry supports managerial strategies in other areas, such as customer service/quality, human resources, risk management/crisis management, purchasing, technology, and communications. The degree of focus on these areas is dependent upon the nature of the individual business, company, or brand and the sector of the hospitality industry.

TECHNOLOGY

In hi-tech hotels such as W Hotels and in automated foodservice facilities, technology leadership has already become a positioning strategy.

While the degree of focus or priority may vary, nearly all companies have managerial strategies in place in most or all of the above-referenced areas. Some are even renowned for their execution of the strategy. For example, Ritz-Carlton, the winner of the Malcolm Baldridge award, exemplifies a customer service/quality–driven managerial strategy. Enterprise Rent-A-Car offers a unique market-driven managerial strategy with its multiple smaller locations and its "bring the car to the customer" concept. Many firms have multiple managerial strategies behind their success. Others have failed at just one and are no longer in business. Some strategies are more appropriate for financial goals such as franchising for development, which provides a faster return on investment, while other strategies such as ownership allow for greater product/service control. In subsequent chapters we will examine the major categories of managerial strategies and provide case examples for each.

Strategy selection is driven by a variety of forces or objectives. For example, lack of financial resources could drive a strong franchising or management contract effort. Abundance of cash could drive an ownership development strategy. Today we see a greater focus on implementing automation, driven partially by a scarcity of human resources and a desire for greater efficiencies and financial returns. The point is that strategy selection is influenced by many factors, ranging from the product or service to the market served to the goals of management. Options are multiple and may change based on market conditions, financial needs, and even changes in leadership.

There are a number of logical starting points to discuss strategy selection. In the hospitality industry it is often the product/service concept and positioning that leads to a business development strategy. For example, if the product/service concept is less capital intensive and limited in geographic introduction, ownership may be the business development strategy. An example would be a fast-food concept being introduced to a selected market. If the concept succeeds, a second, third, and so on, may be added in the same market. As we know from a historical perspective, if the concept succeeds and more rapid expansion is desired, franchising may prove a viable strategy for those with either capital limitations or those who wish to expand more rapidly. In the next chapter we will look closer at business development strategies.

The initial strategy selection process may include the pre–thought/planning related to growing the business; however, the first strategy selected usually relates to the product/service–level positioning upon which the business will base itself. Strategic positioning can be based on numerous concepts and strategies in the hospitality industry. Here are some examples:[1]

- *Highest Quality.* The product/service or brand represents the very best in the market with respect to quality. Hospitality industry firms that have opted for this position strategy include Four Seasons Hotels and Resorts, Ritz-Carlton, Singapore Airlines, Ruth's Chris Steak House, and Seabourn Cruise Line.

- *Least Expensive.* The product/service or brand is the most affordable in the marketplace. Examples include the low-cost airlines and the "rent a wreck" car rental concept.

- *Best Value.* The produce/service or brand is fairly priced, convenient to patronize/purchase, and considered a "value" in the market segment in which it competes. Examples include all-you-can-eat buffets such as Golden Corral, Southwest Airlines (other positioning strategies also apply to Southwest), and Dollar Rent A Car.

- *Best Designed or Styled.* The product/service or brand represents the newest or most advanced in design and style on the market and is likely a leader in innovation. A hospitality industry example is Embassy Suites when it was first introduced. Embassy pioneered the two-room suite concept with its atrium designs and service concepts.

- *Most Prestigious.* The product/service or brand appeals to the ego or the customer mentality that states "only the best will do." Again, Four Seasons or Ritz-Carlton could exemplify this positioning strategy. An exotic auto rental firm or exclusive gourmet restaurant would be another hospitality industry example.

- *Best Performance.* The product/service or brand exemplifies the best in performance. This is usually a strategy that cannot be claimed or chosen until later in the product/service life cycle or until there is external justification, such as being selected the best, most reliable, most durable, or easiest to work with. Hospitality industry examples are Continental Airlines, rated the best in customer service by the prestigious J.D. Power and Associates surveys for 5 consecutive years in the late 1990s and early 2000s, and Southwest Airlines, which garnered the "most reliable" award several times.

- *Most Convenient.* The product/service or brand is convenient in location or access. Again, this type of strategy can only be claimed later in the product/service life cycle when there is more omnipresence to the brand. Examples in the hospitality industry include Holiday Inn, Best Western, McDonald's, and Subway.

- *Fastest.* The product/service or brand offers fastest speed of delivery. A number of fast-food concepts have used this positioning strategy, such as Domino's, who initially guaranteed delivery of your pizza in 30 minutes or less.

- *Safest.* The product/service or brand claims to be the safest. This positioning strategy is one of the more difficult and risky to adopt. An airline may claim to have the safest record and then tragically an accident involving the carrier's brand occurs, thus nullifying the positioning. Sometimes an entire industry segment, such as the airlines, will repeatedly state, "Air travel is the safest form of transportation." This represents an industry positioning strategy.

- *Easiest to Use.* The product/service or brand bases its positioning strategy on being simple or the easiest to use. This can be exemplified by one aspect of the service, such as Hertz's "Go directly to your car," or by a brand's theme, such as Motel 6's "We'll leave the light on for you."

In the hospitality industry there are other positioning strategies such as "more for less" (foodservice concepts) or "more for more" (upgrade offers). And as previously indicated, products/services or brands may "evolve" or change their strategy based on their stage of development and also because of competitive activity.

ETHICS

All management strategies fall under the code of ethics. If the strategy bends or violates the code, it is unacceptable and cannot be pursued or implemented.

Strategy selection and positioning are directly related to the business development strategies and the growth options a product/service or brand pursues. Business development strategies are also a driving force behind the financial and brand strategies selected. In the next three chapters we will examine each of these growth strategies.

CHAPTER REVIEW

The products/services and brands that make up the full spectrum of the hospitality industry appeal to individual and/or multiple segments of the market. Their creation, introduction, and growth are driven by strategies related to their initial introductory positioning and to their growth and evolution as a brand. Successful hospitality industry brands usually adopt a single, clear, and defendable positioning for their brand. The positioning is directly interwoven with the development of the business, its pricing, service levels, and corporate culture; clearly delineating its strategies through positioning and effectively communicating that positioning to its target market results in success as a brand. Success may translate to "highest quality" or "least expensive"; both are valid positioning strategies in the hospitality industry.

KEY CONCEPTS/TERMS

Brand strategy   Target market
Positioning

DISCUSSION QUESTIONS

1. In thinking about different segments of the hospitality industry (airlines, cruise lines, gaming, etc.), which brands do you believe have the clearest positioning strategy in each segment?

2. Other than a unique product design (e.g., Embassy Suites), what other unique concepts might drive a clear positioning strategy?

3. When do you believe it is time for a hospitality industry brand to select a new positioning strategy?

4. Do you feel there is a relationship between the actual "look" of a brand and its selected positioning strategy? Give some examples.

5. Should your positioning strategy move with trends in the market?

ENDNOTES

1. P. Kotler, *Kotler On Marketing* (New York: The Free Press, 2000): 57–61.

CASE 1

Carnival Corporation—Strategy Selection and Positioning

In this chapter we discussed the concept of positioning strategies. The case which follows views a corporation's strategy to be the "biggest" player in its hospitality industry sector. It also demonstrates a strategy that extends to brand collection and individual market segments.

Carnival Corporation, based in Miami, is the world's largest cruise ship operator with control of about a third of the global market. Carnival Cruise Lines is its best-known brand with 16 ships. The company also owns/operates five other brands: Costa Crociere (7 ships), Holland America Line (11 ships), Windstar Cruises (4 ships), Cunard Line (2 ships), and Seabourn Cruise Line (6 ships). Carnival serves 2 million passengers per year. Additional ships are planned for many of its brands over the next 5 to 7 years.

Carnival Corporation generates over 90 percent of its revenue from cruise ships. The balance is generated through other travel- and hotel-related operations. These include a 26 percent interest in Airtours, the second largest tour operator in Britain, and Holland America Westours, which operates Alaska tours and also owns 14 hotels in the area.*

Carnival utilized a corporate management strategy that focused on multiple product/brand positioning in the cruise industry. This case example delineates the different brands' positions with respect to quality, price, market, and lifestyle. Further, its acquisitions strategy and product positioning strategies allow it to exemplify a company that serves not only multiple market segments but also a vast array of geographic markets.

History

Carnival Cruise Lines was founded by Ted Arison in 1972. Arison realized that a market for cruise vacations existed even though the era of the trans-Atlantic line had ended. He persuaded an old friend, Meshulam Riklis, who was the primary shareholder of American International Travel Service (AITS), to fund his purchase of a $6.5 million used vessel, the *Empress of Canada*. Carnival Cruise Lines was established as a subsidiary of AITS. Arison's vessel was renamed the *Mardi Gras*, reflecting Arison's belief that a line could be established to attract young, middle-class tourists who wanted a short seagoing vacation in a warm climate with food, fun, entertainment, music, and gambling at reasonable prices. However, his dream almost ended at the beginning. The *Mardi Gras* ran aground off Miami on its maiden voyage. The company fared poorly, and in 1974, Riklis sold the operation to Arison for $1 and the assumption of some $5 million in debt.

Things soon began to change; sales improved and by the end of 1975, the small line had enough money to buy another used ship. This vessel was the

*Information derived from www.carnivalcorp.com, Investor Overview: Brands.

Empress of Britain and Arison renamed it the *Carnivale*. Again, the name reflected the fun, vacation-oriented concept of cruising, which Arison fostered. An additional used ship purchase was made in the late 1970s. Carnival's first new building venture took place in 1978 when the *Tropicale* was built and delivered in 1981. Additional new buildings followed. Carnival Cruise Lines had become the largest cruise line in the world by 1987. That year it carried over 500,000 passengers and held about 20 percent of the North American cruise market.

Carnival continued to grow. The company went public in 1987, selling an 18 percent interest and raising some $400 million. This move marked a turning point for the company and allowed it to grow even faster. Newer ships were ordered. These included the *Fascination, Fantasy, Ecstasy, Celebration, Elation,* and others. The needs and wants of customers were factored into the design process. More space, more amenities, advanced ship control and propulsion systems, improved safety and fire control, improved fuel economy, and new entertainment options were added. At the turn of the decade, it introduced the *Carnival Triumph,* at over 100,000 gross registered tons (GRT), which represented one of the largest ships ever built. It is considerably larger than Arison's first ship, which was 18,261 GRT. The *Carnival Triumph* carries some 2,750 passengers.

Carnival's growth was accompanied by acquisitions. The Carnival Cruise Lines product was aimed at the mass market. Cruises were predominantly to the Caribbean from the United States, customers were mainly American, and "fun" was the basis of the cruise. Carnival began an expansion program, through horizontal integration, to seek other markets, and acquisitions helped them reach these markets. The names of their acquired subsidiaries were left unchanged. The company's name was changed to Carnival Corporation in 1994 to reflect its growing range of activities to various cruise market segments.

Acquisitions

Carnival attempted to purchase its primary competitor, Royal Caribbean Cruises, in 1988. This move was not successful, however, and it then turned its sights on the venerable Holland America Line. Holland America was active in Alaska and owned 14 hotels in that area under the Westmark brand as well as Holland America Westours, which provided tours in that region. It also owned and operated four sailing cruise ships under the Windstar name. Holland America competed with Carnival in the Caribbean as well. Windstar ships operated in the Caribbean as well as the South Pacific. The purchase was finalized in 1989. It gave Carnival access to the more upscale clientele of Holland America. The adventuresome passenger niche was served by Windstar (sail cruises). This move also positioned the company well in the growing Alaskan tour market, which was to become third after the Caribbean and the Mediterranean in sought-after cruise destinations.

Carnival developed a joint venture with Seabourn Cruise Line in 1992. This move would eventually lead to the buyout of Seabourn in 1999. Seabourn operates six small but upscale luxury vessels on worldwide routes. It is considered by many to be the highest-quality cruise line in the world. Its purchase signaled the beginning of Carnival's entry into the luxury market.

Another move into the luxury market was made in 1999 when Carnival purchased the well-known Cunard Line. This move added additional ships to its fleet, including the world-famous *Queen Elizabeth II* and *Caronia*. Cunard vessels were well positioned in the luxury end of the market. Its vessels operated worldwide, and the *Queen Elizabeth II* remained the only vessel of the liner era to still offer regular trans-Atlantic crossings from New York to Southampton and back for part of the year.

Carnival desired a stake in the growing European market. In 1996, it purchased a 26 percent stake in Airtours, the second largest tour operator in Britain. Together they purchased a 63 percent interest in Costa Crociere, the large Italian cruise operator that at the time held about a 28 percent market share in the European spring-fall market. Costa Crociere was fully purchased by Carnival in 2000.

Carnival Brands

Carnival Cruise Lines   The flagship of all Carnival brands, Carnival Cruise Lines is Carnival's largest and most profitable subsidiary. It is also the most popular cruise line in the world. Its "fun ship" marketing philosophy has successfully defined its position in the mass market sector.

The fun ship theme defines the company as a vacation alternative to land resorts. Carnival emphasizes the cruise experience itself rather than particular destinations. It also emphasizes the advantages of an all-inclusive vacation package. Carnival tries to avoid the stuffiness of the trans-Atlantic liner era by offering a wide variety of shipboard activities. These include Las Vegas–type shows, gambling, and other entertainment. The ships are even designed to foster the spirit of fun. This includes nontraditional interior and exterior features that reflect theme atmospheres.

This practice established the ship as the destination where the fun was and ports as secondary attractions. This marketing effort was a complete reversal of the destination-based marketing of trans-Atlantic–era passenger ships.

The Carnival Cruise Lines fleet of 16 cruise ships range in size from 36,674 GRT carrying about 1,000 passengers to those in the 100,000 GRT category carrying about 2,700 passengers.

The company operates cruises ranging from 3 to 16 days in duration to a variety of ports in the Bahamas, Caribbean, Mexican Riviera, Alaska, Hawaii, and the Panama Canal. Additional ports are regularly added. Vessels generally depart from the ports of Miami, Port Canaveral, Tampa, New Orleans, Los Angeles, San Juan, Ensenada, Vancouver, and Honolulu. Carnival also operates the world's first nonsmoking ship, the *Paradise*, that sails on alternating eastern and western Caribbean itineraries.

Carnival's average per-person, per-diem rate is about $195 (year 2000 U.S. dollars) without discount. Its cruises are strongly supported by those fun seekers whose average age is 43 years and whose average income is about $50,000. Carnival's occupancy rate has stood at over 100 percent for the 1980 to 2000 period, while the industry rate ranged from 70 percent to 88 percent. Its high occupancy rate has been accomplished through broad mass appeal with competitive, all-inclusive pricing. Its wide range of onboard and onshore activities further adds to the product offering. Carnival's "fun ship" marketing technique has brought cruising to the average American and changed forever the conservative, stodgy image of the passenger ships of the trans-Atlantic era.

In 1986, Carnival offered its vacation guarantee. It states that if a guest is not satisfied with his or her cruise experience, the guest may debark at the first non-U.S. port of call and receive reimbursement for coach airfare back to the port of passenger embarkation. This move was undertaken partly to gain first-time cruisers and was a first in the cruise line industry.

The Mediterranean cruising area is the second largest cruise vacation area after the Caribbean. Europeans have been experiencing a growth in leisure time since the early 1990s. In 1994, however, most European cruise lines were high-priced premium and luxury cruises; no cruise line offered the equivalent of Carnival's standard, low-priced cruise vacation. Carnival entered the European cruise business by completing the purchase of Costa Crociere in 2000.

Costa Crociere   Costa Crociere is a Genoa, Italy–based cruise ship operation which had its beginnings over 100 years ago. At that time, it operated cargo ships carrying olive oil. The company developed into one of the first cruise operators in the 1950s by operating trips from Miami. Costa is well known for its "cruising Italian style" theme. Their ships offer legendary Italian cuisine, Italian flair, and hospitality. Their largest ship, the *Costa Atlantica,* has 12 decks named after movies directed by the famous Italian director Federico Fellini.

It is estimated that Costa carries about 28 percent of the European cruise line trade during the spring to fall season. Two-thirds of the fleet operates in Europe; the others operate between Europe and the Caribbean. It owns seven ships, ranging in size from 25,000 GRT to 84,000 GRT. Its customer base is mainly European, with an average age of 45 years and an annual income of $50,000 plus. Average per-diem, per-person rates stand at about $245 (year 2000 U.S. dollars).

Holland America Line   Holland America Line was founded in 1873 as the Netherlands-America Steamship Company. This company primarily operated as a cargo and passenger carrying company. It was a major carrier of immigrants from Europe to the United States until well after the turn of the century. Unable to compete with the growing trans-Atlantic air travel business, Holland America suspended its trans-Atlantic passenger trade in 1971 and turned to offering full-time cruise vacations.

The company operates 11 ships ranging in size from 33,930 GRT to 63,000 GRT and carrying about 1,200 to 1,500 passengers each. Its vessels sail to a wide spectrum of ports in Alaska, Mexico, Europe, Canada, New England, South America, and around the world. Holland America also operated Windstar Cruises, a fleet of four specialty sail/cruise ships operating in Europe, the Caribbean, and Central America. Both fleets were purchased by Carnival in 1989.

Holland America cruises offer a more upscale cruising experience than Carnival Cruise Lines. Typical undiscounted cruises cost about $350 (year 2000 U.S. dollars) per person per diem. Clientele are generally over 50 years of age and a large percentage travel in group tours.

Its ships are well known for their onboard art collections as well as educational programs.

Windstar Cruises   Windstar Cruises was created in 1984 with the vision to offer an alternative to the typical cruise or vacation resort. The company was purchased by Holland America and later by Carnival Corporation in 1989.

Windstar's theme is "180 degrees from the ordinary." This theme clearly defines it as a company providing a different cruise vacation. It operates four sail yachts carrying between 148 and 312 passengers to Europe, the Caribbean, and Central America. Guests are offered unique itineraries and the freedom to be as active or relaxed as they want to be. The company defines this atmosphere as "casual elegance." Passengers range from those in their 20s to those in their 60s. However, the average age is 52 and the average income stands at about $120,000.

The company offers a unique niche or specialty cruise vacation experience that has received awards from both *Condé Nast* and *Travel and Leisure* magazines.

Cunard Line   Cunard Line was purchased by Carnival Corporation in 1999. This purchase allowed it to serve the luxury cruise ship market.

Cunard Line is one of the most famous brands in the history of passenger shipping. The company's founder, Samuel Cunard, began in 1839 by operating steamships for the British Admiralty in carriage of mail between Britain and North America. The company grew into a leader in the passenger ship trade. This company operated such famous liners as the *Queen Mary, Queen Elizabeth,* and *Queen Elizabeth II.*

Cunard customers are typically traditional, well off or wealthy, and generally over 50 years in age. About half of its passengers reside outside of North America, particularly in Britain and Europe. They seek the elegance and tradition that Cunard Line embodies. Typical per-diem, per-person costs, undiscounted, range from just over $400 to $600 (year 2000 U.S. dollars) and up, depending on accommodations.

At this writing, Cunard operates two ships. They are the *Queen Elizabeth II* and the smaller 25,000-GRT *Caronia.* A new vessel, the *Queen Mary,* of 140,000 GRT, is planned to be delivered in the next few years. Cunard ships operate on worldwide routes with emphasis on the Caribbean, Europe, and the Pacific. The *Queen Elizabeth II* continues to offer regular trans-Atlantic service between New York and Southampton for part of the year. It is the only cruise vessel that does so on a regular basis.

Seabourn Cruise Line Seabourn Cruise Line was fully purchased by Carnival Corporation in 1999. This exclusive fleet of "super yachts" has often been rated the best cruise line in the world.

Atle Brynestad, a Norwegian industrialist, founded Seabourn in 1987. The concept since its founding was to provide its customers with the highest level of personal service, equal to any hotel, resort, or restaurant ashore. Spaciousness and elegance is the rule, and guests are pampered in accordance with their own personal tastes and lifestyles.

The company now consists of six ships (all but one is a super yacht). These vessels carry 115 to just over 200 passengers. One vessel, a former Cunard Line ship integrated into the Seabourn fleet, carries about 760 passengers. These vessels operate worldwide, but focus on the Caribbean, South America, Europe, and Asia. Typical per-diem, per-person rates stand at about $750 (year 2000 U.S. dollars). The average Seabourn passenger is affluent (average income is about $200,000 per year). About half of Seabourn's passengers are repeat customers.

A Cruiser Profile

Cruise Line International Association (CLIA) is an industry organization that promotes the cruise industry. It became the sole marketing organization of the industry in 1984 when the Federal Maritime Commission consolidated other industry organizations into CLIA. Its member lines make up about 95 percent of the total North America berths and about 81 percent of all the ships. According to its cruiser profile, based on those who took cruises in the last 5 years (all North American bookings), more than 65 percent of all cruisers are North Americans.

Segmentation of the cruiser of today can also be done by age, income, and psychographic profile. CLIA 2001 studies have segmented prospective North American cruisers as: (1) family folks, 31 percent; (2) want-it-alls, 17 percent; (3) adventurers, 12 percent; (4) comfortable spenders, 25 percent; and (5) cautious travelers, 15 percent.*

Carnival has positioned itself in all major price/quality sectors through its various brands. Royal Caribbean, its chief competitor, is represented in only two areas. Carnival's major berth capacities lie in standard and premium (about 39,000 berths). In luxury and specialty sectors they are about 4,500 berths. Royal Caribbean holds a total of about 33,000 berths in standard and premium. Carnival has also positioned itself well for voyages in all of the major destination areas.

Carnival's competition in the cruise vacation business relates to only four other companies. They are Royal Caribbean, Princess Cruises, and Norwegian

*Information derived from www.cruising.org, CLIA Cruise Industry Overview.

Cruise Line, which is now part of Star Cruises. These four companies are esti-mated to control 64 percent of the total cruise vacation business. Carnival alone controls one-third of the business. It is clear that Carnival has been very successful in its brand acquisition and expansion strategy. Royal Caribbean, the second-rated company in terms of sales (about two-thirds of Carnival's), operates two brands. Celebrity is in the premium category and the Royal Caribbean name brand is in the standard-priced sector.

Carnival Corporation has successfully expanded through multiple posi-tioning strategies. Its brand positioning and acquisition strategies have enabled it to serve the various price/quality segments of the cruiser population with varying products from mass market to niche and luxury. Furthermore, by positioning its various subsidiaries in the top cruiser travel destinations, it is able to serve all the most popular destinations with more than one price/quality product.

Carnival's successful use of segmentation principles has allowed it to control about a third of the total cruise vacation market in this increasingly competitive field.

Discussion Questions

1. Do you believe it is more or less advantageous for Carnival to retain the brand names of the cruise lines it has acquired?

2. Where do you believe Carnival could capitalize on its size while retaining its multiple brands and positioning strategies?

CASE 2

Caesars Palace—Position Retention through Revitalization*

The Las Vegas market is one of the best markets in which to view product positioning in the hospitality industry. The casino hotels, resorts, and complexes have followed and supported the concept of "comparison to the newest" for decades. This case looks at a market leader for many years and the strategic steps it has undertaken over the past few decades to remain competitive and "in the game" with the new and spectacular mega-casinos.

This case focuses on Caesars Palace in Las Vegas. It examines Caesars Palace's positioning technique through its development efforts. It also looks at how it is positioned compared to a few of its primary competitors. The Bellagio (www.bellagiolasvegas.com) and Venetian (www.venetian.com) were selected based on hotel and casino size, elegance and grandeur, and perceived position in the market.

It is difficult to position Caesars Palace in relation to its competitors. All three casinos and hotels have so much to offer their patrons. Each hotel and casino is impressive in its own right and brings elegance, opulence, and grandeur, among other things, to the table. Each has an impressive number of hotel rooms or suites, meeting spaces, restaurants, shopping areas, and entertainment.

However, Caesars Palace sets itself apart from the others because it has always been known and is still known as the "Golden Standard" of the hotel and casino industry. It continuously develops itself to maintain one of the top positions in the casino industry. Caesars Palace hosts major and prestigious events contributing to its "headquarters" positioning. It also hosts only the most well-known entertainers.

Caesars Palace was built in 1966 for $25 million and over the years has had approximately $1 billion in renovations. The Bellagio was built in 1998 for $1.6 billion, while the Venetian was built in 1998 for $1.2 billion.

Although Caesars Palace has been a premier hotel and casino since its inception, in the late 1990s it needed further expansion and renovation to maintain its dominance over the newer mega-hotels. In 1998, Caesars Palace spent $600 million on expansion and renovations. According to the Palace's president, this new construction and renovation "effectively positioned the resort as the leading hospitality facility in Las Vegas." This new construction increased its room count by 1,134 and its meeting and function space by 110,000 square feet, added 23,000 square feet in spa and fitness center space, included a 4.5-acre "Garden of the Gods" swimming complex, and added two new restaurants and a 5,000-seat special events center. The renovation also enlarged and remodeled the front desk area, expanded the front entrance, and enhanced the baggage handling system.

*Information derived from www.caesarspalace.com.

Caesars Palace also planned a $475 million, 900-suite, all-suite wing, which would bring its room total to 3,350. This construction plan also included a 4,000-seat entertainment arena. Although the events of September 11, 2001, temporarily postponed the all-suite wing construction, Caesars Palace continued with construction of its 4,000-seat entertainment arena, the Colosseum. In addition to hotel and casino development, Caesars Palace positions itself through competitive pricing, as shown in Figure 1.

While Caesars has made a massive investment to remain competitive with the newer mega-casinos, it must continue to do even more. The Bellagio, Venetian, and whatever is on the horizon in the future have the strategic advantage of being newer in a market that inherently wants to "try the next thing." Caesars is to be complimented for its efforts to retain both its leadership positioning as "the" events and entertainment headquarters hotel.

Discussion Questions

1. Can you think of any other strategies Caesars' management might utilize to retain or regain its top position now and in the future?
2. Do you think "new" product has an advantage or disadvantage in the hospitality industry? Why?

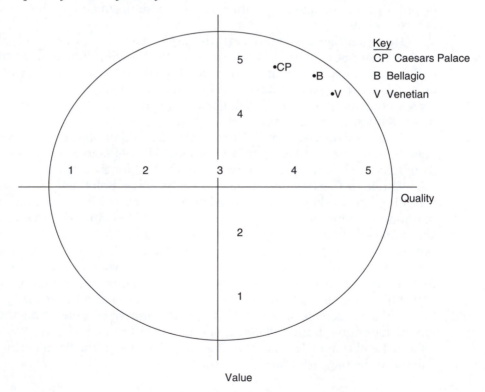

Figure 1 Caesars Palace Positioning Map

PART 2

The Growth Strategies of Development, Financial Options, and Brand Strategy

In Part 2 the growth- and development-related managerial strategies are delineated. In Chapter 4, we look at hospitality industry business development–related strategies. These include a special focus on franchising and management contracts, two of the major growth strategies for many sectors within the hospitality industry.

Part 2 continues in Chapter 5 to focus on the closely related financial strategy options. Strategies are linked to key concepts such as return on investment, return on assets managed, cash flow, and so on. This chapter delineates the various strategies that are most apropos and related to each major industry sector. It also presents a linkage between the pace of growth and the financial strategy selection.

Finally, this part focuses on brand strategy and management in Chapter 6. This chapter discusses the major components of brand development and the major strategic management options for brands within the hospitality industry. It further presents managerial strategies related to purchasing new brands, nourishing existing brands, and rejuvenating tired brands.

Chapter 4

Business Development Strategies

CHAPTER OBJECTIVES

- To describe how various hospitality businesses have developed.
- To identify the major ways in which to expand and grow businesses in the hospitality industry.
- To demonstrate the relationship between selective growth strategies and specific sectors of the hospitality industry.
- To delineate the development process for the major industry segments.
- To define the key techniques related to expanding businesses in the hospitality industry.

In the first three chapters the historical evolution of the industry was discussed. In these chapters we described how the various sectors within the hospitality industry grew from a geographical perspective. Some businesses started with one unit in one market and expanded within that market, then on to other markets in that region and eventually nationwide. Some businesses expanded from one country to another in their pursuit of growth. Today, we see that most sectors of the hospitality industry have a global focus for growth and expansion or for finding and developing new customers. Airlines seek to expand their route systems through code sharing and alliances, as well as acquisitions (e.g., American Airlines' acquisition of TWA or United's many code-sharing agreements). Attractions such as those developed by Disney draw people from markets around the globe. Car rental companies open offices and develop cooperative agreements or joint ventures with sister brands on other continents. Cruise lines acquire both capacity new routes (itineraries) and customers through mergers and acquisitions. Foodservice establishments expand and grow around the globe through franchising and joint ventures, (e.g., T.G.I. Friday's, McDonald's and Burger King). The gaming industry seeks to improve its take/profitability by enticing customers from distant markets through various forms of marketing and related agreements. And finally, travel-related services are offered through extensive "networks" of agency affiliations, global distribution systems, and multiple-partner agreements. All of these factors make the hospitality industry one of the most "global" industries in the world.

INITIAL BUSINESS DEVELOPMENT STRATEGIES

What drove the various players and the overall industry to grow so rapidly and across such a vast geographic horizon? There were many different driving forces behind both individual business growth and the overall development of the industry itself. Individual firms desired to extend the number of markets they served. Others desired to extend their "brand" into new global markets. The growth of business and leisure travel became yet another propellant of industry sector growth. As businesses became more multinational, everything from the allure of an attractive real estate investment to a desire to dilute risk by being in multiple global markets fueled the development of the hospitality industry. The hospitality industry also provided a good venue in which to transfer capital and spread out assets for corporations.

Global Strategies

In general, there were three more-defined global business development strategies that emerged from all of the previously referenced driving forces. First, some expanded globally under the strategic philosophy referred to as *transnational*. A transnational business operates on a global scale but permits each unit to develop in its own right according to local market needs. In this case the overriding philosophy of business development is driven by local (within that country or area of the globe) market needs and nuances. To a large degree, McDonald's functions outside the United States as a transnational when you consider the degree to which its menu may vary in certain markets (for instance, where beef is not consumed and veggie burgers replace the hamburger). Resorts often take on local market flavor in decor and operational aspects such as food and beverage offerings.

The second strategic business development philosophy focused on a *global* perspective. In this case, a product or products, exactly the same, are offered to appeal to as many customers as possible. For example, American Airlines, Japan Airlines, and British Airlines each offer a product (aircraft, brand attributes) with the same look and feel around the globe in any market they serve. We are moving more and more into a marketplace that identifies with global brands. People anywhere in the world expect Coca-Cola to be Coca-Cola or Nescafe to be Nescafe or McDonald's to be fast food (given some transnational adaptations). In essence, as the world becomes more and more a global marketplace, there becomes an increasing advantage to having a globally recognized brand on your product or service.

The third concept or strategic business development philosophy related to global expansion is referred to as *multinational*.[1] A multinational business often uses a flagship unit to provide ideas for new units. In essence, it exports its domestic expertise to a given market and they expand from that base. Examples include hotel chains that develop a flagship hotel in the capital city of another country and then grow their "brand" within the country through local (to that country or region) developers. To a large extent, that is how Holiday Inn and Ramada expanded in their push into a number of foreign markets such as Canada and Germany, respectively.

Global expansion comes with multiple and varying degrees of foreign business practices both from a development and an operational perspective. Understanding that there are various practices and levels of risk associated with political and economic stability in foreign markets is essential. The overall challenge of the new foreign market accepting the product or service offering of an alien business is usually much greater than in domestic development. Certainly, there are operating nuances related to cultural perceptions that may directly affect the business development strategy and subsequent operations. Business protocol is different around the globe, as are cultural considerations and even management perspectives.

Global Challenges

Let's discuss a few of the challenges of operating in a global market and relate them to the overall business development process and strategy, beginning with business protocol. Business protocol can be defined as a set of unwritten guidelines or rules for conducting business. It can also include the related activities of dining, entertaining, and so on. If you are not aware of the business protocol in a country or market into which you wish to expand, you are likely to fail or be extremely frustrated trying to enter the market or develop partnership relations. This brings us to cultural considerations. Business development must take into consideration the "other" side's perspective. The presumption that one's own cultural use and habits are superior (referred to as ethnocentrism) will usually result in no deal or eventually a sour relationship with foreign partners. All cultures can be found guilty of stereotyping individuals from other countries. This can lead to prolonged development negotiations, as well as to deals never culminated due to philosophical differences. These differences will usually manifest themselves in the negotiation phase of a business deal. Just as there are different cultural perspectives between countries, there are different ways and styles of negotiating. A hard-driving, table-pounding executive may well be perceived as "rude" and an unacceptable partner by one whose negotiating style (culture driven) is to establish friendship and trust as an overriding priority.

Finally, differing managerial perspectives may also influence business development strategy. How managers view their jobs, their company, and their employees varies greatly from culture to culture. Perceptions of leadership, power, personal communications, individual rights, and even organizational structure may well be juxtaposed between two neighboring countries or markets. Understanding these differences is often the key to good relationships, successful market expansion, and ultimately strong operations and financial results.

TECHNOLOGY

Software packages, modeling techniques, and instant access to information via the internet have and will continue to influence the decision-making process in the business development area of the hospitality industry.

It is important to understand these overall global perspectives and business development processes to move toward successful partnerships and growth. The companies that understand these perspectives have become global brands, and those that do not have failed to expand beyond their own country borders. Entrepreneurship and individuals drove the early growth of brands, products, and services in the hospitality industry. Growth of business through product and market segmentation within one's own marketplace (country) rapidly followed initial product/service offerings. Domestic franchising and building partnerships and alliances fueled even more growth in the hospitality industry. Both domestically and to some extent internationally, "incentives" led to even further development. These incentives included advantageous tax abatements, franchising rights, and other monetary motivations from governments (local, federal, and international) and from lenders (e.g., the International Monetary Fund and the World Bank).

INFLUENTIAL FACTORS

Business development strategies, both domestic and international, are influenced by some unique factors related to the service sector and hospitality industry itself. Businesses in the hospitality industry may succeed or fail for reasons that are not at all product related. For example, in the hospitality industry, innovation has little or no protection. Your concept, idea, and even perceived uniqueness are readily copied. It is difficult to think of a competitive advantage concept that cannot be readily copied in the hospitality industry, be it an atrium, drive-in, all-suite hotel, or luxury car rental. This translates to a highly competitive business development environment often crowded with multiple choices in products/services. Further, in many parts of the hospitality industry we have simultaneous production and consumption, perishable inventory, and the customer as part of the delivery process. Not only is quality control often in the hands of the hourly waged employee, the assets bearing the brand name are being managed by others. The industry is also labor and capital intensive and highly fragmented.

Selecting the right strategy to grow a hospitality business is often based on the management team's ability to address and execute that strategy as well as the financial capability of the organization. Going from being a domestic company to being a multicontinental or global company requires immense resources and talent. Some in our industry have opted to remain local in nature (domestic or regional); others have opted to go global. Some have had success with a singleness strategy (one product/service offering only), while others have tiered and segmented their product/service offerings. Some like Cendant have sought not only to be a brand collector in one segment of the industry but also to pursue both a horizontal and a vertical integration strategy, vertically adding multiple product types and brands to its lodging holdings (Ramada, Days Inn, Howard Johnson) and horizontally acquiring rental car companies, reservations systems, and direct marketing companies. Some have chosen to evaluate their business and measure their success with indicators such as REVPAR (revenue per available room) or revenue per passenger mile, while others have taken a newer and bigger picture and use REVPAC (revenue per available customer) as an indicator. The public companies' business development strategies must also take into consideration the financial impact of seeking to expand while meeting investor expectations.

Earlier in this chapter we referenced initial business development strategies focused on more units per market or more markets served (geographic expansion). The balance of the chapter will focus on the various strategic options by which a hospitality business is developed and expanded. These strategic options should be viewed along with the financial strategy options delineated in the next chapter. Moreover, these business development options need to be viewed within the context of an organization's total capabilities, often expressed in the form of a strategic business or development plan. Later in the text we will closely examine the strategic planning concept and how it helps to organize and provide direction and goals for business development.

STRATEGIC DEVELOPMENT OPTIONS

Methods to grow a hospitality business include everything from ownership to alliances, and not all methods are compatible with all sectors of the industry. Let's look at the major industry sectors and summarize the major business development options/methods for growth.

Airlines

The airline industry sector is very capital intensive, with a single aircraft costing in excess of $100 million. To grow in this sector, leasing plays a major role for fleet expansion. Leasing allows for the replacement of older aircraft with newer, often larger and more efficient aircraft. Outright purchasing or ownership requires excessive amounts of cash in a very cash flow–sensitive industry sector. Airlines also grow through techniques other than added capacity and efficiencies from leasing. Growth comes from serving new markets with stronger demand than existing markets or where a competitive advantage exists; this is called route expansion. Airlines also grow their business through acquisitions of smaller airlines, gates or slots at airports, and building alliances. With respect to the latter, code-sharing and marketing alliances are most common.

Attractions

The attractions sector of the hospitality industry is very diverse. It includes many different types of attractions, from the mega-parks (e.g., Disney World and Universal Studios) to regional attractions such as Six Flags (smaller parks and more locations) to local attractions of a smaller magnitude. Smaller attractions or single attractions tend to grow through ownership and joint ventures in their initial stages. Licensing and acquisitions are strategies that fuel growth for the larger players. Income is generated from franchising the rights for food, beverages, store/retail outlets, and the like. If the theme park or attraction is successful in developing its brand or characters, it also grows its licensing and ancillary businesses. Land for expansion may be purchased or leased on a long-term basis. Equipment may also be purchased, leased, or acquired, depending on the financial situation of the entity.

Car Rental

Business development strategies for the car rental sector encompass a variety of growth methods. Most major car rental companies have direct relationships with the auto manufacturers who may own all or part of the car rental firm. In addition, the car rental companies' fleets may consist of the auto manufacturers' makes and models provided at special fleet purchase prices. Facilities may be owned, if desired from a real estate investment perspective, but are more likely to be leased. In addition to leasing, the actual growth of the business can be attributed to franchising and joint ventures. Like the airline sector, the large tend to acquire the smaller. Also, joint ventures and percentage ownership may occur to help the economics of the car rental company or to spur more growth. Marketing agreements and alliances in international markets are also common practices.

Cruise Lines

The cruise line sector was one of the fastest growing segments of the hospitality industry at the close of the last century and the onset of the new century. Fueled by market growth from an aging population, newfound leisure activity time for families and singles, and spectacular new ships, this sector has expanded rapidly. The business development strategies include ownership, leasing, joint ventures, and more and more acquisitions and mergers. Capacity has been acquired and increased by replacing older smaller ships with mega-ships. The sector has also grown as new areas of tourism interest have blossomed and created demand for new itineraries or increased capacity on existing itineraries.

Food Service

The foodservice sector continues its remarkable growth as lifestyle and demographic trends propel demand for its product offerings. Common business development strategies to grow foodservice enterprises include franchising, leasing, acquisitions, management contracts, ownership, joint ventures, and retheming existing facilities. By far the dominant business development strategy has been franchising. Later in this chapter, we will discuss franchising and focus on the foodservice sector, as well as other sectors of the industry that have propelled their growth through the business development strategy option of franchising.

Gaming

Another of the fastest-growing sectors of the industry over the last two decades is the gaming sector. Fueled by market demand as well as the desire by states and municipalities to increase or replace revenue (taxes), gaming has enjoyed phenomenal growth. Developing and growing gaming businesses, casinos, and related facilities has been accomplished primarily by ownership and acquisition strategies. Also, in the case of many existing facilities and destinations, a redevelopment strategy has fueled growth. One only needs to look at Las Vegas over the past few decades to see how all three of these strategies have paid off for the major players. Growth in this sector has also come from "local market" facilities (facilities designed to serve the market in which they are located versus destination facilities) and from the rapid growth of Native American–owned casinos. Two excellent examples of the latter are the Foxwoods and Mohegan Sun complexes in Connecticut.

Lodging

Business development options for growth in the lodging sector include acquisitions, franchising, joint ventures, leases, management contracts, ownership, redevelopment, room additions, and new starts (brands). Franchising and management contracts have been the leading business growth strategies, along with acquisitions at the corporate player level. While over one hundred new brands and concepts have been introduced over the last decade, many have grown through franchising. Redevelopment includes refurbishing, retheming, and product hybrids and segmentation. An inspection of the megaplayers reveals the significance of the various options and combinations thereof that have contributed to their growth. For example, Cendant has been collecting brands through acquisitions, most at favorable investment prices. Cendant has purchased primarily franchised brands and then accelerated the growth of the brand through more aggressive franchising. InterContinental Hotels Group (formerly Six Continents, Bass PLC, and Holiday Inn Corp.) also purchased brands, tiered brands, and accelerated its franchising efforts. Inter-Continental Hotels has also changed flags on some of its lodging facilities (for instance, converted Crowne Plazas to InterContinentals). Marriott, after dividing itself into Host Marriott, the real estate ownership company, and Marriott International, the management contract/operating company, has grown through acquisitions of brands (such as Renaissance and Ritz-Carlton), through increased franchising of its lower-tier brands (e.g., Courtyard), and through picking up additional management contracts through its reputation as an excellent operator. Starwood, a real estate investment trust, developed its lodging business through the acquisition of such brands as Sheraton and Westin and development of newer brands such as St. Regis and W Hotels. Hilton has grown dramatically through the acquisition of Promus, which included brands such as Hampton Inn, Embassy Suites, and Doubletree. Hilton has also added a new tiered product—the Garden Inn concept—and fueled the franchising of many of its brands. Hilton also has rapidly expanded its gaming holdings. Overall, the lodging sector business development growth strategy has relied on acquisitions and mergers, franchising, and the concept of management contracts to grow.

Travel-Related Services

Yet another significant sector of the hospitality industry is travel-related services. Travel-related services includes travel agencies (retailers), travel wholesalers, tour operators, incentive travel companies, travel-related credit card companies, travel management companies, reservation services, global distribution services (GDS) companies, and travel/sales rep firms and consortiums. The business development growth strategy of this sector has been exemplified by acquisitions, such as Carlson Companies' acquisition of Wagonlit Travel and other agency groups. Alliances and joint ventures in the GDS area have led to acquisitions and mergers as well as spin-offs, such as AMR (parent of American Airlines) spinning off its SABRE reservations technology into its own entity as a free-standing company. Alliances in airline reservation systems have also been accompanied by shared investment and sales over the past decade. The credit card sector has grown through the issuance of cobranded travel-related cards tied to the second currency of mileage awards for card usage. Today, travel management companies, which originally grew through acquiring or winning new accounts, expand through mergers and franchising. Travel management companies are seeing their business decline as corporations on an increasingly rapid basis implement new software services to manage their own travel.

THE BIG PICTURE

Looking at all sectors of the hospitality industry, it is evident that the primary business development option for growth in the larger sectors such as foodservice and lodging has been franchising. Franchising has also played a key business development role in the car rental and travel-related services sectors. Another major strategy to grow selected sectors has been management contracts—managing the operations of someone else's asset for a fee. While the lodging sector is the primary venue for this, the concept also exists in other sectors such as foodservice and travel-related services. We also see the big getting bigger through acquisitions and mergers in almost all sectors of the industry. Acquisitions as a growth/business development strategy will likely continue in future years. Since the concepts of franchising and management contracts have played such a significant role in the development of the major sectors of the hospitality industry, it is logical that we look more in depth at both concepts.

Franchising

To develop a business one essentially has three choices: start from scratch, acquire an established business, or buy a franchise. The hospitality industry has capitalized on the franchise option to grow in most sectors. In this section we will provide a brief overview of franchising, examine some of the different franchise relationships, and look at the relationships to the hospitality sectors and the overall global growth of the industry. Statistics have demonstrated that buying into an established brand through franchising provides a four-times-greater chance for success than starting from scratch and is actually two times more successful than outright acquiring a business.

Franchising as a business development strategy is said to have originated in the hospitality industry in the 18th century when English and German tavern owners and brewers sought to expand. The real surge in franchising as we know it today took place throughout the 20th century and was launched with the franchising of the A&W Restaurants in the 1920s. Today, franchising remains the dominant and preferred method of rapidly growing a hospitality business. There are many reasons for franchising's preference as a business development strategy. Franchising provides a faster way to market entry and a quicker method to gain market share. Franchising also provides access to the power of advertising, instant brand awareness (awareness equates to sales), and a unique way to expand on a global basis. With respect to the latter, franchising allows for a concept to be exported while capitalizing on a local market partner (franchisee) who already has the working knowledge of that market.

Moreover, franchising is a mutually beneficial financial partnership between a large organization and an independent entrepreneur. In essence, the franchisor sells the right to conduct business using the organization's name, trademarks, products/services, business procedures, marketing and advertising, and everything else to the franchisee. An astounding 90 percent plus of franchises opened in the last 5 years are still open. Success is attributed to three elements: (1) an established identity and exclusive trade name, (2) a finely tuned and proven business format, and (3) a long-term financial relationship between the franchisor and franchisee.

As previously indicated, the primary sectors within the hospitality industry that have deployed franchising as a major business development strategy are lodging, foodservice, car rental, and travel-related services. The industry provides franchising opportunities at many different price points for the independent businessperson or entrepreneur. For example, entry into the travel agency business might involve an initial franchise fee as low as $5,000 to $10,000 and then a small ongoing percent of revenue. In the foodservice sector, to obtain a fast-food franchise usually involves higher investment and ongoing royalty fees. Royalty fees are the amount charged by a franchisor for the ongoing use of the brand name and support. Royalty fees are usually expressed as a percent of sales. The franchisee also has the cost of the facility and operations to bear. Franchisors may provide technical assistance related to construction and training. Some charge separate fees and others provide the advice gratis.

Entry into the lodging sector is usually more costly for a franchisee due to the higher cost of the total business. In addition, the fee structures can be quite complex and change often due to new marketing programs, changes in frequent-stay programs, and technical services.

Franchising provides a quick start with a name brand for the business. It likewise provides an ongoing source of revenue for the franchisor through the various fees and royalties. Franchising is in essence a win-win scenario in the hospitality industry, both domestically and on a global basis. Franchising remains the single greatest business development strategy in the hospitality industry today.

Management Contracts

A major driver in developing the lodging sector and contributing to the growth and profitability of the sector is the strategy option of management contracts. A management contract is an agreement between a management company and a hotel owner (or other type of owned hospitality industry facility such as attractions complex) to operate the hotel/facility. There are two major types or categories of management companies. One is an independent management company and the other a chain management company.

The independent management company provides management and operating expertise to lodging properties it owns, leases, or manages, without the use of a national trademark or reservations system of its own. It may operate a franchised property and have access to a national chain's reservation system. The management or operating company may be a separate entity from the owner, in which case the contract is considered to be an "arm's length" contract. If, on the other hand, the operating company is a subsidiary of the owner or the owner and operating entity have common ownership, the negotiated contract would not be considered at arm's length.[2] There are many large independent management companies in the lodging sector, such as Interstate Hotels & Resorts, Inc., which operates/manages numerous properties under major brand-named trademarks and in over a hundred facilities and thousands of rooms.

A chain management company is a company that provides management and operating expertise to lodging (or other sector) properties it owns, leases, or manages (for other owners), using its national trademark and reservations system as an integral part of the management of the property. Most major brands/chains offer management contracts (services), such as Marriott International, Hilton, and so on.

The management contract process usually begins with a request for proposal. Owners review the management company in depth before committing to a contract. Looking at past performance, actual operating results for similar facilities, reputation, and integrity. Owners focus on the management itself—its accessibility, willingness to share information, and so on. Further, owners evaluate the marketing and sales strength and performance of the management company and assess the overall compatibility of the management company with their type of investment. And finally, there is a detailed review of the actual contract terms offered before any selection occurs. This review focuses on fee structures, all contract terms (including incentives, termination clauses, and penalties), and even reports to be provided.

Fee structures are usually divided into what are referred to as "basic" fees and "incentive" fees. The basic management fee is the remuneration the owner agrees to pay the management company for performing the duties specified in the contract. The basic fee is usually an agreed-upon percentage of gross revenues, but sometimes a fixed dollar amount may be used. The incentive fee is any remuneration the owner agrees to pay the management company for generating a predetermined profit, income, or cashflow level from the operation. The fee may be an agreed-upon percentage of gross operating profit or cash flow after debt service and other specified ownership obligations. The incentive fee may be paid in addition to or in lieu of the basic fee, depending upon the contract provisions.

Fee structures (base and incentive) vary widely and have taken on many different mixes and formulas over the years. Some variations in the mix or structure are related to nuances of the individual property, and some may be related to the prevailing economic climate in the industry. Traditionally, basic fees have been in the range of 1 to 5 percent of gross revenue. The length or term of management contracts also is a moving target or negotiated item in many cases. Traditionally, management contracts were tied to the length of the loan or mortgage, (generally 20 or 30 years). Today management contract terms tend to be much shorter in duration—5, 10, 15, or 20 years. Some may even be for as few as 1 or 2 years.

Other fees related to management companies may include separate fees for technical services such as design and planning. Also, there are usually "pre-opening fees" associated with new construction. Pre-opening fees are fees paid to the management company for developing a pre-opening plan and budget, supervising pre-opening activities such as sales and collateral materials development, and actually overseeing the opening of the hotel or lodging facility.

Management contracts related to international lodging facilities tend to be more complex due to the variety of issues surrounding operating in another country where local laws, business protocol, and cultural considerations all must be incorporated. Selection criteria for international facilities will also focus more on the management company's actual operating experience in the respective market, the actual management personnel to be assigned to the facility, and other related standard operating procedures.

ETHICS

No business development deal merits bending the code of ethics even if the practice is acceptable in the foreign market.

Equally important to both domestic and international owners and operators are the financial strength and proven financial record of both entities.

Key items like risk sharing, redeployment/reinvestment of capital to keep up the facilities, and marketing performance to deliver customers/guests are critical to reaching a successful relationship and longer-term contract or renewal.

There are five areas into which the provisions of most management contracts are subdivided. These are: (1) financial provisions, (2) administrative provisions, (3) operating provisions, (4) marketing provisions, and (5) general provisions. These categories are intended to cover all the key provisions listed in Figure 4-1.

As management contracts are tied to a facility, owner, operator, or constantly changing competitive environment, there is usually considerable attention paid to the termination clause in the agreement. Areas to be clearly delineated under termination usually include failure on agreement, option for property sale, bankruptcy or assignment, owner's option without course, license suspensions or revisions, and operator performance provisions. Finally, there is also usually a process specified within the management contract to which both owner and operator agree to adhere with respect to communications. The process for communications most often includes the specified frequency (monthly, quarterly, or annually) of various types of meetings and reviews. These may involve regular ongoing operations (monthly or quarterly meetings), annual budget reviews, capital/FF&E (fixtures, furniture, and equipment) reviews, and legal issues.

In general, over the past decade management contracts have tended to be of shorter term, be more tailored to the project fees, require less basic fees and more incentive fees, and require stricter operating performance standards and more detailed reporting. Also, of late there is greater demand for operator accountability for charges and greater owner control/approval of capital, as well as more flexible termination clauses.

Both franchising and management contracts are primary business development strategy options due to the fact that both generate income (fees) with minimum investment (capital). This equation allows for more rapid expansion than ownership or joint ventures. Its drawbacks include perhaps a lesser degree of control (quality and brand image) and certainly missing out on real

• Contract terms	• Transfer of ownership
• Management fee	• Exclusivity
Basic	• Insurance and condemnation
Incentive	proceeds
• Reporting requirements	• Personnel
• Approvals	• Reserve for replacement
• Termination	• Restrictions
• Operator's investment in the property	• Indemnity
• Operator's home office expenses	• Technical assistance

Figure 4–1 Key Provisions
Source: C. Borchgrevink, *Perspectives on the Hospitality Industry* (Dubuque, IA: Kendall/Hunt, 1999): 98–99.

estate appreciation. Lodging facilities generally use up large amounts of cash in their early years; thus ownership also depresses cash availability for expansion in the formative years of developing the overall business.

CHAPTER REVIEW

Most major sectors of the hospitality industry have experienced considerable growth over the past decade. This growth while ultimately driven by multiple demand factors such as increasing population, greater affluence, a higher propensity to dine out and travel, and so on, was also a product of the businesses within the industry aggressively expanding. While many different strategies or options were deployed by all the sectors within the hospitality industry, franchising and management contracts propelled growth in the larger foodservice and lodging sectors. Globalization and the exporting of hospitality brands to new foreign markets also fueled growth. Further, new brands, concepts, designs, and services flourished in almost all sectors of the industry.

Finally, it is a business development process marked not only by new starts or brands but also by acquisitions and mergers. As we reflect on today's hospitality industry we see that global mega-corporations have developed in many sectors of our industry. Some of these corporations have also horizontally and vertically integrated components of the industry under their overall umbrella of products and services. Hospitality industry company brands such as McDonald's, Marriott, Hilton, Hertz, Disney, and more are now viewed as global players. In the next few chapters we will examine the financial, brand, and marketing strategies that have all contributed to the successful development of one of the world's largest industries—the hospitality industry.

KEY CONCEPTS/TERMS

Accountability	Independents
Acquisitions	Joint ventures
Alliances	Limited partnerships
Brand collecting	Management companies
Centralization	Management contracts
Concentration	Multinational
Consortiums	Product hybrid
Cooperative agreements	Royalty fees
Franchising	Segmentation
Global	Transnational
Horizontal integration	Vertical integration

DISCUSSION QUESTIONS

1. What are some of the key reasons for the success of franchising in the hospitality industry?
2. Define at least three benefits of a successful joint venture relationship.
3. List some ways to improve return on investment for growing businesses in the industry.
4. What are some of the concerns and implications for a hospitality business that desires to expand outside of its own country?
5. What are some considerations for hospitality businesses that desire to serve the global marketplace?

ENDNOTES

1. M. Olsen, J. West, & E. Ching-Yick Tse, *Strategic Management in the Hospitality Industry* (New York: John Wiley & Sons, 1998): 282.
2. J. Eyster, *The Negotiation and Administration of Hotel and Restaurant Management Contracts* (Ithaca, NY: James J. Eyster, 1988): 4.

CASE 1

McDonald's Corporation—Business Development through Franchising and Joint Ventures

As indicated in this chapter, franchising has been the dominant business development strategy in many sectors of the hospitality industry and especially in the foodservice sector. This case looks at the franchising and joint-venture strategies of a leading global fast-food franchisor with over 5,000 franchisees worldwide.

McDonald's Corporation develops, operates, franchises, and services a worldwide system of restaurants that prepare, assemble, package, and sell a limited menu of value-priced foods. All restaurants are operated by the company or under the terms of franchise agreements, by franchisees that are independent third parties, or by affiliates operating under joint-venture agreements between the company and local business people.*

McDonald's operates primarily in the quick-service hamburger restaurant business. The restaurants offer a substantially uniform menu consisting of hamburgers and cheeseburgers, including the Big Mac and Quarter Pounder with Cheese, the Filet-O-Fish, several chicken sandwiches, French fries, chicken nuggets, salads, milkshakes, cones, cookies, and soft drinks. They also offer a variety of breakfast items and children's meals. In addition, the restaurants sell a variety of other products during limited promotional time periods. The company tests new products on an ongoing process. McDonald's restaurants operate worldwide.

McDonald's is a strong company with a great brand, customer acceptance, and outstanding owner/operators and suppliers. McDonald's is the largest and best-known foodservice retailer, with over 30,000 restaurants in more than 120 countries.

- First franchised McDonald's restaurant: Des Plaines, Illinois, 1955
- First McDonald's franchisee: Art Bender, 1955
- First international McDonald's: British Columbia, Canada, 1967
- McDonald's international division created: 1969
- First twin grand opening: Two restaurants in Cairo, Egypt, 1994
- Seven of the world's busiest McDonald's are located in Hong Kong.
- 70% of McDonald's restaurants, nearly 25,000 restaurants around the world, are operated by more than 5,000 franchisees and affiliates.
- 85% of McDonald's restaurants in the United States are franchised.

Figure 1 Notable McDonald's Franchising Facts

*A. Zuber, "New Brands, Lives Revitalized—McDonald's," *Nation's Restaurant News* 34, no. 21 (May 22, 2000).

McDonald's vision is to be the world's best and largest quick-service restaurant chain. Being the best means providing outstanding quality, service, cleanliness, and value. To achieve its vision, it focuses on three worldwide strategies:

- Be the best employer for the people in each community around the world.
- Deliver operational excellence to its customers in each of its restaurants.
- Achieve enduring profitable growth by expanding the brand and leveraging the strengths of the McDonald's system through franchising, innovation, and technology.

McDonald's business is divided into two main parts, company-owned stores and franchising. It has relied on its franchisees to pay a major role in its success. McDonald's remains committed to franchising as the predominant way of doing business. Approximately 70 percent of McDonald's worldwide are owned and operated by franchisees. McDonald's continues to be recognized as a premier franchising company around the world. Perhaps the fact that McDonald's management listens so carefully to its franchisees is one reason why McDonald's is perennially named as *Entrepreneur Magazine*'s number one franchise for franchisee satisfaction.

Its franchising system is built on the premise that the McDonald's Corporation can be successful only if its franchisees are successful first. The company believes in maintaining a partnering relationship with its owner/operators, suppliers, and employees. Success for McDonald's Corporation flows from the success of its business partners.

The selection of prospective franchisees and owner/operators is based on an assessment of overall business experience and personal qualifications. The company looks for individuals with good "common business sense," a demonstrated ability to effectively lead and develop people, and a history of previous success in business and life endeavors. A restaurant background is not necessary. It franchises only to individuals, not to corporations, partnerships, or passive investors. McDonald's is, by choice, an equal opportunity franchisor, with a proven track record of franchising to all segments of society. In the United States, minorities and women currently represent over 34 percent of McDonald's franchisees and 70 percent of all applicants in training.

McDonald's franchisees need to meet certain criteria, such as:

- Business experience in the market where they are seeking a franchise
- A strong desire to succeed, work hard, and contribute to a winning team
- Demonstrated personal integrity with emphasis on interpersonal skills
- A willingness to participate in a comprehensive training program
- A willingness to personally devote full-time efforts to the day-to-day operations of the business

- A history of success and the ability to work well within a franchising organization
- Personal, nonborrowed resources to be invested in the business

McDonald's provides one of the best support systems in the industry to its franchisees, including:

- Support in the areas of operations, training, advertising, marketing, real estate, construction, purchasing, and equipment
- Personal growth and business knowledge from McDonald's extensive training
- Personal satisfaction both as an owner/operator and as a member of McDonald's worldwide organization

Internationally, there are both franchised restaurants with individual owners and joint-venture partners and affiliates in many countries. A joint-venture partner typically invests 50 percent in the business while McDonald's invests the other 50 percent. In the case of affiliates, McDonald's owns a smaller share of the business. This management represents more fully shared overall management responsibility for the entire company's operations.

McDonald's home office includes all the departments needed to run a large public organization, including administrative, marketing, accounting, legal, communications, human resources, and so on. The company owns and operates about 15 percent of the U.S. restaurants, which means they must maintain a staff to manage a chain of more than 2,000 restaurants. The company-owned restaurants provide a direct source of revenue to McDonald's. Company restaurants allow for testing of many of their innovations in actual restaurant situations and provide an excellent training ground to develop the restaurant expertise and management ability of many future company executives.

The real emphasis of the company is on helping their franchisees to be successful. This includes developing successful marketing, advertising, and promotions for the restaurants; continually enhancing the menu; seeking out and developing new restaurant buildings and equipment; developing new real estate sites; creating successful communications programs for local markets; and training restaurant owners, store managers, and crew members throughout the system. The company develops many programs at its home office and also stays very close to its franchisees in the field. In the United States, McDonald's is organized into five divisions, which are split into 40 regions. Division presidents are the key link between home office management and the regions, each of which has a regional manager directing a staff dedicated to the restaurants in its area. Franchisees work with a business consultant from their region to develop action plans for meeting targets for customer satisfaction, market share, and profitability.

The company's role is a balancing act of making sure that each restaurant complies with strict operating standards while encouraging entrepre-

neurial innovations on the franchisee's part. While all restaurants can participate in national advertising and promotions, local owners within each region
develop and execute their own marketing, advertising, and promotional plans
during the year. Their company structure helps them to communicate winning
local ideas throughout the system—when the partners share, everyone wins.
In international markets, the company frequently grants more responsibility
for running the day-to-day operations to the joint venture partners and affiliates, who are more familiar with the customs and cultures of the people
they're serving. The local partners develop their own organizations to supply
the same kinds of services to their restaurants as McDonald's provides for its
U.S. franchise owners—ensuring the same quality experience in the restaurant
without dampening local ingenuity.

Suppliers also occupy a very important position in McDonald's success.
McDonald's suppliers in the United States operate 40 distribution centers,
strategically located to be accessible to all the restaurants in the country.
These distribution centers carry virtually everything a McDonald's restaurant
would need, including 430 different items ranging from meat and potatoes to
mop heads and light bulbs—supplied by as many as 150 different companies.
A typical distribution center will maintain an inventory of about 80,000 cases
of supplies, which it turns over in two to three days.

Often, company representatives begin establishing a reliable core of local
suppliers two to three years before the first restaurant opens in a new country
or area, in some cases introducing new farming practices, right down to
importing the proper seeds. While every effort is made to obtain suppliers in
the host country, when local suppliers cannot be found or developed the
restaurants import the necessary products. Today as the system's buying
power expands, McDonald's is increasingly using its leverage to capitalize
global purchasing practices.

If there is a single key to McDonald's success, it is the interdependence of
the three major partners—franchisees, suppliers, and the company. The triad
in Figure 2 illustrates its success.

Figure 2   Triad for Success

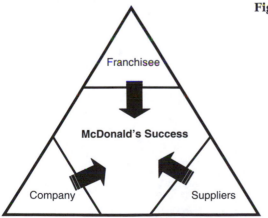

Case Discussion Questions

1. Some of the advantages of franchising with one of the world's largest franchisors have been delineated in this case. What do you think are some of the disadvantages?

2. McDonald's has demonstrated flexibility in adapting its menu to the tastes and cultural practices in specific parts of the world. Do you believe this was a good strategy or hurt its standards?

CASE 2

Carlson Companies, Inc.—Horizontal and Vertical Development Strategies*

In this chapter we have focused on the variety of business development strategies management can select from to grow their company. The case that follows presents a company that has utilized multiple strategies including acquisitions, franchising, joint ventures, and new concept development. The company has also successfully utilized both horizontal and vertical integration strategies from an organizational perspective.

One of the most fascinating companies from a business development perspective is Carlson Companies. Its growth strategies include, but are not limited to, acquisitions, cooperative agreements, franchising, joint ventures, management contracts, partnerships, ownership, and global expansion in multiple hospitality industry sectors. In this case example, we will see how a multi-billion-dollar conglomerate of hospitality-related business grew to be one of the largest players in the industry through strategic deployment of a variety of business development and financial strategies.

It all began with a $55 loan and an entrepreneurial spirit that transcended the years, which were keys in establishing Carlson Companies, Inc., as the Gold Bond Stamp Company in 1938.

Today, Carlson Companies is one of the largest privately held corporations in the United States, with operations in more than 140 countries. Gross system-wide sales under Carlson brands have reached $35.0 billion.

Carlson Companies is a leader in providing services and solutions to two distinct customer groups: corporate customers, who depend on Carlson's expertise in integrated marketing services, business travel management, and hospitality services for business travelers; and consumer customers, who know Carlson through its worldwide restaurant, hotel, cruise, and leisure travel agency brands.

The company's hotel brands include Regent International Hotels, Radisson Hotels Worldwide, and Country Inns & Suites by Carlson. T.G.I. Friday's, Italianni's, AquaKnox, Star Canyon, Timpano Italian Chophouse, Samba Room, and Taqueria Canonita comprise its restaurant brands. Travel-related and other holdings include Radisson Seven Seas Cruises, Carlson Wagonlit Travel (co-owned with Accor of Paris), Travel Agents International, and Carlson Marketing Group.

Marilyn Carlson Nelson became the chairman and CEO of Carlson Hospitality in March 1998, building on a legacy of business leadership, entrepreneurship, and community involvement that her father had nurtured since the beginning of the company.

*Information derived from www.carlson.com.

The Carlson Companies story began with Curtis L. Carlson. The son of a Minnesota grocer, Carlson was a born entrepreneur who organized his own network of newspaper carriers as a teenager and worked his way through college.

While selling products to Twin Cities grocers, Carlson became familiar with the trading stamp, which a handful of department stores had been giving to their customers since the 1800s.

Carlson recognized that the trading stamp provided an enormous opportunity for grocery stores, drug stores, gas stations, and other independent merchants to distinguish themselves from their competitors. Eager to capitalize on the idea, Carlson borrowed $55 from his landlord and began doing business from his dining room table, calling the fledgling operation the Gold Bond Stamp Company.

After a slow start and meager gains during World War II, the Gold Bond Stamp Company hit it big in the early 1950s, when Carlson and his aggressive sales force persuaded the nation's largest supermarket chains that they needed trading stamps to draw and maintain customer loyalty. In fact, during the 1950s and 1960s, Gold Bond and a sister company—Top Value Stamps—helped revolutionize the way retail goods and services were marketed. Given with purchases and redeemable for a vast array of first-class merchandise, the trading stamp became the shopper's friend around the globe.

During the 1960s, the Gold Bond Stamp Company expanded into the hospitality industry with the purchase of the original Radisson Hotel in downtown Minneapolis and the construction of new Radisson facilities throughout Minnesota.

In the 1970s, the company acquired dozens of additional businesses, including the highly successful T.G.I. Friday's and Country Kitchen restaurant chains and the internationally renowned Ask Mr. Foster travel agencies.

In 1973, in order to better reflect its diversified status, the Gold Bond Stamp Company charged its name to Carlson Companies, Inc. Four years later, Carlson Companies achieved its first billion dollars in annual sales as one of the fastest-growing privately held corporations in the world. Today, Carlson Companies is one of the largest travel and hospitality services companies in the world.

The Carlson Companies story is one of continuous progress. It is the spirit of a business that started small, grew, and has positioned itself to grow to greater heights in the century ahead.

Milestones

1938   Curt Carlson founds and develops Gold Bond Stamp Co. in downtown Minneapolis.

1953   Super Valu food stores become the first large supermarket chain in the nation to use Gold Bond trading stamps. Almost overnight, Gold Bond becomes a household word in the United States.

1955   Begins sales in Canada, eventually becoming the largest trading stamp company in that country.

1960   Forms joint venture with Grand Union, with 50% interest in Performance Incentives Co., and also acquires 50% interest in the Radisson Hotel in downtown Minneapolis.

1961   Starts an advertising agency, Adams, Martin and Nelson.

1962   Contract Service Associates (CSA) officially forms.

Acquires the remaining interest in Radisson Hotel in downtown Minneapolis.

1962–   Carlson buys out the majority of partners in Minneapolis Indus-
1963   trial Park.

1963   Changes name to Premium Service Corp. (PSC).

Gift Stars coupons are included on various grocery and grooming aid products.

1964   Acquires Red Scissors Coupons (Premium Associates).

1965   Acquires the Aloha Stamp Co., Holden Stamp Co., and Security Stamp Co.

Acquires a 51 percent interest in the Canning Co. in Trinidad.

1966   Builds the Pacific International Building (four stories) in Honolulu, with a six-story addition in 1968.

Gold Star and Gift Bond trading stamps are introduced in Japan.

1967   Launches Gift Stars coupons nationally on packs of Old Gold cigarettes. Gift Stars coupons are redeemable with Gold Bond stamps at Gold Bond Gift Centers.

1968   In a joint venture with Mitsubishi, the Japanese industrial giant, introduces Gold Star and Gift Bond trading stamps throughout Japan.

Acquires Robinson Seidel, a Twin Cities incentives company, part of which is a travel agency.

Acquires the remaining 50 percent interest in Performance Incentives Co.

The number of trading stamps issued nationally by all companies reaches a peak this year.

Acquires Frontier Stamp Co. (including Family Park Shopping Center, Flintwood Shopping Center, and Park Central Shopping Center, all in Lubbock, Texas).

Acquires a majority interest in May Brothers Co., food wholesalers in Minneapolis.

Starts Direct Mail Division. Acquires Gold Crown Stamp Co.

1969   Launches LMC coupons nationally on packs of Chesterfield cigarettes. LMC coupons are a joint venture with Liggett and Myers. LMC coupons are redeemable with Gold Bond stamps at Gold Bond Gift Centers.

Builds and opens Radisson Mart, connected to the Radisson Hotel in downtown Minneapolis.

1970   Opens Haberdashery Restaurant-Pub in the Radisson Hotel in Minneapolis.

1971   Purchases Melior Stamp Co. in Belgium.

Acquires John Plain/Pick-A-Gift/John Plain Incentives, a direct mail and incentive company.

1972   Acquires the majority of outstanding stock in May Brothers Co., Minneapolis.

Establishes Carlson Properties, Inc., to handle real estate development.

1973   Changes name to Carlson Companies, Inc.

Opens Haberdashery Restaurant-Pub at 7 Corners in Minneapolis.

1974   Opens Haberdashery Restaurant-Pub in downtown St. Paul.

Acquires a majority interest in Superior Fiber Products, Superior, Wisconsin.

1975   Acquires Gold Strike Co. in Salt Lake City.

Acquires T.G.I. Friday's Inc.

1976   Acquires Gold Star Stamp Company in Montreal.

Acquires K-Promotions, Inc. in Milwaukee.

Acquires the Northern Federal Building in downtown St. Paul.

1977   Acquires Country Kitchen International, Inc., in Minneapolis.

Achieves $1 billion in annual revenues.

1978   Acquires Naum Bros. (catalog showrooms) in Rochester, New York.

Acquires NSI Marketing in Canada.

Acquires Omega Sports in Maryland Heights, Missouri.

Acquires WaSko Gold Products Corp. in New York City.

1979   Acquires First Travel Corp. (including Ask Mr. Foster and Colony Hotels).

1980   Premium Group changes its name to Carlson Marketing Group, Inc. (CMG).

Establishes Hotel and Resort Group, which includes Radisson Hotels, Inns and Resorts and Colony Hotels & Resorts.

1981   CMG acquires E.F. MacDonald Motivation Company in Dayton, Ohio.

1982   Achieves $2 billion in annual revenues.

1983   Acquires P. Lawson Travel, Ltd., in Toronto.

T.G.I. Friday's Inc. goes public, with 25 percent or 4.5 million shares sold on the first day.

1984   Launches the Associate (franchise) program for Ask Mr. Foster travel agencies.

Acquires Cartan Tours, Inc., in Rolling Meadows, Illinois.

Acquires Valley Travel in Phoenix.

Radisson launches a franchising program.

1985   Radisson purchases a 25 percent interest in and assumes management of the new Radisson Mark Plaza Hotel in Alexandria, Virginia.

Radisson signs an international partnership agreement with Msvenpick Hotels International.

Achieves $3 billion in annual revenues.

1986   Radisson enters into an international partnership agreement with SAS International Hotels.

Acquires a 50 percent interest in Harvey's Travel Ltd. in Alberta, Canada.

1987   Radisson Hotels Corp. signs international partnership agreements with Park Lane Hotels International and Commonwealth Hospitality Inc. of Canada.

Achieves $4 billion in annual revenues.

1988   Set's a goal of $9 billion in annual revenues by 1992.

Radisson Hotel Corp. is renamed Radisson Hotels International.

Acquires Gelco Travel Management Systems.

Radisson enters the Eastern European market with Radisson Béke Hotel in Budapest.

1989   Moves most of its operations to the new World Headquarters at Carlson Center, Minneapolis.

CMG acquires Promo Marketing (consumer promotions) in Montreal.

Radisson opens its new Worldwide Reservation Center in Omaha.

Acquires all outstanding T.G.I. Friday's Inc. stock to make it a private company again.

Achieves $6.2 billion in system-wide annual revenues.

1990   CMG acquires Forum Organization Pty. Ltd. (a motivation and marketing services) in Australia/New Zealand.

CMG acquires FKB Group (10 marketing and sales promotion companies in Britain) and AVDM in New York City.

The Ask Mr. Foster name changes to Carlson Travel Network.

Achieves $8.1 billion in system-wide annual revenues.

1991   Carlson Travel Network launches a cobranded Visa© bankcard worldwide.

Radisson Slavjanskaya Hotel Moscow opens in Russia as the first American-managed hotel in the former U.S.S.R.

Country Lodging by Carlson expands into Canada.

CMG moves its Dayton, Ohio, employees (formerly of E.F. MacDonald Motivation Co.) to Minneapolis in consolidation.

Achieves $9.2 billion in system-wide annual revenues–one full year ahead of its goal.

1992   The Radisson Diamond cruise ship sails on its maiden voyage.

CMG acquires CMI, a San Francisco–based incentive travel/business meeting management company.

Carlson Travel Network wins the General Electric account—the largest single travel account in history—and creates the "travel agency of the future."

Carlson Travel Network surpasses 1,000 locations.

1993   Carlson Travel Network opens GE Travel Center in Phoenix, the world's single largest dedicated reservation office.

Achieves $10.7 billion in system-wide annual revenues.

1994   Radisson Plaza Hotel La Paz opens in La Paz, Bolivia (the first Radisson hotel in South America).

CMG forms a joint venture with Hermann Marketing of St. Louis (corporate logo merchandise).

Carlson Travel Group and Paris-based Wagonlit Travel sign an alliance to form Carlson Wagonlit Travel (CWT), one of the world's largest travel management companies.

Carlson Wagonlit Travel/P. Lawson Travel launches the Associate Program in Canada.

T.G.I. Friday's Inc. opens a new concept—Front Row Sports Grill in The Ballpark in Arlington, Texas.

T.G.I. Friday's opens the first Italianni's restaurant in Miami.

The Radisson Diamond Cruise and Seven Seas Cruise Line merger creates Radisson Seven Seas Cruises.

1995   Carlson Hospitality Group and Radisson Hotel International are renamed Carlson Hospitality Worldwide and Radisson Hotels Worldwide, respectively.

CWT implements more than $2 billion in U.S. Army contracts, which entails hiring more than 400 employees and opening 250 new locations.

CWT opens its seventh travel academy in Phoenix.

T.G.I. Friday's opens its 16th restaurant in England. Friday's Hospitality Worldwide now operates, franchises, and licenses more than 340 T.G.I. Friday's, Italianni's, and Front Row Sports Grill restaurants in 248 cities and 18 countries.

The largest CWT associate, Murdock Travel in Utah, joins the Associate Program.

T.G.I. Friday's opens a restaurant in Beijing, China.

1996   CWT acquires the corporate travel business of Jetset Travel Pte. Ltd. in Singapore.

Radisson SAS opens four hotels in Italy (Milan, Brescia, Bergamo, and Lodi) and five in Norway (Bergen, Kristiansand, two in Stavanger, and Trondheim).

Country Inns & Suites by Carlson opens 24 new properties.

Friday's Hospitality Worldwide opens Friday's American Bar in Makati/Burgos, Philippines (its first international location).

Carlson Hospitality Worldwide and Four Seasons Hotels, Inc., create a partnership for the future development, management, and marketing of Regent International Hotels around the world.

1997   Marilyn Carlson Nelson is named chief operating officer.

Radisson Hospitality Worldwide acquires Radisson Seven Seas—the world's third-largest luxury cruise line.

Carlson Travel Group splits into two separate operating companies: Carlson Wagonlit Travel (CWT) and Carlson Leisure Group (CLG).

CLG acquires Travel Agents International, becoming the largest travel agency franchiser in North America.

Carlson Hospitality Worldwide debuts a new-generation business support and reservation system, Curtis-C.

T.G.I. Friday's opens its first restaurant in Moscow.

CLG acquires Inspirations PLC in Britain, marking its entry into the airline business through its subsidiary Caledonian Airways.

CMG acquires Aegis Group, a British performance improvement company.

CMG acquires Incentive Dimensions, a San Francisco–based incentive travel, event management, and production company.

Friday's Hospitality Worldwide reaches $1 billion in domestic sales.

1998   CMG acquires S&H Citadel, one of the top five performance improvement firms in the United States, with annual revenues in excess of $100 million.

T.G.I. Friday's teams up with Earvin "Magic" Johnson's company, Johnson Development Corporation, to develop T.G.I. Friday's restaurants in underserved U.S. urban communities.

1999   Achieves $31.4 billion in system-wide gross sales.

2000   Founds the Results Travel Agency franchise.

2001   Acquires Cruise Holidays franchise units.

2004   Curtis Nelson is named President and Chief Operating Officer and Marilyn Carlson Nelson is named Chair and Chief Executive Officer.

As Carlson's milestones and timeline demonstrate, a complete array of business development strategies and techniques have helped shape this very large and fast-growing company.

Case Discussion Questions

1. Why do you believe Carlson Companies has been successful in deploying so many different business development strategies?

2. What do you perceive as the weaknesses and strengths of Carlson Companies' managerial strategies?

Chapter 5

Financial Strategies

CHAPTER OBJECTIVES

- To identify financial strategy options for the major sectors of the hospitality industry
- To delineate the pros and cons of various approaches in financial strategy selection
- To discuss key terms related to strategic financial options in various sectors of the hospitality industry
- To demonstrate the relationship between financial strategy selection and return on investment

Most major sectors of the hospitality industry require substantial amounts of capital to both develop and operate. Therefore, the cost and availability of capital have an enormous impact on the industry. In many sectors, when demand is high large amounts of cash are generated. Likewise, when demand drops, such as was the case immediately following the September 11, 2001, terrorist attacks, cash gets used up very quickly. We saw this occur especially in the airline, rental car, and hotel/lodging sectors. The various sectors and companies within those sectors respond to and operate under a variety of financial strategy options. For example, the airline sector uses leasing as a primary vehicle to obtain aircraft, whereas the foodservice and lodging sectors use franchising and management contracts to expand. Strategy selection also varies by company within the sector. Strategy selection is influenced by the corporation's overall goals and objectives and its mission statement. In many sectors of the industry the business may be viewed with multiple perspectives. For example, strategy selection may be influenced by the organization's need for cash or by its desire to achieve its return on invested capital (ROIC) objectives.[1] Publicly traded companies may be focused on earnings before interest, taxes, and depreciation and amortization, (EBITDA) whereas a private company may have a focus on the acquisition of trophy real estate ownership. Depending on the corporation's mission and goals, financial strategies may vary widely between any two organizations within the same industry sector. Financial strategy selection may also be directly influenced by the corporate structure, such as a holding company, a real estate investment trust (REIT), and a brand collector/franchisor. Almost all companies have financial goals for ROIC and needs for cash generation. Financial strategy selection is about selecting the best ways to achieve these goals, meet ROIC objectives, and satisfy investors. Let's now look at some of these financial strategy options.

TECHNOLOGY

Financial decision input and options are available at the touch of a keyboard. Variables are virtually unlimited and assumptions can be factored in with another touch. Measurements and results are reported in a variety of ways and in real time. Just one more benefit of technology that permeates every area of financial decision making and analysis.

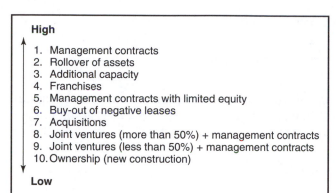

High

1. Management contracts
2. Rollover of assets
3. Additional capacity
4. Franchises
5. Management contracts with limited equity
6. Buy-out of negative leases
7. Acquisitions
8. Joint ventures (more than 50%) + management contracts
9. Joint ventures (less than 50%) + management contracts
10. Ownership (new construction)

Low

Figure 5–1   Return on Invested Capital (Percent Timeliness)

RETURN ON INVESTED CAPITAL

If a corporation's objective is to receive a high ROIC, selecting an ownership strategy that entails new construction for all its operations would likely be disastrous. Very large amounts of investment capital (IC) would be needed, and the R (return) would take years to materialize in most sectors of the industry. On the other hand, if the same company entered into a management contract, or sold an asset (rollover) or franchises, its IC is minimal and its R is very quick, thus resulting in a high ROIC on a percentage or dollar basis (in relationship to the minimal investment). Figure 5-1 presents 10 financial strategy options (not all will relate to every industry sector), ranging from high to low ROIC. They are based on the premise of quicker returns.

There are various ways to mix these strategies to accelerate growth, minimize investment, and improve returns and the timeliness of those returns. The basic formula for ROIC is depicted in Figure 5-2.

The fastest way to improve ROIC is to roll over an asset, that is, sell a hotel or resort or cruise ship. Assuming you receive more for that asset than you owe, or in the case of real estate, assuming you receive a lot more (due to appreciation), your ROIC will improve dramatically—you are increasing your R and decreasing your IC at the same time. Following are five of the faster financial strategies to improve ROIC:

- Rollover of assets (sale)
- Management contracts

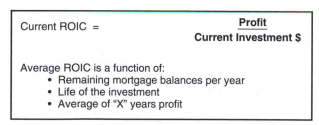

Current ROIC = $\dfrac{\text{Profit}}{\text{Current Investment \$}}$

Average ROIC is a function of:
- Remaining mortgage balances per year
- Life of the investment
- Average of "X" years profit

Figure 5–2   ROIC Formula
Source: Form www.fool.com/school/roic/roic03.htm.

- Additional capacity (assumes high demand)
- Buy-out of negative leases
- Buy-in to joint ventures + management contracts

In the reverse, any financial strategy that requires large amounts of capital and takes a longer period of time to generate earnings (return) is going to be a slower method. Following are the slowest financial strategies to improve ROIC:

- New construction/ownership
- New construction/joint ventures
- Acquisitions

CASH GENERATION

As previously discussed, many organizations in the hospitality industry have to focus on two (or more) different businesses related to their product or service. Obviously, most are in the operations or management of assets business. However, many are also in an asset appreciation/depreciation business, where one focuses on the capital investment in, real estate, cruise ships, casinos, and the like. A high percentage ROIC that doesn't produce a large volume of cash doesn't always help when your business is a major user of cash. Also, if your focus is longer (as with an existing/established business) and you are concentrating on long-term returns, you would likely have cash generation as a priority. Figure 5-3 delineates the greatest and fastest ways to generate the most cash.

There are also a number of other strategies that may be selected to generate cash or improve returns. These include the acquisition of a company that already has a substantial number of management contracts and/or a large franchise base. In this case, the fees and royalty income bring in cash instantly. Certainly, soliciting management contracts or converting others to your brand through a "franchise conversion" will accelerate fees/income. Limited equity positions, which help "buy into" an income stream (such as pur-

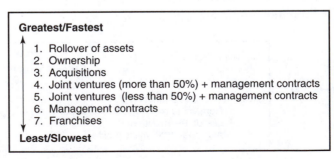

Greatest/Fastest

1. Rollover of assets
2. Ownership
3. Acquisitions
4. Joint ventures (more than 50%) + management contracts
5. Joint ventures (less than 50%) + management contracts
6. Management contracts
7. Franchises

Least/Slowest

Figure 5–3   Cash Generation

chasing 10 percent of an existing hotel and then taking over its management through a management contract) would also accelerate returns (versus new contraction). One strategy, exemplified by Cendant, is the acquisition of franchised brands. This proved an excellent financial strategy, especially when the acquisition prices were low (most attractive) and the royalty income and growth potential of the brand were high (reference the Cendant Case in Chapter 6).

ETHICS
Managers must make a commitment to incorporate the highest standards of business conduct in their financial management functions and strategies.

REAL ESTATE INVESTMENT TRUSTS

One interesting product of the changing tax laws was the concept of the REIT. A financial product, REITs were used by the lodging sector of the hospitality industry as a major financial strategy in the 1990s. REITs provided a tax/investment advantage over the traditional financial structures of lodging companies.

REITS come in a variety of flavors, but the most common type is equity REITs, which invest directly in real estate properties.[2] Others include mortgage REITs, which hold mortgages on commercial and residential real estate properties, and hybrid REITs, which do both.

REITs own and manage all types of real estate assets: hotels, apartment buildings, office buildings, retail space, even industrial buildings, and any combination thereof. But what distinguishes them from ordinary common stocks is that they are required by law, as of January 1, 2001, to pay out 90 percent of their taxable income in the form of dividends to investors, and they don't have to pay ordinary corporate income taxes. So the investment isn't taxed twice—once at the corporate level and once at the personal level. The downside, however, is that REITs can retain only a small amount of their earnings to finance growth, so most REITs resort to some debt when buying new properties, often resulting in moderately leveraged financial structures.

REITs were created in 1960 by an act of Congress as a means of allowing small shareholders to benefit from the tax advantages of investing in real estate. But it wasn't until the Tax Reform Act of 1986 that REITs were allowed to operate the properties they owned. That and changes in how losses from real estate investments could be used as a tax shelter gave REITs the structure to attract investors.

The real estate bust of the late 1980s and early 1990s clobbered the industry's growth prospects, as commercial real estate prices declined as much as 50 percent, according to the National Association of Real Estate Investment Trusts. Borrowing money for further growth became virtually impossible as interest rates soared. As matters improved in the mid-1990s,

REITs could buy properties cheaply, and investors signed on in hopes of participating in the industry's comeback.

The investment potential of a REIT is typically measured against the value of its underlying assets, or net asset value, and its funds from operations, a calculation of the company's earnings and depreciation and amortization expenses.

The lodging sector initially embraced the REIT concept. Starwood Hotels & Resorts Worldwide, Inc., a paired-share REIT, was perhaps the most widely recognized REIT in the hospitality industry[3] (see Case 1). Its recognition came as a result of its acquisitions of the Sheraton and Westin brands, its initial strong performance, and a very visible CEO/spokesperson.

A CHANGING INDUSTRY

The hospitality industry in both its strong and weak cycles provides financial strategy options for the major players. The industry has historically experienced periods of one to two years (e.g., 1990–1992 and 2001–2002) when down cycles occurred. Likewise, the 10- to 12-year up cycles produced very healthy companies, which expanded rapidly—sometimes so rapidly that the growth in supply exceeded the growth in demand. It is in both the down years and the years of substantial profitability that consolidation has taken place. Today, we see fewer major airlines, fewer major car rental firms, fewer major cruise lines, and fewer major lodging companies. However, we see much larger players in almost all sectors that have not only absorbed competitors via acquisitions, but have expanded through product segmentation, new markets, and introducing new brands. The industry remains juxtaposed to some degree when viewed from a financial/developmental perspective. Entrepreneurs continue to introduce new products, services, concepts, and brands, as do the mega-corporations. Private companies, REITs, and public corporations of every size and structure are found within the hospitality industry. Growth comes from all components and new ideas flourish in the form of a new airline, a new theme park, new themed restaurants, new concepts in lodging, and so on. As an industry, the hospitality industry is one in which new brands seem to be an everyday occurrence. The common denominator remains cash, monies to finance growth, cash flow to remain in business, returns or invested capital, and earnings to retain and attract investors.

CHAPTER REVIEW

In this chapter we have stated that the hospitality industry is a capital-intensive industry. Nearly all sectors of the industry require extensive amounts of capital to grow. Most sectors require substantial amounts of cash to operate. And most sectors have the capability of generating substantial amounts of cash when the economic conditions are favorable. We further delineated financial strategies and options that support increasing returns on invested capital on a percentage basis, as well as accelerating the return of capital. Most hospitality sectors can be viewed from the operations and asset investment perspectives. The orchestration of selecting the appropriate mix of financial strategies to achieve the mission, goals, and objectives of the corporation is what the management of financial strategies is all about in the hospitality industry. The industry is one that experiences cycles and one in which the economic/financial cycle produces opportunities for acquisitions and consolidation. Yet, at the same time, the entrepreneurial spirit remains healthy in the creation of new brands, product offerings, and concepts.

KEY CONCEPTS/TERMS

Amortization	Leverage
Assets	Limited partnerships
Break-even analysis	Negative lease
Cost controls	Real estate investment trust
Equity	Taxation
Incentives	Value
Lease buy-back	

DISCUSSION QUESTIONS

1. Which financial strategy options produce the quickest return on invested capital in the hospitality industry?

2. Which financial strategy options provide the most risk? The least risk?

3. What financial strategy(s) would be most compatible with the goal of "controlling" the product/service and the operations and perception of a hospitality business?

4. If your goal was to generate cash and long-term income, which financial strategy(s) would you employ to achieve your objectives?

ENDNOTES

1. From www.investorwords.com.
2. From www.nareit.com/aboutreits/glossary.cfm (September 2, 2002).

CASE 1

Starwood Hotels and Resorts—A Paired-Share REIT*

Hotel industry real estate investment trusts have developed a number of investment models to take advantage of their unique tax situation. These models include paired-share REITs, such as Starwood Hotels and Resorts Worldwide and Patriot American Hospitality. In another type of model, REIT structure, two organizations tie together through an intercompany agreement in which they share certain senior members of management and board members. An example is the REIT formed between CapStar Hotel Co. and American General Hospitality Corp. called MeriStar Hospitality Corp. (also a C corporation called MeriStar Hotels & Resorts). The last model is an REIT in which companies form a strategic alliance with no formal agreement. This is exemplified by the FelCor Suite Hotels, a hotel investment company, and Bristol Hotel Co., a hotel management company. In this model the real estate is separated from day-to-day management elements.* This allows for hospitality companies such as InterContinental Hotels, which owns Holiday Hospitality and holds a 32 percent stake in Bristol, to free up capital for other transactions through a lease-back arrangement with FelCor.

In this case example, we will focus on Starwood Hotels & Resorts Worldwide and view how the REIT concept has played the major role in its financial management strategies.

Starwood is one of the world's largest hotel and leisure companies. The company conducts its hotel and leisure business both directly and through its subsidiaries. The company's brand names include Sheraton, Westin, The Luxury Collection, St. Regis, W Hotels, and Four Points by Sheraton. The company's revenue and earnings are derived primarily from hotel and leisure operations, which include the operation of the company's owned hotels; management fees earned from hotels the company manages pursuant to long-term management contracts; franchise fees; and the development, ownership, and operation of vacation ownership resorts—marketing and selling vacation ownership investments (VOIs) in the resorts and providing financing to customers who purchase such interests. The company's hotel and leisure business emphasizes the global operation of hotels and resorts primarily in the luxury and upscale segment of the lodging industry. Starwood's financial strategy involves acquiring interests in or management rights with respect to properties in these segments. The company's portfolio of owned, managed, and franchised hotels totaled approximately 800 in 80 countries in 2001. This portfolio is comprised of 165-plus hotels that Starwood owns or leases or in which Starwood has a majority equity interest (substantially all of which Starwood also manages); 265-plus hotels managed by Starwood on behalf of third-party

*Information derived from www.starwood.com.
*S. Barney, *The Lodging Stocks* (New York: Salomon Smith Barney, 2002): 45–154.

owners (including entities in which Starwood has a minority equity interest); and 315-plus hotels for which Starwood receives franchise fees. Additionally, the company is currently selling VOI inventory at more than a dozen resorts.

In 1990, Barry Sternlicht formed Starwood Opportunity Fund, using money from private investors, with most of the investment being made in apartments. After success with the first fund, Starwood Opportunity Fund II was created. Properties were bought at deep discounts. In 1994, Starwood acquired Hotel Investors Trust, one of the largest hotel REITs in the United States and one of only two grandfathered under the paired-share structure that allowed the same investors to own stock in a hotel operating company (Hotel Investors Corporation). The names of the two parts of the REIT were changed to Starwood Lodging Trust and Starwood Lodging Corporation. Over the next few years, Starwood continued to acquire individual and small groups of properties. Significant purchases included three Westin Regina resorts in Mexico in 1997—the company's first international properties—and the Flatley Company/Tara Hotels—15 full-service hotels purchased in August 1997 for $470 million. Late in 1997, Starwood acquired ITT Sheraton for $13.3 billion; the sale was approved by shareholders early in 1998. At that time, the company bought four former Ritz-Carltons in Aspen, New York City, Washington, D.C., and Houston for $334 million; they were converted into Luxury Collection properties for a limited time. Early in 1998, on the completion of the Westin purchase, the company's names were changed from Starwood Lodging Trust and Starwood Lodging Corporation to Starwood Hotels and Resorts and Starwood Hotels and Resorts Worldwide, respectively. Late in 1998, the launch of W Hotels was announced. In January 1999, Starwood relinquished its grandfathered paired-share REIT status and became a C corporation, and the trust became a subsidiary of the corporation. In 1999, Starwood sold the gaming interests it had acquired in the ITT Sheraton deal to Park Place Entertainment.

Starwood's acquisition of ITT Sheraton and Westin Hotels & Resorts in early 1998 gave birth to the hotel corporation as it is known today, which encompasses six global brands including Sheraton Hotels & Resorts, Westin Hotels & Resorts, St. Regis, the Luxury Collection, Four Points Hotels by Sheraton, and W Hotels.

As one of the largest hotel and leisure companies focusing on the luxury and upscale full-service lodging market, Starwood has the scale to support its core marketing and reservation function. Its scale contributes to lowering its cost of operations through purchasing economies in such areas as insurance, energy, telecommunications, employee benefits, food and beverage, furniture, fixtures and equipment, and operating supplies.

Starwood has strong brand leadership based on the global recognition of the company's lodging brands. Starwood was designated as the "World's Best Global Hotel Company" by *Global Finance* magazine in their September 2000 issue. Starwood benefits from a luxury and upscale branding strategy that provides a strong operating performance. It is one of the better positioned hotel companies in the world and has a good mix of product (see Figure 1).

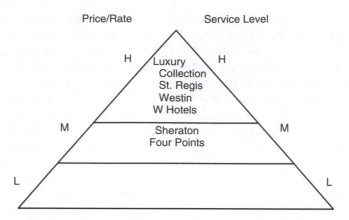

Figure 1   The Starwood Brands Market Position

Sheraton, the largest brand by far, has nearly 400 properties. Growth for this brand is by franchising and management contracts. Four Points by Sheraton with about 140 properties, many of which were Sheraton Inns and Hotels, is the big franchise brand for Starwood. It will continue to grow by franchising. Westin with approximately 120 properties is being overhauled to return it to its four- to four-and-a-half-star heritage. Franchising will continue but on a limited basis; most growth will be in management contracts. St. Regis/Luxury Collection has about 45 properties and almost 10,000 rooms. These are actually two separate brands. St. Regis is targeted for the first or second position in any given market and will not be franchised. With only a handful of properties now, fairly rapid international growth is on the horizon. Luxury Collection is not targeted for growth, although there may be additions to the brand from among properties seeking its international sales and distribution clout. W Hotels, the newest chain, is growing rapidly. Most of these properties are owned by Starwood, although there are a number of management contracts. No franchising is planned at this time.

Starwood's strategies include refining the positioning of the company's brands to further its strategy of strengthening brand identity and, rebranding certain hotels to one of Starwood's proprietary brands to further solidify its brand reputation and market presence. Other major strategies include:

- Continuing to expand the company's role as a third-party manager of hotels and resorts
- Franchising the Sheraton, Westin, and Four Points by Sheraton brands to selected third-party operators, thereby expanding the company's market presence, enhancing the exposure of its hotel brands, and providing additional income through franchising fees
- Expanding the company's internet presence and sales capabilities to increase revenue and improve customer service

- Continuing to grow the company's frequent guest program, thereby increasing occupancy rates while providing the company's customers with benefits based on loyalty to the company's hotels
- Enhancing the company's marketing efforts by integrating the company's proprietary customer databases, so as to sell additional products and services to existing customers, improve occupancy rates, and create additional marketing opportunities
- Optimizing the company's use of its real estate assets to improve ancillary revenue, such as restaurant, beverage, and parking revenue from the company's hotels and resorts
- Continuing to build the new W Hotel brand to appeal to upscale business travelers and other customers seeking full-service hotels in major markets
- Developing additional vacation ownership resorts near select hotel locations
- Becoming the first hospitality company in the world to embrace Six Sigma, the internationally recognized program that dramatically accelerates and maximizes business performance. This initiative is expected to deliver significant long-term financial benefits.

Based on these goals, Starwood has established supporting business strategies. Starwood intends to expand and diversify the company's hotel portfolio through minor investments and selective acquisitions of properties domestically and internationally that meet some or all of the following criteria:

- Luxury and upscale hotels and resorts in major metropolitan areas and business centers
- Major tourist hotels, destination resorts, and conference centers that have favorable demographic trends and are located in markets with significant barriers to entry or with major room demand generators such as office or retail complexes, airports, tourist attractions, or universities
- Undervalued hotels whose performance can be increased by rebranding to one of the company's hotel brands
- Portfolios of hotels or hotel companies that exhibit some or all of the criteria listed above

Also, Starwood selectively chooses to develop and construct desirable hotels and resorts to help the company meet its strategic goals.

Starwood's financial strategies are viewed within the context of a 3-year timeframe (1999–2001) for the purposes of this case example. Analytical focal points include: the balance sheet, the income statement, ratio analysis and competitive comparisons, ROIC and market value, and net income, cap rate, and market value. It should be pointed out that these are examples of financial performance for a historic 3-year period and may or may not be representative of current or future performance.

The balance sheet (see Table 1) is considered a statement of financial position. The balance sheet presents a snapshot of the investments of a firm (assets) and the financing of those investments (liabilities and shareholders' equity) as of a specific time. The balance sheet shows the following balance or equality:

$$Asset = Liabilities + Shareholders' Equity$$

When defining an asset as a potential resource that provides a firm with a future economic benefit, the right side of an asset in the balance sheet presents the method of how to raise the financial resource. As we see in Figure 2, Starwood raises 30.1 percent of its financial resources with liabilities and 69.9 percent with shareholders' equities. In analyzing Starwood's balance sheet for 3 years, there aren't any significant changes. Slight changes can be found in current assets, current liabilities, and long-term liabilities. Cash and equivalents decreased by over 50 percent in 2000, while inventory increased by over 40 percent. Also, Starwood might select the transfer of short-term liabilities to long-term liabilities. The ratio analysis of the balance sheet will be discussed in more detail later.

The income statement (see Table 2) presents the results of the operating activities of a firm for a specific time period. The income statement indicates the net income or earnings for that time period. Net income is the difference between revenues and expenses.

Revenue for 2001 decreased nearly 9 percent to $3,967 million and net operating income decreased approximately 40 percent to $615 million. The decline in operating results when compared to 2000 reflects the impact of lower revenue per available room, primarily attributable to the September 11, 2001, terrorist attacks.

Ratio analyses help managers or outside users of financial statements monitor the performance of the firm's operation or evaluate their efforts to meet a variety of goals.* Ratios are used to communicate financial performance. However, different ratios reveal different conditions or abilities of an operation.

Current ratio (current assets divided by current liabilities), the most common liquidity ratio, can express the ability of a hospitality establishment to meet its short-term obligation. As you see in Figure 3, Starwood's 2001 current ratio is relatively low compared to its competitors and industry averages, spurring Starwood to push up its current ratio.

Debt-equity ratio (debt or liabilities divided by equity), one of the most common solvency ratios, indicates the hospitality establishment's ability to withstand adversity and meet its long-term debt. Figure 4 shows that Starwood's debt-equity ratio is higher than Marriott's and the industry average, but lower than Hilton's; this means that Starwood is at a high leverage level. Starwood

---

*Information on Marriott and Hilton in the following discussion is derived from www.marriott.com and www.hilton.com, respectively.

Table 1 Analysis of Balance Sheet for Starwood

	1999		2000			2001		
	Million US$	Percent	Million US$	Percent	Percent Change	Million US$	Percent	Percent Change
Cash & Equivalents	436	3.37	189	1.49	-56.65	157	1.26	-16.93
Accounts Receivable	468	3.62	538	4.24	14.96	432	3.47	-19.70
Total Inventory	167	1.29	238	1.87	42.51	219	1.76	-7.98
Prepaid Expenses	92	0.71	120	0.95	30.43	89	0.71	-25.83
Other	0	0.00	0	0.00	0.00	0	0.00	0.00
Total Current Assets	**1,163**	**9.00**	**1,085**	**8.55**	**-6.71**	**897**	**7.20**	**-17.33**
P, P & E	8,920	69.01	9,376	73.84	5.11	9,675	77.64	3.19
Accum. Depreciation	-1,133	-8.77	-1,487	-11.71	31.24	-1,840	-14.77	23.74
Net P, P & E	7,787	60.25	7,889	62.13	1.31	7,835	62.88	-0.68
Goodwill	2,872	22.22	2,881	22.69	0.31	2,825	22.67	-1.94
Long-Term Investment	442	3.42	412	3.24	-6.79	400	3.21	-2.91
Other Long-Term Assets	661	5.11	430	3.39	-34.95	504	4.04	17.21
Total Long-Term Assets	**11,762**	**91.00**	**11,612**	**91.45**	**-1.28**	**11,564**	**92.80**	**-0.41**
Total Assets	**12,925**	**100.00**	**12,697**	**100.00**	**-1.76**	**12,461**	**100.00**	**-1.86**
Accounts Payable	205	1.59	186	1.46	-9.27	225	1.81	20.97
Accrued Expenses	1,112	8.60	1,074	8.46	-3.42	1,030	8.27	-4.10
Short-Term Debt	988	7.64	585	4.61	-40.79	332	2.66	-43.25
Other Current Liabilities	0	0.00	0	0.00	0.00	0	0.00	0.00
Total Current Liability	**2,305**	**17.83**	**1,845**	**14.53**	**-19.96**	**1,587**	**12.74**	**-13.98**
Total Long-Term Liabilities	**4,643**	**35.92**	**4,957**	**39.04**	**6.76**	**5,227**	**41.95**	**5.45**
Other Liabilities	2,287	17.69	2,044	16.10	-10.63	1,891	15.18	-7.49
Total Liabilities	**9,235**	**71.45**	**8,846**	**69.67**	**-4.21**	**8,705**	**69.86**	**-1.59**
Preferred Stock	0	0.00	0	0.00	0.00	0	0.00	0.00
Common Stock	4	0.03	4	0.03	0.00	4	0.03	0.00
Paid-In Capital	4,785	37.02	4,796	37.77	0.23	4,861	39.01	1.36
Retained Earnings	-856	-6.62	-592	-4.66	-30.84	-609	-4.89	2.87
Other Equity	-243	-1.88	-357	-2.81	46.91	-500	-4.01	40.06
Total Equity	**3,690**	**28.55**	**3,851**	**30.33**	**4.36**	**3,756**	**30.14**	**-2.47**
Total Liabilities & Equity	**12,925**	**100.00**	**12,697**	**100.00**	**-1.76**	**12,461**	**100.00**	**-1.86**

Source: From www.starwood.com.

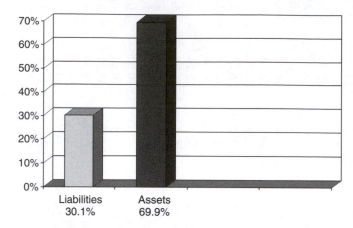

Figure 2   Composition of Financial Resources for Starwood
Source: From www.starwood.com.

raised a large portion of its assets from creditors. On the basis of those ratios analyzed, Starwood's financial strength would not be considered good at this point in time (2001).*

The *accounts receivable turnover ratio* measures the speed of conversion to cash from credit. A high accounts receivable turnover ratio means that accounts receivable is managed well. The *inventory turnover ratio* shows how quickly the inventory is moving. All things fixed, generally the quicker the inventory turnover the better, because inventory can be expensive to maintain. A high inventory turnover ratio indicates a well-managed inventory. Starwood's

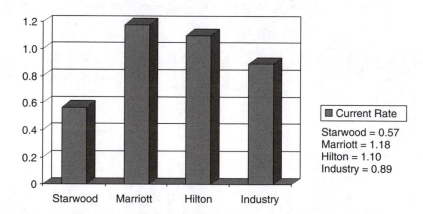

Figure 3   Current Ratio Comparison, 2001
Source: From www.starwood.com, www.hilton.com, and www.marriott.com.

*Ibid.

Table 2 Analysis of Income Statement for Starwood

	1999		2000			2001		
	Million US$	Percent	Million US$	Percent	Percent Change	Million US$	Percent	Percent Change
Revenue	3,391	88.56	3,659	84.21	7.90	3,343	84.27	−8.64
Other Revenue	438	11.44	686	15.79	56.62	624	15.73	−9.04
Total Revenue	**3,829**	**100.00**	**4,345**	**100.00**	**13.48**	**3,967**	**100.00**	**−8.70**
Cost of Revenue	2,313	60.41	2,433	56.00	5.19	2,365	59.62	−2.79
Gross Profit	**1,078**	**28.15**	**1,226**	**28.22**	**13.73**	**978**	**24.65**	**−20.23**
General & Admin Expense	220	5.75	403	9.28	83.18	411	10.36	1.99
Depreciation/Amortization	452	11.80	481	11.07	6.42	526	13.26	9.36
Unusual Income/Expense	3	0.08	0	0.00	−100.00	50	1.26	N/A
Total Operating Expense	2,988	78.04	3,317	76.34	11.01	3,352	84.50	1.06
Operating Income	**841**	**21.96**	**1,028**	**23.66**	**22.24**	**615**	**15.50**	**−40.18**
Interest Expense/Income	−484	−12.64	−420	−9.67	13.22	−358	−9.02	−14.76
Gain/(Loss) on Sale of Assets	191	4.99	2	0.05	−98.95	−57	−1.44	−2,950.00
Other, Net	−15	−0.39	0	0.00	100.00	0	0.00	0.00
Income Before Tax	**533**	**13.92**	**610**	**14.04**	**14.45**	**200**	**5.04**	**−67.21**

Source: From www.starwood.com.

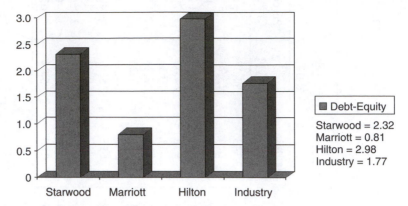

Figure 4   Debt-Equity Ratio Comparison, 2001
Source: From www.starwood.com, www.hilton.com, and www.marriott.com

2001 ratios are low compared to its competitors and industry averages, as follows:

	Starwood	Marriott	Hilton	Industry
Receivable Turnover	8.30	14.60	5.19	12.73
Inventory Turnover	10.29	93.07	11.16	42.42
P/E Ratio	52.30	50.32	31.85	39.92

Return on investment (ROI) is calculated by dividing EBITDA by equity. Following are the ROIs for Starwood and its competitors:

	1999	2000	2001
Starwood	39.24%	46.19%	37.18%
Marriott	14.89%	24.55%	19.15%
Hilton	57.38%	73.81%	48.20%

The ROI of Starwood is relatively higher than Marriott. The debt-equity ratio of Starwood is a lot higher than Marriott. One could conclude that Starwood uses leverage efficiently.

One goal of financial strategy in a company is to increase shareholders' value by increasing ROI and by increasing market value. The ROI and market value of Starwood have been growing in support of that goal during the three years shown below. This shows that Starwood raised and allocated capital fairly well.

	1999	2000	2001
Net Income (millions)	$1,141	$1,509	$1,293
Cap Rate	31%	40%	34%
Value (millions)	$3,681	$3,792	$3,802

Case Discussion Questions

1. Based on the data presented in this case example, which company (Starwood, Marriott, or Hilton) would you invest in and why?

2. Do you think the concept of an REIT has been good or bad for the hospitality industry and why?

Marriott
not Hilton
good recievable + Inventory
Turnover
, currentratio
low debt equity

CASE 2

Foxwoods—Cash for Everyone in Connecticut*

Casinos generate substantial cash flow. Total ownership garners more cash (profits) than a joint-venture or minority position. This case looks at a very substantial cash generator and profitable enterprise.

Foxwoods Resort and Casino, like many gaming entities, could form a good case example in a number of management strategy areas such as communications, human resources, risk management, and marketing, to name a few. However, Foxwoods offers a more interesting financial example, for a number of reasons. Not only is Foxwoods the largest and most financially successful gaming enterprise, it's also one of the largest nongovernmental entities to have positively affected a state's and region's economy. Before presenting a snapshot of its financial significance, let's briefly look at the history and development of this unique facility.

Milestones*

February 1992	The original Foxwoods High Stakes Bingo & Casino opened, in Mashantuket, Connecticut, offering a 46,000-square-foot gaming area with 170 table games, including roulette, poker, and blackjack, but no slot machines. The facility, including the bingo hall adjacent, cost $60 million, totaled 250,000 square feet and contained a retail boutique, museum, three restaurants, and a piano bar. The casino was built next to the original 2,100-seat bingo hall, which opened in 1986 and is now part of Foxwoods. The enterprise employed about 2,300 people, nearly all from Connecticut and Rhode Island.
January 1993	The Mashantucket Pequot tribe (Foxwood's owners) and state negotiated an agreement that allowed the tribe to operate slot machines at Foxwoods. The tribe agreed to pay the state 25 percent of its slot machine win (called net win) each year, or a minimum of $100 million annually. The agreement provided that the tribe's obligation to make such payments would cease if the state legalized the operation of slot machines anywhere else within Connecticut, or if any other entity in the state operated slot machines.

*Based on site visit and interviews with various executives at Foxwoods Resort and Casino.
*Information from www.foxwoods.com.

November 1993   A $240 million expansion increased Foxwoods' size to 1.3 million square feet. Now known as Foxwoods Resort and Casino, the total facility included five large gaming rooms with mixed slots, keno, racebook, table games, a theater complex, 23 retail shops, a beauty salon, and health spa. Four full-service restaurants were now operating, with a fifth restaurant located in the newly opened Two Trees Inn, owned by a limited partnership in which the tribe is an investor. An ice cream parlor, a deli, and a pizza stand were also completed. The two hotels offered a total of 594 rooms. The expansion increased the number of table games to 234 and slot machines to approximately 2,650. Frank Sinatra helped Foxwoods celebrate the formal opening of the new facility with five performances in the new showroom/theater, which offers 1,400 seats and has a large-screen video theater with a seating capacity of 375.

April 1994   After federal recognition of the nearby Mohegan Tribe of Indians of Connecticut, the Mashantucket Pequot Tribe amended its slot revenue agreement with the state. The new agreement provided that both tribes' obligation to make slot payments would terminate upon the legalization or operation elsewhere in the state of *any kind* of commercial casino gaming. Each tribe agreed to make payments of 25 percent of their slot machine win, or 30 percent in any year that the annual payment for the tribe falls below a minimum threshold of $80 million.

June 1994   Foxwoods completed a $65 million expansion, adding another 300,000 square feet. Bingo moved to a new location that offered 3,000 bingo seats and that could be converted into an entertainment center capable of holding up to 5,000 for headline performances and boxing events. The old bingo hall became a slot room, which increased the casino's slot total to 3,864. At this time Foxwoods' gaming area offered nearly 230 table games and a variety of entertainment options for the whole family. The casino gaming area measured 190,000 square feet.

October 1995   The success of Foxwoods' operations and management capability was recognized in October when a selection committee appointed by the governor to review proposals for the development of a casino facility in Bridgeport, Connecticut, selected the tribe's proposal over a proposal submitted by an affiliate of Mirage Resorts, Inc. Authorizing legislation for this development, however, was defeated by vote of the Connecticut General Assembly on November 17, 1995.

March 1996 Foxwoods opened the first full-service, nonsmoking casino on the East Coast. This was the second phase of a two-level, 140,000-square-foot casino expansion project. The first phase, which opened on December 22, 1995, contained a state-of-the-art Racebook, an expanded poker room, and a 30-table high-limit gaming area. Foxwoods now offered its patrons 4,244 slots and 308 table games, as well as many other entertainment options.

July 1997–April 1998 Foxwoods opened the first three levels of the Grand Pequot Tower Hotel. This first phase added 50,000 square feet of casino space, including 958 slots and 60 table games, and an additional 2,500 parking spaces. Two gourmet restaurants, Fox Harbour and Al Dente, along with the Intermezzo Lounge, opened in August 1997. The high-limit gaming area and Club Newport International opened, along with some remaining floors of the Grand Pequot Tower Hotel, in November 1997. The Veranda Cafe, a 24-hour coffee shop/cafe, opened in December 1997, along with the 25,000-square-foot Grand Pequot Ballroom. Additional conference facilities opened in April 1998.

Fall 1998 Foxwoods opened a 20,000-square-foot, state-of-the-art spa and salon along with the Villas at Foxwoods. There are 23 luxury suites with premium amenities located on floors 22 and 23 of the Grand Pequot Tower.

December 1999 *Casino Players Magazine* listed Foxwoods as number one in nearly half of the categories evaluated for casino resorts in the United States and the Caribbean. The resort casino, averaging 40,000 guests per day, is also ranked number one on a composite basis.

February 2002 Foxwoods celebrated its 10th anniversary.

Financial Strategies

The Mashantucket-owned Foxwoods is the largest single casino in the Western Hemisphere and the most lucrative in America. The key to its success and the marketing methods it uses are the issues for this case study.

With nearly 6,000 slot machines and 350 table games, Foxwoods Resort and Casino offers the best in resort amenities, gaming in a relaxing atmosphere, live entertainment with headliners from around the world, and fine dining at Mashantucket, the ancestral home of the Mashantucket Pequot Tribal Nation.

In addition to the massive amounts of money generated by gaming, the tribe runs a successful pharmaceutical division, operates high-speed ferries through its Fox Navigation, and owns the Mystic Hilton, the Spa at Norwich Inn, and Randall's Ordinary restaurant in North Stonington. The tribe also built and operates the $194 million Mashantucket Pequot Museum & Research Center, the largest American Indian museum in the country. It serves not only as a popular tourist attraction, but also as an educational resource for scholars.

The aftermath of the September 11 terrorist attacks might seem like the worst possible time to double the casino's capacity. A well-publicized gaming downturn, after all, led to layoffs throughout the Las Vegas economy at the time. Where the destination resorts of the Vegas Strip reported dramatic declines in fly-in visitors (as much as a 30 percent drop in work-hours), American Indian casinos across the country held up very well, because they draw on day-trippers from the regional market. Foxwoods Resort and Casino rebounded quickly. The shift from airplane to automobile showed up strongly over the Thanksgiving holiday, when a record 87 percent of travelers drove versus flew. At the same time, American Indian casinos reported a surprisingly good turnout. With gamblers at Connecticut's two American Indian casinos losing $120 million in November, the two tribes' year-over-year slot machine win was boosted 16.2 percent. The war on terrorism and uncertainty about the economy didn't deter players from leaving $63 million at Foxwoods in November 2001. Considering the economy and the world situation, these numbers are extremely impressive. The fact that the market sustained a 16.2 percent increase shows how deep a market it is, and it tells a good story about the ability of Connecticut to garner revenues. Moreover, when casinos in Las Vegas faced business declines, Foxwood continued to grow and take market share.

The real financial story is Foxwoods' contributions to the State of Connecticut and the entire region. Prior to Foxwoods, the coastal area of Connecticut and many inland towns were extremely economically depressed. Manufacturing had move out or closed down, leaving ghostlike blocks of empty buildings, stores for lease, and a general economic state of poverty along with high unemployment. Tax revenues were negatively impacted, and state services left much to be desired. Schools were strapped for resources and roads badly in need of repair.

As indicated, Foxwoods agreed to contribute 25 percent of its slot machine win each year to the state. As a result the state began to receive hundreds of millions of dollars from Foxwoods. In addition, Foxwoods' growth was accounting for one out of every two new jobs in the state by the late 1990s. Foxwoods, along with the Mohegan Sun Casino, were significant contributors to lowering the state's high unemployment rate (approaching 10 percent at its worst) to 3 percent.

There is more to this story than Foxwoods' financial impact. As a result of Foxwoods' direct monetary economic contributions, the state developed a multimillion-dollar investment plan, which spurred on new business, new service establishments, and a whole new economy. Connecticut's economy turned around and became very healthy. Its schools are now rated as some of the best in the country. Its roads—once in a state of disrepair—are now rated the best in the country. Land values have dramatically increased throughout the state. And much of the surrounding area in Rhode Island and Massachusetts has also enjoyed a positive spillover effect.

Being the largest and most profitable casino in the nation with the best amenities, Foxwoods has more than a very strong position in the industry. Its financial performance has contributed greatly to the rebirth of a state and regional economy.

Case Discussion Questions

1. What must Foxwoods do to maintain its financial leadership position?
2. Do you believe it was a good idea for Foxwoods to share its profits with the state? Why or why not?

Chapter 6

Brand Strategy and Management

CHAPTER OBJECTIVES

- To delineate how branding and brand strategy plays a role in the hospitality industry
- To identify the evolution of brands within the context of management strategy
- To describe the key components of brand strategy
- To demonstrate the relationship of brand strategy to managerial success and failure

When a family decided to put its name on a building, such as Hilton, Marriott, and so on, it not only "branded" the product/service, it began to establish a positioning statement. The quality of the facility and the level of service now were described by the family name, and vice versa. This was an early form of brand strategy in the hospitality industry. Brand strategy in the hospitality industry has been conveyed by the ownership (names), by the physical product design and packaging (McDonald's and Wendy's), and by the creations of marketing. The latter has created new brand names (W Hotels, Westin, Carnival, and Enterprise). Marketing also created awareness-building logos and icons (e.g., "Jack" for Jack-in-the-Box and Ronald McDonald for McDonald's). Names, logos, and icons are all part of brand strategy in the hospitality industry. In fact, anything associated with the brand's name is part of brand management. Colors, typeface, celebrity spokespersons, lighting, exterior and interior design, supplier affiliations, and so on, all need to be managed to grow and protect brands. In the hospitality industry, the "look" of the brand usually represents the overall product image. One can close one's eyes and picture an American Airlines branded plane, a Motel 6, a Hertz facility, a McDonald's, a Wendy's, or a KFC. One does not only picture the brand but can describe the product, service level, and perhaps even the taste. Brand strategy is very powerful in the hospitality industry today.

IMPLEMENTING A BRAND STRATEGY

In a 10-year time span, over 100 new lodging brands, hundreds of new restaurant brands, and dozens of new airline, rental car, and more brands were launched. Some succeeded, such as Southwest Airlines, and others disappeared, such as Peoples Express. Why some succeed and others fail is what brand management is all about. It is even more complex in certain segments of the industry, due to how businesses are developed and grow (see Chapter 4, Business Development Strategies). Regardless of the growth or development strategy, there are specific areas of focus for brand management that are important to a single brand, hybrids of that brand, and even new brands launched by the same company. The hospitality industry presents multiple examples of many different brand strategies. In fact, in some sectors such as lodging, branding has created confusion through too much management strategy and too many new brands. In this sector we now have resort hotels, express inns, budget suites, extended stays, luxury suites, residential concepts, and so on and so on. Many of these lodging brand strategies are related to "new concepts" in product or market segment needs. Other sectors such as airlines have tried express, commuter, all first class, luxury class, and so on, and food service has juniors, express, and store-in-a-store concepts, and the like. All of these require brand strategy and management.

We have moved historically from product branding to aggressively marketing and expanding brand concepts. There are now mature as well as the new brands (that have grown rapidly through franchising) that have substantial presence and awareness in the hospitality industry. Brands have reached a stage where they now have developed "equity" and are bought and sold on a fairly regular basis during contraction and expansionary periods in the industry. In addition, others absorb the original corporations that developed the brands through acquisition (e.g., Cendent). The latter may result in some brands being retained, such as Ramada and TWA, and others being merged or converted to a new brand.

While brand strategy certainly is closely aligned with overall corporate strategy, the actual execution of brand strategy falls more into the realm of marketing. For branding is a key marketing weapon. Branding is the visible communicator of positioning strategy. Marketing's role is to both lead the creative process and be the "keeper" of the brand (oversee its usage). Branding is complex and involves all elements in the marketing mix.

COMPONENTS OF BRAND STRATEGY

There are multiple components related to brand strategy. These include, but are not limited to: brand equity, brand loyalty, brand awareness; perceived quality; brand associations; the name, symbol, and slogan; brand extensions; and the concept of revitalizing the brand (see Figure 6-1).

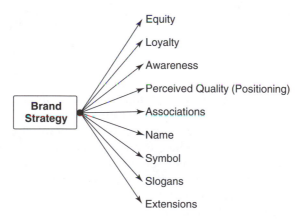

Figure 6–1   Components of Brand Strategy

Before embarking on developing a brand or branding plan, it is essential to understand the components of brand strategy.

Brand Equity

Brand equity is the net result of all the positives and negatives linked to the brand, its name and symbols—that add value to, or subtract value from, a product or service. These assets include brand loyalty, name awareness, perceived quality, and brand associations.[1]

There are considerable pressures for short-term performance, in part driven by the dictum that shareholder wealth is a primary goal of business, and partly by the reality that stock prices are responsive to short-term performance measures. Short-term activities (such as price promotions) can show dramatic results, while brand-building activities (such as image advertising) may have little immediate impact. The challenge is to understand better the links between brand assets and future performance, so that brand-building activities can be justified.

Estimating the value of a brand can help show that the underlying assets do have worth. The assessment of the value of brand equity can be based on the price premium that the name supports, the impact of the name on customer preference, the replacement cost of the brand, and the stock value minus the value of other assets. The most persuasive measure, however, may be a multiplier of the earning power of the brand. The multiplier would be based upon an analysis of the earning power of the brand assets.

ETHICS

One of the fastest ways to destroy brand equity is for management or its representatives to violate the code of ethics.

Brand Loyalty

The core of brand equity is the loyalty of its customer base—the degree to which customers are satisfied, have switching costs, like the brand, and are committed. A loyal set of customers can have substantial value, which is often underestimated. It can also reduce marketing costs, since a customer is much less costly to keep than to gain or regain, and provides leverage over others in the distribution channel. Customers can create brand awareness and generate reassurance to new customers. Loyal customers will also give a firm time to respond to competitive advances.

Brand Awareness

Don't underestimate the power of brand recognition, recall (your brand is recalled as being in a product class), and top-of-mind recall (your brand is the first recalled). People like the recognizable. Further, recognition is a basis for presence, substance, and permanence. Recall can be a necessary condition to being considered, and can have a subtle influence on purchase decisions as well. It also provides the anchor to which other associations are linked.

Building awareness is much easier over a longer time period because learning works better with repetition and reinforcement. In fact, brands with the highest recall are generally older brands. Event sponsorship, publicity, symbol exposure, and the use of brand extensions all can improve awareness. However, developing recall requires a link between the brand and the product class, and just name exposure will not necessarily create that link.

Perceived Quality

Perceived quality pays off. According to recent studies using data from thousands of businesses in the PIMS (profit impact of marketing strategy) database,[2] perceived quality improves prices, market share, and ROI. In addition, it was the top-named competitive advantage in a survey of managers of business units. It provides a reason to buy, a point of differentiation, a price premium option, channel interest, and a basis for brand extensions.

The key to obtaining high perceived quality is to deliver high quality, to identify those quality dimensions that are important, to understand what signals quality to the buyer, and to communicate the quality message in a credible manner. Price becomes a quality cue, especially when a product is difficult to evaluate objectively or when status is involved. Other quality cues include the appearance of servicepeople, public spaces, and other visible first-impression areas.

Brand Associations

A brand association is anything mentally linked to the brand.[3] The brand position is based upon associations and how they differ from competition. An association can affect the processing and recall of information, provide a point of differentiation, provide a reason to buy, create positive attitudes and feelings, and serve as the basis of extensions.

Positioning on the basis of association with a key tangible product attribute is effective when the attribute can drive purchase decisions, but often it can also result in a specification shouting match. The use of an intangible attribute such as overall quality, technological leadership, or health and vitality can sometimes be more enduring. The association with a customer benefit is another option. One study showed that the combination of a rational benefit and an emotional benefit was superior to a rational benefit alone.

The relative price position often is central. Is the brand to be premium, regular, or economy—and, further, is it to be at the top or bottom of the selected category? Among the other association types to consider are: use applications, product users, celebrities, lifestyles and personalities, product class, competitors, and country or geographic area.

Measuring Brand Associations.   Insights about what a brand means to people and what motivations it taps often can be obtained by indirect methods of eliciting associations. A customer, for example, can be asked to describe a brand user or use experience, to generate free associations with the brand, or to indicate how brands differ from each other. Another way to gain a rich profile of a brand is to ask people to consider the brand as a person (or animal, activity, magazine, etc.), and probe as to what type the brand would be.

A companion method involves a representative sample of a customer segment scaling the brand and its competitors with respect to such positioning dimensions as product attributes, customer benefits, user characteristics, use situations, or competitors. The result is a perceptual map that graphically identifies the important perceptual dimensions and shows the position of the brand for the customer sample.

Selecting, Creating, and Maintaining Brand Associations.   A successful brand position will usually follow three tenets: (1) Don't try to be something you are not. (2) Differentiate your brand from competitors. (3) Provide associations that add value or provide a reason to buy.[4]

A key to creating associations is to identify and manage signals. A promotion may signal that nonprice attributes are not important unless it is structured so that it reinforces the desired image. To deliver an attribute and communicate that it exists may not be enough if the appropriate signals are not managed properly. Being consistent over time and over elements of the marketing program is crucial in maintaining associations.

Brand Name, Symbol, and Slogan

The name, symbol, and slogan are critical to brand equity and can be enormous assets, because they serve as indicators of the brand and thus are central to brand recognition and brand associations.

A name should be selected by a systematic process involving the relation of a host of alternatives based upon desired associations and metaphors. The name should be easy to recall, suggest the product class, support a symbol or logo, suggest desired brand associations, not suggest undesirable associations, and be legally protectable. There usually are trade-offs to be made. For example, a name that suggests a product class might be strategically limiting when brand extensions are considered. A symbol can create associations and feelings. A symbol such as IBM or Sony that is based upon the name will have an edge in creating brand recognition. A symbol that includes the product class should help in brand recall where the link to the product class needs to be strong. A slogan can be tailored to a positioning strategy and is far less limited than a name and symbol in the role it can play. A slogan can provide additional associations, or help to focus on the existing one.

Brand Extensions

One way to exploit brand equity is to extend the name to different products. An extension will have the best chance for success when the brand's associations or perceived quality can provide a point of differentiation and advantage for the extension. Extensions rarely work when the brand name has nothing to offer beyond brand awareness.

An extension should "fit" the brand. There should be some link between the brand and the extension. The fit could be based upon a variety of linking elements, such as common use contexts, functional benefits, and links to prestige, user types, or symbols.[5] Any incongruity could cause damage and result in the failure of desired associations to transfer. In addition, there should not be any meaningful negative associations created by the brand name. There is a risk that an extension will damage the core brand by weakening either its associations or its perceived quality. Probably the biggest risk of an extension is that the potential of a new brand name with unique associations may be lost.

Revitalizing Brands

One option for a brand that is old and tired is to pursue one of the seven routes to brand revitalization: (1) Attempt to increase usage by existing customers through reminder advertising or extending the distribution channels. This is both relatively easy and unlikely to precipitate competitive reaction. (2) Find a new product use that can be feasibly stimulated by the brand. (3) Find new markets or attack a neglected market. (4) Reposition by changing associations or adding new associations. (5) Augment the product or service by providing features or services that are not expected. (6) Make existing products obsolete with new-generation technologies. (7) Use the extension option.[6]

Revitalization is not always possible or economically justifiable, especially in the face of a brand that lacks a strong position, is facing a declining market and dominates competitors, is not central to the long-range thrust of the firm, and lacks a revitalization strategy. One option is to divest or liquidate. Another, to milk the brand, would be preferred when there is an enduring niche that remains loyal to the brand, the decline is orderly (with relatively stable prices), and the milking option seems feasible.

In a growing number of contexts, the brand name and what it means combine to become the pivotal sustainable competitive advantage that firms have.[7] The name is pivotal because other bases of competition (such as product attributes) usually are relatively easy to match or exceed. Further, customers often lack the ability or motivation to analyze the brand-choice decision at a sufficient depth to allow specifications to win the day.

Brand equity does not just happen. Its creation, maintenance, and protection need to be actively managed. Further, it involves strategic as well as tactical programs and policies.

The components of a brand strategy need to be orchestrated in a plan in which all the parts work together to achieve the synergy required to market a brand. Planning requires that every detail, from the name, logo, and graphics treatment to the detailed marketing plan, be addressed. Before selecting a name, logo, and so on, it is important to start with the "positioning objective" and then develop related strategies and tactics. In the case of launching a new brand, the perceived quality factor becomes a driving force. When creating an entirely new brand, clear positioning within the product category and in relationship to competitive products becomes a preeminent factor. Therefore, how the brand is portrayed—the actual name and look of the new brand—take a preeminent position in the strategy. Equally important is the front-end planning. A plan needs to be in place to immediately establish a "perceived" brand equity. Positioning the new brand through its visual messages will create the perception.

TECHNOLOGY

Creating a brand "look," logo, icon, or package is but one creative application of software. Managing a brand's performance and meaning, its success or failure are as instantaneous as checking on the screen. Both hardware and software have greatly contributed to effective brand management.

The steps in implementing a brand strategy begin with the positioning objective and are followed by "linking" or creating the visual images that support that objective. These include: name, logo, graphic treatment, and creative approach. Following these "associations" is the next step, implementing a detailed marketing plan which includes but is not limited to: the advertising strategy (creative and media plans), a promotional strategy (introductory promotion and retention promotion), the public relations plan (consumer and trade), the sales strategy for retention of existing business and capturing new business, the sales organizational approach, the direct mail/database marketing program, the electronic marketing strategy, and the packaging.

Brand strategy is usually a "build" or phased activity.[8] Phase 1 is the "declaration" or announcement phase; here you state your intention and positioning objective and reveal your new look. Phase 1 is achieved through public relations and advertising. Phase 2 is the "work in progress" stage—the kick-off plus actions from the marketing plan that state "We are off the pad and ascending," drawing upon all the marketing weapons. Phase 3 begins the "proclamation" or statement of achievement—"We're meeting our goals—delivering as promised." This phase is achieved through public relations and advertising.

Phase 4 usually employs all marketing weaponry and often is accompanied by some form of recognition, such as awards, milestones, and so on.

STRATEGIES FOR A NEW BRAND LAUNCH

The critical steps for launching a new brand need to be put in perspective and involve some key factors. First, timing: The brand needs to be ready to launch. The name, logo, and graphic treatment need to be service marked or registered. The brand identifiers should have been ordered and ready to be put in place. These include the look/design of the brand and any collateral materials. Once the visual associations are ready to go, the brand marketing plan needs to be put into action. This begins with a communications plan, sometimes referred to as "memo or letter 1."

Second, memo #1 delineates the positioning so every employee in the organization can understand and explain what the new brand represents— how it is "better" than the old brand. This communiqué is usually accompanied by highlights from the overall marketing plan. It states when and where the new advertising will appear. It talks about the introductory promotions, the new look, and all the other positive momentum and *esprit de corps* building blocks.

Third, it is absolutely essential to have the "internal launch" take place prior to the "external launch." This ensures that all employees are aware of any changes.

Fourth, every business that adopts a new brand should consider a "new brand grand opening" event that reintroduces the business and people to key local contacts and the community.

Fifth, letters to existing customers should be developed and follow-up calls made to convey the new brand positioning. These letters should seek to excite and entice the customers to return or repeat purchase. An introductory incentive should be included if possible.

Sixth, special familiarization briefings should be provided to all key intermediaries. These intermediaries include middlemen, merchant middlemen, agents, distributors, wholesalers, retailers, brokers, manufacturer agents, jobbers, and facility agents.

Seventh, a comprehensive trade media public relations plan should be rolling at the time of the launch. Interviews with key executives and spokespersons, as well as trade advertising delineating the brand positioning strategy, should be ongoing at this juncture.

Eighth, the consumer marketing plan steps also need to occur in sync with the launch. A new tollfree number, internet address, advertisements, promotions, photos, and the like, all need to be simultaneously lined up and ready to go. These marketing activities need to be executed with a grand opening philosophy and heavy up-front expenditure level (in the first six months of the launch). In essence, spend the largest portion of the annual budget in the months following the brand launch.

Ninth, every month for the first 3 months, recommunicate in the form of an "update" memo #1—then memo #2, memo #3, and so on, to both your internal and external constituencies. Do this again at 6 months and 1 year out.

Tenth, replace anyone who has not bought into the new brand positioning or is not communicating it with enthusiasm. This is poison to a new brand launch with both employees and customers.

In summary, it is critical to be ready before the launch with a detailed communications and marketing plan. It is essential to have the brand identifiers designed, purchased, and in place at the outset of the conversion. Finally, make sure all constituencies have been clearly and thoroughly briefed. The brand launch should have its own critical path chart, with key dates and responsibilities clearly delineated. Regular progress briefings and meetings should also occur. A sound approach is to select the launch date (after planning), then peg all the critical dates/tasks that lead up to that day. Allow for slippage with sign companies, suppliers, design issues, and such. Be sure the new brand signs are within the square foot limitations of the existing zoning regulations before you order signs. And be sure you have taken and completed all legal steps such as registering your brand, slogans, and so forth.

The following can be used as a checklist for a new brand name.

Checklist for a New Brand Name

- Does the name reflect the positioning and product/service attributes or benefits?
- Is it appropriate to the product/service category?
- Is it globally acceptable (translates well)?
- Is it simple and easy to remember and recognize?
- Does it convey emotion or a positive mental image?
- Is it easy to pronounce and visualize?
- Does it relate to the product/service personality?
- Does it lend itself to creative development both visually and in written copy?
- Will it work on packages and signage, and does the logo reproduce in black and white and in small and large size?
- Has it been protected legally (and a search completed also)?
- Will it require any special treatment when used in color in print or broadcast media?
- How does it compare to your top three competitors?
- Have you tested it on your target market, employees, and other constituencies?

CHAPTER REVIEW

In this chapter we have provided a look at how brands have evolved and multiplied in the hospitality industry. Brand strategy, while part of the overall corporation's development and business expansion strategies, is largely a managerial and functional responsibility most closely linked to marketing. For it is marketing that deals with all of the visual and vocal communications aspects surrounding brands. Brand strategy is extraordinarily important, as the execution of such strategy has a direct influence on positioning, customer expectations, and pricing. Further, brand strategy is complex for it involves the management of everything associated with the brand and conveyed about the brand. The sum of all these management activities directly relates to the brand's equity, profitability, image, and actual value in the marketplace.

Building awareness, conveying perceived quality, keeping customers loyal, selecting appropriate associations, and overseeing how the brand is used are all key aspects of brand management. Selecting the proper and appropriate brand partners, extensions, and creative strategy are yet additional managerial focal points. Revitalizing maturing brands and launching new brands have become a regular and significant occurrence in the hospitality industry. Finally, selecting the best brand integration strategies for acquired or merged brands forms yet another managerial strategic task in this industry.

KEY CONCEPTS/TERMS

Brand	Brand extensions
Brand assets	Brand loyalty
Brand associations	PIMS
Brand awareness	Product attributes
Brand equity	

DISCUSSION QUESTIONS

1. Which sector of the hospitality industry do you believe has developed the strongest brands (e.g., airlines, food service, lodging, etc.)? Why do you believe this is so?

2. Select a leading brand in the hospitality industry and list its assets.

3. If you were developing a "new" brand in the hospitality industry, would you seek associations? If so, what would these be?

4. Name two or three brand icons (hospitality industry related) and describe why you believe these contributed to the brand and how they helped.

5. Make a list of five hospitality industry brands you believe do a good job at conveying positioning. State why you believe this is so. Also, do the same for five brands that you believe are not doing a good job of conveying positioning.

ENDNOTES

1. D. Aaker, *Managing Brand Equity* (New York: The Free Press, 1991): 15–16.
2. R. Buzzell & T. Bradley, *The PIMS Principles: Linking Strategy to Performance* (New York: The Free Press, 1987): 106–107.
3. Aaker (1991), 109.
4. Aaker (1991), 273.
5. D. Aaker, *Developing Business Strategies* (New York: John Wiley & Sons, 1995): 264.
6. Aaker (1991), 275.
7. M. Porter, *Competitive Advantages* (New York: The Free Press, 1980): Chap. 2.
8. R. Nykiel, *Marketing Strategies* (New York: Cormar Business Press, 2002): 110.

CASE 1

Cendant—The Brand Collector*

There is perhaps no better example of a brand collector strategy in the industry today than that of Cendant Corporation. Cendant could also be used as a case example for business development, financial, marketing, and leadership strategies. Many of the more widely known brands in the hospitality and other industries fall under the Cendant umbrella.

Cendant's brand collector strategy is based on acquiring name brands at value prices and then growing those brands through its marketing and franchising expertise. Cendant views revenue as revenue per available customer or REVPAC. Cendant offers consumers brands in multiple industries and industry sectors.

Cendant Corporation is a diversified global provider of business and consumer services primarily within the real estate and travel sectors. The company's core competencies include building franchise systems and providing outsourcing services. Cendant is among the world's leading franchisers of real estate brokerage offices, hotels, rental car agencies, and tax preparation services. Cendant is also a provider of outsourcing solutions to its business partners including mortgage origination, employee relocation, customer loyalty programs, vehicle management and fuel card services, vacation exchange services, and vacation interval sales. Other businesses include Britain's largest private car park operator and electronic reservations processing for the travel industry. With headquarters in New York City, the company operates in over 100 countries. Cendant's real estate brands include: Cendant Mobility, Cendant Mortgage, Century 21, Coldwell Banker, Coldwell Banker Commercial, and ERA. Hospitality and travel-related brands include: AmeriHost Inn & Suites, Avis, Budget, Days Inn, Fairfield Communities, Howard Johnson, Knights Inn, PHH Arval, Ramada, Resort Condominiums International, Super 8, Travelodge, Villager Lodge, Wingate Inns, and Wright Express. Other Cendant brands in the diversified services area include: Autovantage, Benefit Consultants, Inc., Cendant Incentives, CIMS, Fisi-Madison Financial, Jackson Hewitt Tax Service, Long Term Preferred Care, National Car Parks, PrivacyGuard, Shoppers Advantage, Travelers Advantage, and WizCom.

Cendant owes its strategy success to Chairman and CEO Henry Silverman, who clearly understands the value of brands as well as how to grow brands. Both his acquisitions and expansion through franchising and marketing have proven exceptional strategies. It is for these reasons that Cendant is an excellent case example of a brand collector in the hospitality industry.

*Information derived from www.cendant.com.

Case Discussion Questions

1. After acquiring a brand, what strategies are implemented to increase the brand's value?

2. Cendant is one of the first corporations to view the customer as a source for multiple revenue/purchases. Do you believe the concept of REVPAC will be utilized by others in the hospitality industry? Why or why not?

CASE 2

Landry's Restaurants—Packaging the Brands*

This case provides an assessment of the overall packaging of the brands owned by Landry's Restaurants, Inc. It examines how well the brand packaging matches the product/service offerings from a positioning perspective.

Landry's Restaurants offers a variety of different concepts that range from theme restaurants such as Rainforest Cafe to restaurants specializing in seafood such as Landry's Seafood House. Restaurants related to the brand are:

- Landry's Seafood House: Offers seafood with a light, lively, and informal atmosphere. It features an array of recipes that include fresh local seafood selections. The atmosphere depicts the pleasantries of the past common to the Gulf Coast.

- Crab House Seafood Restaurant: First opened in Miami in 1975, offering high-quality fresh seafood served in a casual, spirited atmosphere with a casual decor that is inviting and fun.

- Joe's Crab Shack: A great shack full of tasty crustaceans prepared all sorts of delicious ways. It is described as a simple, fun-filled dining experience.

- Kemah Boardwalk: A family get-away entertainment area just 20 miles from downtown Houston. It has quickly evolved from a waterfront dining experience to a weekend destination.

- Willie G's Seafood and Steak House: Known for serving fresh seafood specialties and recognized nationally as one of the top upscale seafood restaurants. Since opening in 1980, it has established itself as a favorite among the local business crowd, area residents, and travelers, offering a multitude of choices for all guests.

- Cadillac Bar: Offers authentic Mexican food and is renowned for its margaritas and lively music, all served in a fun, casual atmosphere. The extensive menu includes old favorites like traditional enchiladas, nachos, and tacos, but specializes in unique dishes found only at the Cadillac Bar.

- Rainforest Cafe: A unique place to shop and eat, where the concept is an adventure through a realistic indoor rain forest. Lush surroundings, cascading waterfalls, and beautiful giant aquariums are combined with good food, providing a unique atmosphere.

- C.A. Muer Restaurants: Offering fine food, service, and entertainment in a more formal atmosphere.

*Information derived from www.landrysseafood.com.

- Chart House Restaurants
- Saltgrass Steak House

History

In 1986, Chairman, President, and CEO Tilman Fertitta bought an interest in the Landry's Seafood House, which opened in 1980, and Willie G's Seafood and Steak House, which opened a year later. Then in 1988, he acquired sole ownership of the company and developed a recognized seafood chain with four distinct concepts. At a time when steakhouses and Italian restaurants were popular, Fertitta felt the seafood restaurant business was untapped and decided to expand, envisioning his high-energy, full-service, casual dining seafood concept throughout the United States. No one since Red Lobster had the foresight to operate a national seafood restaurant chain.

When banks were failing and refusing to negotiate, credit lines were resorting to depletion of all net worth, and businesses were struggling to pay creditors, Fertitta overcame adversity and continued to believe in his product and his dream of expansion. He began in his hometown, Galveston, before branching out in San Antonio, Corpus Christi, Austin, and Dallas. In 5 years, the company grew from 2 to 11 restaurants.

In 1993, Fertitta took the company public, a decision many would consider risky, since 95 percent of restaurant startups fail. However, Fertitta parlayed his cash flow from one restaurant into more, with all earnings invested into company development. Landry's Restaurants, Inc., had become the second largest casual seafood restaurant chain in America. The company continues to expand, aspiring to build a $1 billion restaurant/hospitality company.

Since Fertitta became chairman of the board, president, CEO, and largest shareholder of the company, Landry's Restaurants has grown tremendously, expanding to 150 restaurants in 26 states.

The company was listed fifth on *Forbes* magazine's list of "200 Best Small Companies in America" in 1994, 11th in 1995, and 63rd in 1996. *Business Week* listed Landry's among the "Top 100 Companies for Growth" two consecutive years, while *Restaurants and Institutions* magazine cited it as "One of 1995's Top Growth Companies." *Restaurant Business* listed Landry's as number four of the top 50 restaurant chains based on corporate profit margins.

Landry's is the only restaurant company in the country that has two concepts named as "Hot Concepts" by *Nation's Restaurant News*, citing Landry's as one of nine "Hot Restaurant Concepts of the Nineties" and Joe's Crab Shack as one of eight "Hot Concepts of 1996."

In 1996, the company acquired the 17-unit Crab House Seafood Restaurants, which originated in Miami in 1976.

In 1997, Landry's acquired the Kemah Boardwalk, to create one of the most exciting showplace boardwalks in the United States—an entertainment complex of attractions, restaurants, and retail shops—that it hopes will triple the number of visitors to the area to more than 3 million. In 1998, Landry's bought casual dining Mexican restaurant Cadillac Bar to add a new unit to the Kemah Boardwalk. A series of four tropical storms affected the company's restaurants in May through October of this year. The year 1999 was the official opening of the Kemah Boardwalk, where Landry's planned to open approximately 12 new units and increase focus on existing restaurants.

Later acquisitions for the group were the Rainforest Cafe (2001), a theme restaurant with a focus on environmental protection and awareness, and the C.A. Muer Restaurants (2002) that brought upscale service, entertainment, and quality food to its customers. In 2002, Landry's acquired Chart House Restaurants (35 units) and Saltgrass Steak House (27 units). The company now operates over 275 restaurants across the country.

Brand Characteristics (Packaging) and Awareness

Landry's Restaurants offers different concepts that reach different publics, tastes, and budgets, although most restaurants of the group focus on the seafood segment which facilitates association within the brand.

Another characteristic that makes the company brand strong, besides the exposure due to strategic locations (e.g., the waterfront in Kemah, Texas), is that most of the restaurants have bright colors, cartoon-style logos, and neon movie-style marquees. Some of the restaurants use characters—Joe's Crab Shack uses a pirate; the Rainforest Cafe uses animals. These techniques are used to cause impact and convey the image of a fun and entertaining place. The company's customers want to be part of the Landry's experience and use a brand they trust.

When asked about Landry's, people immediately associate the brand with a fun seafood restaurant. This brand awareness was developed through the years and is the result of full integration of the quality product, training, customer service, and advertising. These are some of the major factors that determined its success in restaurant management and are consistent in all the restaurants of the group. When people go to any of the Landry's restaurants they expect to find good service, tasty food, and a fun experience.

Brand Positioning

Landry's Restaurants' positioning is to be a leader in the casual seafood restaurant category. The company believes not only that it is well positioned to take advantage of the current consumer trends, but that it may actually be responsible for the increased emphasis on the "whole" dining experience (eat and have fun at the same time).

The company is investing in new segments like theme restaurants and bars to diversify the business and reach other target customers.

Another important issue is the maintenance of its market share. This is a time- and cash-consuming process, because restaurant management has to be alert to competitors entering its share of the market, to changes in consumer habits, and to needs that might drive them to their competitors. This is why constant investment in renovation, new concepts, and advertising is done.

Landry's overall packaging illustrates a good match to its service concept and desired image. Landry's philosophy, management strategies, and brand execution have resulted in a profitable and growing restaurant company.

Case Discussion Questions

1. Unlike many multiple-restaurant owners that place their name/brand on all their restaurants, Landry's has opted in many cases to use individual names on its restaurants. Do you believe this is a good practice or bad strategy, and why?

2. Landry's believes in placing its restaurants within a high-activity area (e.g., boardwalks, entertainment complexes, malls, etc.). What do you believe are the benefits of this strategy?

PART 3

The Offensive (Revenue Development) Strategies of Marketing, Sales, and Customer Retention

art 3 focuses on the offensive managerial strategies of revenue development. The part begins with a comprehensive discussion of marketing strategies in Chapter 7. Here, all the major marketing disciplines are delineated and related to strategy selection and implementation. Concepts covered include advertising, promotions, databases, and electronic marketing (the internet, websites, etc.). Marketing strategy selection is related to both market conditions and competitive positioning through strategy selection tools such as the grid concept.

Sales strategies are the focal point of Chapter 8. These include the concepts of proactive and reactive selling, presentation strategies, and motivational concepts. Further, compensation approaches and reward (incentive) concepts are delineated. Sales strategy is presented from an internal managerial focus and from external competitive and customer perspectives. Managerial strategy related to forecasting and budgeting is also covered in this chapter.

Chapter 9 concentrates on managerial strategies related to customer service and quality. This chapter demonstrates the proven relationship between perceived quality and profitability. It further presents the relationship between customer retention and increased sales and reduced marketing expenditures. Chapter 9 also presents managerial strategies related to TQM (total quality management), and CQI (continuous quality improvement).

Chapter 7

Marketing Strategies

CHAPTER OBJECTIVES

- To delineate the internal and external drivers of marketing strategy in the hospitality industry
- To identify the specific research methodologies that assist in selecting marketing strategies
- To provide an overview of the strategic marketing management process upon which hospitality industry strategies are based
- To discuss the applications of the various marketing disciplines and weapons deployed in the hospitality industry today

Marketing strategy within the hospitality industry is determined, set, and orchestrated by the same internal and external drivers as in any industry. Internally, the mission statement, goals, and objectives of the corporation set the parameters. Externally, competitive and environmental factors have a direct influence on the overall marketing strategy. The positioning of the brand and the execution of the brand strategy are usually functions of a strategic marketing plan and the orchestrated selection of marketing weapons. As in any disciplined business process, a number of steps are taken prior to developing a strategic marketing plan.

UNDERSTANDING THE ENVIRONMENT

We are in a transitory and ever-changing period for both business firms and marketing. This applies to every business, be it a new e-commerce venture, retail or service industry enterprise, small firm or mega-corporation. What worked in the past has no guarantee of working in the future as both external and internal change is taking place at an ever-accelerating pace. New technologies, new products and services, new delivery systems, and new competition change the playing field on a regular and frequent basis. Any one or a combination of these external and internal forces may suggest it is time to redefine the business strategy or, if managing a new brand or enterprise, to define it for the first time.

Analyzing the market from customers' expectations and competitive perspectives reveals that a great deal of change is taking place. Internal changes are occurring, such as: utilization of multidisciplinary management teams; managing up, down, and across; and field-based management versus headquarters-based, to name a few. There are changes in how business is being conducted, such as: more outsourcing, more collaborative efforts (alliances and networking), an accelerated development process, use of fewer but more responsive suppliers, and so on. Businesses are seeking to develop new competitive advantages, be more market and customer oriented, improve by benchmarking (measuring themselves against others), and where feasible offer customized products or personalized services. Focal points are also changing, such as looking globally versus locally, zeroing in on the value chain, and refining marketing targets. It is not surprising to find that customers are redefining value to include not just the traditional "quality at a fair price" but adding "speed and convenience" to the equation.

All of these dynamics in the marketplace are changing not only how hospitality entities conduct business but also how they define it. Before beginning the marketing planning process, one must reflect on the company's core competencies and driving forces, with questions such as: (1) Where does the business make a significant contribution to the customer's perceived benefits with the end product or service offered? (2) What do we do or what can we do that is difficult for our competitors to imitate? (3) Are we "market" or "product/service" driven and should we change? The answers form new core values and driving forces upon which the marketing strategy is based.

At this point, organizations relook at or develop a new mission statement. To do so they need to: reexamine and record the philosophies of the firm; develop an overall positioning statement; and focus on the vision of the future—where they want to go and what they want to achieve.

RESEARCH METHODOLOGIES

Most corporations utilize a variety of marketing research methodologies to assess the key focal points for their business. This comprehensive assessment provides the rationale behind their marketing strategies and is considered essential to sound planning. The assessment focuses on: (1) self-analysis (the business itself), (2) the competition, and (3) environmental factors that can impact the business/strategy (see Figure 7-1).

Researching each of these areas is essential to developing the basis for a strategic marketing plan. In fact, before selecting a strategy or deploying marketing weaponry to execute those strategies, one must know the product or service, the target markets and their needs, and the competition. One must

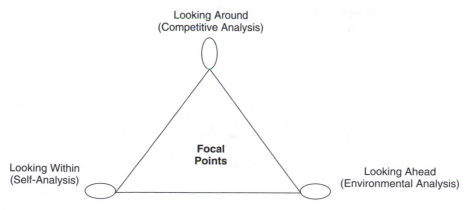

Figure 7–1   Focal Points for Assessment

also know what the road ahead looks like with respect to the business environment in which one will be operating. In essence, marketing strategies must be based on sound research.

Types of Marketing Research

Broadly speaking, marketing research can be either quantitative or qualitative. Quantitative marketing research seeks to quantify data using numbers, projections, forecasts, and the like. Qualitative marketing research seeks to identify, analyze, or profile consumers, looking at consumer attitudes, behaviors, and so on. Both quantitative and qualitative marketing research can be either primary or secondary. Primary research is research you conduct yourself; secondary research is research that someone else has conducted. Marketing research categories are depicted in Figure 7-2. We briefly examine each of the marketing research categories in the following sections.

Market Research   Market research seeks to quantify and segment demand. Focal points of market research include:

- Market share (demand)
- Sales trends
- Market segments/quantification/trends
    Primary target market
    Secondary target market
    Niche/special markets
- Distribution channels
    Outlets
    Penetration
    Coverage
- Geographic markets/trends
- Media markets

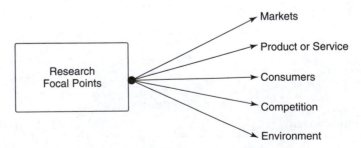

Figure 7–2   Marketing Research Categories

Broadcast (television/radio)

Print (newspaper/magazine)

Electronic (internet)

Direct mail

Outdoor

Other

Product or Service Research   Product or service research usually focuses on your product's/service's strengths and weaknesses in relation to the products/services of competitors. This research focuses on:

- Products/services
  Strengths
  Weaknesses
  Development
  Life cycles
- Positioning
- Branding
- Packaging
- Pricing strategies

Consumer Research   Consumer research takes many different forms and covers a very broad range of customer and potential customer-related issues. It may be quantitative or qualitative in nature. Consumer research may focus on:

- Demographics
- Geographics
- Psychographics
- Behavioral patterns
- Social attitudes
- Habits
- Benefits and needs

Since marketing frequently relies on the media as one method to reach prospective customers, present and future customers can be categorized by designated market area (DMA) (geographic areas reached by clusters of television stations, as defined by AC Neilsen) or area of dominant influence (ADI) (geographic areas defined by the circulation zones of major newspapers, as categorized by Arbitron, an audience research firm).

Consumer research seeks to identify the usage patterns of customers and their preferences. Customer research also seeks to classify consumers by age, income, education, and so on (demographics), as well as discover their habits (psychographics) with respect to likes, dislikes, and so on, always seeking to quantify wherever possible. Consumer research explores everything from the purchasing habits to the attitudes and behaviors of consumers.

Competition Research   One of the keys to successful marketing strategy is understanding how your product or service compares to your top competitors' products or services. Competition research compares your product or service to the products or services of competitors and tries to discover how consumers perceive and experience your product/service offering in relation to those of your competitors. Focal points of competition research include:

- Pricing
- Value
- Quality
- Convenience to purchase
- Customer satisfaction
- Delivery

Environment Research   Marketing must take into account not only what consumers and competitors are doing, but also what is occurring within and to the total industry environment. Environment research focuses on external forces—major issues that will have an impact on your business such as:

- Overall economic scenario
- Social issues
- Political issues
- Technological developments
- Legal implications
- Legislative issues

One key focus of environmental research is to look ahead at what form and shape opportunities and threats may take and how they will affect your activities. Frequently, competition research and environment research are linked. The output of these research assessments is often referred to using the acronym SWOT, which stands for Strengths, Weaknesses, Opportunities, and Threats. SWOT can be analyzed to provide a support rationale for developing marketing strategies. Examples of focal points of a SWOT analysis include:

- Strengths
    Company/brand

Value to the market

Product/service leadership

Brand awareness

Image

Technological

Operational

Marketing (distribution) share

Pricing

Financial

Customer loyalty/satisfaction

- Weaknesses

Consumption/sales trends

Product/service delivery

Technological

Operational

Marketing

Pricing

Distribution

Promotion

Image

Awareness

Reputation

Financial

Obsolescence

- Opportunities

Brand extensions

New products/services

New markets

Incremental purchase

Exploiting competitive weaknesses

Excess demand (pricing)

New distribution channels

Technology

New trends

- Threats

Capacity to deliver

Labor availability

Cost to produce

Superior new competitor

Product/service obsolescence

Regulatory

Competitive pricing

Declining demand

In summary, research focuses on both quantitative and qualitative trends. Quantitative trend research seeks to identify significant increases or declines in customer preferences, methods of purchase, usage/frequency, and other factors impacting future demand. Qualitative trend research seeks to identify changes in consumer attitudes, interests, tastes, benefits sought, and so on. Trend research findings help marketers make strategic marketing decisions.

Marketing Research Techniques

Many types of marketing research techniques can be used to help make sound marketing decisions. Which technique works best depends on many factors, such as the product/service offering, the nature of the problem or opportunity, the amount of resources available, time or urgency, budget, and so on. Basic marketing research techniques widely used include surveys, questionnaires, and focus groups. Of course, there are many other quantitative and qualitative research techniques employed, but the purpose of this section is to summarize these basic techniques. Regardless of the research technique selected, the goal remains the same—to gain information and apply the findings to improve the marketing strategy or marketability of a product or service.

Surveys   A survey seeks to elicit consumer opinion, uncover facts, and gain insights into potential trends. Surveys may be conducted in a variety of ways, at various locations, among customers or potential customers, or even among competitors' customers. Surveys may be conducted in person, by phone, electronically, or by mail.

A survey is a structured document, usually seeking to quantify its findings in terms of percentages of those who agree or disagree with particular statements. It also seeks to measure the depth of agreement or disagreement, often employing a point scale—for example, "Circle 1 if you strongly agree, 5 if you strongly disagree." Five-, seven-, and ten-point scales are commonly used. Surveys are also used to seek qualitative information, especially when open-ended questions are asked—such as, "What else would you like to see or have." Surveys may be conducted only once or periodically scheduled, such as an annual frequent-flier program preference survey. Multiple-period (semi-annual, monthly, etc.) surveys often seek to spot improvements or declines in such areas as service levels or consumer preferences, thus providing a rationale for a marketing, operational, or development decision.

Questionnaires   Perhaps the most widely used research technique is questionnaires. These come in all types of forms and are used for multiple purposes. As data collection vehicles, questionnaires seek both factual information and opinion. Data that questionnaires are designed to collect include customer comments, customer profiles, product and service information, demographic and psychographic data, attitudinal information, consumer usage patterns and preferences, and so on. The data collected may be used to measure performance, improve products or services, qualify prospects, build leads, create mailing lists, determine consumer price sensitivity, analyze menus, and the list goes on. For additional analysis, focus groups may be recorded or observed via one-way mirrors. Focus group members may volunteer their time or be compensated.

Like surveys, questionnaires can be conducted in person, by phone, by mail, or electronically. Questionnaires often are ongoing, such as customer satisfaction comment questionnaires, new customer/purchaser questionnaires, and the like. Also like surveys, questionnaires can use scales or point systems to yield quantifiable data or to rank items in order of importance.

Frequently, the terms "survey" and "questionnaire" are used interchangeably. However, questionnaires tend to be briefer than surveys and are usually less complex in content.

Focus Groups   A focus group is a marketing research technique that combines personal opinion solicitation in the form of group discussion with a structured set of questions. During a focus group session, a "moderator" conducts or facilitates the discussion using a script designed to elicit opinions from focus group members.

There are a number of types of focus groups, ranging from single-area focus groups to regional/market-area focus groups to multiple-area focus groups. Single-area focus groups are focus groups drawn from one market; regional/market-area focus groups are single focus groups held in one or more regions of the country; multiple-area focus groups are more than one focus group held in multiple regions of the country. Also, there are product/service-user focus groups and non-user focus groups. Focus groups may be made up of your customers, your competitors' customers, prospective customers, or any combination thereof.

Focus groups by nature are more time consuming for marketers to conduct and follow through on than surveys or questionnaires. Focus groups involve script writing, hiring a professional group leader, holding the focus group session itself, and then analyzing the focus group and its responses. In general, focus groups provide more in-depth qualitative findings related to attitudes and behavior than do questionnaires or surveys. Sometimes focus groups come up with useful questions that can be placed on subsequent questionnaires or surveys.

Five Essential Marketing Intelligence Tools

As indicated at the outset of this section, prior to developing a marketing strategy/plan you need to "look within, look around, and look ahead." These suggested five marketing intelligence tools provide support for strategic management decisions or a "fail-safe" for any hospitality business (see Figure 7-3). In summary, they are:

1. *SWOT Analysis.* Recording and analyzing your capabilities or resources can improve your competitive position and performance. You develop this intelligence by looking within at your internal company data. Looking within and analyzing any capability or resource that may cause your organization to under-perform or lose market share (weaknesses) may also be identified from this intelligence tool. Your external focus—looking around at the competition and looking ahead at environmental trends—provides you the marketing intelligence to spot opportunities, justify new marketing strategy, and possibly help to identify trends that require changes to marketing strategy.

2. *CSI.* Consistently measuring customer satisfaction is essential to marketing strategy. Developing a methodical marketing intelligence tool such as a customer satisfaction index (CSI) can provide you with an ongoing periodic scorecard on how your business is performing. Wherever possible, your CSI should be closely linked to performance evaluation and reward systems throughout every level of your organization. [Note: The term GSI (guest satisfaction index) is also used widely in the hospitality industry.]

3. *CPA.* A customer perceptions audit (CPA) is a marketing intelligence tool that provides objective (external) evaluation of how your busi-

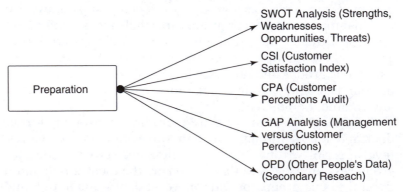

Figure 7–3 The Five Essential Marketing Intelligence Tools

ness is performing and delivering throughout the entire prepurchase to post-purchase experience. A CPA is a step-by-step walk-through of all "points of encounter" with the customer from the customer's perspective. Often "mystery shoppers" or external firms are used to perform the audit.

4. *GAP Analysis.* A GAP analysis as a marketing intelligence tool seeks to identify the difference between management's perspective of how the business is performing with respect to customer satisfaction and how the customer evaluates that performance. The difference is referred to as the "GAP." A good GAP analysis can be quantified/measured using an index. For example, using a 100 percentage point index, management rates unit customer satisfaction at 85 percent and customers rate their experience at 65 percent—thus a 20 percent "GAP" between management's and the customers' perspective.

5. *OPD.* Not every business can afford to conduct extensive marketing research with their limited resources. One solution is to employ the marketing intelligence tool called OPD or Other People's Data. OPD is secondary research that is conducted or compiled by someone other than you, face to face with customers or potential customers. It may be industry or product category information. Many entities (agencies, competitors, the government, etc.) are constantly conducting research (primary research) and reporting or sharing the findings.

Communicating Research Findings

There are many presentation tools that marketers use to help individuals understand and analyze research findings. Some of these presentation tools are simple graphics such as triangles or pyramids, circles or maps, linear diagrams, boxes or rectangles, and grids or matrices. Granted, some may view this discussion as an over-simplification of the presentation process. However, the majority of research findings and models are visually presented using these simple forms. Let's look at a few of these research presentation tools.

Pyramids Pyramids are often used to depict the size of markets, service levels, rates/prices, and product/brand positioning. Figure 7-4 presents a pyramid that profiles three brands by service level and price. This same presentation tool can be used to structure a profile of market and price strategies.

Other uses of the pyramid include segmentation, problem resolution, prioritizing, categorizing, targeting, and importance/weighting. Subdividing the pyramid allows for benefits prioritization, strategy selection, positioning, and cost/quality equations. In these instances, the pyramid is referred to as a "product triad" (see Figure 7-5).

Circles are frequently used for "mapping" purposes, wherein you are comparing your product/service to the expressed needs and wants of consumers and/or in relation to the products/services of competitors (see Figure

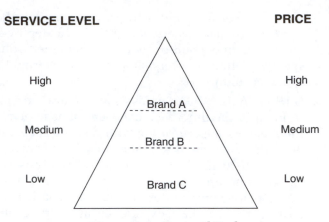

Figure 7–4 Pyramid Tool

7-5). A perceptual map will help you focus on how well your product or service is doing in comparison to others in terms of quality and value, as perceived by your customers. In Figure 7-6, "quality" is plotted along the horizontal axis and "value" along the vertical axis. How consumers perceive your product/service is what locates you on the map. A perceptual map can help identify your problems and opportunities in relation to the market and your competition. A perceptual map can also be of great value in creating advertising or pricing strategies, or in determining the necessity for product- or service-level enhancements.

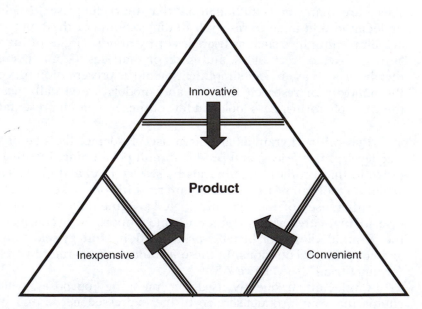

Figure 7–5 Product Triad Tool

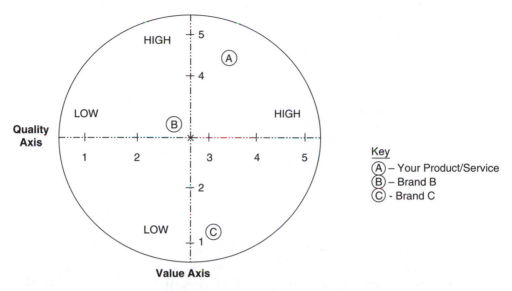

Figure 7–6   Circle Tool: Perceptual Map

Other uses of the circle tool include mapping of product/brand attributes, competitive relationships, inclusion and exclusion of services/benefits, needs assessment, and price/value relationships. In these instances, axis definitions and scales may be customized. In an inclusion/exclusion application, the focus is on what is inside the circle (i.e., within the scope of the business strategy) or what is outside the circle (i.e., excluded from the current business strategy).

Linear Diagrams   Linear diagrams are frequently used to show "pathways" to targets, look at alternative strategies, develop networks and alliances, and aid in the decision-making process. One of the most popular linear diagrams is the "decision tree" (see Figure 7-7), most often used to view product/service extensions and expansions, market segment alternatives, product/service hybrids, and the like. Decision trees show various possible "branches" that you might take to reach an objective or outcome. Decision trees have applicability in the product/service development process, operations, and marketing. Their benefit is to clearly show alternatives or multiple routes to achieve goals and objectives.

Boxes/Rectangles   For many years, "boxes" and "rectangles" have proved to be useful presentation tools for marketers. One of the best known box creations is attributed to the Boston Consulting Group and is referred to as the "portfolio approach to strategy formulation." This leading management consulting firm recommended that organizations appraise each of their products on the basis of market growth rate (annual growth rate of the market in which the product is sold) and the organization's share of the market

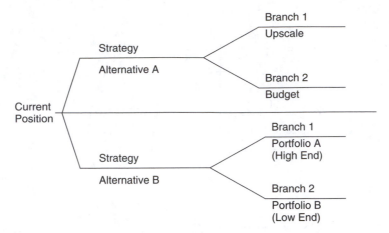

Figure 7–7   Linear Diagram: Decision Tree

relative to its largest competitor. Each product is then placed in the corresponding quadrant of the Boston Consulting Group Portfolio Box. By dividing product-market growth into high growth and low growth and market share into high share and low share, four categories of products can be identified: stars, cash cows, question marks, and dogs. These categories can be summarized as follows:

- *Stars.* Stars are those products in which an organization enjoys a high share of fast-growing (new) markets. Star products are growing rapidly and typically require heavy investment of resources. In such instances, the organization should mobilize its resources to develop stars in such a way that their market growth and market-share leadership is maintained. If the necessary investment is made and the growth proves enduring, a star product will turn into a cash cow and generate income in excess of expenses in the future.

- *Cash Cows.* Cash cows are those products that enjoy a high share of slow-growth (mature) markets. They produce revenues that can be used to support high-growth products or underwrite those with problems.

- *Question Marks.* Question marks are those products that only have a small share of a fast-growing market. Organizations face the question of whether to increase investment in question mark products, hoping to make them stars, or to reduce or terminate investment, on the grounds that funds could be better spent elsewhere.

- *Dogs.* Dogs are those products that have a small market share of slow-growth or declining markets. Since dogs usually make little money or even lose money, a decision may be made to drop them. Sometimes a business, for a variety of reasons, continues to sell dogs even though they are unprofitable. However, managers must remember that the resources that go into maintaining dogs are resources that business can't use for other opportunities.

The Boston Consulting Group Portfolio Box can also be used to analyze companies, brands, or markets.

Another box/rectangle tool is the G.E. Portfolio approach, which expands the Boston Consulting Group concept by adding the dimensions of market attractiveness and organizational strengths to the design. The Boston Consulting Group Portfolio Box and the G.E. Portfolio, as well as other boxes/rectangles, provide visual mechanisms that can help marketers understand data and formulate or select marketing strategies.

Grids   An extension of the box concept is the grid concept. Grids are excellent tools to help a business formulate marketing strategies and plans. The Marketing Strategy Grid, for example, is a dynamic tool that usually views both present and future market and competitive conditions (see Figure 7-8). It

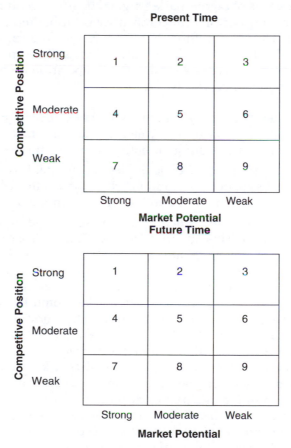

Figure 7–8   Marketing Strategy Grid

allows you to gain perspective on your own product or service through an honest and frank evaluation.[1] In order to objectively select the appropriate marketing strategies, you must understand the conditions (present and future) of the market you are in, where the market is going, and how your product relates to both the current and future conditions as well as to the competition's products.

The Marketing Strategy Grid profiles the success of your product/service. A product/service's position on the grid is a function of both the potential of the market and the competitive position within the market of the product/service. The horizontal axis of the grid denotes the potential of the market sector, while the vertical axis represents the competitive position of the product/service within the market sector. The possible rankings on both axes range from weak to strong. If you are ranking your business or products as a whole, your competitive position is a function of both quantitative and qualitative considerations, such as the amount and quality of competition; your competitive advantages as to amount and quality of competition; your competitive advantages as to distribution, share, image, pricing, and so on; and your ability to meet the needs of target market segments. It is a good practice to develop two grids—one on your present competitive position and the second on your projected competitive position 2 to 5 years into the future. This will help you focus on the dynamics of your marketplace and competition.

Obviously, there is a meaning to the position on the grid in which a particular product or service is placed:

- Boxes 1, 2, and 4 denote a favorable, advantageous, or "go" situation. This situation occurs when at least one factor—market potential or competitive position or both—is strong and the other is moderate.
- Boxes 3, 5, and 7 denote a less favorable, less advantageous, or "caution" situation. A "caution" situation occurs when one factor is weak and one is strong, or both factors are moderate.
- Boxes 6, 8, and 9 denote an unfavorable, disadvantageous, or "no-go" situation. This situation occurs when at least one factor is weak and the other is moderate.

Given these definitions, the optimum position on the grid is the upper-left corner (Box 1), where a strong market potential combines with a strong competitive position within the market. The worst position on the grid is the bottom-right corner (Box 9), where a weak market potential combines with a weak competitive position within the market.

Since both factors being evaluated (market potential and competitive position) are dynamic, movement can take place within the grid framework—that is, the position of a particular product or service can vary over time. Horizontal movement involves changes in the potential of the market. Such changes are due to pressures in either the overall or local external economic or social forces. Vertical upward movement on the grid is possible from the lower six positions. These positions can be considered "action squares," because anyone with a product or service in these squares would want to take action to move up. Such vertical movement denotes changes in the product/service's competitive position within the market and can be accomplished through strategies, product development, technological improvements, and so on.

The use of the grid concept is based on two key assumptions:

1. In order to best meet the needs of each market segment as well as maintain a strong image and market share, we can assume that businesses and products/services will always seek the 1, 2, and 4 positions (favorable positions) on the grid.

2. The position on the grid in which you place your product/service assumes that no major improvement programs or other strategy changes will be undertaken soon, and few, if any, major changes will be made in marketing. As previously stated, you may wish to use two grids—one for the present and one for the future (usually within the next 5 years).

POSITIONING STRATEGIES

Overall positioning strategy takes into account the consumers' perspective. This should include the data collected with respect to the brand's attributes, relationship to competition with respect to value (quality, price, and convenience to and speed of purchase). The above information is derived from the positioning maps produced based on quality, price, and attributes. Combining these findings using an attributes and competitive rating scale (see Figure 7-9) provides a guide and parameters for positioning choices/options. Using this

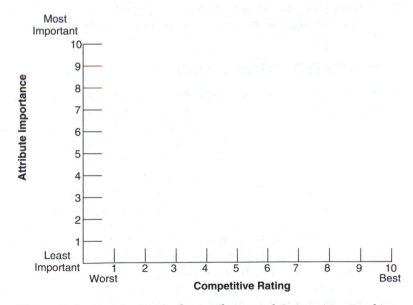

Figure 7–9 Positioning Scale: Attributes and Competitive Ranking

• Best Quality	• Fastest
• Best Performance	• Best Value for the Money
• Most Reliable	• Least Expensive
• Most Durable	• Most Prestigious
• Safest	• Best Designed or Styled
• Easiest to Use	• Most Convenient

Figure 7–10   Positioning Options
Source: Adapted from P. Kotler, *Marketing Management,* 11th ed. (Upper Saddle River, NJ: Prentice Hall, 1999): 5. Used with permission of Pearson Education, Inc.

graphic tool should help to delineate the overall positioning strategy noting qualifiers and rationale.

As discussed in Chapter 3, there are many different positioning options. Figure 7-10 delineates these options.

There are other positioning tactics that have been successfully deployed for hospitality brands, products, and services. For example, "more for less" has been used by foodservice establishments and lodging facilities (such as all-suites). Other positioning tactics include more for more, more for the same, the same for less, and less for much less. Positioning techniques may be based on an attribute (e.g., largest) or multiple attributes (e.g., largest and easiest to work with). Further, hospitality firms have been known to utilize competitive positioning (e.g., we versus they)—witness Ramada and Holiday Inn; "our" first-class seating versus all the other airlines; and so on. The key to positioning strategy is to develop one that gives you the competitive advantage and translates into powerful marketing strategies. Some words of caution: "Over-positioning" is akin to over-promising. Focus, clarity, simplicity, and truth make positioning statements and strategy powerful and easily understood.

MARKETING STRATEGY FOCAL POINTS

Marketing strategy in the hospitality industry has many focal points. Obviously, the number one focus is on the target market. How your marketing message is presented with respect to the core market, price, positioning, and total value perception is what marketing strategy is all about. Further, in the hospitality industry we have a more complex distribution channel upon which to focus. We have end-users and various intermediaries in most sectors of the industry. An end-user is the actual consumer of the product or service such as a business traveler, leisure vacationer, and such, whereas an intermediary can be a wholesaler, retail travel agency, corporate travel manager, and so on. This aspect of the hospitality industry creates the need for multiple communications strategies. These different marketing messages are often required since the motivations and needs of the end-user and the intermediary are not always the same. A business executive as an end-user is looking for quality, crisp, on-time service and reliability. An intermediary is looking for prompt and full

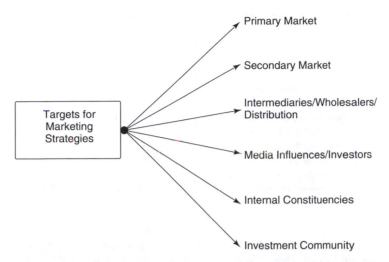

Figure 7–11 Targets for Marketing Strategies

payment of commissions. Figure 7-11 provides some of the targets for marketing strategies.

The perceptions your marketing strategies convey while directed at one focal point can very well influence multiple constituencies. Likewise, if a consumer marketing strategy is found to be distasteful or controversial, there could be major ramifications from shareholders, franchisees, and so on.

ETHICS

In executing marketing strategies, one must stay within the confines of federal, state, and local law. Doing so does not only ensure ethical marketing practices. Consumers will not become customers nor will customers remain buyers if marketing messages and offers violate ethical practices.

Marketing strategy involves not only identifying the targets, but also identifying marketing opportunities. Opportunities are often discovered during the research phase. A marketing opportunity can be identifying an area of buyers' needs and interests and effectively communicating how your brand can fulfill that need. There are many potential sources of opportunity. For example, one might identify a marketplace in short supply and fulfill that need, for instance, an airline serving a new route. Another example could be supplying an existing product or service in a new or superior way, such as supplying rental cars in local communities by delivery like Enterprise, or simply supplying a new product or service such as Krispy Kreme or Starbucks to a market. In some cases, breakthrough marketing strategies result in large

```
Win Through:
  • Ego Appeal
  • Discounting
  • Couponing
  • Value-Added Offers
  • Speed of Delivery
  • Abundance of Availability
  • Convenience of Purchase
  • Targeted Awareness
  • "Points of Encounter"
  • Doing More for Your Customer
```

Figure 7–12 Winning Marketing Tactics

market share gains or creating new market niches. Examples include finding new customers by a new strategy such as a fast-food franchise locating within a super retail store (e.g., a McDonald's within a Wal-Mart). Other break-through strategies might be related to new sales approaches, such as selling through intermediaries for the first time or finding new pricing or financial solutions (e.g., the timeshare concept). Finally, a breakthrough might involve something as simple as adding new product/service features (e.g., check-in on the airport bus or in-room checkout).

Marketing strategy also has a very tactical side, especially within the hospitality industry. As the industry and virtually all sectors within the industry fight for market share, winning marketing tactics are in demand. Figure 7-12 shows some winning marketing tactics; not all will work with every segment, but all have proven to be winners when applied properly.

There are many different perspectives on marketing and marketing strategy, especially in our ever-changing environment. For nearly thirty years (from the 1950s to the 1980s), and still today, marketers have focused on the Four Ps identified by McCarthy and Kotler, as shown below:[2]

- Product
- Price
- Place
- Promotion

In the 1990s, as we transitioned to a predominantly service-oriented economy and marketing environment, marketing strategies shifted to focus on the Four Cs, as delineated by Lauterborn:[3]

- Consumer wants and needs
- Cost to satisfy (wants and needs)
- Convenience to buy
- Communication (creating a dialogue)

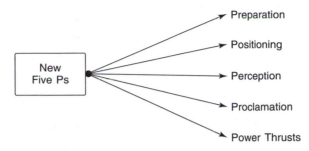

Figure 7–13 The New Five Ps

THE NEW FIVE Ps

In the current decade, while marketing must still focus on the Four Ps and Four Cs, marketing strategies appear to have shifted and are now more and more based on the new Five Ps (see Figure 7-13):

- Preparation
- Positioning
- Perception
- Proclamation
- Power thrusts

Preparation and Positioning

Preparation translates to "assessing your focal points" or "looking within, looking around, and looking ahead." It involves all the research steps and analysis described in the previous section, including deployment of the five essential marketing intelligence tools discussed earlier in the chapter (refer to Figure 7-3). Given the above process output (intelligence), a clear, concise, and most likely advantageous positioning strategy emerges (refer to Figure 7-10).

Perception

The next three Ps of the new Five Ps, *perception, proclamation,* and *power thrusts,* are what marketing strategy is all about today. Successful businesses and brands today are those that succeed in creating "winning" perceptions for their products/services. We are living in a marketing environment that is perception driven. Consumers want to "ride the wave," "have the latest," "go counter to the masses," "want it all now," "seek the newest," and so on. These are perceptions your marketing strategy must convey from a message creation perspective. Creating a perception in tune with your target market is essential for successful marketing strategy in today's world. Perception can be directly

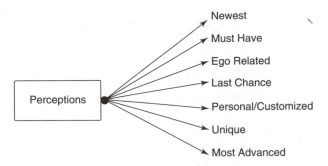

Figure 7–14 Perception Options

linked to positioning; however must be as a "driver" or creator of a compelling call to purchase. In other words, the positioning strategy is the base and the perception message the call to action. Perception options are dynamic—they move with the pulse and mindset of consumers. For some the message is "new," and for others it is "retro." Figure 7-14 delineates some perception options; remember, these are always changing with today's consumers.

Proclamation

Linking your positioning and your perception message requires reading the current and near-term-future pulse of the market. Assuming your reading of the pulse of the market is correct and you have formulated your perceptions strategy, you now need to deploy the fourth P—proclamation. Proclamation is a declaration that your product/service or brand is worth looking at, trying, buying, or repurchasing. Proclamation may take on a different meaning depending upon where your product/service or brand is in its life cycle. For example, if your brand is new or unique, you can immediately proclaim "We are the newest" or "We have the only. . . ." This is a great position to be in, but most brands are not so fortunate. In some instances you will only be able to declare "Look—we are changing/improving," or perhaps you're at the stage of telling the market "We have changed/improved," or "We are like new." And hopefully, you are or will be at the point where momentum is demonstrating itself in sales and revenue gains and you're ready to declare "We are new/the leader/the best" or whatever your positioning and brand strategy support as a proclamation or declaration to the marketplace. Figure 7-15 delineates the phases and thrust (expenditure) levels usually associated with proclamation.

Power Thrusts

Now your marketing strategy has moved to the active or launched phase. This is the time to deploy the fifth P—power thrusts. Remember, just because you have proclaimed you're on the move doesn't mean the consumer world will automatically listen. You will need to focus on a "breakthrough" or unique

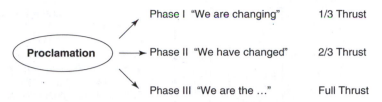

Figure 7–15 Proclamation Phases

message and delivery thereof to be successful. Let's assume you have a very creative, unique, and on-target proclamation/message. This is still no guarantee you will be successful, as the marketing channels are very crowded with other messages. To be heard or seen you will need to have a multipronged approach which should involve as many of the marketing weapons as possible (advertising, promotions, public relations, etc.). These weapons will require synchronization to work most efficiently and effectively. This is the fifth P, power thrusts. Power thrusts are created from a variety of techniques such as "heavy up-front" and "waves" of advertising, overlapping direct mail and direct sales efforts, carrying promotional offers in your advertising, and hyping the offers with public relations. In essence, you are synergistically and methodically using your expenditures and marketing weaponry to create "waves" or "power thrusts" for your product/service or brand offering (see Figure 7-16).

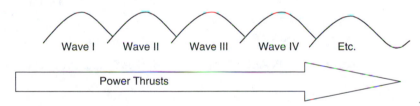

Figure 7–16 Power Thrusts

Not every situation calls for deployment of all of your weaponry in concentrated periods of time or up front. If you have strong brand awareness or are in a market leadership position (Box 1 on the Marketing Strategy Grid, Figure 7-8) you may be better off selecting maintenance-level advertising or reminder messages or utilizing public relations to consistently trumpet your position. Selecting strategies often depends on your market's relative strength (overall consumer demand) and your competitive position. Let's now return to the Marketing Strategy Grid. In Figures 7-17 through 7-25, we depict your product/service or brand in a different position on the grid (Boxes 1 through 9) and provide some potential accompanying marketing strategies that could be appropriate.

The marketing strategies accompanying these nine grid positions are only suggestions. There are many variables to consider, and each product or service may have a uniqueness unto itself that needs to be taken into

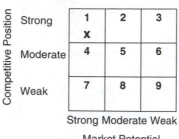

Strategies
1. Maintain position.
2. Cultivate core customers.
3. Maximize profits through pricing.
4. Keep competitively ahead by adding services or upgrading product.
5. Expand your product/service offerings or extend your brand.

Figure 7–17   Position 1: Strong Market/Strong/Best Product or Service

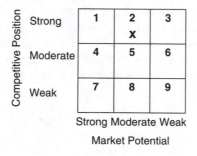

Strategies
1. Go for market share via competitive pricing.
2. If the market movement tends toward strengthening, improve to a #1 position.
3. If the market movement tends toward weakening, go after traditional marketing segments (build core market, consider alternate pricing strategy, etc.)
4. Create and capitalize on perceptions ("the only," ego related, etc.).

Figure 7–18   Position 2: Moderate Market/Strong Product or Service

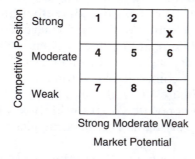

Strategies
1. If the market movement tends toward strengthening, build market core now and retain loyalty of consumers.
2. Go after all market segments with multiple pricing strategies and/or product and service offerings.
3. Strongly emphasize cost control and targeted promotions.
4. Develop new "trial" business with promotional offers to build the customer base.

Figure 7–19   Position 3: Weak Market/Strong Product

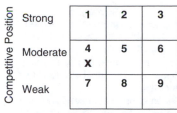

Strategies

1. Maximize profits by pricing slightly below the #1 competitor.

2. If the market movement tends toward strengthening, consider strengthening or upgrading your product/service to move closer to or into the #1 position.

3. Go after the "value-oriented" market segments.

4. Distinguish your product/service as an acceptable replacement for the #1 competitor.

Figure 7–20 Position 4: Strong Market/Moderate/Average Product or Service

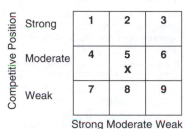

Strategies

1. If the market movement tends toward strengthening, put the product/service in a stronger position with enhancements.

2. Expand the number of market segments you are attracting with specialized promotions.

3. Go after market share through competitive pricing.

4. Distinguish yourself as the value leader.

Figure 7–21 Position 5: Moderate Market/Moderate/Average Product or Service

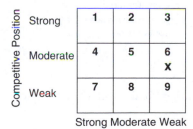

Strategies

1. If the market movement tends toward strengthening, maintain your core market through recognition programs and go after your weakest competitors with special pricing to gain share.

2. If the market is stagnant now and in the foreseeable future, gear your marketing programs to capture as many segments as possible.

3. Create your own markets via specialized promotions and co-op programs.

Figure 7–22 Position 6: Weak Market/Moderate/Average Product or Service

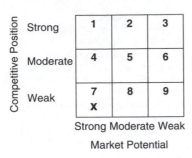

Strategies

1. Repackage, improve, or upgrade the most visible aspects of your product/service.

2. Once this is done, increase your prices to take advantage of strong demand periods.

3. Become the best at servicing the market segments your stronger competitors are not paying attention to.

4. Theme your promotions toward special or unique concepts and go for volume.

Figure 7–23 Position 7: Strong Market/Weak Product or Service

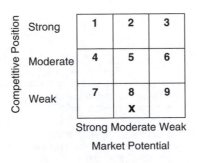

Strategies

1. If the market movement does not tend toward strengthening, look at special price schemes to build share.

2. If the market movement tends toward strengthening, make every effort to upgrade your product/service to move along with the market.

3. If the above is true, work promotions, sales, and advertising to convey your product's/service's availability and value orientation.

4. Consider marketing your product's/service around a theme.

Figure 7–24 Position 8: Moderate Market/Weak Product or Service

Strategies

1. It is time to dispose of your product/service.

2. Consider alternative uses for your product/service that make sense in this poor environment.

3. Look for new markets for your product/service.

Figure 7–25 Position 9: Weak Market/Weak Product or Service

consideration prior to selecting a strategy. The Marketing Strategy Grid is a tool designed to help you think about how to maximize your marketing strategies for the most productive results. In the final analysis, it is your judgment that will dictate the strategy selected; the Marketing Strategy Grid only helps sharpen that judgment.

Figure 7–26   The Marketing Arsenal Weaponry

SELECTING MARKETING WEAPONRY

As previously discussed, one of the new Five Ps, power thrusts, is the deployment of multiple marketing weapons in overlapping "waves." For any business, product/service, or brand, understanding what each weapon in your marketing arsenal is capable of doing and how and when to use it is yet another component of marketing strategy. We will now focus on the weapons and choices/options for development and deployment, as shown in Figure 7-26.

In general, application of the marketing weapons can be viewed within the context of the overall approach. In some cases the marketing strategy is to reach the masses—mass marketing. In other instances, it may be focused on target markets—target marketing. In the latter case, a segment, niche, or market cell may be the focal point. Not every weapon is appropriate for every strategy. In some strategy cases, there will be a need for rapid response, thus eliminating weapons that are time consuming in preparation. In other cases, the marketing strategy will be anticipative—thus requiring a quick but thorough and timely launch. And in still other situations, time will need to be taken to execute need-shaping responses to have a competitive edge. In essence, the strategic option or objective desired will shape or dictate the appropriate marketing discipline and weapons to be deployed. Figure 7-27 delineates strategy applications and appropriate marketing disciplines.

Most organizations in the hospitality industry utilize a mix of marketing disciplines to execute their overall marketing strategy. For example, a fast-food chain such as McDonald's uses network advertising to reach the mass-market target but also runs promotions at select market segments (kids, seniors, etc). Likewise, a hotel chain such as Hilton utilizes national

Strategy Application	Marketing Discipline
Stimulate trade participation	→ Trade promotion
Reward frequency and loyalty	→ Frequency program
Create a sense of involvement	→ Events
Reach a tightly targeted audience	→ Addressable media
Establish credibility and built trust	→ Public relations
Create lifestyle associations	→ Advertising, events
Establish awareness and create images	→ Advertising
Stimulate repeat purchases	→ Sales promotion
Leverage social responsibility	→ Mission marketing
Stimulate referrals	→ Club or affinity group
Stimulate trials	→ Sales promotion
Make a news announcement	→ Public relations

Figure 7–27   Strategy Application and Related Marketing Disciplines
Source: Adapted from R. Heibing, Jr., & S. Cooper, *The Successful Marketing Plan* (Lincolnwood, IL: NTC Business Books, 1996): 187–202. Adapted with permission of The McGraw-Hill Companies.

advertising in print media, broadcast media, along with promotion of its frequency rewards program through various forms of direct marketing and the electronic media. Utilization of multiple disciplines is referred to as the "marketing mix." Successful application of the marketing disciplines results in winning marketing strategy.

TECHNOLOGY

Technology through information systems, market segmentation, transaction analysis, revenue analysis, customer profiling, and many other quantitative methodologies allows today's marketing managers to base strategic decisions on a sound basis of data. Yield and revenue management programs, cost/benefit analysis, market share reports, and simultaneous inventory management systems of reservations centers and units in the field, all contribute to sound selection of marketing strategies.

MEASURING SUCCESS

The application of marketing strategy is measured in numerous ways within the hospitality industry. Financial performance is evaluated, as is marketing performance. Today, market share, customer counts, customer retention (brand loyalty), customer satisfaction (through the CSI), and the various forms of revenue measurements are most common. The latter include: REVPAR (revenue per available room) (lodging), revenue per available seat (airlines and select foodservice establishments), revenue per person (airlines and foodservice), revenue per ticket (attractions), revenue per rental (car rentals), and numerous other measurement techniques. Certainly for those building customer databases and viewing their potential total revenue generated per customer, the ultimate measurement of overall marketing strategy success is REVPAC or revenue per available customer. For a vertically or horizontally integrated company such as Carlson Companies, Cendant, and so on, REVPAC would take into account total revenue production from all sectors of the market by customer.

STRATEGIC ISSUES

Marketing strategy is constantly being challenged not only by competitive and environmental forces but by a number of overall industry issues. Availability of labor (which influences CSI and revenue), security, shrinking margins, and more competition impact virtually all sectors. Some sectors such as airlines, cruise lines, car rental, and the like, must also deal with regulatory changes, escalating fuel costs, and labor (strikes, availability, and competency). Rising sales and promotional costs, declining brand and customer loyalty, media fragmentation, and increased niche attacks present special challenges for marketing strategists. Also, the increasing use of technological applications is affecting almost all areas of marketing. We will discuss technology in Chapter 11.

CHAPTER REVIEW

Understanding the consumer's perspective creates a marketing strategy that sells products and services. The marketing process must be thorough in its research and analysis of the consumer. Product development or changes in services offered should be in line with what consumers express as their needs. Marketing cannot succeed if the product or service offering is not in line with its consumers' needs.

The consumer's perspective centers on the needs fulfilled by a product or service. The marketing challenge is that not all consumers have the same needs. In fact, the same consumer can at different times have a very different set of needs. Much depends on the consumer's purpose or reason for using the product or service.

One key point to remember is that a consumer's perspective of products and services can and does change based on the perception created by marketing.

The nurture, care, and conveying of what the brand stands for and how it meets the needs of the consumer is what marketing strategy is all about. The nurture and care of the brand creates a perception by the consumer. This perception translates into action and to purchases. The perception created by packaging the brand helps to dictate the price consumers are willing to pay. Conveying how the brand meets the specific needs of buyers is one role of marketing strategies and promotional techniques.

Figure 7–28   The Marketing Planning Process in Perspective

Strategy selection is dependent upon the overall strength of your market (demand) and your product/service competitive position. The premise of sound strategy responding appropriately based on your positioning, anticipating the movement of the market (demand), and shaping your message to capitalize on the needs of the market in relation to your attributes. Marketing strategies need to be constantly revisited in a dynamic or ever-changing market. Your most valuable customers will quickly lose their loyalty to your products/services if you do not keep up with meeting their evolving needs. Marketing strategies may also differ based upon the target market selected or the stage of customer development.

Figure 7-28 gives a recap of where we are in the strategic marketing planning process.

KEY CONCEPTS/TERMS

ADIs (areas of dominant influence/domain)	GAP Analysis
	Intermediaries
Benchmarking	Marketing mix
Brand strategies	Mission statement
Core competencies	Perception
CPA	Positioning
CSI	REVPAC
End-users	REVPAR
Four Cs	Value
Four Ps	

DISCUSSION QUESTIONS

1. Give three reasons why research is important to marketing strategy.

2. Why is understanding your positioning important to marketing strategy execution?

3. If your product or service were located in Box 4 of the Marketing Strategy Grid, what marketing tactics would you deploy?

4. Identify hospitality industry firms or brands that represent three different positioning strategy options.

5. Select two different hospitality industry firms or brands and discuss what you believe to be the marketing mix or marketing disciplines to best address their target markets.

6. What do you believe will be the most significant issue to impact hospitality industry marketing strategy in the next decade?

ENDNOTES

1. R. Nykiel, *Marketing in the Hospitality Industry,* 3rd ed. (East Lansing, MI: Educational Institute of the American Hotel and Motel Association, 1997): 59–60.
2. Philip Kotler, (Ed.), *Principles of Marketing.* (Upper Saddle River, NJ: Prentice Hall, 1986): 57.
3. D. E. Schultz, S. I. Tannebaum, & R. F. Lauterborne, *Integrated Marketing Communications.* (Lincolnwood, IL: NTC Business Books, 1993): 187–202.

CASE 1

Starbucks Coffee—The Rising Star*

In this chapter we discussed the concepts of assessing internal, external, and competitive focal points. In the Boston Consulting Group Portfolio Box, "Stars" were identified as companies and brands that demonstrate high market share and high product market growth. This case looks at one company/brand that has been the "star" of the past decade.

Starbucks Coffee Company represents an excellent example of a company that has successfully marketed an "experience."** Moreover, its marketing strategies provide examples of positioning, image development, merchandising, pricing, packaging, and market development. Starbucks' success has helped propel the entire industry segment.

The specialty/gourmet coffee segment has been rapidly growing since the early 1990s. According to the Specialty Coffee Association, specialty coffee beverage retail outlets (gourmet coffee shops) increased more than tenfold in the past decade. Their locations are expected to double by 2015. The growth of this segment was started and accelerated mainly by Starbucks Coffee. Starbucks is the leader in this segment and is becoming one of the most well-known international brands in the hospitality industry like Hilton and McDonald's. In this case study, we will briefly explain the current trends in the specialty coffee segment and then identify the business and marketing strategy of Starbucks.

The thriving specialty coffee segment today differs much from what it used to be. New, growing chain companies are now capturing the segment that used to be dominated by independent mom-and-pop-type shops. Several specialty coffee chains eagerly acquire other chains in order to be a player in the segment behind the market leader Starbucks. Specialty coffee shops frequently charge in excess of $3 for a cup of coffee or specialty coffee. The service style is limited service. The focus is on the quality and quick service of espresso, latte, and cappuccino. The serving of limited food items has given way to adding more items in an effort to be more competitive. It is common for chain companies to have their own roasting facility, where the quality of coffee is controlled and the profit margin is actually preplanned.

Starbucks opened its first shop in Seattle in 1971.* Howard Schultz, the chairman, joined Starbucks in 1982 and introduced the Italian espresso bar concept in 1984. Becoming a public company in 1992, Starbucks accelerated the expansion of business with new capital. Starbucks has over 3,000 outlets in the United States and internationally and is rapidly opening new stores via joint ventures with local companies.

*www.businessweek.com/managing/content/01.
**Information from www.starbucks.com.

The company's retail sales mix (2000) by product type was approximately 73 percent beverages, 14 percent food items, 8 percent whole bean coffees, and 5 percent coffee-making equipment and accessories. The main beverage items are dark-roasted coffee, espresso, latte, and cappuccino.

Interestingly, Starbucks, unlike other chain companies in the foodservice industry, operates 85 percent of Starbucks outlets itself. It does not franchise to individuals, and limits licensing its operations to companies. Starbucks retains total control over the growth and look for logical and appropriate partners.

The mission statement of Starbucks, introduced in 1990, is to "establish Starbucks as the premier purveyor of the finest coffee in the world while maintaining our uncompromising principles while we grow." The principles are as follows:

- Provide a great work environment and treat each other with respect and dignity.
- Embrace diversity as an essential component in the way we do business.
- Apply the highest standards of excellence to the purchasing, roasting, and fresh delivery of coffee.
- Develop enthusiastically satisfied customers all of the time.
- Contribute positively to the communities in which we are located and help preserve the environment.
- Recognize that profitability is essential to future success.

The three basic business strategies of Starbucks are as follows:

- Utilize the recognized and respected brand "Starbucks."
- Expand market shares and develop new markets while keeping the high quality of specialty coffee and service.
- Sell not only coffee but also "coffee experiences" in a place where people can relax and enjoy a conversation.

In order to support the business strategies, Starbucks develops new distribution channels and introduces new products. To extend distribution channels, Starbucks formed strategic alliances with Barnes & Noble Bookstores in 1993, United Airlines in 1995, Aramark in 1996, and Albertson's in 2000. In opening Starbucks coffee shops at Barnes & Noble bookstores, both companies improved their brand image and awareness and improved sales. Starbucks-brewed coffee is served on United and Canada Airlines. With these brand alliances, or cobranding, Starbucks improved brand recognition and sales. Starbucks also expanded its distribution through kiosks and carts in many types of locations. Now, kiosks and carts are at airports, universities, convention centers, and office buildings and are as important a distribution channel as freestanding coffee shops. Moreover, Starbucks has hundreds of kiosks in Albertson's grocery stores and has expanded with shops/stores within stores, such as at selected Targets.

Starbucks introduced cold and frozen specialty coffee drinks mainly for the younger generation, which is fast becoming an important market. Moreover, Starbucks started a lunch program—sandwiches and prepackaged salads priced between $3.75 and $5.95—at over 400 of its outlets to capture a new market.

Starbucks also has extended its products into retail shops, introducing Frappuccino with Pepsi in 1994 and Starbucks ice cream with Dreyer's in 1995. Starbucks coffee is sold in supermarkets as well as at retail shops.

In short, the initial success of Starbucks depended on establishing brand awareness and image. This brand recognition and perception was not established by a large traditional advertising campaign or low promotional prices, but by wide distribution and strategic brand alliances with larger partners. At present Starbucks utilizes the strong brand awareness and alliances to continue to expand.

The products of Starbucks are supported by three elements: quality, wide distribution through strategic alliances, and the well-recognized brand "Starbucks," as depicted in Figure 1.

Case Discussion Questions

1. Do you believe Starbucks is still positioned as a Star in the Boston Consulting Group Portfolio Box? What are your reasons to support this or another positioning?

2. As Starbucks continues both its global expansion and brand extension strategies, what pitfalls should it look out for?

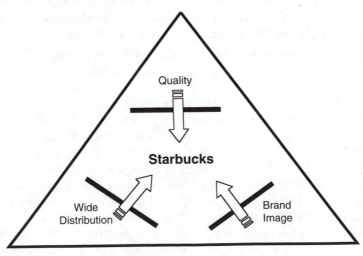

Figure 1   The Starbucks Product Triad

CASE 2

Frequency Programs—Rewarding Loyalty

It has been said that the second currency in the United States is frequency program points/miles. Frequency or loyalty reward programs permeate virtually every sector of the hospitality industry in some form or fashion. Rewards have expanded from airline miles and room nights to just about everything under the sun. Airlines, lodging chains, rental car companies, credit card companies, foodservice entities, themed attractions, and casinos all offer their frequent or loyal customers some type of award/reward program.

Frequency programs have grown to such an extent that their "point" liabilities now add up to hundreds of millions of dollars. Hospitality industry corporations keep the programs because they work to retain customers and in the end lower the expense of attracting new customers. (It costs five times as much on average to attract a new customer as to retain an existing one.)

For this case example, a comparison of Marriott Rewards, Hilton HHonors, and Starwood's Preferred Guest programs is presented.

Marriott Rewards*

The Marriott Corporation's frequent stay program, known as Marriott Rewards, is accepted at any of its participating brands.** Offering over 2,000 hotels worldwide, the program gives the guest the option of earning either points or miles for every dollar spent. Nine distinct hotel brands provide guests the opportunity for a free night or free flight. Marriott offers lodgers of all kinds the chance to earn points, whether at an extended-stay property, a moderately priced property, or a full-service luxury property. Points are awarded based on dollars spent on the full guest folio at full-service properties and on room rate only at all other participating locations. Guests staying at most of the brands earn 10 points for every qualifying dollar spent; however, 5 points per dollar is awarded at TownePlace Suites and Residence Inn locations. Travelers have a few options when enrolling to become a member; they may call the toll free number, sign up at any participating property, or enroll online at www.marriott.com.

Marriott has restructured its program to offer more options, greater flexibility, and better value. The new Stay Anytime Rewards program allows guests to override blackout dates during the most popular travel times—even if it's the last standard room in the hotel—for just 50 percent more points. It has also implemented a One-Call Redemption program that allows members one-to-one point-to-mile conversion rates. These benefits are available to all

---

*Information derived from www.marriott.com.
**Marriott Annual Report 1999, Marriott International Corp.

guests; however, an Elite membership has been set up for more frequent guests. This membership is divided into three levels, Silver, Gold, and Platinum, each offering a more prestigious set of benefits.

Silver-Level Membership   After 15 nights per year, members can become Silver-level members with an added array of benefits. The first is an automatic credit of a 20 percent bonus for those members who have chosen to earn points. Marriott will pay for the Silver-level members' accommodations for the night and will send a check to compensate for the inconvenience should the reservation not be honored. Marriott has set up a dedicated reservation line for Elite members. A priority for the requested room type will be acknowledged upon availability. Silver-level members are also offered a priority for late checkouts. A 10 percent discount on regular Friday and Saturday night rates is offered. Registered Silver-level members are also extended a check-cashing benefit, up to $200 a day. Members receive a 10 percent discount at Marriott-owned and -operated gift shops.

Gold-Level Membership   Once guests have stayed with Marriott for 50 nights throughout the year, they advance to Gold-level membership where they receive all the benefits Silver members receive and more. Guests who opt to earn points are automatically credited with a 25 percent bonus. Upon check-in, Gold-level members are offered an upgrade on their room, to include concierge floors should they be available with no superimposed charge. Select properties also offer Gold-level members access to the concierge lounge where complimentary light snacks, beverages, and continental breakfast are provided. Participating Courtyards, SpringHill Suites, and Fairfield Inn locations also entitle Gold-level members to complimentary, unlimited local phone calls and faxes. Checks of up to $500 a day may be cashed for registered Gold-level members.

Platinum-Level Membership   The 75th night stayed at Marriott properties in a year marks eligibility for the highest level of Elite membership, the Platinum level. This level offers members the same benefits as Gold members with even more. Guests who choose to earn points will be automatically credited with a 30 percent bonus. In addition, Platinum-level members are guaranteed a room when reservations are made 48 hours in advance at participating properties. A welcome package will also be awaiting a Gold-level member upon check-in.

As an added incentive to maintain guest preference, Marriott offers additional benefits in conjunction with Service and Hotel partners. A Marriott Rewards Visa card is available to all guests, with a 5,000-bonus-point incentive for the first purchase. Three points per dollar spent at Marriott locations are earned and one point per dollar spent elsewhere using the card. The Marriott Rewards Visa card also offers guests a complimentary Silver-level membership.

Guests can earn 10 points per dollar spent when shopping at SkyMall online. A total of 500 points can be earned each time a car is rented from Hertz, Marriott's car rental partner. Other Service partners Marriott works in conjunction with include American Express Membership Rewards, ClickRewards, E*Trade, My Points, Diners Club, and AT&T Long Distance. Marriott also offers Travel Rewards with over 20 airline partners, rail travel partners, theme park partners, and cruise line partners. Up to 50,000 points can be earned when meetings or events are hosted at participating properties. Members have the opportunity to combine points with a spouse to qualify for a specific reward under the Joint Ventures program. Up to 10 percent of the required points for a reward may be purchased when sufficient points are not available.

Hilton HHonors*

The Hilton HHonors frequent stay program offers members a variety of services and amenities. These exclusive privileges and benefits strive to set the guest apart from check-in to check-out. Offering over 2,000 hotels worldwide, the program gives guests the opportunity to Double Dip, or earn both points and miles for the same stay. Eight distinct hotel brands provide guests the opportunity to earn points, whether at an extended-stay property, a moderately priced property, or a full-service luxury property. Guests earn 10 points per dollar spent on room rate and incidentals at all participating properties. Travelers have a few options to enroll to become a member; they may call the tollfree number, sign up at any participating property, or enroll online at www.hilton.com.

Members are assured that reservation requests receive special attention, especially during peak periods. In order to achieve this, Hilton offers a dedicated HHonors reservation service. Hilton also offers an expedited check-in once a guest profile is established. A room will be reserved for the guest based on the preferences and credit card information provided on the account. Members are given a complimentary copy of USA Today or the local paper each weekday morning. At participating properties HHonors members are privileged to have their spouses stay free. Late check-out is also accommodated when possible to all members should extra time be needed along with express check-out services. Membership level is determined by stay activity—the more frequent the stays the more generous the benefits become. Some of these benefits include bonus points, complimentary room upgrades, and health club privileges. There are four levels of membership: Blue membership, Silver VIP membership, Gold VIP membership, and Diamond VIP membership, each offering a more prestigious set of benefits.

Blue Membership   Guests can become Blue members simply by enrolling. Blue members receive 2,000 bonus points after four paid stays in a calendar quarter.

*Information derived from www.hilton.com.

Silver VIP Membership After a fourth qualifying stay or tenth qualifying night per year, guests attain Silver VIP membership status. Silver VIP members earn a 15 percent bonus on all points. Members of this group also receive 2,000 bonus points after four paid stays as a Silver VIP in a calendar quarter. Complimentary health club privileges are gained as members earn their Silver VIP status. Silver VIPs can take advantage of check-cashing privileges for up to $200 when staying at participating Hilton hotels. Silver VIPs may also choose from an exclusive selection of rewards at special VIP-only point levels.

Gold VIP Membership After 16 qualifying stays or 36 qualifying nights in a calendar year, guests attain Gold VIP membership status. In addition to the benefits earned as a Silver VIP, Gold VIP members earn a 25 percent bonus on all points. A 4,000-point bonus is earned after four paid stays as a Gold VIP in a calendar quarter. Gold VIP members are offered upgraded accommodations to Towers or Executive levels including complimentary continental breakfast and amenities at participating properties. Gold VIP members also receive a welcome gift upon arrival, which includes a light snack.

Diamond VIP Membership A 28th qualifying stay or 60th qualifying night in a calendar year at HHonors hotels earns a guest Diamond VIP membership. In addition to the benefits earned as a Gold VIP, Diamond VIPs earn a 50 percent bonus on all points. Diamond VIP members enjoy a 4,000-point bonus after four paid stays as a Diamond VIP in a calendar quarter. Reservations availability is guaranteed to Diamond VIPs when reservations are made at least 48 hours prior to check in, although a charge will be billed for not showing up. In addition, Diamond VIP members may redeem points nearly any time. A RewardPlanner Service is also available to members, whether traveling for business or pleasure, that will take care of all the details according to profiles provided with membership; the charge for this service is 20,000 HHonors points.

As an added incentive to maintain guest preference, Hilton offers additional benefits in conjunction with Service and Hotel partners. One of these benefits is the Travel Partner bonus points program, whereby guests traveling with one of over 55 airline or rail partners in conjunction with HHonors stays earn points. Hilton also cooperates with Thrifty, Avis, and National car rental partners and Norwegian and Orient cruise lines which offer bonus points with qualifying stays. Event and Meeting Planner programs also offer bonus points for qualifying events. A 15 percent discount is offered for dinner dining experiences at participating HHonors hotel restaurants. Married members have the opportunity to combine points and stay credits to earn rewards and higher HHonors membership levels under the HHonors Mutual Fund program. The HHonors Reward Exchange program allows guests to turn HHonors points into airline miles and miles into points. Up to 20 percent of the required points for a reward may be purchased when sufficient points are not available, at $10 per 1,000 points.

Starwood Preferred Guest*

Starwood's frequent guest program, Starwood Preferred Guest, is the newest of the three. It serves more than 700 hotels and resorts worldwide, offering guests the option of earning points or miles. Six distinct hotel brands provide guests the opportunity for a free night or free flight. Guests earn two Starpoints for every eligible dollar spent, including dining in the hotels when not a registered guest. Starpoints do not expire so long as the guest stays just once a year. Starwood offers an exchange rate of one Starpoint to one airline mile/point on most major airlines. To enroll, guests may call the tollfree number, sign up at any participating property, or enroll online at www.starwood.com.

Since Starwood's beginning, it has offered a premier policy of no blackout dates and no capacity controls, meaning members can redeem stays anytime, anywhere. As Starwood Preferred Guest members, guests are entitled to a vast amount of benefits. Instant Awards, a spontaneous redemption program, allows immediate use of hotel services during a stay. Numerous award options allow guests the opportunity to enjoy several different vacations and accommodations. These benefits are available to all guests; however, a more exclusive membership has been set up for the more frequently visiting guests. This membership is divided into two levels, Gold Preferred Guest and Platinum Preferred Guest, each offering a more prestigious set of benefits.

Gold Preferred Guests   After 10 stays in a calendar year, members are upgraded to Gold Preferred Guest. A more personalized service is offered in addition to the standard Preferred Guest benefits. As a Gold Preferred Guest, members receive a 50 percent earning bonus (a total of three points) for every eligible dollar spent. Gold Preferred Guests are offered a complimentary upgrade to a Preferred room at check-in upon availability and can choose from leading financial and national newspapers during the week. Gold Preferred Guests are offered a 4:00 p.m. late check-out upon availability. Members are extended a check-cashing benefit of up to $300 a day. Starwood also offers special member events exclusively for Gold Preferred Guests and Platinum Preferred Guests.

Platinum Preferred Guests   After 20 stays in a calendar year, guests are upgraded to Platinum Preferred Guest status. Platinum Preferred Guests enjoy the benefits of Gold Preferred Guest status as well as other added benefits. Platinum Preferred Guests are offered a complimentary upgrade to the best available room, including selected suites, upon availability. A 72-hour room guarantee is extended to Platinum Preferred Guests to ensure that a room is available upon arrival. Platinum Preferred Guests also receive a welcome amenity upon arrival. Should Platinum Preferred Guests choose to fill

*Information derived from www.starwood.com.

out an online profile, they will be given the benefit of having personal preferences met with every stay.

As an added incentive to maintain guest preference, Starwood offers additional benefits in conjunction with Service and Hotel partners. A Preferred Plus credit card from American Express is available to Starwood Preferred Guests along with 1,000 bonus Starpoints on the first paid stay at a participating hotel or resort. Preferred Plus holders earn two Starpoints for every dollar spent at participating properties. One Starpoint is earned for every dollar charged to the card. Starpoints may be redeemed in small quantities or in thousands. Starpoints may be redeemed for gift certificates at retail stores, including Gap and Saks Fifth Avenue. Vouchers are also available for Avis car rentals and AT&T prepaid phone cards.

The wide array of services and benefits offer loyal guests the opportunity to take advantage of several options during travel. See Table 1 for a comparison of the benefits of the three programs. Each program desires to be the best, which creates a highly competitive environment. The programs all target brand buyers, brand switchers, and especially brand loyalists. The ability to market each segment gives companies an opportunity to retain and establish frequent guests. By cooperating with Service partners the potential market is increased and each individual program becomes better known, and this potentially results in increased membership.

Case Discussion Questions

1. From a marketing strategy application perspective, frequency programs reward loyalty. What other marketing strategies help build repeat business?
2. Do you believe promotional concepts such as frequency programs enhance or detract from a brand's image? State your reasons for your position.

Table 1 Comparison of Frequency Programs

	Marriott Rewards			Hilton HHonors			Starwood Preferred Guest	
	Silver Level	Gold Level	Platinum Level	Silver VIP	Gold VIP	Diamond VIP	Gold Preferred	Platinum Preferred
Number of hotels		2,000+			2,000+		700+	
Number of brands		9			8		6	
Redemption Options:								
Ability to earn points		X			X		X	
Ability to earn miles		X			X		X	
Ability to earn both					X			
Points awarded		10 per $1			10 per $1		2 per $1	
Points earned at dining outlets when not registered								
Combine points with spouse		X			X		X	
Point conversion		X			X		X	
Ease of Membership:								
Online enrollment		X			X		X	
Tollfree phone enrollment		X			X		X	
On-property enrollment		X			X		X	
Required nights to become advanced member (per calendar year)	15	50	75	10	36	60	10	20
Service Partners:								
Airlines		20+			50+			
Cruise lines		2			2			
Rail lines		3			1			
Car rentals		1			3			

(continued)

Table 1 *(Continued)*

Other Benefits:	Marriott Rewards			Hilton HHonors			Starwood Preferred Guest	
	Silver Level	Gold Level	Platinum Level	Silver VIP	Gold VIP	Diamond VIP	Gold Preferred	Platinum Preferred
Gift shop discount		X						
Accommodations paid if no room		X						
Room upgrade		•				•	X	
Room guarantee			48 hr. adv.			48 hr. adv.		72 hr. adv.
Welcome package			•		•	•		
Late check-out		X			X		X	
Bonus points offered		X			X		X	
Immediate use of points						•	X	
Guest profile maintained	X				X			
Points for meetings/events		up to 50,000			X			
Ability to purchase points	10% of required points			20% of required points				
No blackout policy		X					X	
Checks cashed		X			X		X	

Note: X indicates applicability to every level of the company; • indicates applicability to the level indicated only.

CASE 3

Gaylord Opryland Resort & Convention Center— The Size Advantage*

In this chapter we have focused on a number of key marketing strategies such as positioning options (see Figure 7-11) and perceptions (see Figure 7-15). In the case study that follows, we will look at one of the world's most successful meeting and convention destinations. We will see how this facility/destination capitalized on being both the "biggest" in its positioning strategy and the "most unique" in its perceptions strategy.

Gaylord Opryland Resort & Convention Center in Nashville is the world's largest combined hotel and convention center under one roof. It has three major indoor gardens that cover more than 9 acres. Opened in 1977 with 600 rooms, it has grown to 2,884 rooms and 600,000 square feet of meeting and exhibit space and boasts a variety of restaurants and lounges and 30 unique shops.

Gaylord Opryland has consistently refurbished and expends millions of dollars to maintain its number one position in the marketplace. Gaylord Opryland has a proud history of being a leader and innovator in the meeting and convention industry. And now it is elevating its performance to new levels so that attendees will experience a complete renewal of the Cascades Lobby, guest rooms and corridors, and many of the fine restaurants and dining venues. An $80 million transformation is in progress to reinforce Gaylord Opryland's premier position for major meetings and conventions. Upon completion, there will be over 4,000 rooms and 1 million square feet of conference and exhibit space. As part of the expansion, a computer-based audio processing and control system with state-of-the-art design has been installed. This entire system can be monitored and controlled, including local control of certain specialized sound systems via wall-mounted, custom designed interface panels located throughout the facility. Each panel is application-specific and simple for nontechnical operation.

As stated, Gaylord Opryland currently features over 600,000 square feet of meeting and exhibit space. Included in this vast expanse are five grand ballrooms and 85 breakout rooms for smaller gatherings. In fact, it's the largest convention center within a hotel in the world. Special services include a fully staffed business center with everything from fax machines and computers to color copiers. Rental car facilities and Opryland International Travel are all located within the complex.

Gaylord Opryland also has 30 specialty shops, a variety of restaurants and lounges, three swimming pools, and a fitness center. Opryland Hotel is

*Information derived from www.gaylord.com.

located in the heart of the Opryland entertainment complex, with attractions like the Grand Ole Opry, the General Jackson Showboat, and Springhouse Golf Club, home of the BellSouth Senior Classic. Other area attractions can be accessed by Opryland USA River Taxi. These include the historic Ryman Auditorium and the Wildhorse Saloon in downtown Nashville and other Nashville riverfront attractions.

There are a variety of rooms to choose from at Opryland Hotel, including traditional rooms with lovely outdoor views, garden terrace rooms with private balconies that overlook acres of indoor gardens, and over 220 magnificent suites. In keeping with its tradition of hospitality, it offers 24-hour room service.

There are a total of three indoor gardens that cover 9 acres. Each of the gardens carries a theme. The Conservatory, which places an emphasis on plants, was completed in 1983. The Cascades is a water-oriented space that was completed in 1988. The most recent addition is the Delta, which opened in 1996. It's a massive subtropical garden complete with fountains, shops, restaurants, and even a river with passenger-carrying flatboats. The combination of these three indoor gardens creates an exceptional destination for convention-goers and pleasure travelers alike.

Located 10 minutes or just 7 miles from Nashville International Airport, Gaylord Opryland provides coach service every 20 minutes. This central U.S. location and proximity to the airport add to its attraction as a meetings destination. Meeting planners and attendees will find not only state-of-the-art group facilities capable of handling up to 6,400 people theater-style or 4,560 people banquet-style, but also state-of-the-art, full-service audiovisual support and an amphitheater. Guestrooms are up-to-date from a technology perspective, with voice mail, fax/modem hookups, and additional telephone lines. Meeting planners will find the fitness center, 18-hole championship golf course, three swimming pools, General Jackson Showboat, and Grand Ole Opry great additional amenities to please their attendees.

In addition to banquet capabilities to serve nearly 5,000 guests, Gaylord Opryland also offers 15 food and beverage outlets, a multiple food facility court, contemporary and regional cuisine, steakhouse, fine dining Italian restaurant, many lounges, and a great sports bar. Consider that all of this is under glass, including more than 9 acres of tropical gardens.

Other aspects of Gaylord Opryland that help put this extraordinarily large facility into perspective include its own powerplant capable of providing enough power for a small town. There is a substantial commissary capable of providing all the supplies for more than 10,000 meals per day plus servicing 15 outlets and multiple banquets and group meal functions simultaneously. There is also a laundry building (not room) to handle the complex's needs. Finally, extensive state-of-the-art computer systems and programs manage everything from inventories to uniform distribution.

Technology and communications provide effective and efficient communications for successful meetings. Gaylord Opryland personnel provide extensive assistance in the areas of internet connectivity and communications services.

Gaylord Opryland is unique in its positioning as the world's largest meeting and convention facility under one roof. It has successfully maintained this number one positioning by consistently upgrading its facilities and technology. Further, its very well-trained staff goes the extra mile to assist meeting planners and attendees with all of their technical and nontechnical needs. There is no other single meeting and convention facility like Gaylord Opryland Resort & Convention Center. It is a great example of the concept of "unique" positioning delineated in this chapter.

ENDNOTES

1. R. Nykiel, *Marketing in the Hospitality Industry*, 3rd ed. (East Lansing, MI: Educational Institute of the American Hotel and Motel Association, 1997): 59–60.
2. Philip Kotler, (Ed.), *Principles of Marketing*. (Upper Saddle River, NJ: Prentice Hall, 1986): 57.
3. D. E. Schultz, S. I. Tannebaum, & R. F. Lauterborne, *Integrated Marketing Communications*. (Lincolnwood, IL: NTC Business Books, 1993): 187–202.

Chapter 8

Sales Strategies

CHAPTER OBJECTIVES

- To provide a review of where and how sales management plays a role in the various sectors of the hospitality industry
- To delineate the overall changing approaches to sales strategy between the industry entity and the customer
- To discuss the importance of knowledge acquisition in support of successful sales strategy
- To describe the different sales strategies and their applications, execution, and measurement
- To provide a perspective on how and where the hospitality industry is changing its approach to sales and sales management

While the hospitality industry and many sectors within the industry provide an ideal product/service to mass market through advertising, sales still plays a significant role in many sectors. For example, selling groups on using a hotel or resort, on an airplane charter, on meeting on a cruise ship, on having an event at a local attraction or foodservice facility are areas where the sales discipline has application in the hospitality industry. In viewing the business or corporate market, sales plays a significant role as well. For example, a travel management company must make a thorough sales presentation in order to obtain the contract to manage a large corporation's travel. Sales presentations are used to help companies (airlines, car rentals, hotels, etc.) achieve selection as preferred suppliers. Sales calls are made to travel intermediaries, associations, and government agencies as well as to almost all sectors of the industry. For some companies such as Marriott, Hilton, and other lodging chains, revenue produced by sales to groups, intermediaries, and so on, can account for 40 percent to 60 percent of total revenue. The sales discipline is the most human resource–intensive marketing weapon and one of the more expensive in the mix. Sales personnel usually require travel and related expenses, office space and related support, and collateral materials. Over the years and dependent upon the sector, there have been various rules of thumb as to how many times the annual average expense of the salesperson should be generated in revenue to validate the function. Some sectors look at 10 to 15 to 1 as a ratio for revenue generation to the salesperson's expense. Much depends on the type of hospitality product or service being sold. For example, a salesperson selling incentive programs (e.g., Maritz Incentive Travel) might sell a very large corporation a total and very expensive incentive sales program. In this case, the single sale could be worth multiples far in excess of 5, 10, or 15 times the salesperson's expense.

The management strategy related to sales will also vary based on many different factors. It may be influenced by the nature of the hospitality product or service, the actual "ticket" or price charge (revenue generated) of a sale, or budgetary or organizational concerns. There are also external influences that have an impact on overall sales strategy today.

TECHNOLOGY

Technology continues to have a dramatic impact on the sales function and related managerial strategies. The use of the internet and extensive software capabilities have allowed sales in many organizations to achieve cost savings through labor reductions and better inventory control. In addition, improved consumer conveniences, streamlined ordering systems, and point-of-sale reporting have all helped to reshape the sales function.

Sales, like a number of other marketing weapons, has undergone many changes as a result of technology, competition, and customer/consumer demands. These changes have resulted in more strategy options, be it for direct sales to the end-user of the product/service or intermediary sales. Technology and consumer trends have had an impact on personal selling in the retail and service sectors, on distribution systems, and on business-to-business sales. While some key principles remain intact, strategies are in general more customized and the sales environment more competitive than ever. In this chapter our focus is on sales strategy, understanding these changes, and management strategy related to the sales function.

CHANGING STRATEGY

Overall sales strategy or philosophy continues to evolve (see Figure 8-1). In the 1950s, sales strategy first began to focus on customer needs and wants and on reflecting these in new products/services. Prior to the 1950s, a "manufacture it and push it on the consumer" mentality prevailed. Consultative-style selling emerged in the late 1960s and early 1970s as an approach that emphasized identification of customer needs through effective communication between the salesperson and the customer. Strategic selling evolved in the 1980s and involved the preparation of a carefully conceived plan to accomplish sales objectives. In the 1990s, partnership selling (providing customers with a quality product *and* a quality, long-term relationship) emerged. In the new millen-

• 1950s	→	Customer-focused selling
• 1960s – 70s	→	Consultative-style selling
• 1980s	→	Strategic selling
• 1990s	→	Partnership selling
• 2000s	→	Customization selling

Figure 8–1 Evolution of Sales Strategy
Source: G. Manning & B. Reece, *Selling Today* (Upper Saddle River, NJ: Pearson Education, Inc., 1997). Reprinted by permission.

nium we have entered yet another era, customization selling.[1] Today, products and services are tailored or customized to meet the buyers' needs. Moreover, selling is customized in the fullest meaning of the word. Buyers expect sellers to provide them products and services designed to their exact needs and wants. Buyers expect to be able to purchase with speed, convenience, and at the best price in any number of ways from sellers. More and more buyers are turning to "self-service," in essence "selling themselves" based on the options offered on the internet. More and more, sellers are going to great lengths to facilitate customized purchasing.

The role of the traditional salesperson has now evolved to what could be termed a "techno-customer" service representative. Sales calls are customer service calls and customer service is a very important marketing weapon (more on this subject in the next chapter). Sales are the direct face-to-face or "screen-to-screen" contact marketing weapon. When human and/or electronic interaction takes place, the interaction has an impact on sales strategies and tactics. Interestingly enough, while the change is dramatic (with respect to the process), some of the basic keys to successful selling are still applicable in the new era of customization. As we look at the sales process and the keys to success, remember most of these, if not all, have direct application in both face-to-face and screen-to-screen sales strategies. Let's begin by looking at personal sales and the sales success triad (see Figure 8-2).

PERSONAL SALES

The basic requirements of successful personal selling are a thorough knowledge of your product or service, thorough knowledge of your client's needs, and thorough knowledge of your sales image—that is, how you come across to clients. If you know your product or service and know how to identify your

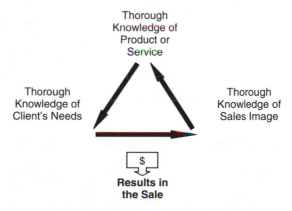

Figure 8–2   Sales Success Triad
Source: R. Nykiel, *Hotel Sales* (Washington, DC: HSMA Educational Publications, 2001): 7.

client's needs, oftentimes you can match your product/service to the needs of the client and make the sale.

Can it really be that simple? The theory is simple, but it takes careful study and a lot of hard work to put it into practice. Let's look a little closer at the three keys of personal sales.

Key 1: Thorough Knowledge of Your Product or Service. You don't possess thorough knowledge of your product or service until you know your product/service so well that you seldom, if ever, have to look up a fact or get back to a client. Your website should provide all the answers and a direct phone link to someone in your organization who has all the answers.

Key 2: Thorough Knowledge of Your Client's Needs. If you've done your homework, then you have thorough knowledge of your client's needs—you know the client's requirements before you try to sell him or her your products/services. Learn as much as you can about your customers and prospects. Access their website and be sure yours is compatible.

Key 3: Thorough Knowledge of Your Sales Image. This is a tough thing to learn especially if you are not looking closely at yourself. What image does your sales personnel convey to clients through dress, speech, mannerisms, and so forth? What images does your website convey? Are these compatible with your image/positioning strategy?

ETHICS

One salesperson's violation of the code of ethics can cause an entire corporation to be viewed negatively. Conversely, an ethical salesperson becomes an ambassador of trust for any organization.

As we move through this chapter we will provide additional steps and tactics for success related to each of these key areas. Let's begin with knowledge acquisition about your own products/services and knowledge of clients/ prospects.

Knowledge of Product/Service and Client's Needs

A salesperson whose product knowledge is complete and accurate is better able to satisfy customers. This is without doubt the most important justification for becoming totally familiar with the products you sell. It is simply not possible to provide maximum assistance to potential customers without this information. Additional advantages to be gained from your sales personnel knowing your product/service include greater self-confidence, increased enthusiasm, improved ability to overcome objections, and development of stronger selling appeals.

A complete understanding of your company by your sales personnel will also yield many personal and professional benefits. The most important benefit, of course, is their ability to serve your customers most effectively. In many selling situations, customers inquire about the company's business practices. They want to know things about support personnel, product development, credit procedures, warranty plans, and product service after the sale. When salespeople are able to provide the necessary company information, they gain respect. They also close more sales.

Your sales personnel should also know your competition. It pays to study other companies that sell similar products to determine whether they have competitive advantages or disadvantages. Salespeople gather information from many sources. Company literature and sales training meetings are among the most important. Other sources include tours, trade shows, customers, competition, publications, actual experience with the product/service offering, and internet searches. Figure 8-3 recaps potential sources of information.

In addition to these sources for knowledge acquisition, there are many other sources from which to develop prospects. These include computerized databases/lists, friends and acquaintances, referrals, cold calling, directories, networking, and your competitors who talk too much.

In the sales presentations, knowledge of the product's services and your company's strengths must be presented in terms of the resulting benefits to the buyer. The information and benefits emphasized will depend on your sales personnel's assessment of the prospect's needs and motivation.

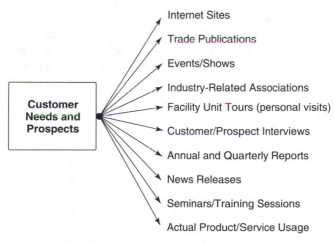

Figure 8–3   Knowledge Acquisition Sources

Knowledge of Sales Image

Understanding the relationship of your sales image to your customers, prospects, and competitors can be vital for sales success. What image, positioning, and reputation do your company, products/services, sales personnel, and internet site portray? How does this relate to your customers and prospects? Can you change anything to better position yourself in line with your customers/prospects? Let's examine a few areas where you might look to address this question of changing sales image.

First, make a list of all "points of encounter" your customers or prospects have with your business.[2] Include all visual, vocal, and electronic points of encounter, (e.g., sales personnel, phone operators for tollfree numbers, internet site, etc.) Ask yourself if your sales personnel (dress, appearance, personality, style, etc.) convey not just the image desired for your business but one that is compatible with your major clients and prospects. With the wide range in business attire in today's world, this is increasingly important. If you err, do it on the side of being overly formal rather than casual. What attitude or message is sent when your phone is answered or your sales personnel visit a client or prospect? Do they demonstrate a thorough knowledge of your product/service and competitive products/services? Are they prepared and sensitive to individual customer needs and nuances? Are they mature and motivated? Can they "read" customers? Can they sell? Now ask yourself similar questions about your internet site. Most important of all, do not hesitate to fix or change any item or personnel that does not convey the desired image or is not compatible with your customer base.

CLIENTS' NEEDS

Your knowledge acquisition should provide you enough in-depth information to develop a customer sales strategy. Are your customers'/prospects' buying motivations and needs clearly identified? Do they purchase with a "social" motive or conscience? What role does emotion play with the customers? Do they prefer deals, bulk purchases, and so on? What are their payment preferences and delivery expectations? What role do they expect your business to play after the sale? The keys to finding the answers to these questions are: (1) analyze past purchasing patterns; (2) listen, listen, listen; and (3) observe your customers/prospects and their relationships with other suppliers, looking closely at their image/positioning and modus operandi.

To be successful as salespeople, your employees will not only need to be knowledgable about your products/services, your customers/prospects and competition, and how to convey the appropriate image, they will also need to know how to present, ask questions, overcome objectives, and "close" or get the sales. In the next few sections of this chapter, we will look at sales presentations and selling strategies.

SALES PRESENTATIONS

When the best price doesn't win, often you will find it was because the best sales presentation did win.[3] Winning sales presentations are the ones that meet the customers' needs and exceed their expectations. And yes, in general, the overall quality or "slick appearance" of the presentation does count (except where the customer profile indicates a bias against such presentations). Let's look at the six keys to a successful/winning sales presentation.

Key 1: Preplanning. This involves ascertaining the customer's needs and expectations and developing a detailed "script." The script includes identification of the type, depth, and flow of the presentation. It is a detailed outline and checklist of every item that should be covered, the logical (from the customer's perspective) order in which each item should be covered, and a listing of anticipated questions and answers.

Key 2: Approach. When setting up the presentation appointment through customer contact, it is important to listen carefully for any additional clues the prospect or client provides. This can alter any number of items in the script, such as length of time, presentation flow/format, and so on.

Key 3: Presentation. There are a number of types of presentations and selecting the appropriate one is a key part of preplanning. Three of the major types of presentations that may be deployed are informative, persuasive, and reminder. An *informative* presentation is designed/scripted to inform customers about new products, major changes (i.e., improvements) to existing products, or unique products. Purchase per se will most likely not occur. Informative presentations should cover all major or new product/service features and benefits and detail how the product/service differs from others. A *persuasive* presentation is what most people believe sales presentations are all about. Persuasive presentations are scripted to produce a sale (close). They are designed to relate to the customer/prospect on a customized basis. Focus is on the needs, beliefs, motivation, and behavior of the customer/prospect. Persuasive presentations often involve demonstrations, options to select from or fall back on, and converting a consumer to a customer or repeat buyer. A *reminder* presentation can serve multiple purposes. It can be to keep awareness levels up (awareness level correlates directly with sales possibility/chance), to reestablish relationships, and to remind the client about your products/services. In addition, reminder presentations afford an excellent occasion to identify any problems or new opportunities.[4] Should any of your presentations actually involve product/service trials or demonstrations, be sure to prepare for this also. Make sure it works and is timed appropriately.

Key 4: Negotiation. Most clients don't sign on the dotted line without some discussion. This interchange is known as negotiation. Buyer resistance and a desire to get a better deal are natural reactions and part of the total sales process. Anticipation and appropriate response are keys to negotiation success. Major reasons for resistance include: the presentation/presenter; not meeting the prospect's/customer's needs; the product/service offering itself; price; time; or external reasons, (e.g., reputation). Any type of sales resistance should always be met with a positive attitude and prepared response.

Key 5: Closing. Closing is an art to be learned and mastered. Often there are different points in the presentation and negotiation phases where an astute salesperson can and should "go for the close." Rehearse the script and note the points. More importantly, listen to the customer/prospect for signals that should let you know they are ready for your close. These may be verbal signals such as "That sounds good to me" or the more subtle "You've given me a lot of useful information." Signals may also be nonverbal and more difficult to recognize, such as the lifting of a pen or pencil from the table. In all likelihood you will misread a signal, so prepare several different closes.

Key 6: After the Sale. This involves everything from the "thank you" process (verbal and written) to the follow-up calls, billing, customer service, and so on. This key is the most important one with respect to developing repeat business, referrals, and keeping competition from succeeding.[5] We will look more closely at the customer services marketing weapon in the next chapter. Figure 8-4 recaps the six keys to successful sales.

One additional method to ensure that your "after the sale" step is well performed, and which may possibly lead to additional sales, is to take notes and record comments. Many times analyzing this information will lead to product/service improvements, new processes/procedures, and repeat/future business. The sales presentation process is sometimes not enough to win the sale, despite best efforts. In the next section, we will look at some additional

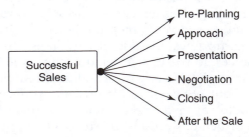

Figure 8–4 Six Keys to Successful Sales

selling insights, strategies, and tactics to help your business succeed in deployment of the sales weapon.

SELLING STRATEGIES AND APPLICATIONS

There are numerous books, theories, and stories about sales strategies and techniques. Our purpose in this section is not to delineate all the techniques, but rather to suggest some overall strategies for hospitality businesses. At the outset, it is important to recognize that you need to be flexible, as no one strategy will work for every customer or prospect. In fact, you will in all likelihood have to employ multiple strategies with the same customer/prospect over time.

Sales strategy selection is dependent upon many different circumstances. Sales strategies may vary based on the "customer type" you are dealing with, the type of resistance you're meeting up with, and the nature of the product/service itself. Are you dealing with a "reactive" or "proactive" sale? Reactive is when the buyer initiates the contact. In this scenario you move almost directly to overcome any objections and close the sale. If the seller (you or your representatives) initiates the contact, you are in a proactive sale. In proactive sales you will use the six keys to successful sales just discussed. In both situations you are going to have to ask "closed" and "open" questions. A closed question requires the respondent to only answer "yes" or "no." A closed question helps the salesperson control the conversation. An open question requires a more extensive response and is best used to let the customer talk or develop a dialogue. The ultimate goal is the same, making a sale or closing.[6]

Making a sale for a new product or service requires a different strategy and tactics than making a sale for an existing or established product/service. The script is going to be different from preplanning to closing.

Selling strategy for an new product/service focuses on changing habits, developing interest, creating a new level of expectation, pointing out new higher standards/benchmarks, building desire for the product, and creating a new customer base or market itself. In fact, in the case of the new product you may have to revert to a few other strategies to get the close. These include:

- **Testimony** by independent testing facilities, research reports, and third-party endorsements
- **Trial offers** where you provide the product/service on a complimentary basis or "you only have to pay if you keep/like it" basis
- **Piggybacks** where you include your new product/service with someone else's or another of your own
- **Samples,** one of the oldest methods to get acceptance of a new product/service offering

Selling strategy for an established product/service focuses on the company reputation, the brand's attributes, the product/service's unique features, incremental sales, and extraordinary customer service. You may find that one of the above new-product strategies turns around a customer who is about to switch. Other strategies to keep existing customers buying your established products or services include:[7]

- Presales contact reminders, thank-you notes, and phone calls
- Special additional product/service offering on the next purchase
- Updates on what's new and improved
- Trade-ups—offering to take back a previous purchase as partial payment for a new or more expensive product line
- Free gifts occasionally bestowed upon your existing customers (including merchandise and other small, legal tokens of appreciation)
- Upgrades. These are always appreciated, especially where there is a real perceived difference in the product or service.
- Surprises. Everyone loves a bonus or surprise, so remember to provide a few to your established customers.
- Extra care/attention. This means going beyond their expectations, such as being there (at the customer's location) when you wouldn't be expected to be (e.g., delivery time).
- "In their favor's." These are simply bending your policies in favor of the customer whenever possible. Extending payments, advancing delivery dates, waiving requirements, are all examples.
- Conveniences—accommodating your customer whenever and wherever possible. Drop-shipping to multiple locations and splitting orders into multiple packs and sequencing their delivery times, are a few examples.
- Special mailers. These are simply incentives or demonstrations of appreciation in the form of an invitation, a special offer whereby you encourage them to repeat purchase or return to use your service again, a special discount, a complimentary next purchase, and so on.
- "Almost theirs." These involve offering a strong incentive (e.g., free upgrade, case of product) if the customer makes just one more purchase.

Selling strategies must be flexible, preplanned, and creatively designed to address what your research/knowledge acquisition has told you will most likely please your established customers or new prospects. Always keep in mind that there is no profit or income until a sale is made. Up to that point all you have generated is expense.

Telephone Sales

Many times a product or service is sold without the opportunity for a direct face-to-face sales call. Obtaining business by telephone is an art in itself. There are several golden rules to telephone sales that will help you achieve success.

The first three are identical to the three keys we discussed in the previous section—thorough knowledge of your product or service, thorough knowledge of your client's needs, and thorough knowledge of your sales image. Let's look at these keys as they apply to telephone sales.

First, just as in personal sales, you should know your product or service thoroughly. You don't want to hesitate or be forced to say, "I'll have to get back to you with those dimensions." Second, know about your prospect by doing research before you call, not while you're talking to him or her. Third, make sure your sales image is professional and positive. Your sales image can be transmitted and detected over the telephone by your vocal expressions and telephone mannerisms.

The fourth key to telephone sales is perhaps the most important of all: Listen! Listen intently to prospects, and be ready with information about options and choices, giving the prospects a clear, accurate, and prompt response to every question. Phone sales should always include a recap, item by item, of all the details before reaching the fifth key. The fifth key to telephone sales is asking for the sale. The sixth key is saying "Thank you."[8]

Remember, in executing any sales strategy, whether personally, over the phone, or on your internet site, to preplan, develop the script, and adhere to the keys to sales success.

INTERDEPARTMENTAL COMMUNICATIONS

Sales are not only dependent upon the marketing weapons of advertising, promotions, databases, pricing, and so on, but are also highly dependent upon functions responsible for getting the product/service offering to the customer when and as promised. Communications and follow-up are essential with manufacturing, operations, transportation, and whatever other functional areas can jeopardize your promises to the customer. Select your external vendors/partners carefully, for they need to be as reliable and flexible as your internal functional departments are if you are to keep your promises to the customer. Customers do not like variations such as: not the amount of product promised; wrong/delayed delivery dates; services not available; erroneous billing terms or calculations; dealing with call-answering systems; and so on. Communicate and eliminate problems before they happen. When you do find a problem, identify options/solutions that you believe will be acceptable to the customer prior to calling the customer. But, by all means, call the customer and be honest.

MEASURING SALES PERFORMANCE

Measuring sales performance can be viewed and performed in numerous ways. Choose the method that has the best applicability for your specific product/service. Be sure to take into account the type of selling environment. If your entire market is declining, be realistic and focus on taking market share or moving units/volume. Take into account the tenure (experience/capabilities) of your sales force. Factor in any seasonal or supply-related issues. Sales objectives, in general, represent the projected levels of products and services to be sold based on an accurate estimate of the market (the growth trend) and the capacity of your organization to realize those opportunities. "Capacity" takes into account all of the above-referenced factors plus the total marketing expenditures allocated. Sales objectives should be time-specific (start date/end date) and expressed in both dollars and units as targets to measure performance. Profits should also be part of any performance measurement.

Establishing sales objectives or benchmarks against which to assess performance can be accomplished using a variety of quantitative methods. You can focus on market share trends and set a market share percentage objective. You can assess your company's overall sales growth compared to the industry's (or your sector's) sales growth rate. You can develop a composite or micro model of your closest competitors (assuming that data are available) and measure yourself against the composite growth index. You can assess your performance against your own previous year's performance. Or you can measure your sales performance against the growth rate of your target market.

It is important to recognize that there are numerous qualitative factors that may influence your sales performance measurements. These include: overall economic conditions (interest rates, growth rates, etc.), competition (new competitors, number of competitors, strengths, etc.), your product's life-cycle stage, the overall mission and personality of your business, and your marketing plan expectations/philosophy (have you intentionally set goals much higher than achievable or realistic?).

In establishing your quantifiable overall sales/revenue objectives, consider using multiple methodologies such as: (1) the outside macro approach, (2) the inside micro approach, and (3) the expense-plus approach. Let's look at each of these approaches.

- **Outside Macro Approach.** This methodology involves establishing a quantifiable target for your sales increase based on the trend in total market or category sales for the next 3 years. In essence, you are comparing your projection of your company's product/service sales share with the market growth trend for that product/service.

- **Inside Micro Approach.** This method is simply taking your own sales history and projecting a 3-year trend line, using your judgment to exclude abnormal deviations from the history or factoring in any major known events (new products, acquisitions, etc.) for future years.

- **Expense-Plus Approach.** This methodology involves estimating the sales levels required to cover expenses and make a projected profit (growth rates and increased expenditures need to be taken into account).

Each of the above approaches will likely result in different sales objectives. Reconcile the differences by using your judgment to factor in the applicable qualitative factors stated above and arrive at your overall sales objective to be measured against for performance purposes.[9]

Sales data broadly include: total sales; sales by product, brand, or department; market share (your product's sales as a percent of the total market's sales); sales by unit (outlets, stores, properties, etc.); sales by season; sales by geographic area; sales by target market segment; sales by location; sales by product/service type; and sales by employee (usually salesperson). With respect to the latter, some segments or product/service categories maintain average ratios of sales to expenses for each employee. For example, in one product/service category you might read that the average ratio of sales to expenses per sales rep is 15 to 1, while in another industry sector it could be 35 to 1 or 10 to 1. These employee average ratios of sales to expenses are simply a guideline to help you establish a minimum threshold for your sales personnel to achieve.

Measurements generally are utilized to measure efficiency (performance) and to form a basis for determining rewards (bonuses, raises, etc.). Other measurements include: number of sales calls per dollar spent; percentage market coverage per dollar spent; number of inquiries/leads per dollar spent; number, size, or value of orders per sales call; number of new customers per dollar spent; and average sales revenue per dollar of selling or distribution expense. Finally, sales objectives for measurement purposes can be split between new and established products/services and also between new and established sales personnel.

REWARDING PERFORMANCE

There are many different ways to reward sales personnel for achieving and exceeding their sales performance objectives. These broadly include, but are not limited to, basic compensation plans, incentives (tangible and intangible), and career advancement. Compensation plans usually involve direct monetary payments in the form of salary and commissions. The mix of the two varies widely and compensation may be purely salary or purely commissions. Many compensation plans also take into account customer satisfaction measures and overall company profit levels (thresholds). Let's examine the major compensation plans usually utilized to reward sales performance from a monetary perspective.[10]

- Fixed salary plus bonus. Salespeople functioning under this compensation plan tend to be more company centered and to have a fairly high degree of financial security if their salary is competitive. The bonus incentives help motivate people under this plan.
- Straight salary. Salespeople who work under this compensation plan are usually more concerned with their financial security and a fixed level of income each pay period.

- Straight commission. The only direct monetary compensation comes from sales. No sales, no income. Salespeople under this plan are very conscious of their sales. Lack of job security can be a strong inducement to produce results. However, these people usually concentrate more on immediate sales than on long-term customer development.
- Commission with a draw provision or guaranteed salary. This plan has about the same impact on salespeople as the straight commission plan. However, it gives them more financial security.
- Commission with a draw provision or guaranteed salary plus bonus. This plan offers more direct financial security than the previous two commission-related plans. Therefore salespeople may adhere more to the company's objectives. The bonus may be based on sales or profits.

In addition to these more or less standard reward programs, some businesses use their own variations. Some modify a plan with rewards for new accounts, incremental commissions for certain items or time frames, and so on.

Incentive rewards include both intangibles and tangibles. Recognition programs are examples of an intangible incentive or reward (e.g., salesperson of the year, new accounts leader, certificate of appreciation, etc.). Incentive rewards may take on a more tangible form such as automobile, merchandise, stock, travel, and the like. Many times incentive rewards are used to increase immediate and short-term performance (e.g., a one-month sales contest or a contest associated with a 90-day new product launch). In the services sector, "mystery shopper" programs can include instant rewards for exceptional customer-related performance.

NEW TECHNOLOGIES/NEW APPROACHES

In many sectors of the hospitality industry new software has been introduced to help the sales effort be more productive as well as improve communications with prospects and clients. Not only has account management software been customized, but multidimensional models can be provided electronically on the website. These models allow both the client and the salesperson to create everything from sample meeting room set-ups to traffic flow and layout of each deck of a cruise ship. Software now allows for "what if" scenarios related to many different aspects of an order/contract and provides instantaneous answers. Variables such as "what if" we change the dates, change the size of the group, change the menu, and so on, are loaded in and the cost or other impact provided. We will discuss more technological applications in a later chapter. Management deploys technology to facilitate sales, increase efficiency, and improve customer satisfaction and to remain competitive. Investment in technology is usually tied to the more prosperous years of the industry economic cycle.

In both prosperous and lean years, management has implemented and experimented with new strategies in an attempt to obtain more effectiveness and more efficiency from the sales function. In some sectors of the industry, select sales forces have been dramatically reduced and more reliance placed on contact with the prospect or customer through the electronic media. Likewise, home office–based and unit/property–based sales forces have undergone a number of changes driven by those seeking efficiencies or seeking to improve customer service. Strategies include "clustering" the sales force in a large market or part of a region. In this case the sales personnel from various units are consolidated in one central market location to serve all units. Another strategy has been to move the sales personnel out of the units and regional offices and let them sell from their own homes. Management believes this strategy is particularly efficient in major urban areas where traffic time and crowded lunch hours cut into productivity. Coupled with both the clustering and work from home approaches is usually an increased focus on customer service at the unit/property level. For example, seven sales personnel would be clustered or home based and at the same time in each of the seven units an onsite customer service representative would handle the client.

There appear to be pros and cons to these sales management strategies. Some customers want to deal with the same person on site and reject having to deal with one person who sold or booked the business and another person at a unit or site. This reaction appears to be especially true of corporate meeting planners. From the side of the salesperson, many like working from home and the flexibility that comes with a home base. The company likes the efficiencies also.

As we move through the next decade, with more and more two-breadwinner households and more and more pressure on earnings, it would appear that streamlining and efficiency-driven managerial strategies will continue to impact the sales function and management thereof. Also, as technology continues to improve in many areas, both software and hardware will support the new strategies. As one senior sales manager for a major hospitality company recently said, "As a result of technology, I actually know more about where and what my sales staff are doing . . . we have both voice and visual communications, that are just a click away."

CHAPTER REVIEW

Sales management plays a significant role in many sectors of the hospitality industry. Sales remains the marketing discipline that utilizes the greatest amount of human resources. Sales is the personal link between the product/service and the customer or prospective customer. Sales management requires seeing that the sales force is knowledgable not only about one's own product or service, but also about key traditional competitors, new nontraditional competition, and the customer's needs. Knowledge acquisition combined with professional presentation skills are two of the keys to successful sales. Management must provide the selling strategies and motivation for its sales team, while setting goals and measuring performance against those goals. Sales management entails the orchestration of the sales strategy as part of the total marketing mix.

Today there is much greater reliance on equipping the sales force with all the support technology to successfully compete and manage the customer base. Organizational options and experimentation are becoming an increasingly important role for management in an era driven by earnings. Sales and customer service remain interlinked in ensuring sales success. Let's recap some key questions for sales management to consider on the sales checklist that follows.

Sales Checklist

- Is your overall sales strategy supported by and interconnected to the other marketing weapons, (advertising, promotions, etc.)? Are the strategies in sync with each other?
- Have you developed specific sales objectives for repeat business?
- Is your sales effort geared to the findings of your knowledge acquisition about your target market customers and prospects?
- Is your sales force knowledgable of your product/service offerings and trained to demonstrate them?
- Is the image conveyed by your sales personnel in line with and supportive of your overall business image and product/service positioning strategy?
- Are research and knowledge acquisition methodologies in place to provide your sales force thorough knowledge of your clients' needs and trends in the marketplace?
- Is your sales force up to date on all competitive product/service offerings?
- Do your internet site, tollfree phone response system, and graphic presentations all reflect the company image and positioning desired?
- Are you developing individual major customer sales strategies?
- Are your sales presentations scripted, rehearsed, and adhering to the six keys to sales success discussed?
- Have your sales personnel received training in negotiation and technical support?
- Do you have an "after the sale" plan/strategy in place?
- Are your sales presentations and techniques appropriate for your new product introductions?
- Have you developed a resource book of product/service testimonials for use by your sales force?
- Is your sales force equipped with "objection overcomers" and are they empowered to use them?
- Are your telephone representatives scripted, trained to answer customer inquiries, and representative of your desired image/positioning?

- Do you have an effective interdepartmental/intrafunctional written communications plan in place?
- Are your sales personnel immediately notified of any product/service delivery changes or problems?
- Have you established quantified and qualified sales objectives and measurements that are appropriate and fair for your sales force?
- Are your reward systems competitive, fair, fairly administered, and challenging but realistically achievable?

Finally, this chapter focused on new technologies and new organizational strategies being applied to sales management. While many of these strategies are driven by efficiency rationale, all recognize that sales and customer service are truly interlinked. In the next chapter, we will look closely at customer service and quality as managerial strategies.

KEY CONCEPTS/TERMS

Alliances	Expense-plus approach
Closing	Incentives
Cold calling	Inside micro approach
Commissions	Outside macro approach
Consultative selling	Partnership selling
Customization selling	Proactive selling
Draw	Reactive selling

DISCUSSION QUESTIONS

1. Why is knowledge about your customer and your competitors essential to sales success?

2. If you were to have your choice of sales compensation plan, which type would you like and why?

3. Select a sector of the hospitality industry where personal sales plays a major role in the overall marketing strategy mix and identify which approach you as a manager would use to set your quantifiable sales objectives.

4. Identify two different firms in different sectors of the hospitality industry and discuss their sales image likenesses and differences. Is their respective image appropriate for the brand they represent?

5. What role do you believe sales should play in the total marketing mix in the hospitality industry?

6. How do you believe technology will impact sales management strategies in the next decade?

ENDNOTES

1. G. Manning & B. Reece, *Selling Today* (Upper Saddle River, NJ: Prentice Hall, 1997): 9–10.
2. R. Nykiel, *You Can't Lose If the Customer Wins* (Stamford, CT: Longmeadow Press, 1990): 18.
3. Nykiel (2001): 10.
4. Ibid., 10–11.
5. R. Nykiel, *Marketing Strategies* (New York: Cormar Business Press, 2002): 126.
6. Ibid., 127.
7. R. Nykiel, *Keeping Customers in Good Times or Bad* (Stamford, CT: Longmeadow Press, 1992): 59–64.
8. R. Nykiel, *Marketing in the Hospitality Industry* (East Lansing, MI: Educational Institute of the American Hotel and Motel Association, 1997): 83.
9. R. Hiebing, Jr., & S. Cooper, *The Successful Marketing Plan* (Lincolnwood, IL: NTC Business Books, 1997): 124–126.
10. Manning & Reece, 398.

CASE 1

A Tale of Two Inns*

At the beginning of the chapter we discussed the importance of understanding your product or service, having knowledge of the your clients and competition, and knowing your desired image. Sales image and related sales presentations are often based on understanding the client's needs. Selling success is directly related to how well your personnel are trained to sell and how much they know about your products/services. In the case study that follows, incidents at two nearly identical oceanfront inns are presented. One has practiced the art of selling based on listening to the client's needs and on image recognition; the other has not utilized these processes.

The Inn at Ocean's Edge received a call from a potential customer who seemed hesitant about the rate. The customer first asked the proprietor if rooms were available during a weeklong period in season. "Fortunately, we still have a few rooms available that week," was the reply. The next question was what is the rate? Sensing potential price resistance, the proprietor responded, "Have you stayed with us before?" The potential customer said no, he was not familiar with the inn and again asked, "What's the rate?" The proprietor then said, "Well, let me tell you a few things you should know prior to making a decision about staying at the Inn." What followed was an extremely informative and enthusiastic description of the property's oceanfront setting, fashion-designer rooms complete with whirlpool/tubs and fireplaces, made-to-order breakfasts, and so on. The proprietor concluded by stating that the Inn is unique in the area because it is the only inn on that section of the coast with the 4 Diamond rating by the American Automobile Association and that he did expect all rooms available for that week to be gone once some of his previous guests call later in the month. The potential customer reserved a room and provided the appropriate deposit.

In this case, the proprietor knew how to sense resistance, knew he had to justify his rates, possessed a detailed knowledge of the product and service, and knew how to move the potential customer to action (close).

Another potential customer called Inn by the Sea in the same state with similar travel dates. The operator at this inn used the top-down selling technique, promoting the top product first. First, she stated they had a very nice suite and cottages available. The rate was just too high for the potential customer who didn't need a multibedroom cottage for four people. Sensing the response, the operator immediately dropped the rate to half for another room that she noticed "just became available." Now, the potential customer had

*This case study is derived from R. Nykiel, *Marketing Strategies* (New York: Cormar Business Press, 2002): 134–135.

previously stayed at this inn on a number of occasions (no one asked this question) and was aware of the fact that a few rooms were less than desirable in terms of location. The customer asked, "Where is that room located?" The operator said, "It is right off the lobby, close to the dining room." The customer knew this was also next to the elevator, underneath the meeting room, and the noisiest room in the inn.

In this case, the inn's personnel had the right idea—go for the rate in season—however, she failed to "qualify" or profile the potential customer. The operator in essence was "selling" without the knowledge that the customer knew the facility. Further, no reasons were provided to justify the initial higher-rated suite. Incidentally, this inn also had the prestigious AAA 4 Diamond award and Mobil 4 Star ranking.

Irrespective of the size of an operation, sound practices related to sales presentation and image need to be followed. Management is responsible for seeing that proper training and adequate knowledge are provided to all sales personnel (including the point-of-encounter phone reservationists). The advantage will always be with the better-trained salesperson.

Case Discussion Questions

1. If you were the manager of the Inn by the Sea, what steps would you take to correct the sales situation described in this case?
2. Knowledge of your customers and their needs is most important. What do you believe would be the best way to provide this knowledge in a smaller operation?

CASE 2

The Worthwhile Investment*

In this chapter we focused on gaining as much knowledge as possible about your customer's needs. Understanding and addressing clients' needs often results in sales success. In this case we will look at an example of thoroughly understanding a client's needs and going more than the extra mile to meet those needs.

The case begins with the step known as knowledge acquisition of the customers' needs by a resort/hotel chain. A large computer company often held training/expo meetings at one or two of this chain's hotels/resorts. It was great business amounting to hundreds of thousands of dollars each year. In one after-the-sale session, the computer company manager responsible for the business casually stated that they had problems with the hotels/resorts they used for these meetings. The alert sales executive for the hotel/resort chain said: "Tell me about these problems." The computer firm manager replied, "Well, they are mostly technical/design problems. You see, the exhibit halls of the hotels do not have enough electrical outlets, high enough ceilings, or adequate ventilation . . . we have wires taped down everywhere and the heat build-up is pretty tough to deal with." The manager went on to say it wasn't just one hotel/resort but all. The sales executive knew this computer company was one of four or five that held the same type of training/expo meetings. The sales executive also knew that one company spent nearly $5 million per year on such meetings.

It just so happened that this hotel/resort chain was planning to add another ballroom/exhibit hall to this resort and also to construct similar resorts/hotels in the middle and western parts of the country. The sales executive asked the computer company client if he could meet with the department head for trade shows and go into detail about these needs. The meeting took place and it was determined that there would need to be heavy-duty electrical systems, tracks of outlets every X number of feet, ceilings 4 feet higher, and superior air conditioning and heat ventilation systems to have the ideal meeting/display show space.

The resort/hotel chain told the client it would build all these needs into the three facilities at a considerable incremental cost. The computer company, in turn, signed a 5-year contract for all of its meetings of this nature with the resort/hotel chain. The resort/hotel chain also signed other companies with similar needs. The end measurable result was $15 million in new revenue in excess of the investment to include the features to meet the customer's needs.

In this case, customization might have been taken to the extreme, but the result was revenue, profit, and a long-term contract. The ability to listen to

---

*This case study is derived from R. Nykiel, *Marketing Strategies* (New York: Cormar Business Press, 2002): 135–136.

your customers' expressed needs, use after-the-sale feedback, and take subsequent action is part of what successful selling is all about.

Case Example Discussion Questions

1. What steps should a salesperson take to understand the client's needs?
2. Make a list of questions you might ask a prospective client and practice with another individual—see how well you listen.

CASE 3

Marriott International and Hilton—The Industry's Trainers

In this chapter we stated that being responsive on a timely basis with well-trained employees is a necessity for a successful sales organization. Not only is extensive training important, but utilizing technology to expedite both customer information as well as provide easy access is extremely advantageous. The case illustrations that follow focus on these aspects and the practices of two of the most successful and sophisticated sales operations in the hospitality industry.

When seeking to identify the best sales and marketing organizations in the hospitality industry, Marriott International and Hilton are almost always cited as the best and most sophisticated. There are many common characteristics that contribute to these accolades, including superior training, sophisticated systems and technology support, and excellent intracompany and customer communications systems. In this case study, we will look at both Marriott's and Hilton's sales operations.

About Marriott International*

Marriott International is a leading worldwide hospitality company. Its humble beginning was a small rootbeer stand which opened in Washington, D.C., in 1927. The founders were J. Willard and Alice S. Marriott.

Today Marriott International has nearly 2,000 lodging properties located in 50 states and 56 countries and territories. The company operates and franchises a broad portfolio of lodging brands worldwide, offering travelers nearly 400,000 rooms and ownership villas worldwide. The company's brands range from luxury to economy and from extended stay to resort timesharing. The Marriott brand name is recognized as a symbol of quality and consistency in senior living and distribution services. The following is a list of current Marriott brands:

- The Ritz-Carlton Hotel Company, LLC—luxury lodging
- Marriott Hotels, Resorts and Suites—flagship upscale hotels and resorts
- Marriott Conference Centers—small to mid-sized conference centers
- Residence Inn by Marriott—extended-stay lodging
- Courtyards by Marriott—moderate-price lodging
- SpringHill Suites by Marriott—moderate-price all-suite lodging

*Information derived from www.marriott.com, in particular, Marriott Annual Reports, 1998–2001; "Marriott Travel Agent Room Night Sales and Commissions Continue to Escalate Significantly," Press Release (Jan. 25, 2000); and "Launches Personalization Features," Press Release (Oct. 3, 2000).

- Fairfield Inn by Marriott—economy lodging
- Renaissance Hotels & Resorts—upscale lodging
- Marriott Executive Residences—upscale department brand
- Ramada International—moderate-price lodging
- TownePlace Suites by Marriott—moderate-price extended-stay lodging
- Marriott ExecuStay—fully furnished corporate lodging
- The Ritz-Carlton Club—exclusive private residences
- Brighton Gardens—assisted living facility (residential design)
- Marriott Maple Ridge—assisted living facility (high-level service)
- Village Oaks—moderate-price assisted living facility
- Marriott Distribution Services—limited-line foodservice distributors
- The Marketplace by Marriott—contracting and procurement
- Other—Marriott International also operates seven New World International Hotels in China and Southeast Asia. Marriott Golf manages 25 golf course facilities.

With one of the broadest portfolios of lodging brands in the industry, Marriott International has a product for most market locations. Many of Marriott's brands have become leaders within their segments, in terms of market share and customer preference.

About Hilton*

Hilton Hotels Corporation is recognized internationally as a preeminent hospitality company. The company develops, owns, manages, or franchises nearly 2,000 hotels, resorts, and vacation ownership properties. Its portfolio includes many of the world's best-known and highly regarded hotel brands. These include:

- Hilton
- Doubletree
- Embassy Suites
- Hampton Inn
- Hampton Inn & Suites
- Hilton Garden Inn

---

*Information derived from www.hilton.com, particularly Hilton Annual Reports, 1998–2001; "Hilton Hotels Corporation Recognized as E-Business Winner in the Travel and Hospitality Industries by *Internet Week* Magazine." Press Release (July 5, 2000); and "Hilton Hotels Corporation Selects New Market's Sales, Marketing, and Catering Automation System," Press Release (Oct. 1, 2000).

- Homewood Suites by Hilton
- Conrad Hotels

Hilton Hotels also owns the famous Waldorf Astoria in New York, Waikiki's Hilton Hawaiian Village, and Chicago's Palmer House Hilton.

Technology Advances

Technology has immensely influenced the sales and marketing of both Marriott International and Hilton. Both lodging chains are witnessing the benefits of sales database storage, the rapidity of intracompany communications, and customer processing speed. The end result is the ability to increase sales by providing up-to-the-minute access to information, thus improved service performance. Both companies have been pioneers in deploying technology to improve their sales performance.

Marriott International and Hilton have recently upgraded technology systems that have already improved sales and marketing department efficiency. Corporate or national sales departments have become recipients of detailed and timely information. This quick access to relevant information enables the national sales department to distribute similar benefits to the sales department of the property level.

Both companies have invested heavily in sales via the internet. This venue, like most industry sales, has taken corporate, group, and vacationing family reservations and information to the home and office. As opposed to the use of tollfree numbers alone, the customer is able to view facilities and make qualified choices of their own. The customers are more informed, which makes the sale of a hotel room a lot easier for a national hotel sales representative.

Hotel Property-Level Sales Benefits   National sales representatives may now provide immediate information to local or property-level sales departments through the internet or the intranet. This accessibility to customer information provides two principal benefits: (1) the marketing strategy may be carried out throughout the property and (2) hotel sales managers are able to utilize this quick access to detailed information to instill a consistent marketing strategy throughout the departments within the property. For example, if the sales and marketing manager is given almost "real-time" reservations of a soon-to-arrive group, he or she may prepare the front desk by loading anticipated room rates into the system. Housekeeping may be notified of anticipated special room requests, and food and beverage may also be prepared to honor special requests. The bellman and concierge may provide more personalized service when made aware of guests' expectations upon arrival, beforehand. This timely data permits a smooth reception and stay for the guests. The customers can receive the service quality, consistency, and reliability that they desire.

Employees are able to feel more relaxed and empowered when properly trained and informed. Tensions are eased, creating a more hospitable environment for the workers as well as the customers. This occurs by internal selling. The sales and marketing department markets to internal customers. Internal customers may visualize from the hotel's sales system how their performance and contribution helped to maximize revenues. Clear and concise data helps employees to be more knowledgable of what is going on in the hotels.

Marriott's Reservations System   Marriott International's worldwide reservations system has the lowest cost per reservation in the industry. The company continues to expand the capacity of the system, which is now handling nearly a million reservations per week. Marriott has only one reservation system. The single system inputs all of the national sales data and loads it for the use of each property sales department. The sales manager then loads the information for reservations at the facility.

Marriott believes that the great advantage of having a single reservations system supporting all of its brands is the cross-selling opportunities of its sales force. These cross-selling opportunities are created when a prospective guest's first choice is sold out. In 2002, Marriott generated nearly 500 million cross-selling bookings through its reservations system. It believes it retains business in this way that might have otherwise gone to competitors.

Marriott solicits feedback in a variety of ways, from guest comment cards to random mail sampling to customer focus groups. Many of the service enhancements implemented over the past few years were initially identified by guests, including automated check-in and check-out, on-demand video, expanded exercise facilities, and additional breakfast offerings.

Hilton's Reservations System   As opposed to Marriott's low-cost, single reservations system, Hilton Hotels Corporation opted for property-level systems that are linked to the national sales system. The Hilton sales system is called the Hilton Intranet. The system was installed in spring of 2000. Only Hilton brands, whether company owned or franchises, have access to the system. Two of the most important sales functions on the system are the Hilton Solicitation Management System (HSMS) and the HilStar. The HSMS is a sales system and the HilStar is a negotiated rate system.

Under the HSMS sales function, the property-level sales managers may load their own rates. This sharing of responsibility gives the local property sales managers control and responsibility of the hotel sales functions. The national sales representative aids the hotel sales manager as well. He or she will load all inquiries of the hotel received at the national level. However, unlike Marriott, the hotel sales manager may choose rooms, negotiate nights, and respond to property and community questions, which results in two benefits—timeliness and span of information.

Prior to the Hilton Intranet, the salespeople of Hilton Hotels Corporation utilized server-based solutions by Newmarket. This system provided Hilton salespeople with up-to-the-minute access to guest room and function room inventories and rate information. In addition, the software offered property data such as meeting room capacities, amenities, and integrated room layout design functionality, as well as information about local attractions. The results were that Hilton's salespeople were able to provide greater amounts of information to customers more efficiently.

While this system proved to be far more efficient than thumbing through yellow pages for local information, it did very little to lessen the workload of corporate sales and to speed up the communication between national and property-level salespeople.

Under the Newmarket system, Hilton's national corporate sales staff was responsible for handling all of the internet and tollfree phone sales. They not only loaded all of the customer information for the hotel sales managers, but also loaded rates, and reviewed their responses to corporate customer questions. Corporations that wished to negotiate a rate and contract for its business travelers had to be informed about ADA compliance, fire code inspections, affirmative action compliance, and even general information. This information encompassed approximately eight hand-typed pages, which along with certificates and rates were mailed or faxed to the national salesperson who handled the specific Hilton corporate account. The process of receiving the information on a potential customer could take several days. This information was loaded based on the priority list of the national sales office, and the loading of the new rates took another 7 days.

The lack of timely communication between the national salesperson and the local sales manager could cause the hotel's service to fail to meet expectations. For example, if a group arrived and their rates were higher than the negotiated rate, it was generally because the national office had not had time to load the rates.

The HSMS shortened this 2½-week process to a 5-minute process. All of the properties' regulations and certifications, layout, and design are now posted on the Hilton Internet. The corporation's bids are posted instantaneously. The property sales manager receives them and may respond instantaneously. To any local questions, the sales manager may then load the hotel's own rates for reservations and the front desk. Although Hilton's national sales continue to provide checks and balances for these transactions, it is done in a timely and efficient manner.

The HilStar is Hilton's negotiated rate reservations site (NetRez) on the Hilton Intranet. The HilStar is primarily used to take reservations and present customers with negotiated rates. The NetRez function takes information on reservations and provides the special rate plan (SRP).

The SRP consists of many different specialized rates based on specific group, specific days of the week and weekends (bounce back), and room category. Accessibility to this site enables local sales managers to input dates, room types, and room rates. This empowerment to local sales managers allows them to govern which rooms would be more profitable under specific rates. For example, the national sales office may have chosen a room, under a specialized rate, that could also be utilized as a banquet room if partitions are removed. The property sales office is more knowledgable about the property and may choose to rent the banquet room to a small convention.

The Hilton Intranet is used to create more efficiency and timeliness by allowing the national sales manager facilitating the local property and the property's sales account manager to work together. Both sales managers may utilize their authority and expertise to create a smoother transaction for the customer. The timing and paired knowledge yields greater results and better hospitality service for the guests.

Online Reservations   An increasing number of travel agents, meeting planners, and hotel guests prefer to do their travel planning and book their reservations online. Marriott developed www.marriott.com in 1996 with the intent of creating the lodging industry's most informative and easy-to-use website. It provides a search and navigation tool for the hotels, with information updated nightly from a central database. Marriott's online bookings have more than tripled over the past few years. Marriott.com is now registering over three million website visits each month. Marriott.com has added an express reservations feature and customized content for business and leisure travelers, travel agents, and event planners.

By voluntarily registering basic profile information on Marriott.com, customers eliminate the need to reenter personal information when making reservations. Site visitors have the option of providing information about their travel habits. Marriott.com can then deliver content that meets the customer's interest.

On the other hand, Hilton Intranet services for guests and customers include a state-of-the-art computerized reservations system that links directly to the company's award-winning corporate website at www.hilton.com. Hilton consistently produces a chain of work shared by the national sales office, property sales office, and hotel departments. Hilton.com is no exception. Both local and national salespeople are able to receive instant reservations and prepare quality service for the guests.

Hilton also provides high-speed internet access for wired laptop travelers in guest and meeting rooms at many of its hotels throughout North America. Hilton has installed other high-speed internet access solutions through guest room televisions and at kiosks in public areas of participating hotels.

Technology and Sales Strategy

Both lodging companies are excelling in REVPAR. They both attribute a large part of this success to outstanding sales performance. They are highly regarded as technologically astute companies. Marriott International and Hilton Hotels Corporation are award-winning companies and receive tremendous support from travel agencies and meeting planners.

In January 2000 Marriott announced that travel agencies had booked over 18 million room-nights in 1999. This is a 12 percent increase over 1998.

In a 1999 independent survey, 36 percent of U.S. business travelers named Marriott as their top choice among hotels. This is nearly three times the number who cited the next most popular brand.

Sales and Marketing Management magazine has rated the Marriott sales organization among the top 25 sales forces in the United States for three consecutive years. Marriott was the only hospitality company to receive this award in 1999.

Internet Week magazine has recognized Hilton Hotels Corporation as the E-Business winner in the travel and hospitality industry category. Hilton was one of only two hotel companies to make the *Internet Week 100*.

Technological innovations customized to meet the employees' and guests' needs have helped advance the sales and marketing programs into a new era at both companies. The instantaneous information and self-help internet services have transformed the sales force into one that can devote much more of its efforts to selling. Technology has become a distinguishing factor in premier service at lodging facilities. Sales systems of both Marriott and Hilton owe part of their success to technological advances.

While needs and preferences of travelers continue to change, both Marriott and Hilton have created sales organizations that are adept at change and service modifications that meet customers' evolving needs. Though technology has greatly influenced the sales departments, the sales departments will also influence technology.

Case Discussion Questions

1. How do you think technology (especially information technology) will enhance the sales process in future years?

2. What are some ways you can think of to ensure that knowledge and up-to-date information reach all employees who have sales/customer interface?

Chapter 9

Customer Service and Quality Strategies

CHAPTER OBJECTIVES

- To identify how customer service and quality strategies are deployed as major managerial strategies within the hospitality industry
- To present a 10-step process that identifies and supports changes in customer service and quality strategies
- To provide a discussion of the various stages of customer development
- To delineate the managerial strategies of continuous quality improvement and total quality management within the hospitality industry
- To assess the likely directions and future trends for customer service and quality strategies within the hospitality industry

Today more than ever, satisfying demanding customers remains the greatest challenge and greatest opportunity in virtually every sector of the hospitality industry. In the hospitality industry, the consumer not only is part of the actual consumption/purchasing process, but moreover often has preset service and quality perspectives. Today's hospitality industry customer is increasingly time poor, more sophisticated, and more demanding. It is important to understand where the customers are coming from and what satisfaction levels they are expressing prior to selecting management strategies for service excellence or quality improvement.

SPEED AND CONNECTIVITY

In general, the consumer of hospitality industry–related products and services is much like any other consumer today with respect to having less time to shop, seeking service and quality, and desiring express services at the speed of lightning. In many industries speed has become the most valued and the new competitive advantage. Speed is shortening product life cycles from years to weeks. Speed and technological progress has made transactions move from days to microseconds. Speed is expected in real-time responsiveness, 24 hours a day, 7 days a week. Speed is what the hospitality industry consumer wants. Those who can fulfill will win, those who can't will be passed by.

Speed is one ingredient in the overall scenario of customer response and satisfaction. Another key factor linked directly to customer retention and satisfaction in the hospitality industry is "connectivity." Connectivity means doing business in a way that is not bound by location. Connectivity means consumers can satisfy their need to access information, make a reservation, and conduct transactions anywhere, at any time, through almost any pertinent medium. Virtually everything in these processes can be done and accessed in some electronic form, be it on the web, phone, screen, modem, and so on. Speed and connectivity mean that the hospitality industry and its sectors must function in real time to satisfy customer needs.

TECHNOLOGY

Technology has enabled hospitality industry firms to improve the customer service experience as well as anticipate and meet the needs of consumers. Customer recognition systems, inventory search systems, frequency and other reward programs, and websites have all contributed to customer retention and new customer development. Property/unit systems feed marketing information systems which in turn feed promotional and product offerings. Certainly speed and convenience, major needs of today's customer, have been dramatically enhanced at virtually every step of the consumption process.

CUSTOMER SATISFACTION

Consumers have control of information with any-time and any-place access. This real-time environment raises the expectations of hospitality industry consumers, sometimes resulting in the "never-satisfied customer." Increased use of the internet to shop, make informed decisions, and purchase reinforces the role of speed and connectivity in customer satisfaction and service expectations. Consumers are savvier, with the difference between the expert seller and the educated buyer becoming increasingly smaller. Consumers are better-informed and more assertive buyers. Today's consumer is also more demanding as a result of having higher expectations of response times. And, perhaps most important of all, consumers have redefined customer satisfaction to include speed of service. Now customer satisfaction and, to a larger degree, the quality/value equation have been redefined. Customer satisfaction is now:

Customer Expectations + or − Perceived Value Received
= Customer Satisfaction

Speed plays a key role in customer expectations and perceived value in the hospitality industry. Consumers are now more demanding—they want what they want where they want it and when they want it. These higher levels of expectations have resulted in overall declines in traveler satisfaction levels in almost all sectors of the industry. Obviously, some of these declines are due to lack of labor, untrained personnel, and more process time related to security issues. For management, there are two over-arching messages that make customer satisfaction a number one goal. First, loyalty increases with satisfaction, especially among frequent business travelers. Second, financial performance increases with loyalty. Remember, satisfied customers return and existing customers cost less than new customers.

WHAT IS REALLY IMPORTANT?

Knowing what is really important to customers allows management to focus resources on those key areas or points of encounter. If one were to look at the lodging, airline, and car rental sectors of the industry, three overall areas contribute most to customer satisfaction. First is speed and ease of reservation/check-in. Second is actual performance versus price. Here the consumer wants the flight to be on time, the car to be there and run well, and the room and related amenities to be ready. The third critical area of importance is the return/check-out or final transaction process. For the foodservice sector this means prompt order taking, service, and presentation of the check. Again, speed and ease (along with accuracy) are expected. Studies have shown that waiting 5 minutes or more to check in or be waited on greatly decreases customer satisfaction. Not surprisingly, membership in a frequency or VIP program increases satisfaction due in part to the program's express check-in, check-out service elements.

In summary, viewing customer satisfaction and quality service must be done from the perspective of the new consumer expectations and mindset. It is no wonder that many consider customer service to be the most valuable managerial weapon and strategy. Customer service plays a role in acquiring new customers, retaining existing loyalty, and taking market share from competitors. Good customer service takes on new importance if you consider that at a minimum it costs businesses five times as much to attract a new customer as it does to satisfy and retain an existing customer. It takes on new importance if you consider that a dissatisfied customer will sometimes tell more than 10 other consumers/prospects about their unsatisfactory experience. So, having a customer service strategy and plan are very important in deploying this valuable marketing weapon. Some businesses fail to recognize customer service as a management weapon and underfund the function or staff it with the lowest paid (and sometimes least trained) employees.

POINTS OF ENCOUNTER

Customer service strategies need to be in place at every point the customer comes into contact with your business or any representation thereof, be it personal, vocal, electronic, and so on. Examine every potential point of encounter and look at all the places/processes that your image and positioning are exposed to. In this section we will present a 10-step process to customer service success.

Step 1: Recognition

The points at which your employees encounter the consumer are opportunities to win (or lose) the consumer.

In an age of increasing customer dissatisfaction, we must take the first step toward achieving service success: recognition. This is not the obvious recognition after the fact that service problems have caused sales to slip or that another company has taken more market share. Such problem recognition is reactive rather than proactive. For recognition to be proactive, observation and analysis of the points of encounter must occur to avoid problems before they occur. Quite simply this means we must focus on the interaction of our product or service with the consumer.

How often have you heard, "They really have a problem here. Too bad they haven't recognized and fixed it." "They" usually refers to top management, which has skipped the all-important thought process known as "recognition." A decline in sales, employee turnover, consumer complaints—these are all reactive indicators.

True recognition in the proactive sense means knowing the points of encounter and assuming the customer's (or prospect's) perspective from pre-sale to post sale.

Step 2: Identification of Problems

Recognition of points of encounter and customer problems is but one proactive step to customer service success.

What is this process by which one can ensure preemptive recognition and prevent loss of market share or customers? Although there are a number of approaches, placing yourself in the role of the customer is one of the best. Ideally it should be done incognito and often. It will make you aware of a service problem or at least give you a fresh look at the customer's perspective. While we shall suggest some periodic acid tests (likely to give you acid indigestion), try to be observant and analytical. Always record the problems and think about possible solutions.

- Call the tollfree number of one of your establishments and analyze the response.
- Go incognito to your outlets, service centers, units, counters, or check-in desks and make notes of your observations (you may need a big notepad). Ask other customers about their experiences at these points of encounter.
- Go to one of your sales offices and read your literature.
- Observe your staff. Are they empathetic with your customers?
- After making these observations, go through the entire purchasing process or service experience and make a list of the direct points of encounter.

Review this list with the following objectives:

- Identification of the critical points at which the sale, purchase, or customer's loyalty can be lost instantly if not handled properly
- Identification of the points that have to be corrected
- Identification of the points that present opportunities for making your service stand out above the competition

Here are some additional strategies and tactics with respect to recognizing problems/opportunities and identifying solutions.

- Use a shoppers' service to check on your business.
- Conduct your own service audit.
- Talk to and, more importantly, listen to your customers.
- Observe and experience the offerings of your most successful competitors.
- Personally review a random sample of complaint letters once per quarter.
- Solicit opinions of your service offering by having a focus group every few years.
- List all points of encounter and have your management focus on one of these points each quarter.
- Check the current relevance of the training material and procedures for all points of encounter. Update where appropriate.
- Spend at least as much time on the points of encounter as you do on the project or development aspects of your business.

Even if you are not in the service sector per se, adapt these steps to check on your sales force, retailers, wholesalers, distributors, agents, and so on. This is what proactive hospitality management strategies are all about in the critical area of customer satisfaction.

Step 3: Plan of Action

Having made your observations incognito, prepared lists, identified points of encounter, and come up with several ideas, you now need a plan of action. Before implementing it on a wide scale, test it to make sure it is executed properly. Not to do so can be disastrous. Test it, modify it, and implement it.

Step 4: Reallocation of Resources

Recognition, identification, and a plan of action are sometimes not enough to make the necessary changes at a point of encounter. To remain competitive and successful, a reallocation of resources sometimes may be required. These resources may be financial, personnel, or equipment. Simple reallocations, such as putting on more phone operators to eliminate the interminable rings followed by a recorded voice telling the caller all lines or service representatives are busy, can set your company ahead of the competition. I would guess that half the callers hang up when the "next available service representative" recording comes on the line—that is, if they haven't been disconnected or forgotten who they called in the first place!

If your firm never puts a customer on hold or if the customers are always connected with a professional service representative, the chances of your winning the customer is pretty good.

Step 5: Prioritization of Execution

The step least often taken and most often needed is prioritization. In a recent edition of the Sunday *New York Times,* I came across two very interesting help-wanted ads that may serve as examples. One fairly large block ad from Beth Israel Medical Center in New York sought a "Director of Guest Relations" (new position). The other ad from a nationally recognized medical clinic read "Wanted—Complaints Clerk." To me it was obvious that Beth Israel had (1) recognized that it was in a service business, (2) identified a point of encounter opportunity, (3) established a plan of action, (4) reallocated resources, and (5) prioritized the importance of relationships with its patients. Note the difference in perspectives. Beth Israel viewed its patients as "guests," and the person who relates to them is at a director's level. These are the obvious signs of a healthy proactive service perspective. On the other hand, the medical clinic had the classical reactive mentality of looking for a "complaints" person and prioritized this function with the label of "clerk." Which medical facility do you think will be perceived as better able to provide service? Here are some additional strategies and tactics to help reallocate and prioritize:

- In order of priority, list the points of encounter that need new or additional resources.
- In order of priority, list all "project" (capital) dollars scheduled for allocation.
- Now prepare a new list which in order of priority blends the points of encounter items and the "projects" items together.
- In prioritizing your "projects" capital needs, place first those that relate to your points of encounter.
- Review your non-point-of-encounter personnel count and payroll costs.
- Review your point-of-encounter personnel count and payroll costs.
- Allocate your resources to the point-of-encounter personnel and the related costs to do their job right on a top-priority basis. Can you imagine a firm that would spend half a million dollars on a project and deny point-of-encounter employees an increase of 50 cents per hour incentive pay or a $5,000 training program? Review all of your firm's expenses; this could be called "current shock."

Step 6: Training of Personnel

Ask yourself if your business is suffering from human incompetence. Today we are experiencing the end product of our formal education process in the form of employees that frequently need to be retrained. It is essential that every one of your point-of-encounter employees are trained or retrained. Also, check on your technology to see if it is functioning properly and evaluate its ease of comprehension and use by the customer and your employees. When your automated systems take over, do they work and really help your customers? Or do they simply help you to lose the customer/prospect and help the competition? Reflect on your own customer experiences and you will quickly perceive the importance of assessing your automation.

Step 7: Recruiting of Personnel

To recruit and hire the appropriate personnel, you have to know the right questions to ask. What are the criteria for those who will be point-of-encounter employees? Do any of these employees sell, quote prices, or directly interface with the potential customer at the critical point of encounter—the actual purchase of your products/services? If so, what type of employees do you want to be responsible for bringing in revenue? Are these employees trainable; are they sufficiently intelligent to hold such positions; or are they overqualified? If you can't answer most of these questions readily, your firm is either already in trouble or will be in trouble before very long.

Well-thought-out recruiting criteria can provide very great returns and should be reviewed frequently. When did you last reevaluate job descriptions and hiring criteria for your point-of-encounter positions? If you believe there is no need for such reviews because the products/services you offer have not changed, you are very wrong; your consumer is changing constantly. Some advocate turning the organization chart upside down, while others suggest that the pay scales be reversed. Obviously, there is no simple answer for all service industry firms. All the steps must be taken into account: recognition, identification, plan of action, reallocation, prioritization, training, and recruiting.

Recruiting should be attempted only after a complete review of each point-of-encounter position. Complexity of job function as well as the types of consumers encountered on a daily basis should be thoroughly analyzed. Do you have (or want) minimum-wage clerks directly interfacing with $100,000-plus executives or large-volume purchasers?

Here are some additional strategies and tactics to facilitate and sharpen your recruiting:

- Have members of top management participate in at least one point-of-encounter position training session.
- Have members of top management work at least one 8-hour day (preferable an entire week) in one of the point-of-encounter positions.
- Review your training resources (people, procedures, and related budgets) annually to determine if they are adequate in preparing your personnel for service leadership.
- Ask customers to evaluate (via questionnaire or direct contact) how well they believe point-of-encounter employees are trained.
- Ask newly trained employees what else they believe should be taught.

- Ask the same question of your seasoned employees.
- Instruct all recruiters of point-of-encounter employees to ask themselves whether they would want to deal face to face with the person they are considering for the job.
- Personally participate in at least one interview session for a point-of-encounter employee.
- Consider upgrading your pay scale to attract seasoned pros away from the competition.
- Make sure your recruiters know exactly what you expect of them, and then periodically check to see that they are doing exactly what you want.

Step 8: Communications

When it comes to communicating with the customer, no one is more important than the point-of-encounter employee. It is this employee that is often the first to know when (and if) your service offering, price, policy, or procedural change is working. He or she is also a great source of information when you attempt to improve service. But when it comes to communicating with these employees, the corporate hierarchy in general does a less than stellar job. This, in tandem with the dissatisfied consumer, works to create the environment for a disastrous customer service experience.

There are many examples of good and bad communication in the service industry. A case of good communication is CEO Bill Marriott, Jr., who was renowned for his visits to virtually every hotel, restaurant, and other facility in Marriott's multi-billion-dollar empire. These were not your typical "presidential" appearances, but detailed inspections as well as walk-throughs to instill motivation. Mistakes were pointed out. Employee suggestions were recorded and implemented on a broad scale if worthwhile.

Adherence to standard operating procedures is mandatory at Marriott. It is therefore no coincidence that Marriott's operations and services are efficient and consistent. There are other examples, but the important point is the same in all situations—good communications. The conscientious CEO goes beyond motivation and inspection. The point-of-encounter employees are made aware of top management's interest in seeing not only how the job is being done but also who is doing the job.

By definition, communication connotes a two-way flow—up and down. Small ideas turn into big winners if communication channels are open. For some reason, it is easier to inform one million customers of your offer than one thousand point-of-encounter employees. There appears to be a logical explanation. Your ad or service offer goes directly from you to the consumer, but the memo describing that offer is often handed down from the vice president of marketing through the managers, to the unit managers, to the department managers, to the shift managers, and finally to the point-of-encounter employees, leaving plenty of opportunity for a breakdown in communication. It happens all the time.

One thing is sure: Never assume that your detailed memo of instructions, the training video, or manual has been read, viewed, or understood by those who must use the information. The best way to find out is to put on the consumer's hat and try to get the service you have offered. Don't be surprised at what you find out. Any form of change may be difficult to communicate, and the difficulty can be compounded when the change involves behavior.

Step 9: Follow Up to Execution

Let's go back to Bill Marriott with regard to communications. All those walk-throughs would not have amounted to much unless there had been a positive form of follow-up. A note was sent to the unit reaffirming the action to be taken or stating the subject to be discussed upon the next visit. Granted, the man had a phenomenal memory, but the key point is that because there was follow-up, employees fixed what needed to be fixed.

Follow-up steps can assume a variety of forms. Some service establishments use "shopper services," which essentially are professional shoppers/customers. They are hired to work as typical consumers, logging their experiences for management. Intelligent use of these findings, of course, is crucial. The results can be negative (employee dismissals) or positive (improved training programs, plans to improve performance and eliminate problem areas).

There are many effective follow-up techniques, and what is appropriate for your particular product/service offering may require special planning. But once a plan is devised, it must be implemented. The procedure must be clearly communicated to those who will implement it, and then you must follow up to make sure it is done. Unless all these steps are taken, all the promises of your promotional ad will only lead to creating a more disappointed consumer.

Here are some strategies and tactics to improve communications and the follow-up process:

- Make a list of all point-of-encounter positions.
- Establish a personal "communications" calendar, scheduling specific frequent dates to deliver your messages to these key people.
- Consider delivering these messages in person, by videotape, or in writing (in that order).
- Make sure all of your point-of-encounter employees clearly understand that their personal contact with customers represents the most critical element to conveying a good service impression.
- Listen. Listen. Listen.
- Communicate the "right" way by showing the employees—not merely telling them.
- Record and remember names and incidents from your employee encounters.
- "Re-touch" those you can with a call or a note.

- Be sincere.
- Repeat all steps regularly. (Employee turnover is the most critical factor in diluting your message and communications in general.)

Step 10: Begin Again

For a number of reasons, this step is perhaps the most difficult. First, to some extent, having to repeat may imply that you have not been successful with the previous nine steps. Second, you need to go back to determine if, indeed, you did not succeed with any of the actions taken. If so, you will need to fix it or replace it. It is only appropriate that we recap the 10 steps to service success.

The 10 Steps to Service Success

1. *Recognition*—Knowing that there is a service opportunity or problem at the points of encounter.
2. *Identification*—Determining what they are.
3. *Plan of Action*—Capitalizing on an opportunity or dealing with a problem.
4. *Reallocation*—Finding the financial and/or human resources to execute the plan.
5. *Prioritization*—Placing execution of the plan at the top of the list.
6. *Training*—Ensuring thorough preparation of those who are charged with taking action at points of encounter.
7. *Recruiting*—Finding the very best people for point-of-encounter positions.
8. *Communications*—Conveying every aspect of your plan accurately, thoroughly, and convincingly to all employees, with special focus on point-of-encounter personnel.
9. *Follow-up*—Recheck all, contact all, and be sure all errors have been corrected.
10. *Begin Again!*—Periodically reviewing all the processes—beginning with the steps of recognition and identification.

CUSTOMER SATISFACTION STRATEGIES

Today's consumer is preconditioned and ready to challenge the product/service provider. Most surveys indicate that consumers in many product/service categories have reached a level of preconditioning that leaves them cynical toward the consumption experience.

Just as there are steps your company (and management) must take, there are steps your employees must take to ensure customer satisfaction. No matter what type of service you provide, there are several keys to effective execution that will create recognition among consumers that your firm goes beyond the point of ENCOUNTER:

- Expectations must be met. Recognize that you must never deliver a service that falls short of what the customer or potential customer expects for the price they are paying. Meeting or exceeding customer expectations is what ultimately determines the level of customer satisfaction. Expectation levels in the mind of the consumer are influenced by the price you charge, their prior experience with your service offering, their prior experience with your competition, and what you promise in your advertising or sales message. Meeting customer expectations is absolutely critical to repeat business.

- Never blame the customer. While some may argue with this categorical statement, you cannot lose by practicing it. The customer is always right, even if he or she is not! Simply stated: Let the customer win! That doesn't mean you should allow the customer to take advantage of you. It means that your employees must understand that they have the flexibility and authority to bend policy when needed to satisfy a customer.

  Most surveys show that less than 5 percent of customers will actually take the time to complain about the service received. However, these same surveys show that almost 25 percent are less than satisfied with that service. And this percentage grows dramatically when customers become increasingly cynical as a result of poor experiences with other companies offering the same type of service. When this occurs, two things can happen. (1) If you insist that your employees adhere so strictly to policy that customers are not allowed to "feel" they have won, you will lose 100 percent of those cynical customers. (2) If you have instilled in your employees the "let the customers feel they have won" philosophy, you will retain (and actually build) the loyalty of these customers.

- Clear communication with customers is essential to problem resolution at the point of encounter or purchase. Your employees must be able to tell customers precisely what they need and want to know or do. This is especially critical when you're involved in a promotional offer. After all, that is why the new customer has come to you in the first place. Make sure that everyone who has customer contact responsibility and their supervisors are thoroughly knowledgable about all aspects of the promotion. If necessary, provide written communiqués and training videos. Augment these with in-person training sessions, and do so in a timely manner. Never start a promotion before all employees have received complete information and thorough instructions. And always provide a central resource for clarification, should questions arise.

- Organize your procedures to reduce the time it takes to purchase your service offering. The number one peeve of today's consumer of services is "standing in line." You must review and then revise your procedures to eliminate or at least shorten the time spent waiting in line. If the nature of your service precludes total elimination of waiting time, develop alternative plans to "fill the time." This can be in the form of a customer service representative who pre-processes the customers or socializes with them. A video entertainment or informational display will distract the customer and fill the waiting time.

- Undo what the customer has done to himself or herself. When customers discover that they are in the wrong, always avoid embarrassing them. The employee must be polite, empathetic, and tactful so that your customers "save face."

- Never use business jargon that is unfamiliar to your customer. You cannot assume that even those who are in other hospitality-related businesses use the same terminology as you.

- Trade-off time management is essential in personal contact situations. Each point of encounter must be analyzed and a determination made as to whether the strategy should be to go for "optimum speed" or special "personal attention."

- Employee job performance criteria for all those in point-of-encounter positions, be they face to face or over the phone, should clearly focus on execution of service with efficiency and politeness. This is what it's all about, and point-of-encounter employees must know that performing their job properly is what they are being paid for!

- Reduce time where service is expected to be fast. Fast and efficient service leads to satisfaction, especially today. In essence, cynical consumers' negative conditioning has led them to expect long lines and slow, inefficient service. Beat that expectation! Provide faster service and you will convert the cynical consumer into one who is more than satisfied.

- Sincere appreciation should be expressed at virtually all points of encounter, not just at the time of purchase. This must be instilled in every point-of-encounter employee. This will ensure reinforcement of the perception that the customer is truly valued.

What follows is a recap of these customer service strategies and tactics.

Strategies and Tactics for Customer Service Success

Expectations must be met.
Never blame the customer.
Clear communication is essential.
Organize to reduce time.
Undo what the customer has done to himself/herself.
Never use unfamiliar business jargon.

Trade-off time management is essential.

Employee performance criteria should focus on efficiency and politeness.

Reduce service time.

Sincere appreciation should be expressed.

WINNING CHARACTERISTICS

There are numerous ways to let your customers win and to win their loyalty. Successful enterprises have "point of encounter" plans and policies in place and widely communicated. These are also the firms that demonstrate lower cost of sales (expenses), higher repeat customer levels, and customer brand loyalty.

Having studied numerous successful companies and award winners at customer service, a number of common characteristics emerge. Here is an encapsulated list of those winning characteristics:

- Leadership
- Formalized process or plan
- Focus on understanding customer needs
- Customer and employee feedback systems
- Responding with action on feedback
- Sales and service synergy
- Customer-retention motivational and promotional programs
- Reading the marketplace and competition and responding appropriately
- Practicing innovation through research and development and through suggestion implementation
- Prominent recognition of the importance of point-of-encounter employees and giving them full support

CUSTOMER SERVICE AND QUALITY STRATEGIES

Customer service strategies and tactics may vary for different types of customers or be tailored based on the developmental stage of the customer (see Figure 9–1). There are hundreds of customer service tactics and ideas for every customer stage and for different sizes and types of product/service businesses. The keys to customer service being successful as a marketing weapon can be summarized as follows: (1) know what stage of development your customer has achieved, (2) recognize the points of encounter, (3) have a plan for customer service success, (4) empower your point-of-encounter employees with an armada of "let the customer win" tactics, (5) have a check system to see that customer service policies are being adhered to, and (6) make sure your employees' evaluations and, where possible, compensation are directly tied to your CSI.

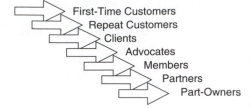

Figure 9–1 Customer Development Stages
Source: R. Nykiel, *The Art of Marketing Strategy* (New York: Amarcor, 2001):146.

Even if an organization doesn't select quality leadership as its positioning, virtually all hospitality industry firms have quality strategies. It is the nature of an industry in the services sector to focus on quality in one manner or another. It is commonplace to find hospitality organizations that have goals to consistently meet or exceed customer expectations by providing services at prices that create value for the customer and profit for the company. This is true for Four Seasons Hotels and Resorts as well as for Motel 6. In the hospitality industry, quality is a moving target and like value may fluctuate in definition with changing customer expectations. So where does management begin to find benchmarks for quality and specific objectives to strive to achieve? Historically, three benchmarks or paths to follow have been delineated. These include: the concept of TQM or total quality management, the concept of CQI or continuous quality improvement, and the criteria specified by the Malcolm Baldrige National Quality Award program.

Total Quality Management

Most TQM programs are based on Deming's 14 points. TQM is based on the overall premise that every area of the enterprise focuses on a total organization concept designed to deliver quality. Figure 9–2 recaps Deming's 14 points.

Continuous Quality Improvement

The concept of CQI originated with Joseph Juran, who suggested the quality of a product or service is determined by its fitness for use by external and internal customers. Juran focused on common language, process itself, and external and internal customers. It was from this philosophy that the hospitality industry concept of treating your employees as your internal customers evolved. The idea is that if management treats employees as customers, employees will treat customers better. The common denominator is that the process must produce value for the customer. According to Juran, quality equals product/service features free from production or delivery defects. This relationship yields the defect ratio, which is frequency of defects divided by opportunity for defects. The lower the defect ratio, the higher the quality rating.[1] By striving to lower the defect ratio CQI is reinforced. CQI leads to breakthrough performances and quality efforts become an integral part of an organization's business plan.

- Create constancy of purpose.
- Adopt the new philosophy.
- Cease dependence on inspection to achieve quality.
- End the practice of awarding business on the basis of price tag.
- Improve constantly and forever the system of production and service.
- Remove barriers that rob employees of pride and workmanship.
- Institute a vigorous program of education and self-improvement.
- Put everybody in the company to work to accomplish the transformation.
- Institute job training.
- Institute leadership.
- Break down barriers between departments.
- Drive out fear.
- Eliminate slogans.
- Eliminate work standards (quotas).

Figure 9–2 Deming's 14 Points of TQM
Source: W. Edwards Deming, *Out of the Crisis* (Cambridge, MA: MIT Press, 1982):
23–24. © 1982 by The MIT Press.

CQI is best delineated by the concept of continuously trying to deliver incremental improvement by enhancing or streamlining the current work process (thus, continuous quality improvement). CQI enforces the concept that striving for improvement will lead to a "breakthrough" or redesign of the work process/delivery of service, which results in unprecedented levels of quality, speed, and savings. The CQI process focuses on the following four steps:

1. Target opportunities.
2. Analyze opportunities.
3. Develop implementation plans.
4. Evaluate the implementation plans.

A fifth unwritten step is to begin again, thus making the process continuous.

The overall CQI process is aimed at improvement in the use and mix of resources. Focal points for resource improvements include organizational concepts, physical facilities, technological systems, workplace and traffic flow design, and training systems. The ultimate goal remains customer satisfaction and retention. CQI recognizes the costs of dissatisfaction including termination costs, recruitment and selection costs, and the cost of "bad press."

TQM and CQI have like goals in seeking to ensure quality service. Both recognize the importance of points of encounter with the customer.

Quality service remains a moving target in the hospitality industry. Quality service is measured by the customer's perception, which changes due to external and internal environmental and competitive influences. Irrespective of the change, at a point in time called the consumption point, quality service is service that meets or exceeds the customer's expectations.

- Customer input
- Competitive analysis
- Empowerment
- Service recovery process

- Brainstorming
- Multi-voting
- Priority determination charts
- Selection matrixes
- Weighted selection matrixes

- Flow charts
- Cause-and-effect diagrams
- Fact-finding planning sheets
- Check sheets
- Bar charts, pie charts, and line graphs

Figure 9–3   CQI Tools and Techniques

High-performance companies in the hospitality industry use components of TQM and CQI to establish guidelines and benchmarks for achieving customer satisfaction and quality service. High-performance companies provide their employees with the skills and information required to do the job of satisfying customers. The entire organization participates in delivery of quality service to reach the point of partnership (see the hierarchy of customer development in Figure 9–1). Finally, compensation, security, and the work environment are all linked to success in the high-performance company. An example of reaching the partnership level (co-owner) comes from American Express. American Express's chairman recently stated that by and large, over 90 percent of the company's product/service improvements have been the direct result of customer suggestions. A high-performance company also listens and acts.

Over the years many different techniques and tools have been developed to apply in a CQI process. Figure 9–3 lists some of the more widely applied tools and techniques for a CQI process.

Empowerment

Perhaps the one tool we hear the most about in today's hospitality industry is the concept of empowerment. Empowerment can be defined as the redistribution of power enabling employees to perform their jobs more efficiently and effectively. Empowerment's goal is to enhance service to the customer/guest by addressing the concern immediately. In the services sector, this process is referred to as "service recovery" or anticipating and handling service problems or failures.[2] Many organizations in the casino/gaming sector and lodging sector have successfully implemented empowerment strategies due to excellent training and specific guidelines for all involved. The concept of empowerment had its origins in the telecommunications industry when AT&T gave notoriety to the concept of "inverted pyramid" organizations (see Figure 9–4). In essence the inverted pyramid places the end-user or customer uppermost in the organizational structure. Next are direct service employees, followed by

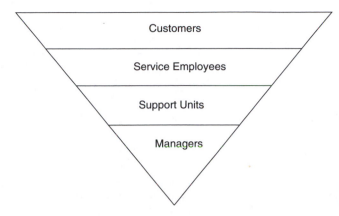

Figure 9–4 The Inverted Pyramid Organization

those who support them, until the bottom of the pyramid is reached where management resides.

Malcolm Baldrige Award

In 1987, the National Quality Improvement Act was established and with it the Malcolm Baldrige National Quality Award. The Baldrige Award established standards of excellence for U.S. businesses with the goal to make the United States more competitive in the global marketplace. The three specific and important roles in strengthening U.S. competitiveness were:

- Improve performance and capabilities
- Facilitate communication/sharing of best-practice information among and within organizations
- Serve as a working tool for managing performance, planning, training, and assessment

As conceived, the Malcolm Baldrige Award would be awarded to six firms each year—two from the manufacturing industry, two from the service industry, and two from the small business arena. To earn the award required outstanding performance in meeting the criteria of enhancing competitiveness with a focus on the delivery of ever-improving value to customers, resulting in marketplace success and the improvement of overall company performance and capabilities. The Baldrige Award application categories include: leadership, information and analysis, strategic planning, human resource development and management, process management, business results, and customer focus and satisfaction. In addition to having to be the best in these categories, the Baldrige Award criteria include "core values and concepts" such as: customer-driven quality, leadership, continuous improvement and learning, employee participation and development, fast response, design quality and prevention, a long range view of the future, management by fact,

Table 9–1 Sample Baldrige Award Point Structure

Category	Point Value
Leadership	90
Information and Analysis	75
Strategic Planning	55
HR Development and Management	140
Process Management	140
Business Results	250
Customer Focus/Satisfaction	250
Total Points	1,000

Source: National Institute of Standards and Technology, "Malcolm Baldrige National Quality Award 1995 Award Criteria" (Gaithersburg, MD: NIST, 1995).

partnership development, corporate responsibility and citizenship, and a results orientation.[3] While all of these core values and concepts are assessed, point values are attached to the award criteria. Table 9–1 provides a sample of the award criteria and point structure.

Over the years of competition, many outstanding firms in the services industry have won the Malcolm Baldrige Award. In the hospitality industry The Ritz-Carlton has won the prestigious award on multiple occasions. The Ritz-Carlton utilizes a variation of the concept of the inverted pyramid called The Ritz-Carlton Interactive Team Pyramid.

DIRECTIONS AND TRENDS

Technology is playing an increasingly significant role in the delivery of customer service and quality experiences in the hospitality industry. Technology that improves value and increases the speed of the transaction is likely to have great impact on customer satisfaction. Management that seeks out such technology and that is in the forefront of implementing the technology will be leading the successful service industry firms of the future. Handheld check-in/check-out devices, scanners, security recognition systems, virtually every form of reliable automated processes will create new benchmarks for delivery time, accuracy, and speed. Customers will demand quality service and value including speed and connectivity in their definition of customer satisfaction. Managerial leadership will invest, train, and implement to succeed. The process will be continuous as the customer redefines expectations due to new technologies, changing needs, and competitive moves in the marketplace. We will take a closer look at technology later in the text.

CHAPTER REVIEW

The hospitality industry is service oriented by nature and as such focuses on customer satisfaction and quality service. Management strategies need to be in place throughout the organization from the points of encounter with the customer to the strategic plan. Fortunately, due to concepts such as TQM, CQI, and the Malcolm Baldrige Award, excellent guides and models are available by which to develop a plan for success. High-performance companies not only develop a plan, they integrate the total organization, reward systems, and measurements for success into the customer satisfaction and quality service undertakings. Management strategies require not only planning but also leadership involvement throughout the process. Management strategies seek customer input and act upon those suggestions by moving the customer through the hierarchy to partnership and ultimately to co-ownership of the process. Utilization of technology to achieve customer satisfaction, improve service recovery, and provide the highest levels of quality service will result in sector leadership in the hospitality industry. Below you will find a customer service checklist for management strategies.

Customer Service Checklist

- Is there a customer service plan/strategy in place?
- Is it adequately supported with both human and financial resources?
- Are you doing everything possible to thoroughly train and support your point-of-encounter employees?
- Do you have an empowerment policy and do all point-of-encounter personnel understand it?
- Is there a customer and (point-of-encounter) employee feedback system?
- Do all your points of encounter (human, vocal, and electronic) represent the image and positioning of your company appropriately?
- Are you performing customer perception audits either internally or with "shopper services"?
- Is customer satisfaction measurement an integral part of your employee evaluation and reward systems?
- Are your recruiting guidelines appropriate for each of your point-of-encounter positions? Is your level of compensation appropriate?
- Is customer service viewed as a marketing weapon of the highest value?
- Do you have recognition programs in place for point-of-encounter employees who provide extraordinary service?
- Is the leadership of your organization actively involved as a champion of customer service excellence?
- Is this message clearly communicated throughout the organization?

KEY CONCEPTS/TERMS

Connectivity

CQI (continuous quality improvement)

CSI (customer satisfaction index)

Empowerment

Expectations

Point of encounter   TQM (total quality management)
Prioritization

DISCUSSION QUESTIONS

1. Why do you think so many hospitality industry companies have stated customer satisfaction is their top goal/management strategy?

2. What points of encounter do you believe are the most critical for a hospitality company in the foodservice sector? Why?

3. Why is it important to move customers through the hierarchy to the point that they become "part owner"? How would you do this in the lodging sector?

4. What do you perceive to be the critical differences between CQI and TQM?

5. Since speed has to be factored into the customer satisfaction equation, list five steps you might suggest a hospitality business take to improve in this area?

6. List three ways a hospitality firm might improve its connectivity.

ENDNOTES

1. R. Woods & J. King, *Quality Leadership and Management* (East Lansing, MI: Educational Institute of the American Hotel and Motel Association, 1996): 39.
2. Ibid., 104.
3. Material adapted from the Malcolm Baldrige National Quality Award 1995 Award Criteria, National Institute of Standards and Technology, Gaithersburg, MD.

CASE 1

Southwest Airlines—The Customer's Airline*

Southwest Airlines could be used as a case study under strategy selection and positioning, branding strategies, marketing strategies, communications strategies, and organizational and operating concepts. However, the more one studies Southwest Airlines the more one must admire their customer service and quality strategies. Quality strategies? Yes, if we recognize quality as a collection of attributes which when present in a product indicate that the product has conformed to or exceeded customer expectations. Southwest Airlines would have to be recognized as the long-term very best. A detailed review of the history, milestones, accomplishments, recognitions, and philosophies of Southwest Airlines provides a case of the best in customer service and quality leadership.

Thirty years ago, Southwest Airlines put itself on the map with low fares, direct flights between three Texas cities, and attractive attendants. Today, the company still offers below-the-belt prices and has expanded its direct service to 58 cities in 30 states. During the past years, Southwest has remained profitable in the face of oil crises, wars, and recessions. And while many major airlines scaled back their schedules following the September 11, 2001, terrorist attacks, Southwest continued at full operation and was the only air carrier to post a profit (for the 29th consecutive year) in one of the most challenging operating environments the air travel industry has ever faced. In 2001, Southwest Airlines also increased its domestic market share, made enhancements to improve its customer service, and ended the year with increased employees and aircraft. The purpose of this case study is to point out what strategies Southwest Airlines has utilized to become and remain so successful.

Milestones

Southwest Airlines began service in 1971 with flights between Houston, Dallas, and San Antonio. Today, it has become the fourth largest airline in America. It operates more than 2,700 flights a day and has more than 33,000 employees throughout the system.

The following years marked the successful steps of Southwest Airlines:

1971	Southwest Airlines takes off on its maiden voyage.
1977	Southwest stock is listed on the New York Stock Exchange as "LUV."
1987	Southwest celebrates the sixth year in a row as holder of the best customer satisfaction record of any continental U.S. carrier.

*Information derived from www.southwest.com, www.iflyswa.com/about_swa/press/factsheet.html (updated June 19, 2001), and www.iflyswa.com/about_swa/financials/investor_relations_index.html.

1988	Southwest is the first airline to win the coveted Triple Crown for a month for "Best On-time Record," "Best Baggage Handling," and "Fewest Customer Complaints."
1989	Southwest announces the billion-dollar revenue mark and becomes a "major" airline!
1994	Southwest introduces Ticketless.
1992–1996	Southwest wins five consecutive annual Triple Crowns.

Awards and Recognitions

- Southwest has ranked number one in "Fewest Customer Complaints" for the last 11 consecutive years, as published in the Department of Transportation's "Air Travel Consumer Report."

- *Fortune* has consistently recognized Southwest Airlines in its annual survey of corporate reputations. Southwest came out on top as the "Most Admired Airline" in the world for 1997, 1998, 1999, and 2000. Among all industries, *Fortune* has listed Southwest as one of the most admired companies in the world, year after year.

- The April 2001 issue of *Fortune* placed Southwest in the list of "50 Most Coveted Employers" voted by MBA students.

- In April 2001, the National Airline Quality Rating (AQR) ranked Southwest Airlines number three among the top ten airlines for performance in 2000. The AQR system uses weighted averages and monthly performance data in the areas of on-time performance, baggage handling, involuntary denied boarding, and a combination of 11 customer complaint categories, all according to DOT statistics.

- Southwest Airlines has been named a charter member of the International Airline Passengers Association's Honor Roll of Airlines among the "World's Safest Airlines." It has also been recognized as one of the "World's Safest Airlines" by *Condé Nast Traveler*.

- In May 2001, *The Wall Street Journal* reported that Southwest had ranked first among airlines for "Highest Customer Service Satisfaction."

- Since 1997, *Fortune* has ranked Southwest Airlines in the "Top Five Best Companies to Work For in America."

- Southwest's Rapid Rewards program placed first in *Inside Flyer* magazine's 2001 annual Freddie Awards in the "Best Bonus Promotion" and "Best Award Redemption" categories. Southwest also placed second in the "Program of the Year," "Best Customer Service," and "Best Web Site" categories.

- Southwest Airlines has been named in the *Forbes* Platinum 400, "America's Best Big Companies."

- In December 2001, Satmetrix Systems named Southwest Airlines the winner of the "Best Customer Satisfaction Award for the Transportation Industry."

- *Business Ethics* lists Southwest Airlines in its "100 Best Corporate Citizens," a list that ranks public companies based on their corporate service to various stakeholder groups.

- Southwest Airlines was listed by *Hispanic* magazine in the 2000 and 2001 Hispanic Corporate 100 for leadership in providing opportunities for Hispanics and for supporting recruitment, scholarships, and minority vendor programs.

- The Secretary of Defense presented the Employer Support of the Guard and Reserve "2001 Employer Support Freedom Award" to Southwest Airlines.

- In 2001, First Lady Laura Bush sent Southwest a personal recognition letter celebrating the company's success with the Adopt-A-Pilot program. Since its inception in 1997, the program has reached more than 25,000 students.

Key Points to Southwest's Success

Southwest has been called America's most successful airline, dramatically outperforming its competitors. It is the industry's most consistently profitable carrier, with a record the envy of its peers. Following are some of the reasons for Southwest's success.

Lower Fare. Boasting the lowest costs among the major airlines, Southwest can profitably offer low fares where others can't.

Simplification. Southwest operates on a point-to-point basis instead of using a hub-and-spoke system. Its planes may land at every point along a journey, which means that the company can schedule flights for maximum utility. In addition, Southwest only uses one type of aircraft—Boeing 737, which considerably simplifies maintenance, spare parts purchase, crew training, and operations.

Efficiency. Southwest boasts some impressive statistics. Its worker-to-customer ratio is the lowest in the industry. Southwest's ground crews take 20 minutes to turn an airplane around for its next flight—half the industry average.

New Technology. In January 1994, Southwest introduced a ticketless travel option, eliminating the need to print a paper ticket. Southwest also entered into an arrangement with Sabre, which was to provide ticketing and automated booking on Southwest's website in a cost-effective manner. In 2002, due to security requirements, Southwest introduced a new computer-generated boarding pass system.

Convenience. Southwest serves many conveniently located satellite or downtown airports, which are typically less congested than other airlines' hub airports. By so doing, Southwest provides greater convenience to passengers, has lower operating fees, and doesn't get backed up with airplane traffic on the ground that slows its quick turn-around operation style.

Focus on Customers. Cheap doesn't have to mean crummy. Sure, there are no hot meals or fancy airport clubs. But Southwest's customer service is legendary. According to the "Air Travel Consumer Report" issued by the Department of Transportation in April 2002, Southwest ranked number one in on-time performance for the last 15 years. Southwest also has the lowest passenger complaint rate—0.47. These outstanding performances provide customers a reliable and comfortable flight experience.

Employee Relationship. Southwest treats its employees as well as its customers. Southwest Airlines has been listed among the top five of *Fortune's* "100 Best Companies to Work For in America" from 1997 to 2000. Although 85 percent unionized, the airline has had only one 8-hour strike in its history while other major carriers have been beset by labor strife for the past several years.

Customer Service at Southwest Airlines

The mission statement of Southwest Airlines is "Dedication to the highest quality of Customer Service delivered with a sense of warmth, friendliness, individual pride and Company Spirit." This mission statement answers the question of why a company focusing on low price and no-frills services has been acclaimed as one of the biggest success legends in American history. As Colleen Barrett, Southwest's COO, stated so succinctly, "Southwest Airlines is not an airline with great customer service. (It is) a great customer service organization that happens to be in the airline business."

In 1971, Southwest Airlines came into being as a little three-jet upstart. Ever since then, service has been recognized as one of the core values it offers its customers. Today, Southwest has become a leader in customer service in the airline industry. Its achievements cover all aspects of service an air travel company provides. Basically, they fall into the following categories:

Safety. Safety has been a number one priority for Southwest Airlines. As a matter of fact, Southwest is the only major airline that has not had any serious accidents as of 2003.

On-Time Performance. According to statistics gathered and published by the Department of Transportation, Southwest has maintained one of the best cumulative on-time performance and flight schedule reliability records in the U.S. airline industry. The company enjoys a legendary turnaround time of 20 to 30 minutes, which allows it to use about 35 fewer aircraft than airlines with an industry-average turnaround time. More amazingly, this is achieved with sometimes half the staff of its average competition.

When delays or cancellations do occur and overnight accommodations are needed for passengers, Southwest is among the few airline companies that address this problem in both its Customer Service Plan and Contract of Carriage agreement clearly and consistently. Southwest provides accommodations to passengers if the delay or cancellation was under the airline's control and the passenger missed the last possible flight or connection of the day to his/her destination.

Baggage Handling. Southwest allows each passenger to check up to three pieces of luggage, which is one more than most other major airlines. The company has also maintained one of the best baggage-handling records in the industry.

Customer Complaints. Southwest Airlines has ranked number one in fewest customer complaints for the past 8 consecutive years as published in DOT's "Air Travel Consumer Report." Correspondingly, the company enjoys the highest customer satisfaction rate. In 2001, it won the Satmetrix "Best Customer Satisfaction Award for the Transportation Industry" with a Customer Loyalty Index score of 8.63, compared with the industry score of 7.79.

Of course, nothing is perfect. Customers do have complaints about Southwest Airlines. The company has a set of valid and effective practices for dealing with customer complaints. A company representative answers each complaint letter personally, and each issue is addressed carefully. If the letter requires an investigation or report, a postcard will be sent to the customer acknowledging the receipt of the letter and notifying him or her how long the investigation should take.

The customer relations department logs and tracks all customer complaints to make sure every issue is addressed properly and timely. The department also prepares monthly reports monitoring trends in customer complaints. Leadership of the company sometimes adjusts customer service policies according to the trends they see.

Warm, Friendly, and Personal Services Sprinkled with Humor. Superb quality of service may sound incongruous with Southwest's no-frills, no-reserved-seating, and no-meals approach to air travel. Yet Southwest's employees have accomplished the miracle by instilling a lot of warmth, friendliness, laughs, and personal attention into whatever simple service they are rendering to the customer.

Southwest's customers constantly write letters to the corporate office praising agents with whom they have developed a friendship just from talking on the phone. In more than one case, reservations agents have met customers at their destination city and driven them to the hospital for medical treatment. One young employee even flew his own private plane to get someone to a hospital in time for a transplant. It is not unusual for an employee to use his or her own car to drive customers 4 or 5 hours to a destination after a scheduling mix-up. Humorous touches in customer service represent yet another famous Southwest way of business that separates the company from its competition. This humorous approach to service helps ease the tension brought on by a long flight and lengthy time in a confined space. It also heightens employees' productivity so they will provide warmer and friendlier services to customers. The company encourages camaraderie between employees and customers. Southwest Airlines has built a reputation as "The airline that loves the customer." The company adopted LUV as its stock exchange symbol to represent not only its home airport—Dallas Love Field—but also the theme of its employee/customer relationship.

Online Reservations. Southwest was among the first airlines to enable online ticket reservation. Now its website is playing an essential role in furthering the low-cost and happy-customer company mission. In 2000, Southwest.com generated 31 percent of the company's passenger revenues, or $1.7 billion. Booking a ticket on Southwest's website is an easy and straightforward process. Since March 2001, the site has also provided rental car and hotel reservations, which allowed Southwest to decide against partnering with other major airlines to form Orbitz. The concern of the company was that it wouldn't be able to control the quality of service a Southwest customer would get from the jointly owned but separately managed travel intermediary.

Innovations in Customer Service. Southwest Airlines has long been acknowledged as one of the most innovative airline companies. It pioneered some practices that are now adopted by other airline companies. For example, Southwest was the first to implement a frequent flyer program that gives credit for the number of trips taken instead of miles flown. In 1974, it began the first profit-sharing plan in the U.S. airline industry. It is also the creator of many unique programs such as senior discounts, Fun Fares, Fun Packs, same-day air freight delivery service, ticketless travel, and so on.

As Southwest has become a customer service star, other companies try to imitate its style. They are seldom successful. Herb Kelleher, the company's cofounder, often said, "It's the intangibles that make the difference at Southwest." Nobody can copy Southwest's success story if they don't understand what the intangibles are. The intangibles of Southwest Airlines are its happy, productive, and creative employees. It is the relentless emphasis the company puts on internal customer service that has made Southwest what it is today.

Internal Customer Service

Internal customer service refers to service directed to the internal customers, or employees, of an organization. It is the level of responsiveness, quality, communication, teamwork, and morale that help the organization succeed. As a company where employees love coming to work, Southwest has created a business strategy that focuses on its internal customers, the employees. Refer to its "inverted pyramid" structure in Figure 1. Following are areas where this strategy is borne out.

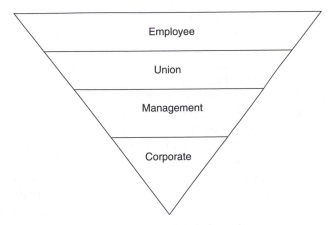

Figure 1   Southwest's Corporate Organization

Caring about the People   Managers at Southwest encourage the "can do" and "let's try" attitude. Employees are encouraged to generate ideas and try them. Internal competition is also encouraged. Competition at Southwest exists in a friendly and motivating way. For example, departments shower each other with ice cream, pizza, or other goodies as tokens of customer devotion. Southwest also accepts failure as a natural and forgivable occurrence. Among the rules it teaches its employees are "Walk a mile in someone else's shoes," "Take accountability and ownership," and "Celebrate your mistakes as well as your triumphs."

As a part of the recruitment process, a "people department" sign welcomes applicants into cheerful surroundings. A popcorn machine is available to staff and applicants—Southwest's "hire for attitude, train for skill" philosophy manifests itself in every aspect of the physical surroundings and operations.

Recruitment and Training   Southwest's primary focus is on its employees. The company has the lowest turnover rate in the airline industry and its employees are hardworking and dedicated. How does Southwest recruit employees? It is through the company's human resources department called the "people department." The recruiting process begins with advertisement in business publications, job fairs, and online promotions. Because of the large number of applicants, the department uses a computer program that matches applicants suitable for the jobs offered. The department chooses people based mainly on their attitudes. Even though Southwest wants its employees to be business oriented, it is not looking for a typical business-oriented person. People who are not afraid to laugh and let their personalities shine are more likely to be recruited. On some occasions, resumes were sent to Southwest in cereal boxes, and people appeared for interviews in gorilla costumes.

The type of interview that an applicant may go through depends on the position he or she is applying for. Basically the company uses a group interview first, which begins with the question, "Tell me how you have used humor to defuse a difficult situation?" Then a paper interview is used. Once the applicant has survived the interview and become an employee, he or she soon realizes that Southwest puts a strong emphasis on continuous learning, training, and cross-training.

Southwest's University of People trains 25,000 people a year. New employees undergo a standardized training session. In addition, every year supervisors, managers, and executives have to undergo a two-day training at the company's headquarters in Dallas, which includes the frontline leadership program for supervisors, the "Leading with Integrity" program for managers, and the "Customer-Care" training program for flight attendants, pilots, and others.

Southwest uses training as an important motivational tool. Employees are re-familiarized with the company's culture, mission statement, and corporate identity. Training prevents mistakes, and employees tend to be more involved in the company and more motivated. Regular training for all ranks of employees also tends to decrease hierarchical thinking.

Communication Good internal customer service depends on good communication. It is a policy at Southwest that every quarter, senior executives must spend one day working in field offices experiencing and seeing firsthand customer service and employment-related issues.

Southwest Airlines uses face-to-face communication whenever possible and always on a first-name basis. This informality helps employees build open and direct relationships and make decisions more quickly. Southwest's people communicate information through *LUV Lines,* an employee newsletter. Every issue of *LUV Lines* carries a segment called "Industry News," which keeps employees informed of what other carriers are doing. Every major event in the company, whether it's the opening of a new location or acquisition of another airline, is announced first to employees and then publicly. Southwest's financial results and performance measures are open to any employees. Southwest believes that when employees have immediate access to critical information, they can make the necessary adjustments to fix significant problems.

According to Southwest's corporate philosophy, bureaucracy exhausts the entrepreneurial spirit, slows the organization down, and constrains its competitive position. Southwest's leanness gives control, ownership, and responsibility to those who are closest to the action. Because of its leanness and informality, Southwest has an atmosphere that fosters active and personal involvement on the part of its managers. The company tries to avoid formal communication channels. Such channels foster communication that is distant and cold. Southwest trusts its employees and gives them the latitude, discretion, and authority they need to do their jobs. Southwest's corporate philosophy of employees first has helped to create a successful and enjoyable communication environment.

Building Employee Relationships Good employee relationships characterize Southwest's organizational culture. Southwest's employees think of the company as a family, feeling personally involved, responsible, and motivated. Southwest is described as a decentralized company with simultaneous loose/tight properties and strong leadership.

A large sign in the main lobby of the home office displays a message by Herb Kelleher: "The people of Southwest Airlines are the creators of what we have become—and what we will be." In Southwest's corporate headquarters, photographs of employees, their families, and even their pets cover hallway walls.

There are two tools applied by Southwest Airlines to build employee relationships. One is creating a good work environment and the other is job security.

Southwest believes that treating employees like family will foster the kind of intimacy that builds strong relationships and makes work fun. The company encourages employees to take their jobs and the competition seriously. On the other hand, it creates an environment where play, humor, creativity, and laughter flourish.

Southwest Airlines is recognized for providing the greatest job security for employees in the airline industry. Although the company does not have a formal no-layoff policy, it has never laid off any employees, in spite of the cyclical nature of the industry. The turnover rate is also low. Instead of pursuing short-term profits, Southwest focuses on the match of employees' and the company's longer-term interests. In order to avoid layoffs, the company hires very sparingly. In 2001, Southwest reviewed 194,821 resumes and hired 6,406 new employees. The strict recruiting procedures and the commitment to job security has helped the company keep the labor force smaller and more productive than their competitors.

The other factor to keep employees at the job is allowing them to feel liberated when they come to work. To foster problem solving and cooperation, Southwest has a "Walk a Mile" program, in which any employee can do somebody else's job for a day. This program helps employees better understand each other's jobs. About 75 percent of 20,000 employees have participated in this program. In 2000, Southwest Airlines was included in *Fortune's* list of the "100 Best Companies to Work For in America," which particularly praised the company's culture, high rate of internal promotions, and job security.

Establishing a Unique Culture   Southwest Airlines has a strong reputation as an employee-centered company with a nonhierarchical culture. The company spends a lot of energy in maintaining this culture. Starting from hiring, it focuses on looking for those who have a good sense of humor, who are interested in performing as a team, and who take pride in team results instead of personal accomplishments.

The other key to the company's culture is communication. Managers spend a lot of time with employees and communicate with them in a variety of ways. The philosophy of the management is to make employees feel fulfilled and happy, treat them as individuals, and be interested in their personal lives. Distinguished from other airlines, Southwest has a culture that values efficiency, hard work, innovation, and simplicity. Southwest established a culture committee in the early 1990s. The committee's mission is to regularly visit all sectors of the company, promoting the original history and spirit of the airline.

Creating Excellent Benefits for Employees   To support the belief that people take better care of things they own, and that this special care is ultimately passed on to the customer, Southwest created a profit-sharing program and a broad-based stock option plan which allows employees to participate in the financial benefits of an ownership culture. Ownership extends beyond just the profit sharing and is manifested in the priority the company places on employee initiative and responsibility. Southwest is built on the principle that employees are expected to take on an entrepreneurial role in being proactive owners who are cognizant of corporate values and confident enough with their empowerment to participate in decision making and the continuous improvement process. This entrepreneurial spirit provides employees with freedom and responsibility to take effective action and the financial participation through ownership that allows them to benefit from the company's overall performance.

Southwest is the only airline to offer stock ownership without asking for wage concessions. The company provides a profit-sharing plan which is at the core of its benefits program. Almost all of the employees are rewarded with a percentage of the company's profits divided up and allocated by relative salary. Employees are free to choose to increase the amount. Twenty-five percent of an employee's profit sharing goes to the purchase of Southwest's stock. Employees as a whole own more than 13 percent of the company's stock through this plan. The shares held by employees are spread broadly among most of the company's workers.

The unique ownership culture has empowered employees to take on responsibility for maintaining the high performance standards with few complications. Southwest has the most productive workforce in the industry, with 2,400 customers served per employee annually, double its competitors' average. Southwest also has the lowest turnover rate among airlines, with less than 4.5 percent of employees leaving per year.

Southwest's internal culture is what sets it apart from other companies in the industry. Every employee is given the general guidelines of his or her responsibilities and role in the company, then expected and encouraged to go outside those guidelines fearlessly. This is an airline that takes the boredom out of flying and makes it fun again. Southwest takes every chance it gets to be funny and out of the ordinary. It seems the employees of Southwest love the benefits of watching their actions create personal financial rewards through stock ownership.

Conclusion

Over thirty years ago, when Rollin King and Herb Kelleher decided to put together a different kind of airline, the philosophy it was based on was: "If you get your passengers to their destinations when they want to get there, on time, at the lowest possible fares, and make darn sure they have a good time doing it, people will fly your airline."

They have lived up to their commitment. All the strategies that have made Southwest Airlines a huge success were smartly built around this original philosophy. Southwest has been famous for its positioning of low fare, great convenience, and no-frills service. Speed, efficiency, and customer service are the three pillars on which the company has built its value. Southwest has achieved its stellar customer service records through a company culture that puts employees first, cares about people, and makes work fun for everybody. When internal customers are satisfied, so are the external customers. Southwest Airlines is exemplifying this business notion each and every day—not for one year but every year. This is why Southwest Airlines was selected for the case study on customer service and quality.

Case Example Discussion Questions

1. Meeting or exceeding customers' expectations results in customer satisfaction. Name three steps you would take to identify a customer's expectations.

2. Building employee relationships and establishing a company/employee "culture" are important in the services industry. What are some of the things you would expect management to do to help develop good employee relationships and a winning culture?

CASE 2

Hertz Corporation—Continuously Improving Product and Customer Service Delivery*

In this chapter we discussed the concept of CQI (continuous quality improvement). For a hospitality company this means continually improving in the delivery of your product or service offering to the consumer. In this case study we look at how technology has played a role in continually improving the service delivery process and customer experience for Hertz.

Hertz is the world's largest car rental company and one of the largest construction and industrial equipment rental businesses in the United States. In total, Hertz operates from approximately 7,000 locations in the United States and more than 140 countries around the world. Its aim is to provide consistent and seamless service and a high level of quality on a global basis generating a perceived value that distinguishes it from its competitors. This case study provides a synopsis of the company's history and looks at some of the many customer service innovations implemented by Hertz. These innovations required management's commitment of substantial resources and even changing the way Hertz conducted its business.**

The pioneer of auto renting was Walter L. Jacobs who in September 1918, at the age of 22, opened a car rental operation in Chicago. Starting with a dozen Model T Fords, which he repaired and repainted himself, Jacobs expanded his operation to the point where, within 5 years, the business generated annual revenues of about $1 million. In 1923, Jacobs sold his car rental concern to John Hertz, president of Yellow Cab and Yellow Truck and Coach Manufacturing Company. Jacobs continued as Hertz's top operating and administrative executive. In 1932, Hertz opened the first airport car rental location at Chicago's Midway Airport. In 1938, the first Hertz location was opened in Canada. In 1950, the first Hertz European location was opened in France. In 1953, the Hertz properties were bought from GMC by the Omnibus Corporation, which divested itself of its bus interest and concentrated solely on car and truck renting and leasing. A year later, a new name was taken—the Hertz Corporation—and it was listed for the first time on the New York Stock Exchange. Jacobs became Hertz's first president and served in that post until his retirement in 1960. In April 1997, Hertz became a publicly traded company, listed on the New York Stock Exchange under the symbol "HRZ." And in March 2001, Ford reacquired Hertz's outstanding stock, making the company once again a wholly owned subsidiary of Ford. Hertz has been headquartered in Park Ridge, New Jersey, since 1988. Prior to that, the corporation was based in New York and before that, Chicago. Car rentals, the largest and best known

*Information derived from www.hertz.com/myprofile.htm.
**R. Nykiel, *You Can't Lose If the Customer Wins* (Stamford, CT: Longmeadow Press, 1990): 121.

of Hertz's activities, are conducted from approximately 1,900 U.S., corporate, and licensee locations and more than 5,100 corporate and licensee locations outside the United States. Hertz offers a wide variety of current model cars on a short-term rental basis—daily, weekly, or monthly—at airports, in downtown and suburban business centers, and in residential areas and resort locales. Today, Hertz's Worldwide Reservations System handles approximately 40 million phone calls and delivers approximately 30 million reservations annually.

Hertz has scored many "firsts" in the industry. Hertz was the first to move car rental locations out of back-street garages and offer a coast-to-coast network of customer-convenient, attractive car rental locations. The company was the first to make available cars in many sizes, makes, and models—allowing customers to choose vehicles to meet various needs. Another Hertz first in the car rental industry has made it easier for customers to find their destination once they leave the Hertz lot. Introduced in 1984, Computerized Driving Directions (CDD) provides customers with detailed directions to local destinations, including estimated time and distance. Today in the United States, customer-friendly, self-service CDD terminals and kiosks are available at most major Hertz airport and downtown locations and provide printed directions in six languages. CDD directions are also available in Canada, across Europe, and in Australia at major airport and downtown locations. CDD in Europe provides directions in nine languages.

Hertz was a pioneer in fast check-in and check-out with such customer-oriented services as the Hertz Number One Club, which preregisters your rental and lets you go right to the car of your choice. Also, Hertz embraced the handheld computer/printer for quick check-ins at almost all locations—a great service to the time-pressured business customer.

While most of the innovative customer-oriented services were made available to all customers, Hertz also developed an extraordinary, popular service for a select list of VIPs called the "Platinum Service." In this case the senior management of Hertz came up with a most interesting strategy. Hertz management targeted only a few thousand corporate CEOs and senior executives for the "by invitation only" Platinum Service. Platinum Service members are individuals who have the power to make or influence key decisions potentially beneficial to Hertz—decisions such as which rental car company to use on a preferred basis for a corporation's travelers and which rental car company should provide leased vehicles to the corporation. These few thousand Platinum Service members receive extraordinary customer service, which includes a private tollfree phone number, reservationists who know the customers by name as well as their car preference history, automatic upgrades to luxury-class autos (when available) at no charge, and personalized service at many airports subject to security restrictions ("meet and greet" personnel bring the car to you or pick it up where you leave it). Many more services and amenities are offered to the Platinum Service members.

In the late 1990s, Hertz introduced a concept called Hertz Local Editions, offering hundreds of convenient locations. This network of local rental

Figure 1   Hertz's Customer Service

locations offers fast customer pickup and return service. All customers need to do is call and Hertz will come and get them at their home or office. This pickup/return service is available with 1-hour advance notice and is usually provided within 15 minutes.

Many things contribute to great customer service. For the hospitality industry customer, especially frequent travelers, much of what Hertz does on a global basis adds up to great customer service. Figure 1 summarizes Hertz's ongoing quality customer service driven by its management and service delivery innovations.

Case Discussion Questions

1. Convenience has become an essential component of successful customer service in today's marketplace. Select a hospitality business and identify three ways you could make the purchasing process and customer service experience more convenient for the customer.

2. In the Hertz case, technology and innovation were combined to offer seamless service. Select another sector of the hospitality industry and identify where you believe technology will have a great impact and improve customer service/satisfaction in the future.

CASE 3

Gleneagles Country Club—Customer Satisfaction through Creative Marketing*

In this chapter we focused on points of encounter and their relationship to customer satisfaction. One of the most challenging areas within the hospitality industry in terms of customer satisfaction and marketing is dealing with club members and marketing clubs. In the case which follows, we will present a club which excels at both satisfying its customers and using creative strategies in its marketing.

Gleneagles Country Club in Plano, Texas, is one of ClubCorp's holdings, which owns or operates nearly 200 golf courses, country clubs, private business and sports clubs, and resorts internationally. Founded in 1957, Dallas-based ClubCorp has $1.6 billion in assets. Among the company's nationally recognized club properties are Pinehurst Country Club in the village of Pinehurst, North Carolina (the world's largest golf resort, home of the 2005 U.S. Open); Firestone Country Club in Akron, Ohio (site of the 2003 World Golf Championships—NEC Invitational); Indian Wells Country Club in Indian Wells, California (site of the Bob Hope Chrysler Classic); The Homestead in Hot Springs, Virginia (America's first resort, founded in 1766); and Mission Hills Country Club in Rancho Mirage, California (home of the Kraft Nabisco Championship). The more than 50 business clubs and business and sports clubs include the Boston College Club; City Club on Bunker Hill in Los Angeles; Citrus Club in Orlando; Columbia Club in Seattle; Metropolitan Club in Chicago; Tower Club in Dallas; and the City Club of Washington, D.C. The company's 19,000 employees serve the more than 215,000 members and households and 200,000 guests who visit ClubCorp properties each year.

Gleneagles was established in 1985. The clubhouse has a very "clubby" feel with the mahogany walls, 10-foot doors, and huge chandeliers. The membership enjoys socializing together. Parties and events have become traditions. As you walk through the front doors you are immediately welcomed by the tenured Gleneagles staff.

Gleneagles Country Club is comprised of members who are looking for an environment that is professional as well as personal. The club has members who need only a place to dine and enjoy the camaraderie of the other members and those who want to have it all . . . golf, tennis, and fitness.

Gleneagles has two impeccably kept championship golf courses, 18 well-lit tennis courts, and pools to enjoy in the summer. The beautifully appointed clubhouse has been ranked top in the area for many years.

Gleneagles also offers a state-of-the-art fitness center with a full line of Cybex resistance equipment, a Cycle Reebok studio, a group exercise and

*Information derived from www.clubcorp.com.

cardiovascular area, a massage and nutrition center, and a tot room. The fitness center is also the home of the Wimbledon Grill as well as the site for the Gleneagles All Star Junior Tennis Program.

Gleneagles is perhaps best known for its golf course, 36 holes of championship golf designed by the team of Von Hagge and Devlin. Bentgrass greens and water views on the majority of the fairways are course signatures.

Gleneagles cultivates its members' children for the future. The club introduces them to the game of golf and what a privilege it is to belong to a club. Year-round instruction and summer clinics give these girls and boys the opportunity to learn the game. Several juniors have competed at the national level and a few have moved on to the PGA Tour.

Gleneagles also provides a private event specialist for members. The event specialist plans the events and works with the executive chef on the menu planning and event details. The facility is available for a full range of events.

The city of Plano, Texas, has an unusually young population and so does Gleneagles. The majority of the membership is families wanting family programs. Many of these younger families live in the large substantial homes surrounding the golf course. A very affluent group of residents are not only Gleneagles neighbors but also the members. Like most clubs, the membership is demanding, and in the Gleneagles case it is very active. Gleneagles staff must relate to the entire family, from the children to the parents, every day of the week.

Gleneagles believes in the concepts outlined in this chapter. Points of encounter, from the moment the valet parks one's car to the doorman's welcome and the greeting upon passing through the doors by a well-trained greeter, make members feel this is "their" club. Further, flexibility is something the entire staff is taught. Staff is empowered to prepare items to the members' request, even if they are not on the very extensive menu. Staff accommodates the membership in every way possible—taking care of errands, retaining forgotten items, and so on.

Satisfying a range of customers that comprises children and adults is no easy task. Gleneagles offers a very creative and comprehensive calendar of events that meets everyone's needs.

In addition to special events related to golf and tennis, the club offers an extensive list of other daily activities each month to keep members and their families involved. Examples include a wine club, happy hour, "two for one" days, and themed dinner nights such as "southern home-style night," "prime rib night, "Italian night," "Caribbean night," and so on. There are ladies' nights and events and children's entertainment, menus, and events. Each holiday is a special event, and the club is themed for the day. For example, on Easter, the Easter Bunny is there for the children along with a magnificent children's buffet (kids have the option of their own seating area) and, of course, the traditional Easter egg hunt. There is a plethora of summer camps, including a golf camp, tennis camp, and swimming camp. From happy hour to happy children's events, there is always something to please the membership irrespective of age.

All of these activities are well marketed with everything from newsletters, to the monthly calendar mailing, to special invitations. Members are encouraged to make suggestions and are often rewarded with small prizes of appreciation. Many of the themed nights, parties, and activities are the direct result of club members' suggestions.

Gleneagles goes the extra mile for its club members. This point can be best exemplified with this actual holiday experience. At Gleneagles like at most clubs, the Christmas holidays often create demand beyond the capacity of the club. Frequently, all December dates and event space are fully reserved and utilized. Such was the case when a certain newer club member tried to hold a holiday event for his company executives at the club. Most clubs would say they were sorry the dates weren't available and offer to book the event for another time. The events staff member at Gleneagles sensed the new member's disappointment and apparent frustration. She offered an alternative idea to the member. Having visited the member's magnificent home, she felt there was more than adequate space in the home for the event. Naturally, the spouse who was planning the event did not want to be cooking and serving. The Gleneagles staff member offered to provide everything from the setup, to bartenders, to the food, to the chef and servers, to the clean-up crew, and yes, even to arrange for valet parking and holiday plants.

The new member couple were amazed the club would go this extra mile for them and agreed to the idea. The event was an immense success, and the new member and spouse received numerous comments from their guests on how warm and nice it was to have this year's executive gathering at a home versus a club. Exceptional service and going the distance for its membership is one reason for Gleneagles' success and satisfied membership.

Gleneagles demonstrates an in-depth understanding of its target market (families) and how to meet their needs. The club understands marketing and creating activities that drive club members to participate and use the club. Gleneagles understands the community it resides in and how to go the extra mile for its members. Moreover, the well-trained staff knows how to serve its membership. From the multiple points-of-encounter greetings to the "exceptions to the rules," Gleneagles aims for member satisfaction.

Case Discussion Questions

1. Many clubs have rules and limitations. When do you believe rules should be broken and flexibility utilized?
2. Having a full activity schedule/calendar is only an informational or planning tool. What steps do you believe a club should take to market the calendar events?

PART 4

The Functional Strategies of Human Resources, Technology, and Purchasing

Part 4 begins with a comprehensive look into human resource managerial strategies in Chapter 10. Focal points within this chapter include personnel management, organizational behavior, labor relations, and community relations. Concepts covered include managerial strategies for employee acquisition and evaluation. The concept of team management is also presented. Finally, this chapter relates the human resource strategies to overall performance success in the hospitality industry.

In Chapter 11, technology applications are viewed from a managerial strategy perspective. A discussion of the driving forces behind technology applications including the supplementing and/or replacement of human functions is also presented. The role of technology in managerial strategy is presented from multiple perspectives such as competitive advantage, efficiency, information application, and managerial decision-making support. This chapter also points out how information technology is changing the managerial perspective of revenue and customers. The concept of REVPAC (revenue per available customer) is presented and discussed. Systems and related strategies that are delineated include reservation systems, revenue and yield management, inventory allocation systems, facilities management applications, and customer retention systems. Finally, this chapter looks at technology in the near and distant future.

Part 4 closes with Chapter 12, which covers managerial strategies related to purchasing focal points including co-ops, outsourcing, and internet applications, all with the common denominator of cost efficiencies while expediting services.

Chapter 10

Human Resource Management Strategies

CHAPTER OBJECTIVES

- To place human resource management strategies in perspective in the dynamic and global environment of today's hospitality industry
- To identify four major focal points for human resource management strategies in the hospitality industry
- To view contemporary and experimental human resource managerial practices and philosophies taking hold in the industry today
- To discuss the successful characteristics of winning organizations from a human resource managerial perspective
- To look at the concept of human resource management in the future and in the global context

In an industry as labor intensive as the hospitality industry, management strategies related to human resources are extraordinarily important. Managing the human asset has a major impact on everything from customer satisfaction to the bottom line. Management strategies are dynamic in today's human resource area. This ever-changing environment is the product of the industry's cyclical growth, downturns, technology and automation, labor availability, new organizational concepts, acquisitions and mergers, and new approaches to doing business. In managing the human asset there is a cost from the moment the recruitment begins to the final paycheck. These costs include training and other normal ongoing expenses such as salary and benefits. Numerous studies in virtually every segment of the industry have addressed the cost of turnover, which is very significant in most sectors of the hospitality industry where turnover rates can exceed 100 percent in a year.

Managerial strategies in the human resource area need to be flexible, for in any given business cycle the hospitality firm can go from an emphasis on employee acquisition to a focus on layoffs. In growth periods, managerial strategies may focus on the reassignment and development of managers and supervisors, whereas in a period of decline in demand the focus can shift to reducing managerial personnel to new, more efficient means of organization. In any given 10- to 12-year cycle, human resources will likely experience numerous changes in direction, priorities, and roles within the overall management of a hospitality business.

TYPES OF HUMAN RESOURCE MANAGEMENT STRATEGIES

In general, there are four major areas of focus into which most human resource management strategies can be classified, depicted in Figure 10-1.

Personnel Management

In most sectors of the hospitality industry, personnel management frequently focuses on strategy, especially in growing organizations. Acquisition of personnel (recruitment) has traditionally been a high priority for management.

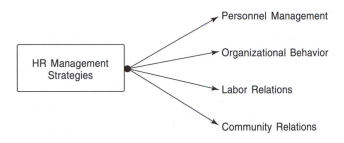

Figure 10–1   Focal Points of Human Resource Management Strategies

Management strategies include: assessing acquisition targets (managers) from key competitors, seeking individuals with desired strengths and skills that may enhance the balance and scope of the overall management team, and seeking to diversify the managerial pool. For the multinational organization, the acquisition of managerial talent with specific experience in a given country or region of the world is an additional focal point. Also, in an industry where the asset may be owned by another entity (i.e., management contract), acquisition of personnel requires seeking those who will also be compatible with the ownership of the asset. Companies may elect to recruit on their own or to outsource the acquisition process through an executive recruitment organization or a combination.

Managerial strategies must also address the development and administration of those who become employees. These activities require performance evaluation processes, promotion and transfer policies/strategy, and training and education. Today, in many sectors and areas of the hospitality business, a managerial strategy often has to be in place to provide for the counseling of employees. In most multinationals, a strategy to address relocation to and from foreign countries (expatriation and cultural assimilation) needs to be in place. In this vital area of development of personnel, many hospitality organizations have frequent meetings to assess the needs of the organization and to seek to fill these needs from within their own ranks. Individuals' performance and development are monitored and tracked against the needs and expectations of the organization. Career movement, including frequent relocation, are all part of the overall managerial development process.

Personnel management strategies must also address compensation and all activities associated with compensation. These include salary guidelines, levels, and ranges; benefits; bonus and incentive plans; stock options; and fringe benefits. Managerial strategy involves seeking to be competitive with or more attractive than key competitors. Management strategy also includes being creative and developing fair and rewarding motivational and performance incentives. In the multinational marketplace, this involves cost-of-living considerations as well as sometimes complex tax considerations. In general, management's focus is on retaining good employees and rewarding performance.

Organizational Behavior

The hospitality industry provides examples of a wide variety of different types of organizational behavior. Strategies for organizational behavior are those that deal with the "climate" of the firm and productive working relationships. Due to the variety of types of businesses and sectors within the hospitality industry, there are many different organizational behavior approaches and models. The models and approaches often change as companies grow, CEOs arrive and depart, and the operating environment changes. One general statement that does apply in the hospitality industry is that it remains a people-oriented business and as such organizational behavior usually has a great impact. Organizational behavior involves not only the climate (feeling) of the work environment but also the structure in which the business conducts itself. Structure includes formal hierarchy, inverted pyramids, team concepts, outsourcing, and philosophical approaches to running the business.[1] In general, nonunionized companies and areas within hospitality firms tend to have greater flexibility in their structure.

At both the corporate level and operational level, the hospitality industry continues to adopt and experiment with many new practices. In some companies "team management" has replaced the traditional hierarchy. In other companies centralization has given way to decentralization under the premise that managerial strategies are best decided upon and implemented in the field or region. And in still other firms, some functions are centralized, such as marketing and purchasing, and others such as operations are decentralized. Smaller companies and those focusing on efficiencies or streamlining elect to outsource select functions as part of their overall management of the business. Areas that have been outsourced include recruitment, benefits and compensation management, human resources, payroll, security, and more. Other organizational behavioral strategies include the concept of employees working out of their homes relying on technology for their communications. As we know, business cycles often create an ebb and flow of various organizational behavior practices.

Labor Relations

Most sectors or functional areas of the hospitality industry have a history of unions or organized labor. Labor relations strategies are the managerial strategies that directly relate to or deal with organized labor. Managerial strategy in this area ranges from an embracement of organized labor or the "we" theory to a conscious strategy to avoid unions. Labor relations tend to receive high visibility in the hospitality industry due to the nature of the travel and hospitality businesses themselves. A strike or labor unrest in the airline sector, for example, has a ripple effect throughout the industry and beyond. The same holds true within a given major market. Successful organizations within the hospitality industry seek to develop good (win/win or give/give) relationships with organized labor if it applies to their operations.

Labor relations managerial strategy also encompasses the concept of "imported" labor in the hospitality industry. In fact, it has been said that the hospitality industry would suffer dramatically if it did not use substantial imported labor. Many, if not most, sectors of the hospitality industry rely on labor from other countries being imported into a variety of jobs within the industry. Given these circumstances, management must have policies and strategies in place to train and deal with this unique labor pool. As the industry continues to globalize, the use of imported labor will continue. How management addresses this issue will ultimately result in healthy or unhealthy labor relations.

Community Relations

The hospitality industry serves the local community, the host country community, and the global community in all its diversity. From a managerial strategy perspective, community relations focus on developing and maturing the relationship with each constituency in the communities. In most cases and sectors of our industry, hospitality organizations aim to have a "partner" or "good citizen" relationship with the communities in which they operate or with which they deal. Examples are abundant, such as: hotels housing local victims of natural disasters; foodservice establishments feeding the hungry on holidays; and numerous community outreach programs and training. Some companies such as Marriott have established schools. McDonald's actually developed the infrastructure within a country to help supply its restaurants. Many have minority development initiatives, such as Cendant. There are few industries that can boost so many positive managerial strategies related to the human and economic resources of the communities (local to global) in which they conduct business.

GOALS OF HUMAN RESOURCE MANAGEMENT STRATEGIES

Acquisition and Retention of Employees

It has been said that the hospitality industry is a people business. In fact, one definition of the industry is "taking care of the needs of people who are away from home." As a people-oriented business, hospitality management strategies focus on and are built around people. The most pressing need of the hospitality industry remains the acquisition and retention of the labor pool. Human resource management strategies that focus to this need include: sign-up and stay-on incentive programs, monetary and other rewards for longevity, and organizational experimentation to assist in both better service and higher job satisfaction. The latter is also a management strategy aimed at achieving greater efficiency.

ETHICS

Being a moral person does not necessarily equate to one becoming a moral manager, and it is not enough to assume that one's employees will observe these qualities based on the limited interaction that occurs between manager and employee. Moral persons must possess distinct traits and exhibit certain behaviors, but moral managers must become visible role models and communicate their ideals about ethics and values openly to all those around them. There is a delicate balance between a moral person and a moral manager.

Efficiencies

A key target of many human resource management strategies can be summarized in one word, efficiencies. Efficiency management strategies include outsourcing, human replacement by automation and technology (see Chapter 11), product and service delivery redesign, elimination of labor, expediting the experience, and customer involvement (self-service). These efficiency-oriented management strategies rise to the top of the strategy implementation priority list if they meet certain criteria: problem resolution, cost and/or time reduction, better customer service, and competitive advantage. The rapid development of new technologies (e.g., wireless applications) is having a major positive impact on these efficiency strategies.

Performance

Managerial strategies with a target of improved performance include succession planning, equity position program development, and employee shared ownership programs (ESOPs). Avis was a pioneer in the hospitality business when it changed its corporate ownership structure to an ESOP. At the time of that transition and for years thereafter, its customer satisfaction indicators went straight up. Performance-driven strategies also include the concept of high-performance teams. These teams involve a variety of structures and can be made up from a variety of functional levels or functions. The team may be at the corporate level (actually running the business or a significant part of the business) or it may be at the unit/field level or departmental level in its makeup. Teams may involve players from corporate management, different functions, and different expertise. Teams may focus on specific tasks such as new openings, CQI, new program implementation, or even overall daily operations. Successful teams have some common characteristics. Figure 10-2 delineates some of these successful characteristics and keys to success for the team strategy approach. Overall management strategy related to successful team concepts usually includes an evaluation/assessment of the outcome and a consensus decision-making process.

Figure 10–2   Successful Characteristics for Team Strategy
Source: R. Woods & J. King, *Quality Leadership and Management in the Hospitality Industry* (East Lansing, MI: Educational Institute of the American Hotels and Motels Association, 1996): 249–250.

MANAGING FOR CHANGE

At the outset of this chapter we emphasized that the hospitality industry is in a dynamic and ever-changing environment, which has a direct bearing on management strategies. Competition, market behavior, technology, and human behavior require strategy reassessment and change. To manage change itself requires a strategic thought process that can involve doing things differently, learning new ideas, and mastering new devices. Change can be either unplanned or planned. Internal forces such as intentional re-engineering, reinvention, a CQI process, or a crisis can drive change. External forces can also cause change, such as technology, the market, competition, the labor market, and an external crisis. In fact, nearly all of the internal and external forces that drive changes in management strategy can be exemplified within the hospitality industry. For example, technology has required hotel rooms to have internet access to meet customers' needs. TWA's and Pan Am's demise was due in part to two crises, financial woes and a fear-driven decrease in demand caused by terrorism. Brands constantly reinvent themselves; for example, in the foodservice sector there are new concepts, menus, and decor.

Every day there are new examples of change-driven strategies emerging in virtually all sectors of the hospitality industry. We see new security steps implemented by the airlines and cruise lines due to external forces. We see self-check-in and self-check-out systems, driven by both the internal force of labor shortages and the external force of new technology. Management's role in dealing with change can take on a number of different strategic perspectives. Senior management may be the sponsor of change, in essence by influencing and motivating its own management to seek to implement change. Here the power is given in the form of empowerment to make changes at the operations levels. Changes may be driven by the board of directors or shareholder pressure, or it could be simply part of a strategic plan. In the first scenario, the board sponsors the change (either allocating resources or changing policies) and management becomes the change agent or entity responsible to implement or execute the directives. Most change directives are aimed at specific targets such as a new organizational structure, a massive "retheming" or refurbishment, or a new brand image.

TECHNOLOGY

Technology has had and will continue to have a dramatic impact on virtually every aspect of human resources. Employee acquisitions (hiring) are aided by resume generation and candidate profiling on line. Automation has helped lower labor costs across the industry. Payroll and benefits management have been improved through analytical software applications. Training in a complex, multicultural global environment has been enhanced through video technology and assessment and feedback systems. Every day new hardware and software help improve productivity, increase knowledge, and disseminate information. Literacy has been redefined in terms of "tech-knows" and "tech-know-nots."

Human resource management strategy is often influenced by economic change: In upturns in the economy or industry cycle, look for the accordion to expand, and in downturns look for it to contract. Human resource management strategies also need to adapt to sociocultural changes and political changes, which usually manifest themselves in new regulations or modified regulations, changes in supplier relations, customer perceptions, technological advances, and competitive activities. For example, consistently losing good employees to a competitor usually sends a signal to examine salary levels and benefits and ultimately to alter these compensation strategies. This is especially true in labor-tight sectors or markets. Human resource management strategies are often complex due to the range of the activities themselves. Not only do externally driven factors cause change, simple changes in internal management can alter the entire corporate philosophy, vision, or climate.

CHAPTER REVIEW

In this chapter the place of human resource management strategies in the hospitality industry was discussed, with a focus on the total environment and the external and internal factors that impact strategy. The four major areas of focus for human resource management strategy were delineated. The first area was personnel management, which includes the acquisition of employees or recruitment, the development of personnel (training), and strategies related to compensation and benefits. The second focal point discussed was organizational behavior, which includes the company/organizational climate, the approaches to structure, and team management strategies, among others. The third area reviewed was labor relations, which involves management strategies related to the desired relationship with unions. And fourthly, community relations strategies encompass both the local community in which the firm resides and the totality of communities (including foreign countries) in which the company operates. Here we stressed the importance of managerial strategies that incorporate the distant communities into the decision process.

We also examined the numerous areas of human resource management where strategy is a dynamic process due to multiple internal and external forces of change taking place. We further looked at the change process itself and its impact on human resource management strategies.

KEY CONCEPTS/TERMS

Automation	Labor importation
Equity positions	Labor relations
ESOPs	Outsourcing
Incentives	Teams

DISCUSSION QUESTIONS

1. Which focal point of human resources do you believe would be the most important in a multinational organization?

2. In the hospitality industry most organizations are very service oriented. How do you foresee automation and technology positively contributing to higher service levels in lieu of labor?

3. How do you feel hospitality executives should be compensated? Suggest a specific mix of incentives you feel would best motivate a global executive.

4. Do you feel the hospitality industry could use more ESOPs or concepts of greater employee ownership? Why?

5. Would you prefer to work in a traditional hierarchy organization, an inverted pyramid organization, or within a team concept during your career in the hospitality industry? Why?

ENDNOTE

1. J. P. Kotter, L. Schlesinger, & V. Sathe, *Organization* (Homewood, IL: Richard D. Irwin, 1986): 7.

CASE 1

Chick-fil-A—The Exception to High Turnover*

In this chapter we stated that organizational behavior involves the "climate" or feeling of the work environment. In the hospitality industry a good climate helps to reduce turnover. And in industry sectors such as food service, this becomes especially important as turnover rates run very high. This is a case study of one company that does an extraordinary job at beating the industry with substantially lower turnover rates.

You know your human resource management strategies are working when your hourly employee turnover rate is 100 percent less than your competitors and the industry sector. You know your human resource managerial strategies are working when many of your new investors come from within the ranks of your own employees. Both of these astonishing facts are true for the fast-food Chick-fil-A chain.

Chick-fil-A Inc. is one of the largest privately held restaurant chains and the third-largest quick-service chicken restaurant chain in the nation, currently with 975 locations in 34 states and South Africa. Chick-fil-A serves nutritious food products in malls, freestanding units, drive-through outlets, Chick-fil-A Dwarf House, and Truett's Grill full-service restaurants, and through licensed outlets in college campuses, hospitals, airports, businesses, and industrial sites. Their mission statement is to be America's best quick-service restaurant and satisfy every customer. Their sales in 2001 reached more than $1 billion. Amazingly, the restaurant chain maintains a "closed-on-Sunday" policy for all types of Chick-fil-A restaurant concepts, in keeping with the Christian faith of the founder and his family.

Chick-fil-A has three simple business rules:

1. **Listen** to the customer.
2. Focus on getting **better** before trying to get bigger.
3. Focus on **quality**.

In national surveys conducted by leading market research firms, Chick-fil-A's core menu products have consistently ranked number one in their respective categories for "product quality."

One unique human resource strategy that contributes to Chick-fil-A's low employee turnover rate is allowing hourly employees to determine their own work schedules (within reason). Other human resource strategies include encouraging employees to grow and reach their potential by providing $1,000

---

*Information derived from www.chick-fil-a.com/Company.asp; S. T. Cathy, *Eat Mor Chickin* (Nashville: Cumberland House, 2002); and S. T. Cathy, *It Is Easier to Succeed than Fail* (Nashville: Thomas Nelson, 1989).

scholarships to all restaurant employees. These scholarships may be used at the college or university of the employee's choice. Chick-fil-A's philanthropic efforts include a children's summer camp program and supporting foster homes.

Chick-fil-A employs multiple managerial strategies that have resulted in an extraordinarily low turnover rate and resultant cost savings and performance enhancements. Its human resource strategy to retain and reward its employees and its flexibility in relating to employee needs have proven a success.

Case Discussion Questions

1. Correlations support the fact that satisfied and motivated employees contribute directly to higher-quality performance and a better customer service experience. Name two or three steps you would take as a manager to improve your employees' satisfaction with their jobs.

2. Do you think it is a bad or good idea to allow hourly employees to determine their own schedules?

CASE 2

The Ritz-Carlton—Great Training and Targeted Recruiting*

Two critical functions of human resources management are effective and ongoing training programs and employee acquisitions (recruitment). How does a company win the prestigious Malcolm Baldrige National Quality Award on multiple occasions? One answer is effective training and sound employee acquisitions. The Ritz-Carlton is the first and only hotel company to win the Malcolm Baldrige Award and the only service industry sector company to win the award multiple times. While The Ritz-Carlton management certainly is driven by the pride of its heritage, training excellence also plays a major role.

History as a Driving Force

The history of The Ritz-Carlton provides the number one driving force of its pride of excellence. The legacy of The Ritz-Carlton Boston begins with the celebrated hotelier César Ritz, the "king of hoteliers to kings." His philosophy of service and innovations redefined the luxury hotel experience in Europe with his management of The Ritz in Paris and The Carlton in London.

César Ritz died in 1918, but his wife Marie continued the expansion of hotels bearing his name. In the United States, The Ritz-Carlton Investing Company was established by Albert Keller who bought and franchised the name. In 1927, Edward N. Wyner, a local Boston real estate developer, was asked by Mayor Curley to build a new hotel. Wyner, who was building an apartment building and was up to the second floor at the time, agreed to change the apartment building into a hotel. Because of the reputation of The Ritz in Europe and the cosmopolitan nature of Boston, Wyner knew The Ritz-Carlton would secure immediate success. He received permission from the Carlton Investing Company and the Paris Ritz for use of the name and set out to create a luxury hotel. The Ritz-Carlton Boston opened on May 19, 1927, with a room rate of $15. Other hotels followed in New York (at Madison and 54th), Philadelphia, Pittsburgh, Atlantic City, and Boca Raton. However, by 1940 none of the hotels were operating except The Ritz-Carlton Boston simply because a wealthy owner was able to maintain its operation.

In the tradition of César Ritz, Wyner was meticulous about maintaining the privacy of his guests, a policy adhered to today in all Ritz-Carlton hotels. Therefore, the elite were drawn to his hotel. However, he was acutely aware of the role and reputation the hotel had in the community; during the Depression, Wyner kept the lights on in the vacant hotel rooms to portray an aura of success.

The Ritz-Carlton Boston revolutionized hospitality in America by creating in a luxury setting:

*Information derived from the Ritz-Carlton Human Resources Department.

- Private bath in guest room
- Lighter fabrics in the guest room to allow for more thorough washing
- White tie and apron uniforms for the waitstaff, black tie for the maitre d', and morning suits for all, conducive to a formal, professional appearance
- Extensive fresh flowers throughout the public areas
- A la carte dining, providing choices for diners
- Gourmet cuisine, utilizing the genius and cooking methods of Auguste Escoffier
- Intimate, smaller lobbies for a more personalized guest experience

The Ritz-Carlton logo is a combination of the British royal seal (the crown) and the lion. Every dining room and café at Ritz-Carlton hotels and resorts worldwide set their table with the signature blue glasses. For as long as The Ritz-Carlton Boston has been in existence, blue goblets have been part of the hotel. These goblets were designed to match the blue Czechoslovakian crystal chandeliers in The Dining Room that still hang today. Coincidentally, blue glass was considered a status symbol in 1920s Boston. Window glass from Europe underwent a chemical reaction when hitting the Boston air and turned blue.

The Ritz-Carlton Hotel Company, L.L.C., originated with the 1983 purchase of The Ritz-Carlton Boston. The standards of service of this Boston landmark serve as a benchmark for all Ritz-Carlton hotels and resorts worldwide. The company quickly grew from this one hotel in 1983 to 45 hotels. Several of these hotels are historic landmarks and follow a commitment of The Ritz-Carlton Hotel Company to preserve architecturally important buildings. Examples are The Ritz-Carlton Schlosshotel, Berlin; The Ritz-Carlton, San Francisco; The Ritz-Carlton, New Orleans; and The Ritz-Carlton Huntington Hotel & Spa in Huntington Beach, California.

In 1995, Marriott International purchased 49 percent interest in Ritz-Carlton. Three years later, that interest was raised to 99 percent.

The Ritz-Carlton Gold Standards are the foundation by which Ritz-Carlton functions. They encompass the philosophy by which the company operates and include The Credo, The Motto, The Three Steps of Service, The Basics, and the Employee Promise.

The Credo is as follows:

The Ritz-Carlton Hotel is a place where the genuine care and comfort of our guest is our highest mission. We pledge to provide the finest personal service and facilities for our guests who will always enjoy a warm, relaxed, yet refined ambience. The Ritz-Carlton experience enlivens the senses, instills well-being, and fulfills even the unexpressed wishes and needs of our guests.

The Motto is:

We Are Ladies and Gentlemen Serving Ladies and Gentlemen.

The Three Steps of Service are:

1. A warm and sincere greeting. Use the guest's name if and when possible.
2. Anticipation and compliance with guest needs.
3. A fond farewell. Give them a warm good-bye and use their names, if and when possible.

The Employee Promise is:

At The Ritz-Carlton, our ladies and gentlemen are the most important resource in our service commitment. By applying the principles of trust, honesty, respect, integrity and commitment, we nurture and maximize the benefit of each individual and the company. The Ritz-Carlton fosters a work environment where diversity is valued, quality of life is enhanced, individual aspirations are fulfilled, and The Ritz-Carlton mystique is strengthened.

The Basics are:

1. The Credo is the principal belief of our Company. It must be known, owned and energized by all.
2. Our Motto is "We are Ladies and Gentlemen serving Ladies and Gentlemen." As service professionals, we treat our guests and each other with respect and dignity.
3. The Three Steps of Service are the foundation of Ritz-Carlton hospitality. These steps must be used in every interaction to ensure satisfaction, retention and loyalty.
4. The Employee Promise is the basis for our Ritz-Carlton work environment. It will be honored by all employees.
5. All employees will successfully complete annual Training Certification for their position.
6. Company objectives are communicated to all employees. It is everyone's responsibility to support them.
7. To create pride and joy in the workplace, all employees have the right to be involved in the planning of the work that affects them.
8. Each employee will continuously identify defects [CQI] throughout the Hotel.
9. It is the responsibility of each employee to create a work environment of teamwork and lateral service so that the needs of our guests and each other are met.

10. Each employee is empowered. For example, when a guest has a problem or needs something special you should break away from your regular duties, address and resolve the issue.

11. Uncompromising levels of cleanliness are the responsibility of every employee.

12. To provide the finest personal service for our guests, each employee is responsible for identifying and recording individual guest preferences.

13. Never lose a guest. Instant guest pacification is the responsibility of each employee. Whoever receives a complaint will own it, resolve it to the guest's satisfaction and record it.

14. "Smile—we are on stage." Always maintain positive eye contact. Use the proper vocabulary with our guests. (Use words like "Good morning," "Certainly," "I'll be happy to," and "My pleasure.")

15. Be an ambassador of your Hotel in and outside of the work place. Always talk positively. Communicate any concerns to the appropriate person.

16. Escort guests rather than pointing out directions to another area of the Hotel.

17. Use Ritz-Carlton telephone etiquette. Answer within three rings and with a "smile." Use the guest's name when possible. When necessary, ask the caller "May I place you on hold?" Do not screen calls. Eliminate call transfers whenever possible. Adhere to voice mail standards.

18. Take pride in and care of your personal appearance. Everyone is responsible for conveying a professional image by adhering to Ritz-Carlton clothing and grooming standards.

19. Think safety first. Each employee is responsible for creating a safe, secure and accident-free environment for all guests and each other. Be aware of all fire and safety emergency procedures and report security risks immediately.

20. Protecting the assets of a Ritz-Carlton Hotel is the responsibility of every employee. Conserve energy, properly maintain our hotels and protect the environment.

Training as a Driving Force

The second driving force behind Ritz-Carlton's human resources management strategies focuses on training. Imagine a hotel where every employee has over 100 hours of customer service training annually. Where guests always check in efficiently and quickly. Where a guestroom is guaranteed to be defect-free because of a revolutionary maintenance program. Where every employee is the customer service department and will break away from their duties to help a guest. Consistent, reliable services such as these are just a few of the reasons why The Ritz-Carlton Hotel Company has been named a winner of the Malcolm Baldrige National Quality Award by the U.S. Department of Commerce.

How does The Ritz-Carlton maintain a culture of service excellence while continuing to grow and expand? One very important element in this effort is The Ritz-Carlton Leadership Center.

Since opening its doors in 1999, more than 10,000 senior executives and middle managers have benefited from a diverse mix of benchmarking seminars and leadership development workshops. The Leadership Center was originally created to support the growth and expansion of Ritz-Carlton products and services. However, it serves as a resource center for leading organizations interested in benchmarking many business practices.

Programs include innovative ways to increase employee retention and loyalty, increase customer retention and loyalty, achieve service excellence, apply sound TQM practices, and effectively drive your organization's culture, philosophy, vision, and mission.

The mission of The Ritz-Carlton Leadership Center states "Partnering to Create a World-Class Service Promotes Knowledge and Sustainable Change." The knowledge and information participants receive transcends all industries and all types of leadership.

Other Driving Forces

The third and fourth driving forces behind the Ritz-Carlton human resources management strategy are the integration of their quality philosophy into daily operations and the utilization of team concepts and empowerment on a regular basis. The Ritz-Carlton displays the daily SQI (Service Quality Indicator) throughout the hotel, enabling all departments to monitor the key production and guest service processes up to the minute to address challenges and areas that need immediate attention. The SQI of all hotels is displayed on flat-screen monitors in the corporate office, ensuring immediate communication of hotel issues and strategies. All Ritz-Carlton employees are empowered to make a difference. Using tools ranging from nine-step quality improvement teams to guest surveys, Ritz-Carlton employees examine every process in the hotel to ensure that the most efficient, customer-service-driven practices are in place.

The following are some examples of SQI:

- A front desk project team at The Ritz-Carlton Osaka reduced check-in time by 50 percent.
- A cross-functional team from the two Atlanta hotels developed a guest-room child safety program, POLO (Protect Our Little Ones), in response to an increase in family travel. The team reviewed benchmarking children's programs, interviewed customers, tested products, and piloted the program to ensure successful implementation.
- A cross-functional corporate and hotel team created the functional model for CLASS (Customer Loyalty Anticipation Satisfaction System).

This guest recognition database is the company-wide tool used to meet and anticipate repeat customers' preferences and requirements.

- Hotel engineers from resorts and city hotels developed a system called CARE (Clean And Repair Everything) to create the most defect-free guestrooms in the industry.

- Merging the deep-cleaning housekeeping processes with the engineering preventive maintenance schedule ensured that all guestrooms are guaranteed to be defect-free every 90 days.

- At Hotel Arts Barcelona, a cross-functional team of hourly employees and managers tackled the problem of guestroom readiness when a guest checks in. Staggering the lunch hours of the housekeeping supervisors streamlined the guestroom inspection process and eliminated the problem of ensuring that a guest's room is always ready when he or she wants to check in.

- Based on the results of a nine-step customer problem-solving team, business and leisure travelers on The Club level of The Ritz-Carlton Buckhead are checked in according to their specific needs. Business travelers are checked in quickly and efficiently, whereas leisure guests are given the option of a more pampered check-in with champagne and a more lengthy presentation of the hotel services and amenities.

- A team of catering managers from Ritz-Carlton hotels worldwide created the first comprehensive wedding program in the hospitality industry. After 2 years of surveying guests, benchmarking the competition, and meeting with wedding experts and media, a five-tier program designed to meet the bride's needs from initial telephone call to the first anniversary was successfully launched.

This extraordinary focus on human resource management strategy has provided great returns for The Ritz-Carlton. In addition to the Malcolm Baldrige National Quality Awards (1992 and 1999), The Ritz-Carlton hotels have been widely recognized with other awards. *Worth Magazine* gave The Ritz-Carlton its 2000 Readers' Choice Award for the "Best Luxury Hotel Chain." *Business Travel News'* 2002 Top U.S. Hotel Chain Survey ranked it number one in its category. *Training Magazine's* 2002 Top 100 selected Ritz-Carlton's Leadership Center as number eight on its list. And the American Automobile Association (AAA) has awarded more than a dozen Ritz-Carlton hotels its top AAA Five Diamond Award.

The Ritz-Carlton and its individual hotels have been recognized with many more awards and top rankings from organizations and publications such as: *Travel and Leisure's* Best Awards, Top 100 Hotels; *Condé Nast Traveler's* Gold List of Best Hotels in the United States; *The Asian Wall Street Journal and Far Eastern Economic Review's* "Best Employer" award; and the Singapore Quality Award.

Case Discussion Questions

1. How important do you believe it is to measure service quality and customer satisfaction in the hospitality industry? Why?

2. Ritz-Carlton exemplifies an organization with a very liberal empowerment policy. What do you see as the benefits and pitfalls of such a policy?

Chapter 11

Technology Management and Applications

CHAPTER OBJECTIVES

- To identify the driving forces behind the ever-increasing demand for technological applications in the hospitality industry
- To delineate where technology plays a role in hospitality management strategies
- To provide an overview of how technological applications impact the industry and what types of technology are having the greatest impact
- To look to the future, both near-term and distant, to ascertain the influence of technology on managerial strategy

Technology is having a dramatic impact on everything from the pre-purchase to the post-purchase process in virtually all industry sectors. At the center of this revolution is the customer. Revenue generation is pushing technology for new applications and new solutions in its ongoing battle to win and retain customers. In this chapter we will examine how technological advances are likely to impact the consumption process. We will look at how technology may well be on the way to solving labor shortages, improving customer satisfaction, and adding more dollars to the bottom line. Let's examine some of the driving forces behind the upcoming changes in the consumption process.

TECHNOLOGY

Management strategy selection in virtually all corporate functional areas has been dramatically enhanced by technology directly or indirectly. In an age when one key competitive advantage is speed, the "tech-knows" have the inside track. New wireless technologies, sophisticated interface systems, communications devices, order expediting systems, virtual reality applications, and multiple linkages will continue to revolutionize every managerial function in the hospitality industry in the foreseeable future.

DRIVING FORCES FOR NEW TECHNOLOGIES

There are five overriding driving forces propelling new technologies that will impact how we will make purchasing decisions, consume products and services, and actually pay for these products and services. These are: expediting the consumption process, speed/time, human scarcity (labor shortages), revenue growth, and cost/efficiencies. Let us briefly examine each of these five driving forces.[1]

First, new technologies are and will continue to evolve that dramatically and positively expedite the actual consumption process. These same technologies will also function as feeders of consumption information to marketing databases. While we will address three such technical devices, we should remember that product forms evolve rapidly in this exciting technological environment. Given this caveat, it would appear that advances in chip capabilities, scanner technology, and a whole new array of "multitask" mechanisms will result in "smart products" that change the pre- to post-consumption process. Later in this chapter we will focus on the "how" portion of the process.

The second driving force derives from current lifestyle patterns. Today, we see lifestyle patterns that are driven by speed of delivery and time. In marketing terms, this means customer convenience. Recently it was stated that consumers in the service sector have redefined value. The new definition includes not only a basic quality and price component but moreover the "convenience factor."

The third driving force can be categorized as "human scarcity." Many employers say they now reach out to applicants they would normally send to the rejection pile . . . because there are so few of them around. Yes, labor shortages, job alternatives, and decreased competence are all contributing to a reduction in customer satisfaction. In fact, customer service ratings in key sectors of the service industry have been steadily declining while in manufacturing sectors such as automobiles and electronics, ratings have dramatically improved.

The fourth driving force is the need for revenue growth. Financial analysts, shareholders, and the investment community at large respond to revenue growth (along with corresponding profit achievement). It has been proven through the PIMS (profit impact of marketing strategy) research efforts that there is a direct correlation between quality of service and profitability. Increasingly, the focus has expanded from simple measurement of revenue growth to the more meaningful extraction of maximum revenue from the customer—thus the value of the customer as an account, name, source of revenue, and so on. Historically, the most widely used approach to lifestyle management/marketing has been AIO (activities, interests, and opinions) rating statements. Today and most likely in the future we will see management and marketing focusing on REVPAC or maximizing revenue per available customer. The data collected by technological devices such as chips, scanners, and multitask mechanisms do now and will continue to directly feed other technologically driven electronic marketing systems focused on purchasing patterns, promotional responses, and match-up offers.

The fifth driving force centers on cost/efficiencies. New technologies will have to meet what might be referred to as the "test of five."[2] Before a new technology is introduced into the consumption process, it will have to meet one or more of these criteria: (1) Does it solve a problem? (2) Does it save money and/or reduce labor? (3) Will it help increase revenue? (4) Does it provide a strategic competitive advantage or create a perception of favorability? (5) Will the technology life cycle justify the investment? Most likely, the new technology that meets all of the above criteria will have the greatest chance for success.

TECHNOLOGICAL ADVANCES AND THE CONSUMPTION PROCESS

Now that we have delineated five driving forces behind the development and delivery of new technology, let's examine how these advances in chip technology, scanners, and multitask mechanisms will impact the pre-consumption process, the consumption process, and the post-consumption process. In general, marketing activity within our society will be greatly expanded and the consumption process greatly expedited as a result of these technological implications.

The pre-consumption process will see potential customers offered more access choices with respect to all products and services, resulting in more convenience and time savings. The latter should be noted as highly significant as it meets the needs of both the consumer and the provider. Using travel as a product/service example, think how dramatically technology is changing the decision and pre-consumption process. Access has progressed from vocal (phone) to online to virtual reality videos. Access is everywhere—at the office, at home, onboard the aircraft, in the hotel room, and so on. Pre-consumption decisions are based on better information, customer preferences, and the consumer's control. Yes, Priceline.com and many other services have reversed the concept of selling, putting the advantage in the consumer's hands versus the salesperson's.

At the actual consumption points, technology is also advancing by expediting the process or in some cases actually eliminating it. Let's look at a simple example of the application of a "smart" multitask mechanism developed by Nokia. In select European markets consumers can use their Nokia (cell phone/smart chip, multitask hand-held device) to bypass the check-out line at the supermarket, access their credit, and so on. In the very near future this same technology could eliminate the front desk and cashier functions (labor-intensive areas) in lodging facilities while also improving security for the guest. Think of how these types of applications would lead to increased customer satisfaction and reduced labor/costs. Moreover, the dollars saved could be channeled to other critical customer services. In this example technology meets several of the "test of five" criteria—reducing costs, providing better service, retention of customers, and so on.

These promising new technologies will help to redefine the experience points of the consumption process. Better work and home access, more information, greater product/service offerings, higher satisfaction levels, and more likelihood for repeat purchases are but a few of the likely results from the marriage of technology and the consumer in the hospitality industry. Significant post-consumption benefits include: a more customized on-demand (by the consumer) product/service focus; smarter marketing (more in line with the needs of the individual consumer as well as instantaneous); and database retention and development to maximize REVPAC.[3]

The implications of the marriage of technology and marketing are profound for not only the consumer but also the provider of products and services. Technology is redefining and redesigning the consumption process for most products and services. Providers must think through how these technologies will impact not only the delivery of the product/service offering but everything from customer interface points to actual product design. Management strategies will need to be redefined and dynamic to adapt to the new technologies and be responsive to the customer. Service levels are likely to improve as resources are redirected and consumption processes are redefined and refined.

We must also refocus educational and training programs to address preparing individuals to work with competence in delivering and applying these new technologies. Technology applications provide a great opportunity to retrain and redeploy human assets to reverse the downward trend in customer satisfaction ratings through the use of new technology. We have the opportunity to not only have customers for life, but to maximize REVPAC for life, thus resulting in greater profitability. The age of technological acceleration will have a positive impact on the consumption pipeline if hospitality management chooses to embrace the strategic opportunities presented by new technology applications.

THE ROLE OF TECHNOLOGY

The role of technology in the hospitality industry might best be defined by simply stating that technology will have a role everywhere, directly or indirectly. Up to this point we have alluded to its role in customer service, marketing, training, and operations. We have stated that technology will affect database strategies, electronic marketing, systems management, and purchasing strategies. From a functional perspective, virtually all functions will be impacted by technological applications: human resources, finance, operations, marketing, and business development. Many different trends in technology do now and will continue to have an impact on the hospitality industry, including internet usage, wireless applications, personal communication devices (PCDs) and multitask mechanisms, database sophistication, online business partnerships, internal communications, and training and labor/time efficiency-related applications, to name a few.

The Role in Marketing

From a functional perspective, management strategies related to technology applications will involve marketing. Electronic marketing through websites, global linkages, and vastly improved database systems; new pricing models; and revenue and yield management systems will all enhance the marketing arena. Closely linked to marketing will be customer satisfaction and retention-related areas of focus. The common goal of all the marketing and customer service–related managerial strategies will be revenue. New revenue sources (databases), more revenue from existing customers, and maximizing revenue from supply and demand models/forecasts (revenue management and yield management systems) will all be key managerial focal points.

```
                        ETHICS

  Information technology is an extraordinary tool for management strategies and
  decision making. This same technology requires its applications to be ethical and
  consumer privacy to be protected.
```

The Role in Operations

The second major focal point or area for technology applications will be in the total scope of operations. Areas of impact include security, electronic entry systems, HVAC (climate control and utility cost management), scheduling, replacement of labor by automation, and process expedition. Management strategies' overall focus in this area will be the cost or expense reduction side of the equation. Technology application decisions will have a direct impact on everything operational from legal expenses and labor costs to purchasing. Also, technology applications will involve redesign of facilities, reinvestment in facilities, and enhanced systems for transactions (check-in, check-out, ordering, simultaneous transmission of data such as food orders, refrigerator stocks, etc.). Management strategies will be guided by efficiency (cost reduction) and expediting (speed).

The Role in Product/Service Development

The third area for management strategy from a functional perspective will relate to product/service development. Technology applications will allow for greater focus on modifications, new designs, new delivery systems, and enhanced delivery time. The focal point of management strategies in the development area will be innovation. Applying technology applications to provide innovative solutions to solve problems, improve systems, and develop competitive advantages are all strategic areas.

SYSTEM STRATEGIES AND TRENDS

While virtually every aspect of a hospitality organization will be affected by technology, there are seven major areas where system strategies will likely apply: reservation systems, order-taking process, revenue/yield management, purchasing, facilities management, time/labor management, and customer retention systems. Some of these areas may have a higher priority in select sectors of the industry; however, all seven will be strategic focal points for management.

While we have commented on a number of these seven system areas, customer retention systems may provide the greatest return on investment. As we have previously pointed out, it is much less expensive to retain an existing customer than to attract a new one to your hospitality industry enterprise.

Consumers/customers will demand that hospitality organizations provide them the same level of services and technology away from home that they are accustomed to at their home or office. This means more than just high-speed internet access. It includes everything from the ability to pay bills to being entertained to communicating in the total scope of the term with home or office. It also includes a secure environment but yet easy access or entry and exit from the hospitality provider. Further, it is likely to include personalization of services through guest/customer history systems. One futurist and international globetrotter stated he expected it would be possible for him someday to travel without a suitcase, as his destination hotel would have a record of his needs (in total, including his clothes) and literally have these supplies in his room upon arrival. Another futurist indicated she expected to be able to use a PCD anywhere at anytime to do anything she desired from bill paying to wireless transmission of memoranda, to security clearances to room entry to rental car activation.

While some of these needs may appear extraordinary, there is absolutely no technical reason they cannot be accommodated today. The increasing level of computer literacy, growing internet usage, mushrooming growth of wireless applications, and global communications improvements all support these desires becoming full realities. Technology applications and systems that meet customers' needs will result in brand preference and loyalty.

CURRENT AND FUTURE TECHNOLOGY APPLICATIONS

Today hospitality industry management must make a wide array of technology-related decisions. Each decision to apply or upgrade technology has an impact on performance, costs, revenues, and ultimately the bottom line. The list that follows may not be all-inclusive; however, it will give you an idea of the scope and breadth of technology applications currently requiring management decisions and strategies in most sectors of the hospitality business.

Current Applications

- High-speed internet access
- Global distribution channels (relationships)
- Facility management systems
- Security systems
- Revenue management systems
- Telecommunications systems
- Forecasting and business planning
- Point-of-sale applications
- Training and education systems
- Inventory management systems

- Purchasing systems
- Wireless applications
- Entertainment systems
- Order processing systems
- Websites
- Electronic marketing systems
- Database systems

As if the above list of current strategy considerations weren't enough, technology keeps inventing new technologies and applications. The list that follows delineates some of the foreseeable areas for management decisions/ strategies in the near future.

Near-Future Applications

- Integration of systems
- Convergence of databases
- New knowledge resource systems
- Executive information systems
- Web-based customer access policies
- More sophisticated customer information/interface systems
- Alliances and linkages
- Employee replacement systems
- Virtual meetings, travel, etc.

The companies that will have the competitive advantage are those with the most knowledgable employees and management. Knowledge for decision making and strategy application will be provided through information technology systems. Having employees who are technology savvy will accelerate the knowledge acquisition and decision process. Today, wireless technologies allow knowledge/information to be obtained anywhere and in virtually any format. Sophisticated software applications enable accurate decisions or recommendations at speeds unimaginable just years or even months ago. Smart cards/chips provide heretofore-unimagined task performance and interfaces. Prioritization will be a challenge for managerial strategies. The current and future lists of technology applications are substantial in content. The future's list is perhaps infinite in scope.

Where the parameters of knowledge, technology, and applications take us is only limited by our imaginations (biotechnology is seeking to expand that substantially!) What will be the ultimate PCD or multitask wireless device is probably yet to be defined. What will be the universal security identification process may be yet to be identified. How we go through the pre-consumption to post-consumption experience in the hospitality industry perhaps hasn't been fully refined. One thing, however, is for sure: Technological applications will play a major role in virtually every aspect of the hospitality industry and consumption process. Managerial decisions and strategies in this dynamic environment will need to be visionary to keep up with the pace of change technology will bring us. The managers with the best information and knowledge base will be the driving forces behind the winners in the hospitality industry.

CHAPTER REVIEW

In this chapter we identified five driving forces propelling new technology applications in the hospitality industry. These included: expediting the consumption process, improving value through convenience, the shortage of labor, the need for revenue growth, and cost reduction and/or greater efficiencies. We then delineated the extensive role of technology in the hospitality industry, touching upon the many functional areas where technological applications are critical for competitive and managerial success today. These included but were not limited to marketing, operations, and product/service development. We then looked at major areas where system strategies emerge as significant to the hospitality industry enterprise. Finally, we listed current and future technology applications that would demand managerial strategies now and in the near future. We concluded that technology will continue to reinvent itself with new applications and that the pace of change in technology applications will accelerate as we move into the future.

KEY CONCEPTS/TERMS

Database	Prioritization
Electronic marketing	Revenue management
Linkages	REVPAC (revenue per available
PCDs (personal communication	customer)
devices)	Scanners

DISCUSSION QUESTIONS

1. What functional area(s) of hospitality organizations do you believe will receive the greatest benefit from technological applications in the next 5 years?

2. Do you feel consumers will accept more self-service provided by technological applications in the hospitality industry?

3. What are the potential downsides to technological applications in the hospitality industry?

4. How will technology play a role in training the workforce in the hospitality industry?

5. New technological applications will require substantial investment by hospitality organizations. How would you justify funding or making such an investment?

6. How do you believe technology will impact the customer/guest in any given sector of the hospitality industry?

ENDNOTES

1. R. Nykiel, "Technology, Cost, Convenience and Consumption," *Hospitality Business Review* 3, no. 4: 42–43.
2. Ibid., 44.
3. Ibid., 45.

CASE 1

The Peninsula Group and the Peninsula Hong Kong—
Technologically Advanced*

The impact of accelerating technology is rapidly changing the business environment, with the most far-reaching effects being produced by access to information on a worldwide scale. As a consequence of the fast pace and ready access to new developments, today's customer is more demanding and impatient and expects higher and more efficient standards of service. The hotel industry therefore must meet and exceed their expectations of excellence by staying abreast of the rapidly changing and expanding world of technology. However, the use of technology must be carefully incorporated so as not to infringe upon the personal aspects of hospitality service. In many respects, this traditional part of the business will become even more important in light of the rapid changes.

Today's hotel customers are driven by several important factors such as immediate information requirements, quality service, the most cost-effective solutions, and the desire to be multitasking and proficient.

The hospitality industry is increasingly relying on technological components such as in-room internet services, in-room entertainment and games, and multipurpose bedside control systems to achieve customer satisfaction and to maintain a loyal client base.

An excellent example of a company utilizing the latest in-room technology is the Peninsula Group. Established in Hong Kong in 1973, the Peninsula Group is the operations and marketing division of Hong Kong and Shanghai Hotels, Ltd. (HSH), a publicly listed company whose principal business is the ownership and management of prestige deluxe hotels and commercial and residential properties.

The Peninsula Group of hotels consists of the Peninsula and the Kowloon Hotels in Hong Kong, the Peninsula Bangkok, the Peninsula Manila, the Peninsula Palace Beijing, the Peninsula New York, the Peninsula Beverly Hills, the Peninsula Chicago, and the Quail Lodge Resort & Golf Club in Carmel, California.

At the company's flagship property, the Peninsula Hong Kong, panels strategically located around the room access various room functions. For example, a bedside panel controls lighting, air conditioning, radio, television, and curtains. At the New York property, rooms include a mood switch that allows guests to select their preferred lighting and air-conditioning levels. A panel inside the entry of each room records outdoor temperature and

---

*Information derived from www.hotelshongkong.com/hotels/peninsula, www.hongkong
.hotels.net/kowloon/peninsula/guest_room.htm,   and   www.fastrack.hongkong.peninsula.com/
accommodation.

humidity or UV levels and wind chill factors. Refurbishment at the Peninsula Hong Kong allowed for installation of an interface at check-in which automatically captures and feeds a central guestroom server with information specific to each guest. A fax machine signals via the bedside and door panels whether a fax has been received, and the group is currently working on automatically programming the fax header with the guest's name upon check-in. These innovative implementations could change the technological standards for hotel rooms around the world.

Looking to the future, it is predicted that a new era of television transmission built on digital TV will make the TV set closer to a computer than today's traditional television. Many choices currently include video-on-demand and video libraries. In the future, telephony will merge with the television receiver of each room, which will also likely undergo major physical change. The Peninsula Group is currently designing furniture around the new, ultra-thin 16:9 plasma TV, which virtually eliminates the need for armories. It may not be long before telephones with a video capability will offer guests a virtual reality link-up with their company or family.

The Peninsula Group assessed the implications for hotels of hi-tech phenomena such as high-speed internet access. Its research found that 65 percent of business customers travel with laptops, and over 50 percent of these use them to check their e-mail and connect to their company. Over 60 percent of them have ethernet cards, which allow for 30 times faster connectivity than conventional dial-up.

High-speed internet access brings a number of benefits for hotels. It frees up PBX lines, brings in incremental revenue, and boosts guest satisfaction. The challenge is the infrastructure required to accommodate the new technology. Hotels have to leverage their existing infrastructure by adopting a data-over-voice solution, using voice connection to connect from the room to the local area network, or using wireless solutions via the desktop PC, thin client, or a set-top box.

Areas of emerging technology include: the increasing use of smart cards, identification and verification technology (door locks that recognize guests and open automatically), tracking and location, and technology and applications that allow for complete customization of the hotel room according to guests' needs before they check in.

Other emerging trends are the technological convergences between voice and data and between standardization and consolidation, as well as mass customization, or one-to-one marketing.

The Peninsula Group is developing a competitive advantage by accommodating guests' needs at a higher level of service. Today's clients are demanding and fast-paced. On-the-road travelers need the resources of their offices while staying at hotels. Their expectations are for convenience coupled with state-of-the-art technology. In addition, guests anticipate exceptional service to be delivered with the technology. The product's assets and the staff's training and skills must work together to achieve a successful operation.

In order to maintain a sustainable competitive advantage, it is imperative that the staff is well trained to handle the equipment, answer questions, deal with computer issues, and promote the new technology in a confident and educated manner. In addition, a technologically trained professional should be available around the clock to fix any unexpected glitches that might occur with the operation of the equipment. During large meetings and conferences, an entire team must be available on site to assist with the usage of the technology.

An important target market for the Peninsula Group is the business traveler who will come to expect this level of service from other properties and hotel companies as well. Their frequent visitors will share their experiences with their clients and business associates, which could generate new business for the Peninsula Group.

The successful and reputable name recognition of the Peninsula Group brings credibility to the changes. The Peninsula Group is a well-established and respected luxury hotel leader in the hospitality industry. An effective management team with a service-focused philosophy backed by a quality product supports the company.

The strategic vision of the Peninsula Group is clear. The property's objective is to accommodate guests' needs by providing them with the essential resources that their demanding lives and schedules require. The implementation of in-room technology is obviously a major capital investment, so the strategic vision also provides the rationale for investment that may require years to achieve a payoff. Most importantly, the Peninsula Group's technological offerings are "forward-looking" into the future, and the investment entails a long-term perspective and goal to exceed guest expectations.

The in-room technology offered by the Peninsula Group is a major point of differentiation from competitors.

Case Discussion Questions

1. Do you believe state-of-the-art technology for customer use can be a major competitive advantage? Why or why not?

2. Do you feel it will be important to standardize technology on a worldwide basis for the hospitality industry? If so, how would you recommend this be achieved?

CASE 2

Pleasant Holidays—The Interactive Website*

In this chapter we pointed out the increased utilization of the internet by the consumer of travel-related products and services. We also pointed out the need for speed and convenience and the fact that the internet helps fulfill that need. However, not all internet information gathering or purchasing experiences are speedy and convenient due to flows in website designs and applications. In this case study we will see how one hospitality firm addresses the website for the benefit of their customers.

Ed Hogan, CEO and founder of Pleasant Holidays LLC, and his wife Lynn began Pleasant Holidays as a simple travel agency in 1959. They are pioneers in packaged travel and today operate the largest travel company serving Hawaii, sending nearly 500,000 visitors a year to the islands. In 1998, the Hogans formed Pleasant Holidays LLC, which now serves as the parent company of Pleasant Hawaiian Holidays, Pleasant Mexican Holidays, Pleasant Tahitian Holidays, Pleasant South Pacific Holidays, Pleasant Fiji Holidays, Pleasant Australia/New Zealand Holidays, Japan & Orient Tours (now Air by Pleasant), Destinations Plus, Pleasant Island Holidays, Vacation Acceptance Company, and other travel-related businesses.

The company has a positioning which is the best and largest packaging product agency for Hawaii travel from the United States. It has built its position through several key strategies: developing its website; co-oping with many of the largest, most recognizable brand name companies; concentrating on "group tourists"; developing channel distribution; and contributing toward future tourism.

Pleasant Holidays launched its internet site in 1996. The website was designed for the customer's convenience and ease of use. In 1999 Pleasant Holidays was awarded an unprecedented two Select Site Awards from GlobalDiscoveries.com, a company specializing in website evaluations. Pleasant Holidays' site was the first known to have multidestination and online booking capability for its Hawaii products. Today, its website has expanded to include Mexico, Tahiti, Australia, and New Zealand travel products.

Co-oping with many of the largest, most recognizable brand name companies in the travel industry has also provided extensive reach through website linkages, thereby strengthening its products. These companies include AAA Travel Agency, American Airlines, American Express, Ritz-Carlton, Aston Hotels & Resorts, Starwood Hotels & Resorts, Hilton Hotels Corporation, Norwegian Cruise Line, and United Airlines, just to mention a few.

Technology has allowed Pleasant Holidays to offer major package plans, allowing customers to personalize package features. Pleasant Holidays encour-

*Information derived from www.pleasantholidays.com and www.divine.com/pr/archives/040302.asp, as well as an interview with Ed and Lynn Hogan, founders of Pleasant Holidays.

ages customers' participation in group tours to Mexico and Hawaii by letting customers select package components in line with their own interests. Through the website customers can easily request their preferences of the class of service, departure date, departure city, return date, seating assignment, destination, hotel, type of room, number of days, ground transportation, car rental, and so on. After the members of the group specify their choices, specialists in the company's group tour department customize the plan for the group customers. This is a win-win situation for both Pleasant Holidays and its group customers.

Case Discussion Questions

1. Pull up two different hospitality industry websites from the same sector (airlines, cruise lines, hotels, etc.). Which site do you believe was faster and more convenient in its design and operation? Why?

2. How important do you believe it is to have a website that offers customization features or choice options such as described in the Pleasant Holidays case study? Why?

Chapter 12

Purchasing Concepts

CHAPTER OBJECTIVES

- To identify the significance of purchasing within the context of hospitality industry management
- To provide an understanding of the various areas of purchasing and their relationship to the hospitality industry
- To delineate the traditional purchasing functions/activities
- To define the concept of e-procurement
- To focus upon current trends related to management and strategic options for purchasing in the hospitality industry

Until a few years ago purchasing was primarily viewed as a function to save money through seeking the best prices for all the various needs of a hospitality organization. Management's focus was to view the function as a provider of everything from badges and uniforms to major furnishings and equipment. The larger the entity, the greater the purchasing power and to some extent the competitive advantage. Management recognized that purchasing could influence the bottom line through both cost savings as well as quality control. In franchised organizations the parent company or joint-ventured purchasing function could also pass some savings on to its franchisees. This helped the franchisees and the parent company drive prices lower based on higher volumes. On occasion the controlling entity of the purchasing function could also benefit from a small services fee.

Purchasing in this traditional model requires staff, systems, and other related costs such as administrative needs, receiving facilities, and a processing/shipping function. Purchasing also is a time-consuming function that requires going out for bids, negotiating with vendors, ordering, and communicating with internal and external constituencies. In essence, while purchasing's goal is to provide the best merchandise at the most competitive price and when needed, the traditional method of purchasing entails substantial labor and systems-related expense. One goal of many hospitality organizations was to move purchasing from a cost viewpoint to a breakeven venture and then to a revenue generator. With respect to the latter, the historic and more aggressive goal involved establishing an internal ROI factor for the purchasing function. Some organizations were content with a 5 percent return, while others placed the ROI objective more in line with their overall corporate ROI goal (expressed on a percentage basis).[1]

ETHICS

In purchasing, adherence to a code of ethics and core values is not optional. Integrity must be a focal point in every activity.

CHANGING MARKETPLACE

A number of external and internal forces came together in the late 1990s and early 2000s to set the scene for some major changes in management's perspective on the purchasing function. Externally, pressure to increase stockholder value, consolidations, and electronic procurement began to change the thought process or perspective of purchasing having to be an internal function. Co-ops first emerged and led to considerable cost savings due to volume purchasing. Electronic purchasing also dramatically streamlined the function as more and more vendors and products could be accessed on line.

Ultimately, management began to explore everything from outsourcing the entire function to forming consortiums with others in the same industry sector including competitors.

ELECTRONIC PROCUREMENT

Due to the development of internet sites, hardware and software capabilities, and cost efficiencies, e-procurement has emerged as a new and often preferred way of purchasing. Management recognizes that speed, convenience, and lower costs all support a focus on e-procurement. Like traditional procurement, e-procurement also requires a structured process, which includes:

- Internal needs analysis
- Market evaluation
- RFPs (Requests for proposal)
- Formal evaluation of responses
- Negotiation

E-procurement also allows for faster comparisons of bids and even simultaneous or instant negotiations.

TECHNOLOGY

Every second of every day, more and more purchasing is conducted on line. Technology has contributed greatly to knowledge requisition, competitive bidding, and rapid response times. Technology has fostered customization, logistics, and enhanced delivery processes. Current benefits include, but are not limited to, cost savings, staff reductions or elimination, and the economics of scale through purchasing co-ops.

Internal Needs Analysis

Selecting an e-procurement model or solution is a major management undertaking for any hospitality organization. Management must strategically focus on everything from internal needs identification to actual implementation.

The first step in the internal analysis is to understand just what it is e-procurement can do and how an organization will adapt to e-procurement. Next is to look at overall business strategies and understand how the procurement initiative fits into that. If cost reduction is the major driver in the strategy, an e-procurement solution that requires creating and maintaining a marketplace isn't a good fit. If the culture is to command, control, and communicate, and there are extensive internal technology and procurement infrastructures in place, then an in-house solution might be appealing, not to mention politically salable. Some questions management should ask are:

- What are we trying to do with e-procurement? What problems are we trying to solve?
- How do we expect to fund the costs associated with e-procurement?
- To what extent do we want to control our marketplace versus join in with others?
- Does this initiative have the support of top management?
- To what extent do our existing accounting, communications, and control processes support this effort? Will some of these key areas have to adapt?
- What will be the impact on the vendors we use today?
- Will this effort lead to changes in any critical strategic vendor relationships? Are there contractual commitments to current vendors that we need to consider?

Market Evaluation

The next step is market evaluation. A thorough needs analysis process requires an intimate understanding of the offerings in the marketplace. One must understand the differences between the various structural forms and business models found in the marketplace today, and where those forms will go in the future.[2]

At this point it is appropriate to look at the overall e-procurement marketplace, recognizing that the hospitality industry is a unique vertical market and an interesting subvertical market to some of the major players in e-procurement.

Assessing the marketplace can be done in several ways. Informally, salespeople (vendors) can be interviewed. Formally, an RFI (request for information) can be issued. Most likely, with different service providers there will be variations on the business models provided. Selecting the model that best fits the company's needs requires an objective comparison. Defining the different offerings along these critical dimensions will assist in making an objective decision:

- Is the offering open to all comers that register and establish a relationship with the operator?

- Does the operator or some other party control what buyers are admitted?
- Does the operator or some other party control what sellers are admitted?
- Who funds the use of the system?

Request for Proposal

Now comes the RFP step. This is the phase in which it's actually time to go shopping with a formal document. Defining your needs in detail is vital in the RFP. It is good practice to frame the RFP in a format that requires respondents to answer exactly as specified in detail. Management should identify exactly what purchasing functionality is needed in the software solution.

In order to launch an e-procurement function, additional services such as custom programming, business process consulting, training, and deployment services may be required. Some services that may be required on an ongoing basis include content management, customer care (both technical support and the more difficult transaction support), retraining, and more. Management must also factor in expectations for future growth and take into consideration how to protect against fee increases. With new providers of e-procurement services, it is essential to take a thorough look at the vendors' financial stability and cash flow prior to entering into any relationship.

Formal Evaluation of Responses

The next step is the formal evaluation of responses. In the evaluation process, management should be satisfied that the proposal accurately reflects the specified model or needs and, moreover, that there is software functionality to support that model. It should be clear who will conduct the crucial and laborious tasks of vendor acquisition and content acquisition, who will handle the training process, and who bears the expenses.

Negotiation

Finally comes the negotiation phase. Finalizing price, timing, and implementation schedules are all critical elements in a final decision process. Once management buys into an e-procurement system it is transition time. Management must be prepared to redefine responsibilities, have backup systems, and move quickly toward the e-procurement way of doing business.

CHAPTER REVIEW

In the hospitality industry today, there are several options for purchasing replacing the traditional model. First is co-oping and joining a purchasing consortium. Second, the historic perspective of purchasing generating percentage fees or returns is being replaced with the concept of eliminating or severely restricting the cost side of the equation and using an external firm or joint venture entity for purchasing. Third, those who have opted to have a purchasing entity have sought to have its profit goal equal or exceed the EBITDA percentage goal of the company. Fourth, e-procurement is replacing the traditional procurement process. Overall, the winning strategy appears to be reducing the overhead expenses by going outside and taking advantage of better purchasing leverage offered by the new purchasing co-ops and consortiums such as Avendra, the Starwood Group, and PurchasePro.com, to name just a few.

KEY CONCEPTS/TERMS

Consortium	Outsourcing
Co-op	RFI (request for information)
E-procurement	RFP (request for proposal)

DISCUSSION QUESTIONS

1. What are the advantages of participating in a purchasing co-op?
2. What are the drawbacks or disadvantages of outsourcing the purchasing function?
3. Why would a hospitality organization want to maintain a traditional purchasing function?
4. What do you see as the primary attributes of an e-procurement system?
5. How would an e-procurement system limit an organization?
6. Do you believe there should be an ROI objective for the purchasing function?

ENDNOTES

1. R. Nykiel, *Procurement Practices and Services—A Proprietary Study and Survey of Procurement Functions In the Hospitality Industry* (Houston: World Institute Associates, 2001).
2. M. Haley, "*Caveat Emptor!* Simple Steps to Selecting an E-Procurement Solution," *Hospitality Upgrade Magazine* (Spring 2001): 24–26.

CASE 1

Avendra—The Electronic Procurement Co-op*

In this chapter we indicated that the rapid growth of e-procurement points to a win-win scenario for the hospitality company and the vendor of products. In the case study that follows we will focus on the benefits of e-purchasing for the company.

Avendra is an independent company formed in early 2001 by Marriott International, Hyatt Corporation, ClubCorp USA, InterContinental Hotels Group (formerly Six Continents Hotels), and Fairmont Hotels & Resorts—all leading companies in their respective hospitality markets. Today, Avendra is the largest procurement service company serving the hospitality industry in North America and the Caribbean.

Avendra matches customers' needs to suppliers who meet those needs. Customers can access and take advantage of the programs by telephone, fax, or the internet. Customers' benefits include:

- Avendra's expertise in selecting appropriate products
- Cost savings derived from a large committed customer base
- Supply chain management efficiency
- An internet-enabled purchasing system that streamlines processes and easily integrates with other enterprise systems

Avendra serves everything from large luxury chains to golf facilities and single properties. Avendra helps lower procurement costs through one of the largest committed purchasing volumes in the industry. This translates to the most attractive terms. Working with manufacturers and distributors, Avendra offers exceptional prices on goods and services at a variety of quality and price points, all from suppliers who have undergone a thorough review and inspection.

Avendra is dedicated to delivering quality-assured procurement programs to the hospitality and related industries. Suppliers play a critical role in the success of this venture. The integrity and quality of the services and products supplied must meet Avendra's expectations/standards.

At the same time Avendra's industry-leading procurement service offers substantial benefits to the suppliers of products and services, including:

- Increased access to hospitality customers and related industries
- Improved communication of available products and specifications

*Information derived from www.avendra.com and www.hotel_online.com/neo/trends/kpmg/articles/2001_estrategyplan.html.

- Enhanced customer service through better reporting and real-time information access
- Standardized and simplified business processes
- Increased sales volume potential
- New customers
- Heightened market exposure through Avendra's national marketing campaigns

Avendra's first priority is to save its clients time, effort, and money. The expertise of Avendra's founding companies has been combined to offer the most complete way to address virtually all procurement needs.

Avendra organizes products and services into "programs" that are grouped according to their use in the hospitality venue. There are currently 10 programs that encompass the full range of products and services Avendra offers, each uniquely tailored to meet the needs of its specific venue. They include: food and beverage; room operations; engineering and energy; administrative; financial and professional services; furnishings, fixtures, and equipment; building and construction; technology and telecommunications; golf and grounds maintenance; retail and spa; and replenishment services.

Avendra appears to be successful in saving money for its individual and corporate participants as well as providing suppliers with an ongoing flow of business. The ability to provide better service and greater cost efficiencies has dramatically changed the purchasing function in the hospitality industry. Avendra demonstrates that thoughtful utilization of technology can have a substantial impact on the way the purchasing business is conducted. After all, greater efficiencies, faster service, and saving money are all great objectives for a purchasing function.

Case Discussion Questions

1. Avendra is an excellent example of outsourcing a total function and represents perhaps a better way of performing the function. What other functional areas do you think would lend themselves to outsourcing?

2. You have been asked to develop an e-procurement function for your company. Name the steps you would undertake to do so.

CASE 2

SYSCO—Volume and Customization Fuel Success*

In virtually every sector of the hospitality industry, when one thinks of purchasing the initial response is likely to include SYSCO Corporation. The history of this supplier to the industry exemplifies multiple managerial and business strategies. SYSCO created a purchasing concept from the supplier perspective that has been unmatched to date. SYSCO strategies include acquisitions, branding, co-oping, delivery systems, e-commerce, customization, and product development, to name a few. SYSCO's rich history is the best starting point for this case study.

Company Profile

In 1970 SYSCO Corporation was established as nine entrepreneurs merged their companies in an initial public offering. One of them came to be SYSCO Food Services of Houston, LP. Through the innovative services and product, the company led its industry by 1977. In 1988 SYSCO became the first distributor with the capability to provide total, uniform services to customers across the country. Taking advantage of innovations in food technology, improved packaging, and advance transportation techniques, the company continues to provide its customers with quality products, delivered on time in excellent condition, and reflecting the quest for ever-improving efficiencies at reasonable prices.

SYSCO is the largest marketer and distributor of foodservice products in America. Operating from distribution facilities nationwide, the company provides its products and services to approximately 356,000 customers. The SYSCO distribution network covers virtually the entire continental United States and includes all of its 150 largest cities as well as the Pacific Coast region of Canada.

SYSCO provides customers with over 12,000 foodservice products—fresh and frozen meats, seafood, and poultry; fresh and processed produce; beverages; china; glassware, and tabletop items; kitchen supplies and equipment; paper and disposable items; and chemical and janitorial supplies.

The foundation of SYSCO's success is superior customer service, extensive product knowledge, consistent quality of product offerings, and business-building support services. A distinctive mix of ever-evolving branded products and dedicated employees has thrust SYSCO into a new dimension from a distributor to a brand provider, supported by a depth of service unparalleled in the foodservice distribution industry. Brand width and service depth have

---

*Information derived from SYSCO Corporation Annual Reports, 1999, 2000, and 2001, as well as www.sysco.com and www.sysco.software.com.

made SYSCO the distributor of choice for the "meals prepared away from home" market.

Six strategic acquisitions completed during 2000 strengthened both its geographical presence and its product offerings. They include three custom-cutting meat operations, two broad-line distributors, and a specialty produce company (Buckhead Beef Company and Tyson Foods, Inc.), to form the Electronic Foodservice Network (EFS Network), an internet-based, business-to-business network. Open to suppliers, distributors, and chain restaurant operators, EFS Network is aimed at cutting costs in the foodservice supply chain by more efficiently managing the flow of information and products to the marketplace.

Commitment to Quality Control

SYSCO Corporation maintains the largest foodservice distribution technical quality assurance staff in America with over 150 representatives. SYSCO quality assurance has developed finite specifications for products marketed under brands. SYSCO quality assurance staff inspects products during production, inspects incoming and outgoing loads at redistribution centers, and audits products at each distribution center. SYSCO's high level of control of the products packed is extended to all of its high-usage products. The staff travels nationally and worldwide to conduct ongoing plant inspections and evaluations. SYSCO's commitment to quality assurance not only controls its products' quality, but also results in the highest-quality products in the marketplace.

Fold-out Strategy

SYSCO's internal growth strategy involves building distribution centers in established markets that previously were being served by another SYSCO company from a distance.

When a fold-out company is formed, domiciled sales and delivery personnel become employees of the new company, a core management team is transferred from the original or other SYSCO companies, and additional employees are hired locally. Supported by a state-of-the-art facility and the SYSCO Uniform System, the new company is better able to serve its customers, and SYSCO grows more rapidly in both the original and the fold-out markets.

Milestones

1969	Incorporated in Delaware.
1970	Acquires the following companies: Frost-Pack Distributing Co. and its subsidiary, Global Frozen Foods, Inc.; Houston's Food Service Co.; Louisville Grocery Co.; Plantation Foods Corp.; Texas Wholesale Grocery Corp. and its subsidiary, Thomas Foods, Inc., and its subsidiary, Justrite Foods Service, Inc.; Wicker, Inc., and its affiliate, Albany Frosted Foods,

Inc.; and affiliates Allied Langfield, H&R Wholesale Co., Inc., and Sam Symons & Co.

1971	Acquires Arrow Food Distributors, Inc., Koon Food Sales, Inc., Rome Foods Co., and Saunders Food Distribution, Inc.
1972	Acquires Hallsmith Co., Inc., Miesel Co., Robert Orr & Co., and Hymie Fiakow Co.
1973	Acquires Lauber, Inc., Baraboo Food Products, Inc., E.R. Cochran Co.
1974	Acquires the following companies: Harrisonburg Fruit and Produce Co., Theimer Food Services, Sterling-Keeley's, Inc., Complete Foods, Inc., and Swan Food Sales, Inc.
1975	Acquires the following companies: Tri-State General Food Supply Co., Marietta Institutional Wholesalers, Monticello Provision Co., Oregon Film Service, Inc., McBreen Trucking, Inc., and Mid-Central Fish & Frozen Foods, Inc.
1978	Acquires Glen-Webb & Co.
1979	Acquires Select-Union Foods, Inc.
1982	Acquires General Management Corp. and its subsidiaries, S.E. Lankford Co. and Frosted Foods, Inc.
1984	Acquires Pegler & Co. and Bell Distributing Co.
1985	Acquires the assets of PYA/Monarch of Texas, Inc., and acquires B.A. Railton Co., New York Tea Co., CML Company, Inc., and DiPaolo Food Distributors.
1986	Acquires Trammell, Temple & Staff, Inc., Deaktor Brothers Provision Co., and Bangor Wholesale Foods, Inc.
1987	Acquires General Food Service Supply, Inc., Lawrence Foods, Inc., Vogel's Inc., and Major-Hosking's, Inc.
1988	Acquires for cash the net assets of Staley Continental, Inc.'s foodservice distribution business known as CFS Continental; acquires Fresh Start Foods Ltd. Partnership; sells Havi Corp. to TFP Acquisition Ltd. Partnership; sells Continental Coffee Co. of Houston to Quaker Oats; and sells Gregg/RE-MI to Borden, Inc.
1989	Sells NCD Detergent, Inc., to Ecolab, Inc.
1990	Acquires Oklahoma City Foodservice Distribution Business of Scrivner Inc. and Twin City Fruit, Inc., and sells Sysco Military Distribution Division and Select-Sysco Foods.
1991	Acquires certain assets of Scrivner, Inc.
1992	Acquires certain assets of Collins Foodservice, Inc., and Benjamin Polakoff & Son, Inc., and sells its Global/Sysco division.

1993   Acquires Perloff Brothers, Inc., St. Louis Assets of Clark Foodservice, Inc., and Ritter Food Corp. (which it renames Ritter Sysco Food Services, Inc.).

1996   Acquires Strano Foodservice Limited (which it renames Strano Sysco Foodservice).

Recent Strategic Acquisitions

In order to meet customer needs, six strategic acquisitions completed during 2000 strengthened both geographical presence and product offerings. These acquisitions included three custom-cutting meat operations:

1. **Buckhead Beef Company of Atlanta:** The number one distributor of Certified Angus Beef™ products in the world in 1999; provides customers access to the largest inventory of wet- and dry-aged USDA Prime.

2. **Malcolm Meats of Toledo, Ohio:** Distributor of custom-cut meats and other protein products to customers and SYSCO broad-line companies throughout Illinois, Michigan, and Ohio.

3. **Newport Meat Company of Irvine, California:** Now SYSCO Newport Meat Company, one of the largest purveyors of fine meats, poultry, and seafood in southern California, offering products, services, and training to SYSCO broad-line companies in California, Arizona, New Mexico, and Utah.

Through the custom-cutting meat operations, SYSCO now offers precision, custom-cut steaks and other protein products to customers in certain areas. These three meat-cutting operations have taken customer service to a higher level, and each operation is a leader in its market area. They also supply other customized and portion-controlled meat and protein products, complementing SYSCO's existing broad-line capabilities. Strategically located across the United States, they offer SYSCO's operating companies in certain areas the opportunity to benefit from their product range and expertise while expanding their own market reach.

SYSCO's acquisitions also included two broad-line distributors: Doughtie's Food Inc. of Portsmouth, Virginia, and Watson Foodservice of Lubbock, Texas. These broad-line distributors enhanced customer service in the mid-Atlantic and southwestern United States. Annualized sales of these five companies together totaled approximately $500 million.

The sixth acquisition in 2000 was a specialty produce company, FreshPoint, Inc., which distributes specialty produce to 22 locations across the United States and Canada. Customers choose from a variety of produce items, from the conventional to the exotic. The company also specializes in value-added services including ripening and repacking.

This addition of FreshPoint, with approximately $750 million in annualized sales, positioned SYSCO for significant future growth, as broad-line customers may now access a wider spectrum of unique specialty product items. Along with increased produce sales and enhanced product offerings, the FreshPoint acquisition also allowed SYSCO customers to enjoy the benefits of FreshPoint's in-house ripening and repacking procedures.

SYSCO now offers a full spectrum of produce in numerous varieties, from everyday staples to the exotic. Opportunities also exist for strategic product cross-selling through both customer bases. Recently, SYSCO acquired certain operations of The Freedman Companies.

Autonomy Strategy

SYSCO is using the autonomy strategy for its acquisition process. There is no change in management when an acquisition is made. The acquired company continues its operations with its own employees—only the capital structure changes. If the acquired company has a strong brand perception in the market, the acquired company can keep its original name along with SYSCO, such as Nobel/SYSCO. The acquired company has power to manage its own company. Only capital expansion or equipment investment decisions need SYSCO approval. The autonomy strategy has benefited both SYSCO and the acquired company. Table 1 illustrates the benefits of the autonomy strategy.

Branding Strategies

SYSCO is determined that every product is pure, wholesome, and consistent with the high standards set by name brand products. The largest North American foodservice supplier, SYSCO has the industry's largest and most respected quality assurance department. SYSCO is dedicated to creating quality products that are a part of millions of lives every day, a responsibility that is taken very seriously. Unparalleled measures are taken to ensure that each product offered is as safe as possible. The quality assurance personnel's

Table 1 The Benefits of the Autonomy Strategy

Feature	Advantages	Benefit
Efficiency	Savings of time and cost in the acquisition process Savings of time and effort in regular operations and decision making	More profit generated
Market	Brand perception maintained	Market segment maintained; sales increased
Security	No employee lay-offs	Security for employees in the workplace
Expertise	Employees expert in the field	Better products and services

objective is to ensure that every SYSCO product, at every level, meets or exceeds the toughest industry standards. SYSCO has made food safety a top priority for over 25 years. The recalls on millions of pounds of ground beef reinforce the importance of quality assurance in the foodservice industry.

The produce department of SYSCO has a quality assurance program that was developed to improve upon the performance of the daily fresh produce inspection—a unique characteristic to the foodservice industry. These programs assist in the identifying and branding of the highest quality in fresh produce in the foodservice marketplace.

The quality assurance inspection department has developed and maintains coffee specifications for each SYSCO brand product. These specifications define every aspect of the product, which includes blend, minimum quality of raw materials for each blend, decaffeinating process, grind, roast color, moisture, oxygen, and packaging and labeling.

The SYSCO Canned Lot Set-Aside program is a unique industry program that assists in providing consistently high-quality products, categorizing canned fruits, vegetables, and tomatoes. Another monitoring program focuses on boxed beef, to ensure that every customer receives boxed beef products that meet all specifications set by the industry.

The commitment to delivering consistent products and exceptional value at all quality levels is unprecedented. SYSCO proudly stands behind each and every SYSCO brand product displaying the Guaranteed Quality Assured emblem and guarantees that these products conform to stringent standards for food safety, sanitation, and consistency.

Branding   SYSCO has four levels of quality for every product: Imperial, Supreme, Classic, and Reliance. Imperial products are the best available quality that are produced in prime growing regions and packed to extremely high specifications. Supreme are top-quality products, similar in quality to Imperial, but exclusive in that they are rare in the industry and unique to SYSCO. The Classic brand is SYSCO's lead-quality level under which the finest-quality products are marketed. Classic products meet and even exceed top-of-the-line competitive labels and account for the largest array of products. Products with the Reliance label, an economy position, are equal to competitive labels and offer consistency and value.

Specialty Products   Arrezzio is the family of authentic, Old World products specifically created for foodservice operations that feature Italian cuisine. Ottimo is the complete line of Italian products that provide quality at an exceptional value and are comparable with Italian distributors' brands. The Casa Solana brand, south-of-the-border-style products, is best suited for Mexican food. Block & Barrel is a collection of prepared products that features a variety of deli meats and cheeses, which is used mostly by delicatessen operations. Jade Mountain are the Asian products designed for Oriental meals. The House Recipe line consists of premium-quality tabletop products providing exceptional value to foodservice operators.

Specialty Companies SYSCO had the desire to create a cafeteria, food court, or freestanding mobile cart line with attractive signage to market the complete line of delicious, easy-to-prepare, heat-and-serve foods. The desire led to the creation of several different specialty companies. The Arrezzio Pizza program is an easy way to offer pizzeria-style pizza, by the slice or whole. Arrezzio Italian Café offers an appetizing display of Italian pastas and sauces, from a four-cheese Alfredo sauce to delightful, fresh pasta varieties. The Casa Solana Mexican Cantina offers exciting Mexican menus, featuring south-of-the-border favorites. Satisfying the hunger of the health conscious, as well as those with hearty appetites, the Potato Gourmet features huge baked potatoes and a large selection of hot and cold toppings. To enjoy the taste of Asian cuisine, there is the Mein Street Wok, featuring a variety of popular Asian rice bowls that are convenient and easy to prepare. National Floor Insurance Program provides a number of dry goods to suit the front of the house, back of the house, bar, cutlery, healthcare, janitorial, and the outdoors. National Floor Insurance Program is able to meet the equipment needs of every type of company or establishment.

Marketing Strategy

Considering the very fast expansion SYSCO has had, one can understand why the corporation only does a short-term (usually 1-year) marketing plan. There is separate marketing for different brands. However, there are some basic strategies SYSCO utilizes to maximize its market share.

Be Present Everywhere SYSCO is the leader in total dollar purchasing volume of food and related nonfood products in the "away-from-home" market. Included in the away-from-home market are restaurants, delis, hospitals, retirement homes, schools, colleges, hotels, cruise lines, and entertainment facilities. This market is served by three distributor categories, as defined below, and SYSCO has its presence in every category.

- Broad-line distributors supply a wide array of food and related items to all types of foodservice operators. These operators generally require a broad spectrum of products, and their menu offerings may change frequently. SYSCO's 62 "traditional" operating companies are broad-line distributors.
- Customized or systems distributors, also known as chain restaurant or quick-service restaurant distributors, supply chain restaurant operations. This customer segment generally serves a relatively fixed menu and requires a more limited product line. FreshPoint and the SYGMA Network, Inc., are systems distributors. SYSCO built SYGMA 15 years ago to accommodate this market. It is operated from the corporation level and has its headquarters in Denver. Its customers include some of the major national chains such as Wendy's and Papa John's Pizza.

- Specialty or niche distributors specialize in supplying a specific product category or a specific customer segment such as ethnic restaurants. SYSCO's custom-cutting meat companies are specialty distributors.

Take Different Approaches to Different Markets   SYSCO divides its market into two segments:

- Marketing associate–served customers include independently operated foodservice locations serviced by a SYSCO marketing associate. Sales to these customers represented approximately 55 percent of total sales at SYSCO's 63 broad-line, or traditional, locations. SYSCO has a team of nearly 7,000 commissioned sales professionals, or relationship managers, who provide customers with services tailored to undergird their operations and profitability. Their responsibilities include assuring that orders are submitted timely and completely, presenting new products that will enhance the customer's menu or reduce the labor required for preparation, and assisting with inventory control and menu costing and pricing.
- Multi-unit customers include local, regional, or national foodservice operations that have multiple locations and, due to their more centralized purchasing operations, generally do not require the same degree of personalized, value-added services that Marketing Associates offer, but are supported by other sales personnel within the SYSCO companies. Multi-unit customers contribute approximately 45 percent of total sales at SYSCO's broad-line locations.

Categorize Customers   Eighty-five percent of SYSCO's total sales come from only 25 percent of its customers. Therefore, SYSCO brackets its customers into four groups based on their order size, gross cost per stop for them, and SYSCO brand percentage in sales. It defines the top 10 percent as its Gold Customers, next 15 percent Silver, next 20 percent Bronze, and the rest "everybody else." They offer different special services above their standard service to different customer categories other than "everybody else." For example, they make special delivery arrangements for Gold Customers. By offering the special treatment, they want to motivate their customers and move them up to higher levels.

In summary, SYSCO's leadership success in the procurement arena can be attributed to the following four major management strategies:

- Acquisition of key players in the industry
- A fold-out strategy that economizes the system
- Concentration on SYSCO brands and specialty companies
- A responsive marketing plan

Case Discussion Questions

1. What advantages does SYSCO have over its competitors?
2. Acquisitions are a primary management strategy for SYSCO. Can you identify a product/service or brand which might fit the SYSCO acquisition strategy?

PART 5

The Defensive (Business Preservation) Strategies of Risk Management, Crisis Management, and Communications

Part 5 relates to the defensive managerial strategies and disciplines aimed at business preservation. Chapter 13 deals with the various aspects of risk management, including defensive, offensive, and preventive strategies. Loss prevention, security, and terrorism issues are presented. The chapter delineates the changing role of security in a world which must deal daily with the threat of terrorism.

Chapter 14 focuses on the appropriate steps in the crisis management process and the strategies managers must focus upon. This chapter outlines a comprehensive plan for crisis management. The nature of a crisis is subdivided into pre-crisis, actual crisis, and post-crisis strategies. In addition to the multiple-part plan, the chapter provides managerial strategies for dealing with the media, shareholders, and employees.

The final chapter in Part 5 focuses on communications strategies. Chapter 15 looks at all the focal points for communications management strategies such as employees, customers, investors, franchisees, the financial community, and the local community. The Four A's of communications strategies (attention, awareness, attitude influence, action or desired behavior, and action for motion toward consumption) are covered. Also, the role of publicity (proactive) and overall public relations strategies and tactics are presented. Both external and internal public relations strategies are discussed, as well as a description of all the tools and weapons of public relations.

Chapter 13

Risk Management

CHAPTER OBJECTIVES

- To describe the scope of risk management in the hospitality industry
- To delineate the major focal points for risk management and loss prevention strategies
- To discuss the role of security from a management strategies perspective
- To identify risks including terrorism and discuss preventive steps and other management strategies

In today's world the scope of risk management has both broadened and become increasingly important to hospitality industry organizations. Risks may be external threats, such as terrorism and arson, or internal occurrences, such as employee crime and violence. Table 13-1 provides some examples of external and internal risks.

FOCAL POINTS OF RISK MANAGEMENT

Management strategies must focus on the financial and legal implications associated with both external and internal risks. The managerial focus must also take into consideration self-inflicted risks such as those that are accidental. In general, management strategies related to risk fall into three broad categories: defensive, offensive, and preventive.

Table 13–1 Partial List of External and Internal Risks

External Threats	Internal Risks
Arson	Accident
Bomb/threat	Allergic reaction
Civil disorder	Asset theft
Counterfeiting	Break-in
Demonstration	Crisis
Earthquake	Death
Flood	Drugs
Former disgruntled employee	Employee-on-employee crime
Hijacking	Employee-on-guest crime
Hurricane	Financial loss
Insect invasion	Fine
Intrusion/holdup	Health crisis
Kidnapping	Infectious disease
Litigation	Kidnapping
Natural disaster	Lawsuit
Robbery	Guest-on-employee crime
Shooting	Medical emergency
Terrorism	Poisoning
Tornado	Strike
Toxic chemical release	Sanitation problem
Weather	Shooting
	Structural failure

Defensive, offensive, and preventive strategies are many and include: access control and monitoring, accident prevention patrols and accident insurance, quality monitoring, alarms, allergy treatment kits, building/evacuation procedures, facility inspections, carbon monoxide detectors, consumer product safety reports, emergency procedures, employee training, evacuation procedures, financial control systems, fire safety systems, guest protection systems, handrails, health insurance, liability insurance, key control, metal detectors, medical emergency training and supplies, natural disaster survival procedures, radon monitors, required immunizations, safes, sanitation systems, screening and testing of employees, security training, nonslip floors, well-lighted stairwells and other critical points, telephone and intercom procedures, training, travel accident insurance, and zero tolerance policies.

In risk management, the importance of training, systems and procedures, and adherence to policies cannot be overemphasized. These three areas provide the best defense and prevention for any organization. Crisis management procedures, insurance, and security are equally critical. Today's global environment is redefining the concept and role of security, especially the wave of terrorism sweeping society. While security and risk management are both dedicated to preventing losses, each approaches its mission differently. Security tries to prevent all forms of loss, yet knowing that some are inevitable, its secondary goal is to keep the dollar amount of the loss as low as possible. These twin objectives also mandate security's involvement in plans and preparations for dealing with emergencies and disasters. Risk management's role is to provide protection against losses, including those that might be caused by security operations, through the medium of insurance.

In planning and preparing for a proper response in the case of an emergency or disaster, the security/loss-prevention effort has to focus on a wide range of incidents that can result in the loss of life or assets or injuries to customers and employees. Plans mean that employees will know what to do if an incident occurs, as well as what to do and how they can be accounted for if evacuation is necessary. Preparations involve having available the resources needed to respond.

While by definition emergencies and disasters are sudden, unanticipated events that require immediate responses, in some cases, such as acts of nature, forecasting can help with preparations. Many other situations, such as bomb threats or acts of terrorism, cannot be predicted. Nevertheless, by weighing probabilities against vulnerabilities, training, and establishing priorities in terms of resources, meaningful programs can be designed to deal with many of these occurrences.

THE CHANGING ROLE OF SECURITY

Security has always been viewed as an important function in many sectors of the hospitality industry. However, historically it seldom was viewed by senior management with the frequency and urgency it is today in nearly all sectors. Granted, the airline sector viewed security as a major priority, as did the cruise and casino sectors prior to September 11, 2001. Thereafter, security took on a whole new priority in all hospitality sectors. To put this in perspective, with the exception of the aforementioned airline, cruise, and casino sectors, security reports were not board of director–level, executive committee–level, or even senior management–level meeting agenda items, unless something major had actually occurred. Today, security-related matters are priority items on these agenda.

ETHICS

Risk management focuses on both the internal and external violators of a code of ethics. Communication helps to reduce risk and can be vital in loss prevention.

Senior management now not only recognizes the importance of security as a function, but more significantly understands the role and the urgency of security. Hijackings now cause the entire air travel system to shut down. Terrorism activities have generated a whole new generation of preventive measures and acquisitions of sophisticated equipment and newly trained human resources throughout the industry. Insurance premiums have skyrocketed for buildings, facilities, and infrastructure, and for the potential liability for injury or death of employees, visitors, and bystanders. We have moved in a giant step to the point where security is now the number one concern (or one of the top concerns) of travelers and in most other sectors of the hospitality industry.

From a management strategies perspective, there are many implications beyond the elevated attention levels now given to the security function. These implications have resulted in changes in hiring criteria, training, labor force levels, equipment requirements, and human and financial resources in virtually every sector of the industry. Senior management must now focus on a daily basis on everything from potential terrorism threats to serious reallocation of resources to meet these new needs. A balancing act between individuals' (guests' and employees') rights and offering reasonable security is now an ongoing issue for the courts. It has been said that too little security or too much rights intrusion results in the same outcome—litigation. Senior management must continually strive to balance these issues while protecting the human, physical, and financial assets of their corporation.

TECHNOLOGY

Today we live in a world obsessed with security yet demanding speed and convenience. Security technology includes audio and video surveillance, scanning equipment, high-speed data transmission, and a plethora of other features that assist in providing enhanced security, safer environments, and quicker response times when crises or events occur. In the hospitality industry technological applications such as heat sensors, traffic flow/management systems, and numerous life safety applications have also reduced risks while enhancing customer and employee experiences.

Some of the duties and functions go by the same names—such as loss prevention, risk management; protection of assets, and so on—however, their magnitude and scope has taken on new meaning. Loss prevention now deals with the loss of lives, buildings, and perhaps the corporation itself, versus traditional focuses such as theft and fraud. Risk management now requires a whole new level of, and types of, insurance coverage and protection systems. Protection of assets is no longer only applicable to third-world countries or what were considered high-risk hot spots. Today assets need protection at home as well as abroad. Not only does this global perspective apply to physical and human resources, but also to financial resources, as the internet and technology have developed rapidly as tools of the criminal who can operate from anywhere on earth. Let there be no mistake, security as an issue has risen to the top of the organizational hierarchy and is certainly receiving senior management's attention in today's hospitality industry.

RISKS AND TERRORISM

In its simplest form a risk can be defined as a potential occurrence that can impact an organization, customers, or employees. Terrorism can be categorized as one of the most uncontrollable and severe forms of risk that exists today. Terrorism is one of the worst risks because of the character of the acts, which often result in major loss of human, physical, and financial resources. Terrorists' acts are crimes and include homicides, bombings, kidnappings, and destructive acts. All acts of terrorism involve violence or threats of violence and are frequently directed at civilians. Terrorism is disruptive not only to businesses, but to the way people go about their daily lives.

Management strategies to protect an organization and all of its assets from terrorism begins with assessing the threat and taking preventive measures. It has been said that the individual and the organization may be best equipped to protect itself against terrorism by being aware of possible risk. Personal vulnerability must be a principal concern. Those who attract terrorists' attention are persons of apparent wealth, people who represent something important or of particular value to others, or who are accessible.

Most terrorist groups need money; therefore, wealth or access to wealth makes people and organizations targets. Terrorists also need publicity to keep their cause in the eyes of the public. Kidnapping someone unimportant does not get sufficient publicity. However, kidnapping someone who represents a prominent firm or business, with a worldwide image, raises the stakes.

Terrorists also take the path of least resistance. The more accessible one is, the more likely one is to become a target. One way to evaluate risk is to assess the number of social or political demonstrations in the destination, the number of terrorist incidents and the subject of these acts, and the type of security procedures designed to discourage terrorist activity and their effectiveness. The U.S. Department of State issues bulletins relating to travel safety in countries throughout the world.

Intense attention has been given to airport security since September 11, 2001. In the United States, the Federal Aviation Act of 1958 established the Federal Aviation Administration (FAA) to provide for a safe and efficient utilization of the nation's airspace. Since 1973, the FAA's Office of Civil Aviation Security has been responsible for the implementation and coordination of security measures to deter acts of criminal and aircraft piracy. After September 11, President Bush established an Office of Homeland Security reporting directly to the president to oversee and coordinate all activities related to security including terrorism.

The Middle East has become the primary source of international terrorism, accounting for about one-third of the incidents. However, international travel has permitted the export of Middle Eastern terrorism elsewhere. The targets of Middle Eastern terrorism are typically Israel, Western governments and citizens (especially of democratic nations and in particular the United States), moderate Arab governments and officials, and critics of radical regimes.

While the Middle East generates most of the terrorist groups, historically, Europe has been the location of the largest number of incidents (40 to 50 percent). Latin America is the third center of terrorist incidents, accounting for approximately a fifth of the events worldwide. Most of the terrorist groups in this region have emerged from the social, economic, and political turmoil that confronts the region. There also has been some spillover into Latin America of terrorism from the Middle East and Europe. Hospitality industry management should constantly assess destinations and consider what the local terrorists are doing, who they are doing it to, how frequently they do it, whether past attacks have been successful and why, and the stability of the government in the proposed destination. This will help to develop preventive measures for business entities and visitors to the regions.

Until September 11 and in large part due to the effectiveness of U.S. law enforcement agencies, Americans seemed to think that they were protected, anywhere they go, at any time. In reality, there is a limit to the protection any country can offer its citizens. No country can guarantee protection for its citizens wherever they go. Citizens of all countries need to take protective measures and be vigilant about terrorism, especially when traveling. Figure 13-1 provides preventive steps to help in protecting oneself and others.

There are additional steps one can take to avoid being a target of terrorism or criminal activity when traveling. Deliberately vary your mode of trans-

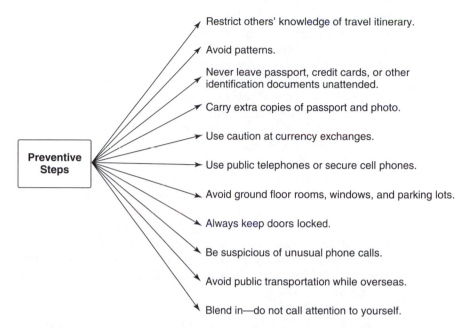

Figure 13–1 Preventive Steps for Terrorism and Crime While Traveling
Source: Foreign Service Institute, *Terrorism: Avoidance and Survival* (Washington, DC: Government Printing Office, 1979).

portation, travel routes, and times. Most of the larger hotels have several entrances and exits. Use them all. A complicated, unpredictable pattern makes the traveler a very difficult target for terrorists or others considering a kidnapping, mugging, or other criminal activity.

Business personnel should especially vary departure times and routes to and from work; use different entrances and exits from work; understand where help can be obtained along routes to and from work; travel well-trafficked roads; eliminate parking spaces marked with name and title; avoid regularly scheduled meetings each day, week, or month; and lunch at different locations.

One of the biggest threats while overseas is kidnapping. In contrast to other terrorist tactics, all of which are deployed against a variety of targets, kidnapping primarily involves a single entity, often a corporate executive.

Kidnappings can occur anywhere the traveler is not adequately protected. The risk of kidnapping is directly related to the security of the space the traveler is in at any given moment. When terrorists plan a kidnapping, they pick the point in a routine where security is minimal. Typically, protection from kidnapping involves being aware of one's own habits and routines and being willing to alter them, deciding what level of security is acceptable, and developing a positive attitude toward security.

Kidnappers are drawn to prominent persons, because they can gather information about such persons with relative ease. Precautions to keep such information to a minimum include: keeping personal publicity to a minimum; avoiding exposure in the local or national press, except where it is absolutely essential; keeping public exposure in advertising and promotional campaigns to a minimum; not publicizing memberships in social, religious, or fraternal organizations; corporations never releasing photographs of key executives; avoiding mentions in social columns; and key executives of an overseas corporation granting interviews to the media only when absolutely necessary.

Bombings and attempted bombings in the United States and abroad are on a rapid increase. A well-placed bomb in an underground garage or under a modern building in which the first floor consists largely of supports holding up the rest of the building can bring the entire structure down. Nothing is immune to bomb attacks and bomb threats. Office buildings, restaurants, stores, churches, hotels, hospitals, buses, and tourist attractions are all possible targets. Precautions and protection include physical barriers to intrusion, including such items as alarms, fences, and locks; controlling entry and monitoring movement of employees and visitors; and hiring practices. Today, pre-employment screening is an absolutely essential step to risk management and loss prevention.

From the standpoint of prevention, therefore, much can be done on the basis of careful analysis and flexibility in both planning and preparing a response. This does not alter the fact that the most difficult problem arises when the possibility of terrorist activity exists. There are limits to what can be done in the way of preventive action, but the importance of good communication and relations with police and appropriate federal agencies, as well as the hospitality organization's own ability to collect and analyze intelligence, cannot be overemphasized. If an act of terrorism does occur, the response is the same as in any other disaster.

CHAPTER REVIEW

In this chapter we have described the scope of risk management and the roles of loss prevention and security within the hospitality industry. We stated that risks and threats may be from both external and internal sources. In order to address these risks and threats, hospitality management strategies must encompass defensive, offensive, and preventive strategies. In today's global environment we stated that threats and terrorism can be directed at human, physical, and financial resources and that preventive steps should be part of training for all employees. We also discussed the changing role of security, especially since the events of September 11, 2001. Included in these changes were both a broadening of the scope of security and an elevating of the topic/function to senior managerial levels.

Next, we examined a number of risks including terrorism, bombing, and kidnapping. We suggested assessment and preventive steps that can be followed to increase awareness of these risks/acts as well as potentially help prevent becoming a victim of the acts. Finally, we emphasized the importance of pre-employment screening as a major step to avoid or reduce risks and losses.

KEY CONCEPTS/TERMS

Crisis   Risk management
Liability   Terrorism

DISCUSSION QUESTIONS

1. List three defensive measures you would take for a hospitality industry firm.
2. List three offensive risk management strategies.
3. Identify an external threat and state what you would do to monitor and respond to the threat.
4. What steps would you undertake to prevent a major crisis from occurring? Identify a crisis and related steps.
5. Why do you believe hospitality organizations should have a comprehensive risk management plan?
6. How do security/loss prevention and risk management differ?
7. If an act of terrorism occurs, how should management respond?
8. Name three types of resources that are at risk from criminal or terrorist activities.

CASE 1

McDonald's Corporation—Monitoring Suppliers Can Reduce Risk*

A risk may come from either an external or internal source. In the case study that follows, the risk is external, from a contracted or supplier source.

This is the case of McDonald's "Pick Your Prize Monopoly" game promotion; the case of a company's most famous and lucrative promotion turning into a front-page headline about fraud. It is an excellent example of turning a potentially disastrous event into one in which the risk was minimized and the problem effectively shifted to another party.

Headlines read: "McTheft" and "FBI Arrests 8 in Fraud Scheme Targeting McDonald's Game." Eight people were arrested and charged with rigging the popular McDonald's promotion game to fraudulently collect more than $13 million worth of prizes. Fortunately, no employees of McDonald's were involved in the scam. Those charged were employees of Simon Marketing Inc., the Los Angeles–based company hired to run the promotion/game for McDonald's. Where there is a brand as famous and well respected as McDonald's, the risk is always there to associate the blame and the liabilities. In this case, post-crisis, McDonald's did just about everything right to minimize its risk and to repair the bad publicity of the initial event. On the other hand, McDonald's may not have done its best pre-event in selecting a vendor for its most famous promotion. Let's look at both of these risk management performances by McDonald's Corporation.

Here is what happened. The FBI arrested eight people involved in a scheme to defraud the McDonald's Corp. of some $13 million by rigging several of the fast-food company's promotional games since as early as 1995.

The scheme—involving friends and close-knit family members, including a husband and wife—was initially reported by a citizen who "came forward and roughly described a conspiracy" that was confirmed by further investigation.

The eight suspects were charged with fixing the outcome of the contests—including the "Pick Your Prize Monopoly" game—by controlling the distribution of the high prize values. The ringleader was identified as a security official with Simon Marketing, Inc.—the company that McDonald's hired to run the Monopoly game.

The complaint alleges that the security officer provided the winning game pieces to his friends and associates who acted as recruiters. These recruiters then solicited others who falsely and fraudulently represented that they were the legitimate winners of the McDonald's games.

Simon Marketing handles virtually all of McDonald's major promotions, including its "Happy Meal" menus. The security officer with the firm had been

*Information derived from www.cnn.com/2001/law/08/21/monopoly.arrests.

responsible for placing the winning high-prize pieces into circulation since at least 1995.

Prosecutors alleged that for a $1 million winning piece, the security officer and his recruiters would charge $50,000 in cash from the winner, often money he demanded in advance before giving over the piece. The recruiters also got a cut.

On lower prizes, such as luxury vehicles, the recruiters would sell the winning game pieces to other family members or friends. According to court documents, Simon Marketing's policy called for constant supervision of the high-level game pieces from printing to distribution by at least two or sometimes three people.

Obviously McDonald's Corporation has been through crises before this, as evidenced by its response and handling of the event.

McDonald's chairman and CEO (at that time), Jack Greenberg, announced that the fast-food chain was terminating its relationship with Simon Marketing "effective immediately." He said it would impanel an independent task force to review all future promotions and ensure their integrity.

McDonald's said it was "delighted" with the arrests and announced a new $10 million instant cash giveaway, lasting for five days, to make up for the fraudulent games. "We are committed to giving our customers a chance to win every dollar that has been stolen by this criminal ring," Greenberg said. "This initial $10 million giveaway is the first important step toward fulfilling this commitment." During that five-day period, McDonald's gave away five $1 million prizes and 50 $100,000 prizes at randomly selected restaurants.

Greenberg said that when the FBI concluded the investigation and determined the total amount stolen, McDonald's would give customers an opportunity to win any additional dollars taken.

A McDonald's spokesperson said the company "was victimized by a long-time supplier in a sophisticated inside game of fraud and deception. . . . Protecting our customers' interest has been our goal since the investigation began."

The FBI praised McDonald's for its role in the investigation, saying the corporation and Greenberg were "model corporate citizens."

A sample of corporate press releases from McDonald's demonstrates the methodological manner in which McDonald's handled the crisis and related risks.

Corporate Press Releases

08/21/2001
McDonald's Applauds FBI Action, Announces $10 Million Instant Give-Away for Customers*

Oak Brook, IL, August 21, 2001—McDonald's Corporation today thanked and congratulated the Federal Bureau of Investigation, the U.S. Attorney's Office and the U.S. Department of Justice for their investigation that led to the arrest of a suspected criminal ring that has been charged with stealing high-level McDonald's game prizes.

According to the FBI, no current or former McDonald's employees or franchisees were implicated in the compromised promotions. The criminal ring was allegedly led by the security director for Simon Marketing, Inc., the outside company responsible for game security.

"Quite simply, this office could not have built the strong case we now have against the subjects without McDonald's cooperation and support," said Thomas Kneir, F.B.I. Special Agent in Charge from the Jacksonville, FL bureau. "This case is an excellent example of how cooperation between corporate America and the FBI can work to protect the American people from those who would victimize them for their own selfish gains. In this case, McDonald's was the consummate 'good corporate citizen' and for this we thank you."

"Customer confidence is at the very heart of McDonald's business," said McDonald's Chairman and CEO Jack M. Greenberg. "We're determined that nothing gets between us and our customers, and we're outraged when anyone tries to breach that trust. Once the FBI contacted us, we agreed immediately to cooperate fully with them in an effort to ensure our customer interests were protected. And today, we are pleased to see this objective accomplished."

Mr. Greenberg also thanked the hard-working investigators and pledged the company's continuing support to the U.S. Attorney's Office prosecution team. "Their professionalism and diligence throughout this investigation have been a credit to America's law enforcement community. Let me underscore the point that this is an on-going investigation, and McDonald's is fully committed to providing our continuing assistance and cooperation to the FBI."

Additionally, McDonald's announced several action steps related to this investigation, including:

McDonald's 2001 Instant Give-Away
"Even though millions of McDonald's customers legitimately won prizes over the years, this criminal enterprise has been charged with stealing many of the highest value prizes from our customers, and that is completely unacceptable," said Greenberg. "To right this wrong, we are announcing today the opportunity for McDonald's customers to participate in an instant give-away from August 30 through September 3, 2001, to win cash prizes valued at $10 million."

*From www.cheril.com/mcdonald/fraud.htm.

During the five-day period, 55 major cash prizes—five $1,000,000 prizes and fifty $100,000 prizes—will be given away at randomly selected McDonald's restaurants. To reach customers with news of the McDonald's 2001 Instant Give-Away, McDonald's will be publishing newspaper ads on Wednesday, August 22, 2001. Full details of McDonald's 2001 Instant Give-Away will be available today on McDonald's website, www.mcdonalds.com, and will be posted in McDonald's restaurants from August 30 to September 3, 2001.

"McDonald's is committed to giving our customers a chance to win every dollar that has been stolen by this criminal ring," said Greenberg. "This initial $10 million give-away is the first important step towards fulfilling this commitment. When the FBI concludes its investigation and ultimately determines the total amount stolen, we will announce plans to give our customers an opportunity to win any additional dollars taken."

Independent Security Task Force
In order to ensure the integrity of future promotions and protect its customers, McDonald's announced the creation of an independent task force to review all procedures for future promotions. "We're particularly pleased that Dan K. Webb, former U.S. Attorney, Northern District of IL, and Chicago partner at the law firm of Winston & Strawn, has agreed to chair this security task force," said Greenberg. "The task force will include leading independent anti-fraud and game security experts and is charged with scrutinizing our promotion processes to identify the ideal mix of checks, balances and oversight to ensure the integrity of future promotions."

McDonald's Terminates Supplier
Separately, McDonald's announced that it is terminating its relationship with Simon Marketing. "Given the duration of the alleged conspiracy, the lack of any meaningful oversight and the magnitude of the losses, it was the only responsible course of action," said Greenberg.

McDonald's is the world's leading food service retailer with nearly 29,000 restaurants in 121 countries serving 45 million people each day.

08/21/2001

Statement from Jack M. Greenberg*

Chairman and Chief Executive Officer, McDonald's Corporation

FBI Arrests Suspected Criminal Ring Charged With Stealing High Level McDonald's Game Prizes
Today's arrests are a powerful reminder that McDonald's will never let anything get between us and our customers. Customer confidence is at the very heart of McDonald's business.

When the FBI first contacted us, we were shocked and stunned. However, we agreed immediately to cooperate fully with the FBI in an effort to ensure our customer interests were protected. And today, we're pleased to see this objective

*From www.cheril.com/mcdonald/press_release_chairman.htm.

accomplished. We are proud of the role McDonald's played in this investigation, and pleased that no McDonald's employees were involved in any way. The FBI has made it clear that McDonald's was betrayed by a long-time supplier in a highly sophisticated inside game of fraud and deception. We are delighted that the perpetrators were arrested today.

On behalf of McDonald's, our franchisees, employees and customers, we want to thank the FBI, the U.S. Attorney's Office, and the Department of Justice for their extraordinary work. In piecing together this challenging case, this federal law enforcement team has earned our heartfelt thanks for the arrest of this criminal ring. Moreover, we recognize that this investigation is ongoing, and McDonald's has pledged its continued cooperation and support to the FBI's efforts.

Let me underscore one important point. Millions of McDonald's customers legitimately won prizes over the years, from free food and drinks to cash and merchandise. We now know, however, that this criminal enterprise has been charged with stealing many of the highest value prizes from our customers . . . and that is completely unacceptable. To right this wrong, we are announcing today the opportunity for McDonald's customers to win prizes valued at $10 million between August 30 through September 3 in a McDonald's Instant Give-Away.

McDonald's is committed to giving our customers a chance to win every dollar that has been stolen by this criminal ring. This initial $10 million give-away is the first important step towards fulfilling this commitment. When the FBI concludes its investigation and ultimately determines the total amount stolen, we will announce plans to give our customers an opportunity to win any additional dollars taken.

Finally, we want to emphasize again that McDonald's will do whatever it takes to ensure the integrity of our brand, our restaurants and the trust of our customers.

The theft of $13 million in prize money from the McDonald's promotional contest provides powerful evidence of the inherent risks a business takes when outsourcing a function to a business partner. In this case, McDonald's outsourced the promotion of its Monopoly and "Who Wants to Be a Millionaire" contests to Simon Marketing, Inc., and were victimized by the very person who was in charge of the promotion's security.

This is an example of the type of damage that a third-party vendor can have on a business's financial health and hard-earned reputation. Hundreds of billions of dollars each year are spent on the marketing of consumer products for such things as contests, coupon programs, cooperative advertising, and trade spending. Many companies do not monitor the activities of the vendors that make up the marketing supply chain and thus run the risk that millions of dollars intended for those purposes are diverted for someone's personal enrichment. Putting the following sound risk management practices in place can prevent some of these crimes.

- Conduct a complete background check of the vendor company and thoroughly investigate any red flags generated by that check.

- Get a complete list of the employees the vendor will have working on your account and fully verify their personal backgrounds for any history of malfeasance.
- Ensure that no one employee of the vendor has complete control of the security process.
- Assign one of your own employees supervisory responsibility for the vendor relationship.
- Conduct periodic audits of the companies to whom fiduciary responsibilities have been outsourced.

McDonald's is sure to closely adhere to these risk management practices in the future. Even if one does an excellent public relations job on the crisis, avoiding it and its inherent risks are the better road to take for any corporation.

Case Discussion Questions

1. In this chapter we indicated that there is a major movement toward outsourcing, and in the McDonald's case we see that the risks can be incurred from suppliers. What steps would you take to limit your risks with external suppliers?
2. Do you believe McDonald's "fix" or response was adequate?

CASE 2

MGM Grand Hotel and Casino—Taking Risks and Taking Chances*

Risk management, like any other managerial function, requires planning and thoroughness prior to decision implementation. Many times corners are cut, details ignored, and planning and thoroughness shortcut. The net result is often a substantial increase in problems or the creation of risks of a major and potentially costly magnitude. In the case study of the MGM Grand Hotel and Casino in Las Vegas, risks taken resulted not only in huge costs but also in one of the hospitality industry's most memorable tragedies. From this tragedy came major changes to laws that affect every property in the industry—every employee and every guest.

Two decades ago, the idea of a high-rise hotel fire killing dozens of people in Las Vegas seemed impossible. Building designs and codes were too advanced. Las Vegas was too modern a city. But, on the morning of November 21, 1980, 84 people died and 679 were injured as a result of a fire at the MGM Grand Hotel in Las Vegas. This was the second largest loss of life from a hotel fire in U.S. history.

Wiring behind a wall in the resort's deli overheated and then burned undetected for hours. The result was a flash fire that spread at a rate of 19 feet per second through the casino. The smoke from this super-fire whisked through the resort's air circulation system and trapped victims in hallways, rooms, and stairwells.

About 5,000 people were inside the resort when the fire started shortly after 7:00 a.m. Eighty-four of those would die at the scene or in Las Vegas hospitals. Within a year, three more victims would succumb to fire-related injuries. They were largely tourists and MGM employees. An investigation found the fire seized on the hotel's cost cutting in constructing the resort and on a series of installation and building design flaws.

Fire marshals had insisted that sprinklers should be installed in the casino during the building's construction in 1972. The hotel refused to pay for the $192,000 system, and a Clark County building official sided with the resort. Authorities later said the sprinkler system could have prevented the disaster at the hotel, which is now Bally's.

Where the fire started, a wire that was not properly grounded could have been discovered had the area been inspected. A compressor was not properly installed. A piece of copper was not insulated correctly. A fire alarm never sounded. A supposedly smoke-free stairwell that was a crucial escape route filled with smoke. The laundry chutes failed to seal, and defects existed in the HVAC systems—all contributing to the spread of the smoke. The fallout was

---

*Information from E. Koch, "MGM Grand Fire Altered Safety Standards" (November 2000), accessed online at www.lasvegassun.com/dossier/events/mgmfire.

$223 million in legal settlements. There was a public—yet not criminal—dressing down of those responsible for enforcing building codes and of the resort and those who built it.

The lesson was learned, and Las Vegas is now the undisputed leader in the world when it comes to fire safety.

Officially 87 people lost their lives, and many other lives arguably were shortened as a result of the smoke and toxins inhaled that day. Many survivors including the hundreds who were injured returned home and told their stories to lawmakers to help pass laws that changed fire safety practices in high-rise buildings worldwide. Nevada became one of the first states to enact what remain some of the world's toughest safety standards for public buildings.

After the fire, then-Governor Robert List put together a blue-ribbon panel of fire prevention experts, building inspectors, and government representatives to strengthen safety regulations in resorts statewide.

Although some progress had been made by the panel in the first weeks following the MGM fire, the February 10, 1981, arson blaze at the Las Vegas Hilton killed eight people and drove home the need for immediate change. Since then, there has not been a fire death in a high-rise building in Las Vegas.

It wasn't just the MGM Grand or Hilton that were virtually without sprinklers in November 1980. A report prepared for the Clark County manager's office named 11 other hotels as lacking sprinklers.

Five months after the MGM fire, the Nevada legislature passed a bill mandating sprinkler systems in all hotels, motels, office buildings, and apartments higher than 55 feet and requiring sprinklers in showrooms and other public gathering places of more than 15,000 square feet.

The MGM, which was at 99 percent capacity the day of the fire, only had sprinklers in a galley and in the basement, areas where the fire was stopped dead in its tracks by the heavy flow of water.

In 1980 there were no smoke detectors in any MGM rooms. Today, every room of every hotel in Las Vegas has one or more smoke detectors depending on size.

The MGM, like other local hotels, had shared-air supply vents that funneled toxic fumes into rooms, killing people as they slept that Friday morning. Today, the vents operate independently, blocking fumes.

The MGM and other resorts did not have fire control rooms. Today, every major public building in Las Vegas has such rooms with computers that can pinpoint the origin of fires and vent smoke out of areas to help firefighters.

There was no way for the MGM to contact hotel guests. Today, all hotels in Las Vegas have voice communication paging systems, enabling hotel and fire officials to talk to guests and give them evacuation instructions.

The MGM and other hotels had flammable cellulose acoustical ceiling tiles as well as plastics in carpets and slot machines that fueled flames and spread toxins. Those materials have long since been replaced. One subcontractor who used an adhesive banned elsewhere illustrates how risky such substitutions can be. "Use of that adhesive cost that company $26 million in damages."

Underinsuring was another costly risk for MGM. The underinsured MGM paid a $40 million premium for $120 million in retroactive insurance to cover huge claims. The insurance companies banked on a long settlement process in order to make money from investment of the premium. The settlement came too quickly—within 5 years—and the insurance companies refused to pay.

MGM Grand owner, Kirk Kerkorian, took the money out of his own pocket to pay the remaining fire victims, and then sued the insurance companies. This prevented the victims and their families from suffering while the matter was argued in the courts.

The trial was to be financed by the litigants, not Nevada taxpayers, but days before it started the insurance companies settled, paying $87.5 million.

The MGM restitution trial and the subsequent legal action in which the hotel sued insurance companies that balked at paying off retroactive insurance policies had profound legal ramifications. The restitution trial had 2,000 plaintiffs and several hundred defendants, including the MGM, suppliers, engineers, architects, chemical companies, and elevator firms. The MGM case paved the way for how today's massive consumer trials, like those involving tobacco and breast implants, are conducted.

This case brought about the realization that retroactive insurance is just bad policy because it makes the insurer insensitive to settling quickly. This trial ended retroactive insurance. But while insurance and legal issues dominated the aftermath of the fire, public safety always remained the central concern.

Since the MGM catastrophe, there have been some close calls, but no resort disasters. Most hotel fires are caused by a carelessly tossed cigarette, an electrical malfunction, or grease ablaze in the kitchen.

As recently as 1998, the Hilton hotel-casino in Las Vegas suffered $1 million in damages and evacuated six floors during a two-alarm fire, but no one was injured. Also in the late 1990s, a four-alarm fire at the Rio Hotel All-American Grill evacuated the hotel as the fire blazed in a kitchen duct.

While fireproofing major resorts that are the size of small cities is expensive, few of today's owners balk—still well aware of the consequences of an MGM-type fire. When the Aladdin was resurrected, every smoke alarm was required to be tested three times. Any failure requires replacing the faulty alarm.

Safety measures are now so exhaustive that a water pump has to work at all times and have a backup generator in case the power goes out—and electricity has to be restored within 10 seconds.

Remember, prevention (pre-planning and thoroughness) is one of the keys to successful risk management practices.

Case Discussion Questions

1. Select any potential risk or threat from Table 13-1 and list the preventive steps you would undertake for this threat.

2. What steps would you implement to monitor and deter employee crime?

Chapter 14

Crisis Management

CHAPTER OBJECTIVES

- To delineate the significance of crisis management
- To provide a comprehensive understanding of the crisis management process and related planning
- To set forth an evaluation and assessment process for a crisis
- To suggest a multifaceted checklist to assist hospitality management in strategically managing a crisis

Crisis management and related strategies are among management's most important responsibilities in the hospitality industry. A crisis can cause any organization to suffer revenue declines, loss of consumer and investment community support, and ultimately the death of the brand, product/service, and even the organization itself. Nearly all sectors of the hospitality industry are highly vulnerable to a crisis situation, and multiple crises could severely hurt even the industry itself. A crisis is an unexpected event that can immediately threaten the lives of shareholders and the ability of the organization to function/survive, and potentially the loss of all revenue.[1] Crisis management is the management of operations during the actual crisis (in the midst of the event) and the management of the business before, during, and after the crisis. Most crises require management from the outside-in and the inside-out by the management team. The crisis management of the organization needs to include even the "perception" of crisis as a major event to be managed. A situation that is left unaddressed jeopardizes the ability of a company to function and ultimately hurts the brand. A crisis can happen at any time to anyone. Organizations that have experienced a major crisis include: airlines (American, United, USAir, etc.); foodservice establishments (McDonald's, Burger King, Jack-in-the-Box, etc.); gaming and lodging firms (MGM, Hilton, Cendant, etc.); attractions (Disney, Six Flags, etc.), cruise lines, car rental firms, and virtually all segments in the industry. In fact, even the industry itself experienced a massive crisis as a result of the terrorism events of September 11, 2001. There are thousands more that could be listed. What strategies should be ready and put in place when a crisis occurs? Who is in charge? What are the responses? Who is the spokesperson? All of these questions and more should be scripted and addressed in a crisis management plan.

TECHNOLOGY

State-of-the-art life safety systems driven by the newest technology, such as fire and smoke detectors, air monitors, and sensors, are reducing costs, saving lives, and preventing crises for many firms in the hospitality industry. Advances in security screening equipment are making travel safer, as are redundant computer-driven systems in air transportation.

CRISIS MANAGEMENT PLAN AND PROCESS

Let's look at the planning process and the major parts of a crisis management plan and at the strategies in each.

Part 1: Mission/Approach

It is essential to be organized prior to any crisis occurring. Since you have no prior knowledge of what is likely to occur or what questions might need to be addressed, the need to organize critical data about a company is essential. Included information is the mission statement; a statement on the company's philosophy, related behavior, and standards; and statements on overriding values, objectives, and performance standards. Any key benchmarks and records should be identified and their location made known to those who will respond to the media, public, and authorities. Most important of all, it must be determined what and who need to be protected (e.g., patents, brand equity, the CEO and CFO) and the crisis management team members must be identified. It must be clearly identified who is in charge, who is the backup, and who is the next backup; who will address the media; and how all the team members will be reached (24 hours a day).

Part 2: History and Potential Crisis

The next step is to develop and record any significant historic information on crises or problems with your product, brand, facility, personnel, and so forth, that has previously occurred. Also list any future potential crises you foresee. These include but are not limited to: fires, crashes, murders, deaths, major accidents, poisonings, health hazards/occurrences, thefts, violence, employee crises, and electrical/mechanical and financial crises. Identify levels, categories, and related definitions for each type. Keep information on the business, the plan for handling each potential crisis, topical related information, key industry and trade association related data, competitive information, potential external resources, and so on. These files can make the difference between timely response and late response or successful crisis management or failure. It is important to have crisis files up to date at all times. Figure 14-1 provides a partial list of types of crisis files for a hospitality organization to keep.

Remember, the smallest crisis can be organizationally debilitating if mishandled. In fact, usually the mishandling results in a bigger crisis unto itself. Recognize that crises occur in stages. The time leading up to the crisis is

• Fire	• Employee crisis
• Murder/death	• Electrical/mechanical crisis
• Poisoning	• Accident
• Theft	• Terrorism
• Violence	

Figure 14–1 Types of Crisis Files

referred to as pre-crisis. There is the actual occurrence, or "event." Then there is the post-crisis period, where damage control needs to be effective. If damage control fails or the crisis is mishandled, you have the next stage, which is the resultant new crisis.

Part 3: Walkthrough

Simulate a crisis and conduct periodic walkthroughs or drills for the crisis management team. When it comes time to face the media be sure to do another "walkthrough" with all "spokespersons." Be prepared, always anticipate, and don't create another issue or crisis for misstating a fact.

Part 4: Initial Crisis Strategies

Immediately notify the crisis team leader and members the instant a crisis or potential crisis is identified. Notify the CEO, CFO, and board of directors. Pull the crisis team together and get into motion. The team leader should immediately establish a "gatekeeper" whose job is to control all contacts and inquiries in an organized and predetermined manner. The leader needs to restate each team member's responsibilities.

A crisis room should immediately be set up. This becomes a gathering place for response control and also eliminates looking for people, data, and so on. It further "contains" the crisis and related data to one locale. The crisis room should have a complete array of communications vehicles such as phones, faxes, video equipment, TV, computer, printer, and the like. Stock a crisis management packet including all the information described in Part 1 and any current "official" statements.

It is extremely important to quickly establish a media center, usually a room to which you can readily control entry and that limits the media's movement. Equip this room with everything the media needs and make them comfortable, as no one wants the media roaming around the facilities or catching employees and pressing them for comments.

By all means, do not hesitate to pull in outside advisors. Cross-check with other departments to keep them alert and appraised to the degree you deem necessary to control the crisis. Collect all data on the crisis and control access to the data to those who need to know and to those who are designated spokespersons. In Figure 14-2 the key initial strategy steps are highlighted.

Part 5: Audience Strategies

Immediately define and identify all audiences (e.g., victims' families, impacted employees, the media). Prioritize a key list of data for your stakeholders. Identify the best mechanism to reach each audience (e.g., personal meetings/briefings, telephone, videoconference). Know each audience well and anticipate any potential problem individuals as well as any potential allies. Know and follow government rules, regulations, procedures, and laws to the letter.

- Notify the crisis team leader/members.
- Notify the CEO, CFO, and board.
- Pull the crisis team together.
  - Establish a gatekeeper.
  - State responsibilities.
  - Furnish a crisis room.
  - Stock a crisis packet.
  - Establish a media center.
  - Pull in outside advisors if necessary.
  - Cross-check with other departments.

Figure 14–2   Initial Strategy Steps
Source: Adapted from J. Gottschalk, *Crisis Response* (Detroit: Visible Ink Press, 1993): 416–417.

Part 6: Media Strategies

Identify the corporate media policy and spokespeople. Be sure the appointed gatekeeper for the media is in place as soon as possible. Have a media database ready at all times with any meaningful data/facts noted. Have data from any third-party source which supports the company or its brands, products, personnel, or processes readily available. Have all rules and regulations understood by the spokesperson prior to meeting with the media. Put in place a "media inquiry system" including a list of information available, a list of available/authorized spokespersons, control process for media questions, and so on. The company's spokesperson will in all likelihood not be able to respond to or answer every question. Therefore, have a "fast-check process" in place to quickly follow up with answers for those questions. Remember to control and limit access by the media, and most of all be honest with them. Figure 14-3 recaps the key strategy steps with respect to the media.

ETHICS

Violating the code of ethics is one management strategy that usually results in a crisis of significant magnitude for any hospitality business

Part 7: Evaluation

Establish an item-by-item checklist and evaluate the crisis team's performance on each item. Make notations and take corrective actions on any items you feel did not go well. Contact external sources to get their reading and survey all internal constituencies. Conduct a complete content analysis of all clippings, video, footage, and the like, on the event. Make detailed notes of what was done correctly and what could have been done better. Express appreciation to all those who helped handle the crisis and to the media who treated your organization fairly. Reevaluate the crisis plan and make any modifica-

- Identify corporate media policy.
- Identify spokespeople.
- Set gatekeeper in place.
- Have media database and third-party source information ready.
- Understand all rules and regulations.
- Have a media inquiry system and fast-check process in place.

Figure 14–3 Media Strategy Steps
Source: Adapted from J. Gottschalk, *Crisis Response* (Detroit: Visible Ink Press, 1993): 421–423.

tions that better the plan or eliminate problem situations. Remember to reward employees who performed well during the pre-crisis, actual crisis/ event, and post-crisis periods. Figure 14-4 recaps the evaluation steps.

FIVE KEY COMMUNICATION STRATEGIES IN CRISIS MANAGEMENT

1. Respond appropriately based on the type, severity, or degree of the crisis. It is always best to provide only that information which is required.
2. The degree of urgency should be directly related to the type of crisis and the timing required.
3. Provide enough detail to dispel false rumors.
4. Issue a statement of resolution (the crisis has occurred and been resolved) or an assurance statement (the crisis has been identified and is being handled/addressed).
5. Remember to thank and recognize all that helped.

CRISIS MANAGEMENT CHECKLIST[2]

- Who is in charge when a crisis occurs? Who is on the crisis management team? Who are the team leader and backups?
- Who are the spokespersons?
- Who needs to be involved in each potential type of crisis?

- Check on how handled.
- Contact external sources.
- Survey internal publics.
- Conduct contact analysis of clippings.
- Analyze impact on the bottom line.
- Express appreciation to the team.
- Evaluate and modify the plan.
- Reward employees for performance.

Figure 14–4 Evaluation Steps
Source: R. Nykiel, *The Art of Marketing Strategy* (New York: Amarcor, 2001): 153.

- Where will the crisis management room (center) be set up?
- Who will be the gatekeeper?
- Where will the media room be located? Who will monitor/manage/gatekeep the media?
- What is in the crisis management packet? What should be updated?
- Is there a monitoring and data collection system or procedure to obtain and record information on similar crises within our industry when they occur?
- Is there up-to-date contact information (phone numbers, etc.) for all key stakeholders, crisis management team members, board of directors, and external resources?
- Is there an internal "need to know" crisis communications plan and policy in place?
- Is there a recovery plan in place which addresses concerns of customers, intermediaries, and the like?
- Are internal and external counsel versed on all federal, state, and local laws, rules, regulations, and procedures related to the potential crisis?

CHAPTER REVIEW

In this chapter we pointed out that virtually every organization in the hospitality industry is likely to experience a major crisis. We defined a crisis as an unexpected event that can immediately threaten the ability of the organization to survive or function. We suggested that a multifaceted plan and process make up the key management strategy for managing a crisis. The process incorporates addressing the three phases of a crisis—pre-crisis, the crisis itself, and post-crisis. Moreover, crisis management strategies include a dual focus. One focus must be on managing the outside entities (e.g., media) and the second on managing the inside entities (employees, the crisis itself, etc.). We further pointed out that any situation left unaddressed during a crisis is likely to turn into another crisis itself. Crisis management strategies require planning, organizing, and defining responsibilities prior to any crisis. Finally, we stated that all crisis files and plans be constantly updated.

KEY CONCEPTS/TERMS

Benchmarks	Crisis management
Crisis	Walkthrough

DISCUSSION QUESTIONS

1. Why is it important to have a crisis management team versus an individual to handle a crisis?
2. How should media inquiries be managed on site?
3. What do you believe is the major role of managing the crisis internally?
4. What types of other crises can develop from not managing the original crisis properly? List three.
5. List all the potential audiences who might need to be notified and addressed when a crisis occurs.
6. Why is the "need to know" concept important in crisis management?

ENDNOTES

1. J. Gottschalk. *Crisis Response* (Detroit: Visible Ink Press, 1993): 410.
2. R. Nykiel. *The Art of Marketing Strategy* (New York: Amarcor, 2001): 154.

CASE 1

Jack in the Box—Recovering from a Mega-Crisis*

Earlier in the chapter, we stated that one definition of a crisis was any event that jeopardizes the existence of an organization. Jack in the Box Inc. is an appropriate example of "how not to" and "how to" handle a crisis of this magnitude. In this case, we will look at a brief profile of the company and how the company handled a major crisis both initially and over the longer term.

In 1951, Robert O. Peterson, the owner of a chain of successful local restaurants, developed a drive-through restaurant called Jack in the Box. Located primarily in California, Texas, and Arizona, Jack in the Box restaurants featured a smiling clown named Jack, who greeted motorists ordering through a two-way speaker device encased inside Jack's head.

During the early years, Jack in the Box business operations were conducted under various names and structures, including Foodmaker, Inc. In 1968, Jack in the Box was acquired by the Ralston Purina Company as a wholly owned subsidiary. Jack in the Box's management performed a leveraged buyout in 1985, and the company went public 2 years later with a common stock offering of 4.6 million shares.

In late 1988, Jack in the Box management took the company private once again. The company initiated a recapitalization program in 1992 and went public with a common stock offering of 17.2 million shares.

In October 1999, the company changed its name from Foodmaker, Inc., to Jack in the Box Inc. The company's NYSE stock ticker symbol also changed from FM to JBX. On the first day of trading under the company's new name, Jack, the company's fictional founder, rang the closing bell at the New York Stock Exchange.

Known as a trendsetter and innovator, Jack in the Box has created some of the most powerful ideas and distinctive menu items in the quick-serve industry. It introduced the industry's first breakfast sandwich as well as the first prepackaged portable salad.

Today, Jack in the Box tailors its menu primarily to adult tastes and features one of the most varied and high-quality menus in the fast-food industry. The company continues to explore new food trends, including ethnic and regional foods, snacks, and healthy offerings—all aimed at satisfying changing consumer demands.

In 1993, a major crisis hit Jack in the Box. Hamburger meat was contaminated with the bacteria E. coli, resulting in over 600 Jack in the Box customers becoming ill and three deaths. In handling this crisis, Jack in the Box made a number of mistakes, including moving too slowly to recall the product and not managing the company's reputation with the media and consumers.

*Information derived from www.jackinthebox.com/pressroom/index.php?section=6.

Further, Jack in the Box initially and perhaps inadvertently tried to blame its supplier (a scapegoat) rather than address the problem. After these initial mistakes, Jack in the Box did a number of things to handle the crisis much better. First, it agreed to pay all medical bills without question. And second, after the loss of customers and revenues, it instituted a new recovery plan to win back the consumers' and investors' confidence.*

In 1994, Jack in the Box implemented the fast-food industry's first comprehensive Hazard Analysis & Critical Control Points (HACCP) system for managing food safety and quality "from farm to fork." This HACCP system includes a microbial meat-testing program, as well as a series of inspections that monitor restaurant activities daily to ensure safe food.**

Then, in 1995, Jack in the Box turned to marketing to help reintroduce itself and target a new market segment. In January of that year, Jack was reintroduced as the company founder, "spokesman," and icon in a new advertising and marketing campaign. Targeted at young adult males, the ads help build brand awareness and showcase product initiatives. Independent consumer research shows that the Jack ad campaign is more memorable than ads of competitors who have a greater share-of-voice. Nearly 4 years after the campaign launch, consumer research confirmed that the ads were still considered fresh and memorable. Furthermore, consumer research found that they are highly effective and have been successful in building brand equity for Jack in the Box restaurants.

In his bid for the White House during the 1996 presidential elections, Jack was the top vote-getter in a national independent Virtual Vote poll, beating out Bill Clinton, Bob Dole, and Dogbert (a popular cartoon character).

Over 11 million antenna balls in Jack's likeness were sold in 5 years. In the ad campaign, the balls act as Jack's sales force in the field, promoting the Sourdough Jack burger to fast-food lovers everywhere.

Although the company is now considered the industry leader in food safety, Jack in the Box continues to support tougher legislation to mandate food safety systems throughout the industry. Company executives have testified before state legislative committees, the U.S. Department of Agriculture, and other food industry organizations in support of state and national laws aimed at enhancing the safety of the nation's meat supply.

The company also partners with national consumer organizations to educate the public about the best techniques families can use to protect themselves against food poisoning, since most outbreaks occur in the home.

All Jack in the Box restaurant management personnel go through ServSafe®, a rigorous nationally recognized food safety training and certification program. Jack in the Box is a member of the Industry Council on Food Safety, a coalition of the National Restaurant Association charged with

---

*From www.foodquality.com/jjcov99.html.

**Colorado State University Cooperative Extension, "Safe Food Rapid Response Network," *Safe Food News* 1, no. 3 (Spring 1997).

demonstrating the industry's commitment to safe food service through food safety training.

Jack in the Box has completed a dramatic turnaround from both the consumer's and financial communities' perspectives. As many articles have recently stated: "Jack is back."

Case Discussion Questions

1. Make a list of what you believe would be the top five crises a fast-food chain might encounter.

2. What steps would you take to train your employees to deal with a major crisis?

CASE 2

Pan Am—A Catastrophic Crisis

As indicated in this chapter, a crisis can arise at any time and from both internal and external sources. Some crises can be catastrophic in their own nature and to an organization. The case which follows describes one such crisis.

The long, pioneering history of Pan American World Airways, which began in the sunny skies of the Caribbean in 1927, ended 61 years later on the night of December 21, 1988, on the cold, windswept hills around the tiny village of Lockerbie, Scotland. That night 270 people—259 aboard Pan Am Flight 103 bound from Frankfurt via London to New York and Detroit, and 11 on the ground in Lockerbie—died, victims of one of the most vicious terrorist attacks in aviation history.

Though Pan Am would struggle on for another two and a half years before bankruptcy forced the end of all operations, few would doubt its final chapter began that night at 6:25 p.m. (GMT) when Flight 103 departed Heathrow Airport, 25 minutes behind schedule. Half an hour later, a powerful bomb tore through *Clipper—Maid of the Seas* as it approached 31,000 feet, 175 miles north of London. A storm of debris—shredded aircraft, flaming jet fuel, luggage, cargo, brightly wrapped presents, and horribly mangled bodies—rained down over several hundred square miles of the Scottish countryside. The largest pieces, including one of the massive Pratt & Whitney jet engines, fell directly on the center of Lockerbie, igniting a firestorm of incredible proportions.

Word of the tragedy crossed international news wires within minutes after the radar controllers in Scotland lost contact with Flight 103. NBC and ITN, the British television network, were credited with the initial reports. At Pan American headquarters in New York, where it was mid-afternoon, a well-rehearsed crisis disaster plan went into action. Guards restricted access to the company's executive offices on the 46th floor of the landmark Pan Am Building. A dedicated tollfree telephone line for relatives and friends of passengers was activated. At the Pan Am WorldPort at Kennedy International Airport, New York, arriving flight status boards flashed "SEE AGT" ("See Agent") next to Flight 103. Specially trained teams of passenger service agents prepared for the grim task of meeting and assisting relatives and friends.

In response to the first wire service queries, a Pan Am spokesperson was able to confirm only that radar controllers had lost contact with Flight 103. Moments later Pan Am confirmed that a crash had, indeed, occurred, that there were no indications of survivors, and that there were casualties on the ground. Inevitable confusion developed over the number of passengers on board. Reuters wire service initially quoted a Federal Aviation Administration (FAA) spokesperson who reported that there were 244 people on board and that the crash had occurred 10 minutes after takeoff.

Both misstatements were quickly corrected. Pan Am's initial count was 255 on board, subsequently increased to 259. By the time Pan Am's chief spokesperson addressed assembled reporters at the company's headquarters at 7:00 p.m., he was able to confirm the actual passenger count. Following standard procedure, he declined to release passenger lists, pending notification of next of kin. He also declined numerous requests to speculate on the cause of the accident.

A Pan Am spokesperson answered questions at headquarters; the scene at the WorldPort was growing increasingly frantic. Still, from the outset the families were well disposed to Pan Am. The first accounts tell of escorts providing help and support for the families.*

In fact, wire service reports noted the grief and attendant rage directed at television news cameras and photographers. Associated Press reported that one grieving relative knocked a camera from a photographer's hand and added, approvingly, that a Pan Am security guard intervened asking for understanding from the assembled photographers and escorted the person from their prying lenses.

Unaware of the real cause of the disaster, reporters initially speculated about a mechanical or structural failure. They recalled an accident earlier that year in which an Aloha Airlines Boeing 737 came apart in midflight, a result of stress fractures in its frame and skin. The crippled aircraft landed safely thanks to the heroic efforts of pilot and crew.

Both Pan Am and the FAA quickly produced the *Maid of the Seas'* maintenance logs and answered questions. The aircraft was delivered to Pan Am in 1970, the 15th 747 built by Boeing. There was nothing out of the ordinary in its log.

In fact, two years earlier the aircraft had been completely rebuilt as part of the U.S. government's Civilian Reserve Air Fleet (CRAF) program. CRAF was intended to ensure that there would be sufficient high-quality airlift capacity available in the event of a national emergency.

Officials in the United Kingdom and the FAA and FBI knew that 747s did not simply disintegrate in midair. At the time, the plane had one of the best safety records of all commercial aircraft. They quickly dismissed the possibility of mechanical or structural failure. They knew there could be only one explanation for what happened. And within an hour of the first reports, they were organizing what would become the largest manhunt in the history of international terrorism.

It is often said that how an organization is perceived to be managing a crisis is determined by its actions in the first 12 to 24 hours. While an expert response will not necessarily resolve the crisis, the contrary proposition should be self-evident: A bungled response will worsen the problem and prolong the recovery.

Pan Am executives did as much as they could that night and the next day to organize an effective response. Once questions about the aircraft's integrity

*R. O'Rourke, *Disaster at Lockerbie, Crisis Response* (Detroit: Visable Ink Press, 1993): 253–262.

were disposed of, media reports acknowledged the company's concern for those with family and friends on Flight 103 and firmly positioned the company among the victims of that tragedy.

However, the destruction of Flight 103 had profound long-term implications for Pan Am, and no amount of short-term damage control would change that. In fact, Pan Am's experience after Lockerbie illustrates the point that there is no objective standard of success in crisis management. Each situation is unique. Judging a company's performance requires a thorough understanding of the underlying conditions that predated the crisis and some reasonable definition of what constitutes success, given those preexisting conditions.

Pan Am ultimately succumbed after Lockerbie, but also after years of financial distress, contentious labor relations, and operating in a fiercely competitive, deregulated market. Against that backdrop, and through the Lockerbie crisis, the management team quickly recovered a large share of its customer base, minimized the sense of despair among shocked and beleaguered employees, and preserved a large measure of the company's historical reputation for safe, professional operations.

How they managed the issues that emerged in the weeks and months following Lockerbie is instructive for those interested in the complexities of crisis management.

If a terrorist group had wanted to strike out at a symbol of American prestige and leadership around the world, they could hardly have chosen a better target.

Pan Am had pioneered international aviation, starting in Latin America. The airline expanded service throughout the Pacific and, finally, across the Atlantic. Few companies were so identified with the United States around the world. Even the name *Clipper—Maid of the Seas* evoked the rich heritage of the Pan Am flying boats and the ideals of ingenuity, adventure, and pioneering spirit.

In 1988, despite years of financial difficulties, a shrinking international route system, and a problematic service image at home, Pan Am's blue and white logo still scored high in international brand recognition studies. In fact, the logo was as well known overseas as it was in the United States.

As a practical matter, in 1988 Pan Am was still the largest American carrier to Europe, serving more cities with more flights and carrying more people than any other U.S. airline. On either score—visibility or opportunity—Pan Am was a likely target. These facts did not escape the attention of the families of the victims of Flight 103. They asked, "If Pan Am was such an obvious target, why wasn't security better?"

If international visibility was the terrorists' objective, they accomplished more than they could have hoped. And more, it seems, than they had planned. Investigators quickly surmised that the bomber had intended that his device explode as Flight 103 proceeded out over the North Atlantic, taking with it all clues to his handiwork. However, as noted, Flight 103 departed 25 minutes late. The delay at Heathrow, and a northerly routing, resulted in an explosion over land, enabling investigators to gather enough evidence to identify a likely suspect and the route his bomb followed to Lockerbie.

More important, from a communications perspective it also enabled television crews to record the gruesome results. The *Maid of the Seas'* cockpit lying in a Scottish meadow became the visual symbol of the horror of Flight 103. The power of the visual images helped this act stand out among other terrorist attacks.

One day before the crash at Lockerbie, Pan Am CEO Thomas Plaskett, who had been at the helm less than a year, told Dow Jones News Service he was optimistic about the airline's prospects for the coming year. He predicted that year-end results for 1988 would be substantially better than the $265 million loss recorded in 1987. He even raised the prospect of a modest operating profit for the year. Overall, Pan Am's prospects at the time were better than they had been in recent memory. In 1988, a significant rebuilding of transatlantic traffic ensued from depressed, terror-conscious lows of 1986 and 1987.

Pan Am, given its dominant position in the market, had capitalized on the surge. Its share of the transatlantic market rose to 16.7 percent compared with 13.5 percent in 1986. Though still cash strapped, Plaskett and his team were confident that the improved performance could make lining up additional cash—or an outright buyer—considerably easier. Pan Am employees, if not quite optimistic, were justifiably proud of their tenacity. They had earned a grudging respect from competitors and analysts for their ability to keep the airline going.

In one sense, that pride and dogged determination was another victim of the crash at Lockerbie. With the crash, many Pan Am employees resigned themselves to the idea that the airline would not, in fact, survive and that the end was coming sooner rather than later. It was against those prevailing currents that Plaskett and his team set their course in the days immediately following the disaster at Lockerbie.

On day two reporters began asking about a new story from Moscow. Early in December, FAA officials had issued a warning to other government agencies about an anonymous threat received by the U.S. Embassy in Helsinki from a caller who said a Pan Am flight bound from Frankfurt to New York would be bombed and that the bomb would be carried on board by a woman.

Officials at the U.S. Embassy in Moscow posted the warning on an embassy bulletin board advising staffers that despite the warning they were not relieved from their obligation to fly on U.S. carriers. Word that government employees had the benefit of a warning that was denied to the American public was reported the next day. And though Pan Am had no control over the government posting, the issue became one of the organizing points for families of the victims of Flight 103.

Ironically, law enforcement and intelligence organizations knew of the Helsinki threat and had dismissed it as meaningless long before it was posted in Moscow. Finnish intelligence sources knew the caller and said that he was a disturbed man who had made similar threats before. Word that the threat was in all likelihood empty was communicated to U.S. officials and to Pan Am. Still, the idea that Pan Am negligently failed to warn its passengers of a threat fueled the growing anger of the families.

In the days following the crash—after notifications of next of kin were completed and it had been firmly established that Flight 103 was the victim of a terrorist bombing—Plaskett and his team turned to the question of how to appropriately express the genuine grief and sorrow that was so palpable throughout the organization.

A national day of mourning was scheduled in the United Kingdom for January 4, 1989, with a special memorial service in Lockerbie. It quickly became the focus of international attention. Members of the royal family, the prime minister, and numerous foreign dignitaries attended. Plaskett, as CEO, represented Pan Am. He was accompanied by employees representing every Pan Am location around the world. The gesture was widely noted in the United Kingdom and served the important purpose of unifying a disheartened work force.

In a prepared statement that Plaskett brought with him to Lockerbie, Pan Am expressed its gratitude "to the many heroic men and women who have emerged in the face of this tragedy, (who) have worked virtually without rest for 15 days to bring order to chaos, aid to the injured, and comfort to the bereaved."

In addition, a simple statement was prepared and ran in newspapers in the United Kingdom. It stated simply: "We extend our deepest sympathies and condolences to all who lost relatives, friends, and co-workers in the tragedy of Flight 103."

If the efforts helped to restore Pan Am's reputation in the United Kingdom or better position the company among the victims of the tragedy that was never its stated purpose. Therefore, no assessment was ever undertaken to measure "effectiveness." The delegation, the statement, and the newspaper notice were Pan Am's best efforts to express the organization's grief over the uniquely horrifying event.

In the weeks following the Lockerbie disaster, normally slow winter Pan Am traffic across the Atlantic dropped dramatically. In an effort to understand the decline, Pan Am surveyed air travelers, specifically those who intended to fly in the next 6 months. The results were disturbing. Although 81 percent of those who responded said they had no plans to change their travel itineraries, 36 percent said they were able to identify particular carriers about which they were concerned. Of those, 45 percent said they were concerned about flying Pan Am, compared with only 13 percent who said they were concerned about flying Delta or TWA and 9 percent who expressed concern about American.

More than three times as many travelers expressed concern about Pan Am than about their nearest competitor. Pan Am officials were also aware of recent survey results that indicated that the traveling public at large expected airlines and airport operators—not government officials—to bear the primary responsibility for the safe, reliable operation of the air transportation system. The surveys were particularly troubling because they contrasted sharply with similar research that had been done in the summer of 1986 after a series of terrorist incidents in Europe, including the hijacking of a TWA aircraft in Beirut, caused a dramatic fall-off in traffic to Europe. In that case, travelers identified Europe—the destination—as the source of their concern. In the current research, travelers cited a particular carrier—Pan Am—as the source of their concern.

Anecdotal evidence tended to support the data. Pan Am sales executives reported that travel agents were having difficulty convincing travelers that Pan Am was a secure choice. In response Pan Am produced an eight-page brochure on safety and security that was eagerly accepted by travel agents around the United States. Distributed by travel agents and Pan Am ticket offices in response to any expressions of fear or concern, either the airline or safety generally, the brochure attempted to familiarize passengers with the level of security already in place at airports and aboard aircraft.

Plainly identified as a Pan Am brochure, it instructed the traveler on what to expect at the airport and in flight. It also noted that some of the most critical aspects of air travel security were consciously kept out of public view. It noted Pan Am's cooperation with law enforcement and government intelligence organizations "to ensure that the most up-to-date intelligence is always available." The advice applied to all international flights. And while the focus was definitely on the actions and responsibilities of the airline and airport operators, the traveler was reminded several times about the need to guard against letting one's luggage out of one's control and accepting any packages to check in or carry on.

While the brochure was being prepared, Pan Am's commercial sales staff—those calling on corporate customers—learned of plans by some major customers to book all their transatlantic flights on foreign carriers, fearing that U.S. airlines were to be the target of a new wave of terrorism. In a letter to the chief executives of one thousand of the largest service and manufacturing companies in the United States, Plaskett called such actions "unprecedented, unwarranted and unlikely to increase the safety" of American business travelers.

He noted that U.S. carriers, particularly Pan Am, were operating at maximum security levels and that since supplemental security measures ordered by the FAA in January 1989 for flights inbound to the United States applied only to U.S. carriers, flying on foreign flight carriers provided, at best, a false sense of security.

"Unfortunately," the letter stated, "all airlines operate in the shadow of terrorist threats. In fact, there appears to be no meaningful distinction in the level of threats faced by the major Western nations. Terrorists seek targets of opportunity, and in recent years foreign flag carriers have been the targets of more incidents than all U.S. airlines combined."

Plaskett offered to have his chief of security meet with travel managers and security directors at any concerned company. The response was overwhelmingly favorable. Chief executives and travel managers who responded expressed their sympathies over the disaster and their continued support for

Pan Am. Volume levels among this critically important segment showed no drop traceable to a "corporate boycott."

Pan Am executives recognized that their immediate response to Lockerbie did not address the underlying vulnerability of the international air transport system to terrorist attack. The reality was—and remains—that a determined terrorist, with access to the best available technology, could repeat the attack on Flight 103.

Plaskett mounted an aggressive effort to raise awareness among key government and industry officials about alternatives to the current structure of the aviation security system. In government testimony, and in speeches before the International Conference on Airline Operators and the American Society of Industrial Security, Government/Industry Conference on Terrorism, Plaskett laid out a six-point plan that called on governments, air carriers, and airport operators of all nations to:

1. Recognize that all airlines are subject to the threat of terrorism, and agree that strong actions are required to safeguard passengers and crew members of all nations.

2. Agree to establish and implement a uniform international standard of practices and procedures for airport and airline security, worldwide.

3. Recognize that governments of all nations must take direct responsibility for airline security as distinguished from a solely passive, rule-making, or regulatory role, by providing whatever resources are necessary for improving the security of international air travel.

4. Concur on the means to fund the necessary resources, including law enforcement personnel and equipment to screen passengers, cabins, checked baggage, mail, and freight.

5. Accelerate development of advanced technology, equipment, and qualified operating personnel.

6. Establish a timetable for implementing these new standards, focusing initial efforts on airports deemed to be most in need of improvement in view of their threat profile.

Pan Am and Lockerbie are forever related; part of each other's story. Pan Am has now entered the annals of aviation history, to be listed among the great pioneering accomplishments of the 20th century. Lockerbie remains very much with us today, part of the darker reality of this era. It neither will—nor should—be forgotten.*

This case study provided insight into both the good and bad aspects of handling a major crisis. It also pointed out the unfortunate fact that many

*An additional source for this material was http://web.syr.edu/~vpaf103/update.html.

times after such a catastrophic crisis the damage is so severe that the organization finds it virtually impossible to recover.

Case Discussion Questions

1. "Misstatements" and false news reports from the media frequently occur in a major crisis like Pan Am 103. What would you do to help avoid such misstatements or expeditiously respond to a false report?

2. Many times a major crisis will reveal flaws in a process, product, or delivery system which require an action plan to correct. A number of such flaws appeared in this case. Do you believe Pan Am's management strategies and action steps to correct these were adequate?

Chapter 15

Communications and Public Relations

CHAPTER OBJECTIVES

- To identify major focal points for managerial strategies with respect to communications within the hospitality industry
- To delineate the various target audiences for management communications strategies
- To provide an example of a communications process
- To discuss public relations as one of the major communications vehicles
- To provide some guidelines for dealing with the media and press

Most successful senior managers tend to be excellent communicators. This also holds true within the managerial ranks of the hospitality industry. Communications strategies must be focused on many different audiences by hospitality industry management. These audiences include: employees, customers, financial analysts, investors and shareholders, franchisees, the media, the influential, and the community in which the company and/or its operations reside. Figure 15-1 delineates the focal points for communications.

To reach these target audiences with a planned message is what communications management strategies are all about. Among the keys to success is understanding of the objective for each focal point. For example, for employees, the objective might be motivational to improve performance and reduce turnover. For franchisees and investors/shareholders, the objective may be to stimulate incremental investment. Continuing on with these two examples will help understand the strategy and tactical executions management might choose to deploy. For reaching employees, a speech, video, or personal letter could be utilized, whereas, to reach franchisees and investors/shareholders, meetings and targeted "advertorials" might be selected. The key to overall management success in

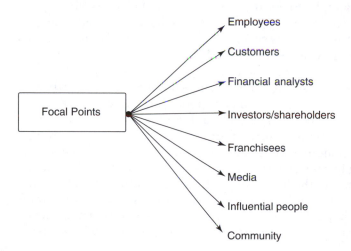

Employees

Customers

Financial analysts

Focal Points — Investors/shareholders

Franchisees

Media

Influential people

Community

Figure 15–1 Focal Points of Communications Management Strategies
Source: R. Nykiel, *The Art of Marketing Strategy* (New York: Amarcor, 2001): 31.

communicating is to have a plan, objectives, targets, and strategies and tactics well thought out and in a proactive mode.

THE FOUR As OF COMMUNICATIONS STRATEGY

Communications objectives and strategies should be preplanned and aimed at all target markets. Strategies planned and aimed at consumers should seek to spur purchases, consumption, and retention of loyalty. They may also stimulate referrals and trial business. The results of most can be measured or quantified if planned for in advance. News announcements should be timed for the greatest impact on the preselected target market. Influencing all constituencies in a positive manner is a major leadership function for hospitality industry management. Even the management of a crisis can be turned into a positive if acted upon promptly and effectively by management.

TECHNOLOGY

Communications technologies deliver pertinent business information instantaneously to the office, home, automobile, or individual. PCDs (personal communications devices) now offer multifaceted capabilities. The wireless revolution is enhancing service delivery and productivity. And, of course, the internet and related internet technology have dramatically improved communications.

Normally effective communications strategy encompasses what are referred to as the four As. First is *awareness* or getting your target audience's attention. Calling a press conference, staging a web telecast, or holding an employee meeting or franchise convention can exemplify this. The next A is to influence *attitudes;* for example, to get the media to write favorably about your brand, have employees leave a meeting motivated, or have franchisees feeling good about their brand. The third A is *action* or causing a desired behavior. This is when employees go back to work and perform better, your company is featured in a positive manner in a major media story or report, or franchisees ask for a development person (franchise sales) to call them. And, finally, the fourth A or *action 2,* which is defined as a motion or consumption. Employees' performance improves, the media calls for more interviews, and the franchisee buys another franchise from you. Figure 15-2 depicts the four As of communications strategy.

Successful management involves good communicators who plan and execute their plan, resulting in motion and consumption. Senior management has many other responsibilities in the hospitality industry and must often leave the tactics and scheduling up to public relations professionals. Some companies elect to have a formal public relations and communications person/staff, while others opt to contract outside the organization. Many elect to do both, using

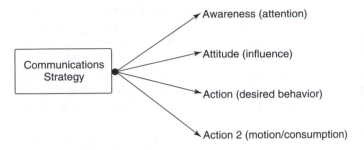

Awareness (attention)

Attitude (influence)

Communications Strategy

Action (desired behavior)

Action 2 (motion/consumption)

Figure 15–2 The Four As of Communications Strategy *Source:* R. Heibing, Jr., & S. Cooper, *The Successful Marketing Plan* (Lincolnwood, IL: NTC Business Books, 1996): 205–206. © The McGraw-Hill Companies, Inc.

an internal staff as well as external contracted expertise. In the next section we will take a closer look at public relations as it relates to communications.

PUBLIC RELATIONS

Public relations is a strategic weapon. It is a communications vehicle connecting your strategic messages to a variety of audiences. Public relations must include the total audience, which includes the investment community, shareholders, and franchisees, among others, as well as intermediaries and individual consumers of products and services. Public relations can effectively reach and affect everyone in this broad external audience. Furthermore, public relations can prove to be a very effective internal device to communicate with and motivate employees.

Publicity is only one facet of public relations. Publicity can be free, but it can be negative as well as positive. We will discuss publicity in more detail later in the chapter.

There are many fallacies about public relations: "PR is B.S." "Public relations is undefinable—it doesn't do anything and can't be measured." "Public relations is a waste of time and money." "Anyone can do PR work." People who make these comments either do not understand public relations or have only been exposed to disorganized public relations efforts. It's true, public relations does not directly make sales; however, it can be very influential in seeing that sales are made. Let's look at some ground rules for public relations strategies and explore what public relations is, how it can be applied, and later, how it can be measured.

What Public Relations Is

Public relations is a powerful tool that is capable of reaching all target audiences. In positive applications, public relations is on the offensive; in negative situations, public relations can provide a strong defensive strategy.

Public relations involves dealing with all publics, including individual consumers and potential consumers, the financial community, the local community, the media, and even your own employees. Effective public relations can provide a competitive advantage within your own business area or hospitality industry sector. Even public relations personnel frequently overlook this competitive advantage. In essence, a well-executed public relations/communications program can provide a good image within any industry segment. That image pays dividends in consumer preference for products or services, and it may also result in attracting and retaining good employees.

Public relations can create a favorable environment for a company, product, or service. It creates this favorable environment most effectively if it is part of the firm's overall strategic plan and management objectives. Objectives, strategies, target markets, expected results, timetables, and measurement can and should be established for all public relations programs. Of equal importance in a formal plan for public relations is the selection of the trained professionals to create and execute the plan. It is an absolute fallacy to believe "anyone can do public relations."[1]

The resources that can be used in public relations are unlimited. Here is a brief list of some of the vehicles public relations personnel use to reach various audiences:

- Announcements
- Broadcast media (TV and radio)
- Print media (newspapers, magazines, etc.)
- News conferences
- News releases
- Civic, social, and community involvement
- Employee relations
- Speeches
- Interviews
- Photographs

In addition, there are many different public relations and communications techniques that can be employed to obtain media exposures. Numerous articles and texts provide list after list of ideas and suggestions for generating positive publicity, but many authors forget one basic thing—the planned purpose or strategy for achieving such exposure. Even if your relationship with the media is superb, the use and placement of publicity must support your overall management objectives. The caution is simply stated: "Make your PR count." Some ideas for making your PR count are included in the list below. Each of the ideas listed should be placed within the context of an overall managerial strategy.

Applying Public Relations

Following is a partial list of public relations/communications opportunities:

- Accomplishments of employees or the firm
- Activities involving your company employees
- Anniversary dates
- Appointments of key people
- Awards received by the firm or employees
- Celebrities who use your products/services
- Community awards
- Contributions to charities and the local community by the firm or employees
- Displays of all types
- Events
- Events of special interest—humorous or creative
- Grand openings of all types
- Industry-related events
- Interviews
- New management, ownership, employees, etc.
- Organizational and/or operating changes of major significance to the public
- Public service events/activities
- Receipt of certificates, awards, etc.
- Recognition of people, places, things
- Special displays, features introduced, etc.
- Special events of all types
- Speeches of employees

Once the ideas and objectives for your public relations plan have been established and tied into the overall strategic plan, it is time to consider how to apply or execute those ideas. You must first answer some questions: (1) What medium can best execute this strategy? (2) Who are the key contacts for this task? (3) Is it necessary to establish or resolidify any personal relationships with the media before executing the strategy? (4) Do we have a delivery package ready for the media?

The delivery package—a package for the press containing news items, names and phone numbers of contact persons, property information, photographs, brochures, and so on—is essential. Although there is no guarantee the copy or materials you provided will be used, it is much more likely that your public relations message will correspond to your intentions if you make a delivery package available. The list below delineates the delivery package.

Delivery Package Requirements[2]

- Addresses and phone numbers of key media contacts
- Addresses and phone numbers of key corporation personnel
- Biographies of key personnel
- Briefing sheets on individuals, company, products, etc.
- Approval procedures and required forms
- Brochures, if applicable
- Product/service policies and procedures
- "Canned" formats, releases, letterheads, logos, symbols, etc.
- Confidentiality statements/procedures
- Contact list and phone numbers/procedures
- Ad copy samples and actual copy
- Displays, podiums with logos, etc.
- News conference procedures list
- Name and phone number of public relations contact
- Photo inventory of products, people, etc.
- Photo library and selection ready for press
- Previous problems file and checklist
- Previous questions file and checklist
- Price/information
- Procedures for distribution
- Promotional package on firm or product
- Request forms—data, photo, product information, etc.
- Scrapbook or clippings files
- Speech copies for distribution

Some public relations/communications opportunities—speeches, press conferences, meetings, interviews, and so on—involve personal contact with media personnel and others. Employing one of these direct-contact PR methods requires preparing the individual(s) who will be making the direct contact with the media. Thorough preparation is essential for successful direct-contact public relations. Ground rules and suggestions abound as to how to prepare a speech or other public presentation. Assuming the spokesperson follows the rules and makes a good presentation, there is still one critical mistake that can be made—using the wrong person. Simply stated, management must put the right speaker in front of the media. If the talk is on technical matters, be certain that the speaker has total command of the technical terms. If the talk is on corporate strategy, be sure the individual has enough authority within the corporation to be credible. If the talk is on the product or service, make sure the speaker can relate it to the audience's perspective. The following is a brief list of public speaking dos and don'ts:

Dos

- Carefully organize and allow yourself enough time to prepare.
- Be prepared—write out the talk, memorize it, and keep notes.
- Rewrite, review, and rewrite again.
- Create an outline or plan for your speech and follow it.
- Use pauses for emphasis.
- Check and doublecheck the visuals, equipment, room, visibility, etc.
- Speak out clearly and deliver smoothly.

Don'ts

- Don't speak on subjects about which you are not qualified.
- Don't ad lib.
- Don't guess or estimate numbers.
- Don't read in a monotone.
- Don't use excessive pauses, either in number or length of time.
- Don't prepare unreadable visuals.
- Don't mumble, slur, laugh to yourself, etc.
- Don't wait to read what you are going to say until the plane ride or cab ride there.

Dealing with the Press

Dealing with the press is one of the most difficult tasks management and public relations personnel undertake. Press relations are difficult for many reasons, but most of all because the press is powerful. It reaches many consumers with a message in writing, so you must be absolutely certain that the press has the facts correct.

Again, many good articles have been written on public relations and the press, many golden rules laid down, and many dos and don'ts listed. The recognition factors that follow represent a composite of a number of such lists. These are not all-inclusive, nor are they intended to be golden rules. They are factors that keep public relations efforts on a positive note—on the offensive rather than in a defensive position.

RECOGNITION FACTORS³

1. *Identify the purpose.* What is the purpose or reason for seeking the public relations exposure? If the purpose is to make others aware of the new product/service, be sure that is exactly what is conveyed— don't let it be lost in a story about the production process. Be precise and be sure the intent is communicated.

2. *Identify the target and objectives.* Who is the target? Is it prospective consumers? Is it the financial community? Is it employees? What are the objectives? Is it to boost employee morale? Is it to increase sales or brand awareness, support a new promotion, etc.? Think it out and identify how and where in the media you will best achieve the objectives.

3. *Understand the press's perspective.* You know your purpose and your target; that is your perspective. What is the press's perspective? Identify and understand the press's interests. Determine how you can place your purpose and target within a package that directly meets the interest of the press or other media. Think about what will help increase their circulation.

4. *Tailor the preparation.* Having identified the purpose, the target, and the media's perspective, tailor the preparation to include all three. Be sure to include everything that the press will need to convey the story—photos, names, and releases. Be sure the story is typed, double-spaced, and in the style the media is currently using. Follow the editorial style of the selected media at all times.

5. *Know the transmission channels.* Knowing where to send the material means knowing the difference between news and a feature story. News should be directed to the city desk, and feature stories should go to the appropriate editor. Better yet, get to know the editors who can be of most help and cultivate those relationships (but don't wear them out).

6. *Deal with the human element.* People do not like extra work or being pressured, and most cannot afford the time to tell you the ground rules. People basically want the easy way out. This sounds harsh, but it should help you understand how to deal with the human element. Find out the media's deadlines in advance. Do not waste time or the valuable time of media contacts. Do as much of their work as you can. Remember, if the material is well prepared and you do most of the work for them, your material may be used. If you do not do the work, you can expect nothing to appear. Also, remember to be available to respond to any media questions or requests for clarification. If you are unavailable, your material may be scrapped or come out wrong.

Management should have guidelines for answering questions from media representatives. The keys that follow are not all-inclusive, nor are they original, but they are very practical:

1. *Tell the truth.* The message management wants to convey should be pure fact. The media want credible, straightforward, and truthful material and relationships. This simply means the materials should be thorough and honest. It does not mean there is a need to reveal confidential data or private sources, nor does it mean confidentiality should be violated.

2. *Be responsive.* You may not have all the answers at your fingertips for every question or inquiry. Do not lie or guess; say, "I do not have that information with me; however, I will call you and provide it today." Then get the information fast and provide it accurately.

3. *Provide the facts and follow up.* Supply the key facts in print to lessen the chance of being misquoted on key data. If at all possible, follow up with media personnel by going over the facts or key numbers with them to ensure accuracy. If you do not have a requested statistic, get it and call or send a note to the person who requested it. Be sure accurate numbers reach the media.

4. *Be concise.* People usually get into trouble with the media for what they say, not for what they do not say. Provide the facts in a concise, uneditorialized, and unexaggerated manner. Be precise and accurate. Ranges may be okay, but pulling numbers out of the sky is a disaster.

5. *Build the relationship.* If you follow steps 1 through 4 by being truthful, responsive, factual, and concise, you are on your way to achieving the fifth practical key—building good relationships with media personnel. Hostile attitudes, reactionary statements to sensitive questions, aloofness, or a combative position damage relationships with the press. Work hard at being in control of yourself and your responses, no matter what you think of the media or a particular media representative. After all, someone who dislikes you is not going to be eager to give you space or airtime.

Tools of Public Relations

A press kit is usually a two-sided folder of high quality, often customized with the firm's logo or other identification markings. Background materials are normally placed in the left pocket, timely news items in the right. Examples of background information might include biographies of key property personnel, property fact sheets, and photographs. Timely news items include the actual press releases. The cover of the kit should not only convey your firm's image, but also be of a practical weight, size, and nature to protect photos. Photos should be clearly labeled on the reverse side. Few things are more embarrassing to marketers than to have the wrong photo get picked up with a press release.

Press releases may sometimes be picked up verbatim. Therefore, all releases should be "in form" and grammatically flawless. "In form" means the release should be exactly in the form you would want a publication to present your story. More often, the press release will be used as background or a resource from which the magazine or newspaper editor or reporter will work to mold an actual story. Here are seven keys to creating a press release with the proper form:

Key 1: The top right or left corner is almost always used for the name of the *contact person(s);* sometimes this appears at the end of the release. These contacts are the people who are readily available to provide more information. This means they should be knowledgable enough to speak to the press. Under the names should appear their telephone numbers, fax numbers, and addresses.

Key 2: A specific *release date* should be noted at the top of the page, slightly below the contact information. If the information is for a feature story that can appear at any time or is otherwise not date sensitive, the words "FOR IMMEDIATE RELEASE" should appear there, usually capital letters and sometimes underlined.

Key 3: The *headline* should be presented in capital letters and underlined (if desired) about one-quarter to one-third of the way down the first page. Considerable effort should go into developing the headline, because it is the "hook" that might catch the editor's eye or make your release stand out from any others seeking the same precious space.

Key 4: The *"dateline"*—the city and state in capital letters followed by the month and day—should be the lead-in to the actual text of the release. Datelines are important because they tell the reader where and when an event is occurring.

Key 5: The *body* or main part of the release should always be double-spaced. Paragraphs should be short, journalistic, and to the point. Like the headline, the lead or first few sentences are a "hook" that must grab the attention of the reader and address the key questions (who, what, where, when, and why—the five Ws).

Key 6: Including a few *quotes* is almost standard procedure with a press release. Whether the quote is from an internal source (someone employed by the organization issuing the release) or an external source, it is imperative that the individual quoted is aware of and approves of the quote. It is best to also let the individuals being quoted know of the date and time of the release so there are no surprises. When multiple quotes are used, it is usually best to alternate direct quotes (those in quotation marks) and factual nonquoted information.

Key 7: *Photographs* almost always enhance a story. You cannot always read the minds of those picking up your releases/stories; therefore, if you do not know the specifications, it is usually better to provide black and white photos as well as color photos. Color slides or negatives (assuming the publication uses color) are generally better, but send the actual photo to help the editor see what is on the slide or negative. Many publications now request that digital photos be e-mailed. You should also have this capability.

ETHICS

Through a concerted and sustained communications effort, an organization can transform its code of ethics into a genuine management tool.

How Can Public Relations Be Measured?

You frequently hear this comment: "PR is useless because you can't measure it." This is absolutely false! If a public relations program is well organized, it can be measured in many ways. One way is to measure the number and type of media exposures received. Keep a scrapbook of clippings and a current log of exposures—newspaper stories, magazine articles, mentions on the local television news, and so on. Set goals for the number and type of exposures, and then measure actual performance versus target.

Specific public relations activities may be measured by increases in sales. For example, if a major event or product is promoted through PR, and sales volume directly increases as a result of additional customers coming in for the event or for the product, you know public relations is likely working for you.

The following is a short checklist to assist in managing the public relations function:

Public Relations Checklist[4]

____ Does a PR plan exist and does it support the current priority areas of marketing?

____ Does the director of marketing and all staff members understand their responsibilities with respect to the press, the PR firm, and other outsiders?

____ Do key managers have good relations with the local media?

____ Are press release mailing lists up to date, accurate, and readily available?

____ Are fact sheets readily accessible to all and near the phones?

____ Are photo files up to date and fully stocked? Is there an up-to-date black and white photo file?

____ Are brochures and other collateral material accessible?

____ Are there definite plans, budgets, reviews, and measurement procedures in place for PR?

____ Is there a property or product press kit? Is it up to date?

_____ What is the quality of photos and stories, and how are they to be used?

_____ Are all key employees briefed and knowledgable about the value of public relations? Do they know the procedures to follow for press inquires?

_____ Are PR network memos kept on file? Where? How often are they looked at or discussed?

_____ When was the last PR audit? What were the results, and were all follow-up steps completed?

INTERNAL PUBLIC RELATIONS

The jobs of many people in the hospitality industry are challenging and require long hours. Keeping employees motivated and proud of their jobs is a difficult task. One of the most effective managerial strategies for accomplishing this is a well-organized internal public relations effort. This does not mean promoting the goods or benefits of the company to the employees. It can take many shapes and forms. An especially effective technique is to promote or provide special recognition of employees, their efforts, or even their interests. "Employee of the Month" awards, posters, photos, and so forth all work well. Special incentive awards and related public relations also are valuable motivational tools. Giving cash, prizes, or even novelty awards or plaques to deserving employees will help boost morale. Activities and events employees and managers participate in together—a bowling club or a joggers' group, for example—will help build a team spirit. A common goal, such as company-wide support of a selected charity, is another type of internal PR device for building unity. Perhaps most important of all is the continual recognition of employees' human dignity, pride, and desire for respect. Make internal public relations one of your key strategies for helping your employees be productive and happy.

There are a few measurement methods geared to evaluating the effectiveness of internal PR efforts. Look at questionnaires that assess employee morale, as well as employee turnover rates, breakage, pilferage, and so on. If your internal PR is working, certain quantifiable trends should emerge. Do not, however, ignore a more subjective yardstick of your efforts: Have you improved the esprit de corps in your organization? Are employees busy and enthusiastic?

PUBLICATIONS AND TRADE MEDIA

Most industry sectors have publications dedicated to the types of firms, products, and services within the industry sector. These are referred to as "trade" publications. They are often widely read by those who have an interest in your industry such as wholesalers, distributors, agents, and other intermediaries. These are excellent sources in which to publicize a new product, explain a change in policy or in management personnel, and so on. In general, it is also

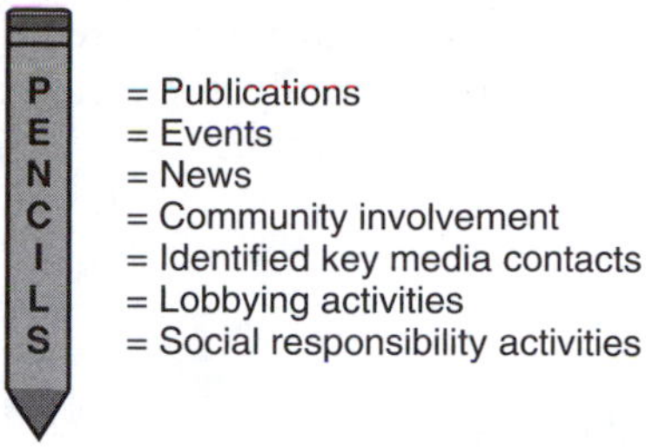

P = Publications
E = Events
N = News
C = Community involvement
I = Identified key media contacts
L = Lobbying activities
S = Social responsibility activities

Figure 15–3   Public Relations Tools
Source: R. Nykiel, *Marketing Strategies* (New York: Cormar Business Press, 2002): 72.

usually less expensive to advertise in the trades and easier to obtain coverage for your releases, stories, and the like.

Should your product or service lend itself to advertising in consumer-related publications, be sure your ad agency and public relations function/agency work together. Frequently, in order to secure your advertising, consumer publications will provide "advertorial" space or agree to include your product/service in a story or article. The synergy of advertising and public relations working together is a win-win scenario.

There are a number of types of materials that publications will pick up or that can be "pitched." These include new releases, announcements for an event, feature stories, concept articles, opinion pieces, and public service announcements. Remember that publicity is a nonpaid media communication that helps build target market awareness and positively affects attitudes for your products/services, brand, and firm. Just like all other marketing weapons, public relations should be planned and work in concert with your total marketing strategy. Public relations is your best marketing weapon for establishing credibility and building trust. Figure 15-3 is a simple way to help you remember six tools for public relations.

CHAPTER REVIEW

In this chapter we identified many audiences and focal points for management communications strategies ranging from employees and customers to the investment community. We suggested that a communications/public relations plan be directly linked to overall corporate strategy and objectives. We discussed the four As of a communications strategy: awareness, attitude, action (desired behavior), and action 2 (motion/consumption). We suggested that public relations is a very potent strategic weapon if executed properly and in concert with other managerial strategies. Further, we delineated various public relations/communications techniques and tactics to help get messages to various target audiences. We stated that public relations/communications has both internal and external constituencies or targets. The concept of a delivery package for the press was reviewed, along with a list of dos and don'ts for speaking to the public. Specific guidelines and suggestions were provided for dealing with the press. The "tools" of public relations were discussed including the press kit and press release mechanics. Finally, we concluded that sales, changes in attitudes, and exposures are measurement tools for gauging the success of public relations efforts.

KEY CONCEPTS/TERMS

Audiences

Delivery package

Exposure

Four As

Publicity

Public relations

DISCUSSION QUESTIONS

1. What are three proactive ways public relations can communicate a corporation's business strategy?

2. How would you address a turn-around or recovery in profits, and to which audiences would you convey the message?

3. Senior management wishes to convey a new compensation program for all unit managers. What techniques should be employed to do so effectively?

4. What guidelines would you provide your president/CEO if the media were calling with respect to a negative crisis?

5. Why is it a good idea to cultivate media contacts as well as provide them a detailed delivery package?

6. Why should a corporation's communications plan be linked to and driven by its strategic plan and objectives?

ENDNOTES

1. R. Nykiel, *Marketing Strategies* (New York: Cormar Business Press, 2002): 63–64.

2. Ibid., 65–66.

3. R. Nykiel, *Marketing in the Hospitality Industry* (East Lansing, MI: Educational Institute of the American Hotel and Motel Association, 1997): 117–119.

4. Ibid., 122.

CASE 1

Continental Airlines—The Power of the Survey and the Award*

In this chapter we stated that public relations can be deployed as an offensive weapon. Offensive weapons require not only the firing power of good media placement but must also have sound ammunition to work effectively. The case that follows points out the benefits of one type of great ammunition.

There are two ways to use the power of the survey or the award. One is to be fortunate enough to be ranked number one in an external objective consumer survey of products or services in your category. The other is to conduct and report on your "own" survey. This latter practice is frequently used by politicians and political parties to create perceptions that their policies are on target, or to create momentum for a candidate campaign. The former is an extraordinarily valuable strategic weapon if used to the fullest extent and if lived up to (remember the level of expectation concept).

Continental Airlines won the J.D. Power and Associates number one ranking in customer service in 1997. It went on to win J.D. Power and Associates rankings for 5 consecutive years. Granted this is a highly visible award/survey; however, once it is released it could be yesterday's news unless you reinforce it in a methodical manner. Continental Airlines did a masterful job of doing just that, reinforcing its accomplishment with all constituencies. It provided employee-based internal public relations programs and incentives. External advertising campaigns, promotional literature, timetables, and frequent traveler programs all repeated the accomplishment. In fact, its then-CEO even wrote a book, *From Worst to Best*, that further publicizes the achievement. In a business where "service" is the business and a major competitive advantage, Continental has the edge as a result of reinforcing its achievement through an aggressive internal and external public relations program that is also interlinked to its other strategic weapons.

Public relations is at its best when closely reinforced or linked to the other marketing disciplines or weapons such as advertising, sales, and promotions. The Continental Airlines case demonstrates how both public relations and advertising are used in concert for maximum effectiveness.

Case Discussion Questions

1. Discuss the pros and cons of participating in a survey that would publish the rankings of a hospitality industry brand or service offering.

2. Assuming your organization was highly ranked in the above-referenced survey, what would you do to exploit this finding?

*Information derived from R. Nykiel, *Points of Encounter* (New York: Amarcor, 1999): 77–78.

CASE 2

American Express—Listening to Your Needs*

This case could easily be included in the chapter on customer service and quality. However, it would be difficult to offer outstanding customer service and a quality experience without an excellent communications process, both within the organization and between the organization and the customers. Listening to your employees and to your customers personifies good communications. For this reason American Express is the case study for communications.

At American Express quality service is defined by excellence in communications. This excellence in communications extends from the credit card application process to the disputed charge inquiry—all along the way, exceptional written and verbal communications by well-trained professionals. To American Express quality equals outstanding customer and employee communications processes.

American Express has long believed that quality should be the goal of its business worldwide. The chairman of the company also carries the title of "chief quality officer" to help convey this goal to the entire organization. American Express goes beyond the signals by supporting its quality performance with substance, all focused on one goal—better customer service.

Basic substance begins with superior training (at its "quality university") and full support of senior management. American Express publishes an annual quality management report. Its focus is to emphasize that the corporation is in the customer service business. Employees are routinely expected to go beyond the normal procedures to provide outstanding customer service. Those who do are recognized by a corporate awards program.

Like many service organizations, American Express has numerous customer bases to cover. The two largest are its cardholders and those who use its worldwide travel services. Necessarily, a lot of time is devoted to see that the relationship between these two provides synergy instead of becoming a source of conflict.

American Express recognizes and successfully satisfies an immense and diverse group of customers around the globe. It focuses on its customers' needs for timeliness, accuracy, responsiveness, and immediate resolution at the first point of encounter.

Customer satisfaction is constantly monitored, and when new customer needs emerge, new services are implemented to meet these needs. These new services come from one principal source, according to company executives, who stated: "Virtually every new service introduced by American Express during

*Information derived from R. Nykiel, *Points of Encounter* (New York: Amarcor, 1999): 73–74.

the past 10 years came directly from listening to the suggestions and expressed needs of the customers themselves." In addition to listening to its customers, American Express employees are asked to spend 10 percent of their time striving to improve their job of delivering quality service. The result is many internal and procedural changes culminating ultimately in better service to the customers.

American Express sincerely believes that the key to success begins not only with pride and motivation of its employees, but with ongoing research into both job enhancement and customer needs identification. It utilizes sophisticated research techniques and the latest technology to quantitatively and qualitatively assess the needs of the customer. From these assessments, delivery of service improvements and new services is developed for its card membership. Ultimately, American Express wants its customers to feel that it is the only company they want to do business with.

The common elements of its success formula include: getting employees involved to redefine their jobs so they can better serve the customer; a passion for listening to the customers' needs; responding with action; prompt implementation of new services; addressing the needs accurately and with targeted marketing messages, reinforcing its quality image in how it promotes and markets its brand; and having the basic quality systems fully operating at all customer contact points.

American Express often "begins again," as exemplified by the innovative services introduced year after year. Many of these things, we now take for granted—because American Express is there doing it for us. Things like: cash when and where we need it, replacement of lost traveler's checks; global assist programs which help its card members with virtually any need, anywhere on earth; Gold Card holder account statements and categorizations at year-end that help in preparing tax returns; a product/service guarantee program that makes returns simple and workable; very high credit; translation services; lost luggage assistance; and the list could go on.

In essence, American Express quality service levels and innovative new service offerings have improved an entire industry as competitors strive to keep up with the leader. Leadership, quality service, customer satisfaction, and outstanding communications are what make American Express a winner.

Case Discussion Questions

1. Listening, especially to your customers, is one of the most effective steps a hospitality industry firm can undertake to improve its service and product delivery. Describe the process you would employ to take these findings to action or implementation.

2. Do you believe it is a good practice to actually have a "chief quality officer" in a hospitality industry corporation, or should quality be the focus of everyone?

CASE 3

Days Inn*

The expansion of nationally recognized brands across America is one of this century's greatest business success stories, a story in which franchising has been a key contributor. In fact, one out of every six businesses today belongs to a franchise system.

As brands grow in today's vitalized economy, it becomes increasingly challenging to maintain a strong relationship with owners and managers whose efforts dictate the success or failure of a franchise company and its reputation.

In the competitive field of lodging, where over 180 major brands exist, franchisors are faced with the risk of distancing themselves from their franchisees. For the sake of maintaining brand integrity, unity, and harmony, national-brand franchisors need to recognize the importance of communication and understanding in order to ensure the success of the brand with consumers.

A lack of attention in this critical aspect could invite apathy and a negative attitude that can affect service performance and product consistency.

The notion of maintaining solid communications isn't new. It has become a necessity as brands continue to grow. Franchise systems across the globe have come to recognize that when a franchisee isn't happy or feels they are not getting enough value for their royalty dollars, the franchisee could explore the countless pastures that perhaps offer greener grass. So, in order to attract new investors and retain existing ones, a brand should strive toward personal relationships that focus on adding value and demonstrating that the franchisees are your number one priority.

At Days Inn, with over 2,000 hotels, they have a saying, "24—Not an Hour More," which means that when they receive a call from a franchisee regarding a question or an issue, they will respond within 24 hours with an answer. Usually a question can be answered on the spot by a capable team of franchise service managers, but if it requires more research their goal is to get an answer for the franchisee within 24 hours. Every day, 365 days a year, the franchise service managers can be reached by franchisees for help and assistance.

Another initiative to solicit input and participation by franchisees is Days Inn's Alliance Program. Days Inn subdivided the United States into 36 marketing alliances; these alliances create regional advertising with co-op funds to augment the national marketing effort. These alliance efforts strengthen the brand message and at the same time ensure solid communications throughout the organization. While membership in these alliances is voluntary, 85 percent of Days Inns participate. These alliance hotels generate 30 percent more revenue per available room than the nonalliance locations.

Another strategy to ensure strong relationships is face-to-face meetings with the franchisee. By practicing this Days Inn is able to see how the brand is

*J. Kane, "How to Ensure Strong Franchise Relationships," *Hospitality Business Review* 3, no. 2: 27–30.

really performing and delivering in reality. Days Inn's senior management spends more than half their time in the field with franchisees. Rather than have national conferences, Days Inn recently held 11 regional meetings called Super Summits. These day-and-a-half meetings were designed to create a sense of positive energy regarding the brand and its franchisees, as well as focusing on superior guest service.

These meetings provided direct and open communication—including an interactive "town meeting" with the brand leadership, which led to many new ideas and initiatives that will add value for both the franchisee and the consumer.

Many franchisee companies have an active franchise advisory committee (FAC) as does Days Inn. An FAC consists of owners working as advisors to the brand. They are nominated and elected for specific terms outlined in the bylaws of the committee. Typically, owners in good standing elect other property owners to represent their views to the brand. Days Inns' FAC is comprised of 11 member owners who provide an excellent cross-section of opinions, geographical representation, and diversity. By defining objectives together, the brand and the FAC work collaboratively to strengthen the system. Discussions are open and wide ranging, from a new ad campaign to adding new amenities. FAC boards are probably the most misunderstood concept in hotel franchising. Days Inn's FAC is not a rubber stamp organization run by management. Spirited, sometimes contentious debates occur on key issues that affect the brand. It's a powerful group whose job is to help find solutions that work for the benefit of everyone—guests, owners, and the franchisor.

How do you know you're hitting the mark with your franchisee? You need feedback. One method that works for Days Inn is to host monthly brand conference calls, with a small group of owners chosen at random to participate. This is a very effective way of keeping in touch—listening to the franchisees and making them feel that their input is valuable and important. As well, many successful ideas have come from such meetings.

In short, Days Inn uses whatever creative method is available to encourage harmony between owners, managers, and the franchisor. Days Inn wants all parties to be seeking the same end result—success and a profitable bottom line. By keeping the channels of communication open and receptive, coming to an understanding will be easier. Here are a few more principles practiced by Days Inn.

First, they really listen to their customer the franchisee. When a franchisee voices concerns about something, Days Inn looks into it immediately by identifying and discussing possible solutions so the franchisee feels a part of the decision process. Days Inn's management answers franchisee questions within 24 hours, developing trust and demonstrating that the brand cares about the success of its franchisees.

Second, when developing new programs or ideas, Days Inn uses its franchisees as a sounding board to ensure program acceptance and success. The corporation endeavors to inject reality to a new idea or initiative.

Third, Days Inn has established a "Think Team" focused on the mission of the brand. As an example, its FAC and the brand's senior management team worked collectively to create a series of Key Result Area (KRA) objectives to formalize specific goals and actions for the brand. Each KRA statement includes critical success factors, measurements, and accountability and has been the framework of many of the last several years' most successful initiatives.

Fourth, Days Inn and its franchisees work within industry associations that can serve as a means to provide franchisees with additional resources and keep them updated on legislative issues. Franchisees are kept abreast of events that shape their business beyond the world of the franchisor.

As indicated in this chapter, practicing excellent communications must include all "audiences." Certainly in the hospitality industry today there are few audiences more important than franchisees.

Case Discussion Questions

1. What process or steps would you have in place to ensure that you were receiving your franchisees' opinions and input?
2. What mechanisms would you use to fully communicate with your franchisees?

PART 6

The Implementation of Strategic Planning, Organizational and Operational Concepts, and Leadership

Part 6 focuses on managerial strategy implementation and begins with Chapter 16 on the strategic planning process. This process provides the blueprint (plan) for implementing in an organized and measurable fashion the total array of managerial strategies. Actual examples for each step/component of the strategic planning process are presented.

Strategy implementation frequently influences and affects organizational and operational structures and procedures. Chapter 17 focuses on both organizational managerial strategies and techniques and various models of operational strategy. The chapter begins with a discussion of how the external and internal forces of change create the need for responsive organizational and operational strategies. A four-phased change model is presented, and a discussion of the complexity of change is included. Organizational philosophies and structures such as centralization and decentralization are presented. The concept of Six Sigma, including the six-step process, and KRAs (key result areas) are covered.

In the final chapter of the book, the concept of leadership profiles and strategy relationships are presented. Also in Chapter 18, a multidimensional model that matches leadership strengths with the product/service life cycle of an organization is presented. The concept of business acumen, with strategic focal points for management, is delineated. Finally, the traits and characteristics of successful leaders are presented along with the leadership profiles of 10 hospitality industry leaders.

Chapter 16

The Strategic Planning Process

CHAPTER OBJECTIVES

- To define the strategic planning process within the context of hospitality industry organizations
- To look at various organizational strategies utilized by management to conduct the strategic planning process
- To provide a step-by-step walk-through of the key components of the strategic planning process
- To delineate managerial responsibilities and strategies related to the strategic planning process

In most hospitality organizations the board of directors and the CEO focus on the overall direction and growth strategies for the company. To facilitate organizational harmony and commonality in direction, a strategic plan becomes the blueprint or guide for recording the decisions and defining the mission, goals, and objectives of the organization. Historically, many strategic plans were of a longer-term nature, looking out into the future 7 to 10 years or more. As the business environment changed by moving at a much faster pace, the planning cycle shortened to a 3- to 5-year perspective.

The overall perspective of the strategic plan begins with the corporate-level perspective and might be summed up with a question—What do we want this corporation to look like 3 years or 5 years into the future? Or, what businesses or segments do we wish to participate in or dispose of in the next few years? These types of questions usually lead to a "mission statement" or redefining an existing "mission statement." The mission statement is usually a concise narrative statement that summarizes the organization's ultimate goals. The mission statement represents the end result of achieving all the objectives and goals. It is what the organization wants to be.[1]

TECHNOLOGY

Due to the increased pace of change as a result of technology and improvements in analytical software and communications devices, strategic planning is also undergoing change. The entire concept of strategic planning in the hospitality industry has changed from a long-term to mid-term to tactical short-term process. In essence, technology caused 10-year planning cycles to drop to 3 to 5 years with constant revisions and updates. The net result is better planning and managerial strategy implementation.

PHASES OF STRATEGIC PLANNING

Prior to any mission statement or even goals being defined, the strategic planning process involves a comprehensive *competitive and environmental assessment*. This assessment focuses on both the external as well as internal environment. It represents a look at how the organization is performing and what factors are most likely to challenge or enhance the performance. The analysis focuses on what trends are going to impact the business or sections of the business. The competitive and environmental assessment looks at what is referred to as the SWOT analysis—that is, strengths, weaknesses, opportunities, and threats related to the business.

The comprehensive competitive and environmental analysis forms the rationale behind the next overall component of the strategic planning process known as the *strategy formulation phase*. In this phase various scenarios or models of the business are formulated. "What if" scenarios are played out, along with alternative models. Everything from the least likely to the most likely is modeled. Eventually, a number of best-choice scenarios emerge that capitalize on the outcomes of the competitive and environmental assessment and meet certain predetermined growth rates. These growth rates may be expressed in "ranges" or related to a multidimensional strategic plan. In the latter concept a "base case" is often utilized to look at the growth of existing businesses within the context of a business-as-usual assumption. The next dimension is often referred to as an "accelerated case" and puts additional resources or accelerated timetables in place to speed up the existing business growth. The third dimension or level is called the "new starts case" and builds upon the base and/or accelerated cases by identifying new businesses, acquisitions, and so on, that are above and beyond the other two levels. This multilevel strategic plan is depicted in Figure 16-1.[2]

After strategy formulation comes the intellectual process of determining the actual mix of strategies to be selected. This is known as the *strategy determination* or *strategy choice phase* of the strategic planning process. Selected strategies may be categorized or subdivided as related to the base, accelerated, or new starts case.

Given the completion of the strategy determination or choice phase, the strategic planning process moves into the active mode or *strategy implementation phase*. In this phase specific objectives are assigned to various areas of management for implementation. For example, business development may be charged with the objective of "accelerating franchise growth by 15 percent" or finance charged with restructuring the corporation's debt. An acquisitions

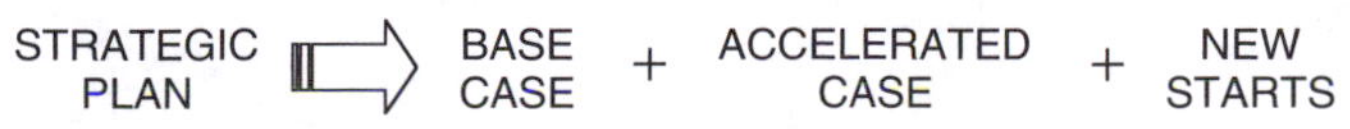

STRATEGIC   ⟹   BASE   +   ACCELERATED   +   NEW
PLAN   CASE   CASE   STARTS

Figure 16–1   A Multilevel Strategic Plan
Source: R. Haigh & R. Nykiel, "Future Shock and the Crossroads of Planning," speech to the Harvard Business Club, New York, NY (May 1970).

team might be formed and charged with doubling the size of the business by pursuing one or more acquisition candidates, and so on. As in most planning processes, the strategic plan has benchmarks or milestones by which achievement of objectives is targeted to be complete. This phase of the process is usually labeled "milestones" or "timetable." Progress is then measured and reported upon to the board in the *measurement phase*.

Today, strategic planning is more fluid than fixed, always allowing for reassessments, new opportunities, and adjustments to goals and objectives. Thus, the next step is to either *adjust* the plan or *reassess* and begin the overall strategic planning process over again. Figure 16-2 depicts the overall phases of the strategic planning process.

ORGANIZING THE STRATEGIC PLANNING

Within the hospitality industry, corporations utilize various approaches to organizing the strategic planning process. Some firms use a formal organizational approach by having a corporate staff function in charge of strategic planning. Some corporations utilize a "team" approach that involves selecting the "best strategic thinkers" and letting the group undertake the process. Others use an inside/outside approach by having either the formal organizational function or an internal team work with external consultants to formulate the plan. And in still other organizations the process is carried out by a committee of the board of directors with or without internal and external

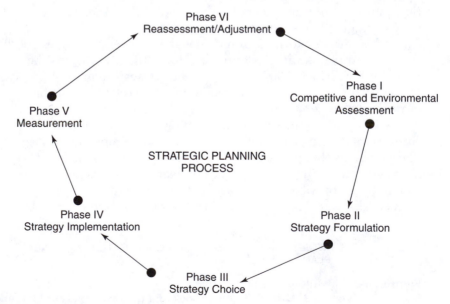

Figure 16–2 The Overall Phases of the Strategic Planning Process

assistance. In all scenarios, the CEO is likely to play the key role of team leader or facilitator, either directly or defacto.

ETHICS

A code of ethics serves as a central guide to support day-to-day decision making at work. It clarifies the cornerstones of an organization—its mission, values, and principles and helps managers, employees, and stakeholders understand how these cornerstones translate to everyday decisions, behaviors, and actions.

Once completed, the strategic plan becomes the grand design or framework for managing resources and the growth of the entire organization. Strategic direction is provided to corporate officers, business-level strategies are implemented or adjusted, and functional levels such as finance, marketing, human resources, and operations are given their objectives. Organizations that embrace the strategic planning process share it widely with employees, shareholders, analysts, and so on. Key overriding elements for a successful strategic plan are communications and coordination. Everyone needs to be on the same page and marching to the same directives.

ETHICS

A well-crafted code of ethics should be up front of every strategic planning document.

KEY COMPONENTS OF STRATEGIC PLANNING

Preface and Executive Summary

Actual strategic plans in written document form usually begin with a brief preface or introduction which describes the scope of the document and lets the reader know the flow and what to look for. The preface is usually followed by an executive summary. This executive summary is the key to presenting, communicating, and convincing all audiences (ownership, investors, shareholders, and stakeholders) to read on and be convinced. The executive summary should articulate the organization's mission statement, goals and objectives, strategies and tactics, and milestones. Further, it should address issues and highlight the planning documents' recommendations. Inclusion of a broad statement about the business environment (competitive and environmental assessment) may also be included. Executive summaries are concise and usually highlight key points using bulleted points, italics, boldface print, and the like—the objective is to allow for the reader to scan the summary and understand the key points and lead the reader into the document should detail or rationale be desired.

Competitive and Environmental Assessment

After the executive summary, the competitive and environmental assessment should be provided. This section of the plan should be written with the facts/findings presented in a fashion that directly supports or provides the logical rationale for the recommendations contained in the executive summary. The competitive and environmental assessment provides a realistic assessment of the business's strengths and weaknesses and its surrounding opportunities and threats (it is commonly referred to as the SWOT analysis) and then takes a close look at its competition. A strength is an asset or resource of the business that can be used to improve its competitive position, such as strong brand equity, a new product, or a strong distribution system. A weakness is just the opposite—a deteriorating resource or lack of capability that may cause the business to have a less competitive position, which can adversely affect market share. For instance, an antiquated distribution system and lack of a major market are categorized as weaknesses. Opportunities are developed from the business's or brand's strengths or set of positive circumstances, and can include superior products, high awareness levels, or the opportunity for unique products within your category. Threats are viewed as problems that focus on weaknesses and which can create a potentially negative situation. Depressed wholesaler activity and new competitors with substantial financial resources are examples of threats.

Strategic plan strategies should be based on a realistic assessment of the operating environment and competitive position. This assessment should include a factual SWOT analysis that is both objective and subjective in nature. The perspective should also include looking around at your competition, looking within at the business itself, and looking ahead to the next 1 to 5 years.

One note: Often competitive and environmental analysis is very comprehensive and contains many findings/facts useful to various functions and individuals in the organization. When this is the case the competitive and environmental assessment is usually summarized in the strategic plan and then presented in its full context in an appendix or reference document to the plan.

Driving Forces

On occasion a thorough competitive and environmental assessment/SWOT analysis may reveal critical forces related to the business itself. These are referred to as "driving forces" as they may actually drive the outcomes of the plan or substantially influence the outcomes. As a conclusion to the competitive and environmental assessment or as a lead-in to the goals and objectives, it is important to recognize that there are major driving forces. These are of such magnitude that they need to be discussed separately from the strategic issues. These driving forces, although interrelated to a large degree, should be viewed both individually and collectively as they support the objectives and strategies of the plan. Here are some samples of driving forces.[3]

Driving Force #1—Perception

We are clearly positioning as the current "value" leader in terms of quality product at a fair price. Our brands and sales force are perceived as the finest in the industry. Our overall perception by customers and competitors is one of leadership. We need to reinforce this perception or lose this advantage.

Driving Force #2—Pricing

Our pricing strategies have made us the most attractive company to deal with and provided us great sales advantages. Supported by our lower cost structure and quality product we have been able to take the number one market share position in most product/brand categories. We will need to capitalize on this and be even more aggressive to thwart new competition and maintain share in the upcoming economic downturn.

Driving Force #3—New Product Development

Our competitors and customers know us as the new product innovator. Our ability to develop and launch new products ahead of the competition is only threatened by the many new specialty product upstarts and our deteriorating distribution system. We can protect this driving force by rapid implementation of the new/proposed distribution system and an accelerated schedule of new product launches.

Mission Statement

The core of the strategic plan begins with the mission statement. This is a brief sentence or two that describes the purpose for which an organization exists and defines the scope of its operating domain. It clearly states the business's ultimate goals. The mission statement is shared with everyone in the organization and all external constituencies. It provides a clear direction for everyone working in the organization, serves as a basis for communication, asserts a philosophy for doing business, and provides a basis for evaluating the organization. In essence, a mission statement outlines why you are in business.

A mission statement once agreed upon becomes the benchmark against which all strategies and human and financial resource allocations are measured. Furthermore, a mission statement is a communications vehicle, whose purpose is to be clear, concise, and directional while focusing on the planning period as well as the future. A mission statement expresses what the leadership see as the end product of the organization in a few succinct sentences. Here is a sample mission statement:

> To become the industry leader known for product innovation, extraordinary customer service, and the best "value" in the marketplace.

Goals and Objectives

The next section, which immediately follows the mission statement, is the Goals and Objectives section. Goals are both qualitative and quantitative, which means that they are comprised of both databased estimates and educated guesses, although realistic estimates are preferred. Objectives outline what needs to be accomplished during the time frame of the plan. They must be specific, measurable in a quantifiable manner, related to a specific time period, and focused on affecting behavior. Although the overall goal is the fulfillment of the mission statement, very specific and quantifiable objectives are delineated. These specify the desired outcome or end results expected from successful execution of the strategic plan. Here is an example of a Goals and Objectives section.

Goal

To seek to offset pending economic declines (as a minimum target) with the achievement of actual growth through new product introduction producing an annualized rate of (up to) 15 percent incremental revenue growth during the plan's duration.

Primary Objectives

Reaching this goal is based upon the achievement of the following primary objectives:

1. Enhance the overall product offering both quantitatively and perceptually.
2. Broaden the customer base by providing new products.
3. Develop a new distribution infrastructure to be user friendly and maximize marketing resources to facilitate repeat business.
4. Increase market share by 5% per annum during the planning period.
5. Improve communications to all audiences, including current customers, suppliers, distributors, investors, and employees.

Each of these primary objectives is supported with a set of strategies and tactics for their implementation in the strategy section of this plan.

Strategies and Tactics

The next part of the strategic plan focuses on "how" the goals and objectives as previously outlined will now be achieved. This section is the Strategies and Tactics section. Strategies simply detail how the plan's objectives will be achieved. Tactics are the detailed items related to the strategies. Here are some sample strategies and tactics.

Reference: Objective #1—Enhance the overall product offering both quantitatively and perceptually.

Supporting Strategies

- Launch all brand extensions in the next 18 months.
- Introduce one new product per quarter.
- Implement the new package and signage designs over the next 6 months.

Tactics

- Begin brand extensions on the West Coast first.
- Introduce the first new product in New York for media proximity and coverage.
- Unveil new signage designs at the new unit opening in Chicago during the Franchise Convention.

Reference: Objective #2—Broaden the customer base by providing new products.

Supporting Strategies

- Expand the database list program and electronic marketing efforts.
- Launch a new advertising campaign at twice the GRPs (gross rating points).
- Implement new, more aggressive promotions and co-op programs.
- Expand the sales coverage into Canada and Mexico through new alliances.

Tactics

- Mail new prospects special introductory offers.
- Purchase incremental prime-time network television time.
- Increase the number of promotions and include a minimum of three trial offers during each business cycle.
- Sign alliance agreements by December 1 and have fully in place by March 1.

Reference: Objective #3—Develop a new distribution infrastructure to be user friendly and maximize marketing resources to facilitate repeat business.

Supporting Strategies

- Design the new system to allow online customers access for order tracking.
- Increase the discount percentages for multiple-term contracts.
- Launch a new frequent-purchaser incentive rewards program.

Tactics

- Provide major (category 1) customers with complimentary software at the time of system implementation (co-op with vendor).
- Run a sales contest when discounts are announced.
- Unveil at the Franchise/Convention.

Program Plans

In some cases, an objective and related strategies may be of such magnitude or so extraordinary in nature that a separate detailed "program plan" or "action plan" is delineated within the actual body of the strategic plan, incorporated in the appendix, or provided as a separate document (even though summarized in the strategic plan). In our example, the "new distribution infrastructure" might be meritorious of this type of treatment.

Certainly it is appropriate to include items such as a new franchising program, a massive refurbishment effort, and the like, within the Program Plans section or in tabled appendices.

Recommendations

Now that the strategic plan detail has been outlined, it is time to provide specific recommendations for both a short- and longer-term perspective. Typically, these recommendations are related to the objectives previously detailed in the goals and objectives section of the plan. This interrelationship between the recommendations and objectives should permeate decisions and actions in a manner consistent with the long-term success of the overall strategy. Once the necessary decisions are made, specific action takes place. Let's now look at some sample recommendations.

- To enhance the overall product offering, we recommend the acquisition of a new line of products (brand X and/or company Y). This will also help us quickly broaden our customer base (supports Objectives #1 and #2).

- Immediately reallocate an additional $5.0 million to expedite the implementation of the new distribution system (supports Objective #3).
- Retain our outside design expertise to refresh all packaging, brands, and the corporate logo (supports Objectives #1 and #5).
- Establish a new "communications" group to oversee all communication functions, and coordinate all efforts including the newly proposed "customer-friendly" order/distribution system communications (supports Objectives #1, #3, #4, and #5).

Vision Statement

In many strategic plans a section outlining the company's vision is included. The "vision" is a statement that vividly describes the desired outcome of the overall strategic plan.[4] Often the section including the company's vision will present alternative scenarios for its future while providing both direction and purpose for its interim strategies and activities. Let's review a sample vision statement:

- To be viewed as the industry leader by customers, investors, employees, and shareholders as a result of our innovative products, service-oriented employees, and strong financial performance.
- To achieve preeminence as the industry leader through award-winning customer service, flawless product quality and delivery, and dedicated personnel worldwide.

Slogans

In many business or corporate strategic plans, a company's mission, vision, goals, and objectives become reflected in a slogan. Slogans help build identity and can convey a company's position in the marketplace, as demonstrated by examples such as: "Quality IS Job Number One" or "Innovation Through Investigation." Ultimately, a slogan becomes a brand association or image with which almost everyone can identify. Let's take a look at some sample slogans:

- "Leadership Through Innovation"
- "The Quality/Value Leader"
- "Beyond Expectations"
- "Customer Driven Product Excellence"
- "The Company of Tomorrow"

Issues

In the process of undertaking any strategic plan, various issues will surface. We recommend that these issues be collected during the planning process and set aside for appropriate discussion at the end of the planning process. Although some issues may resolve themselves during the planning process, others may divert the process or cause delays. Addressing the issues at the end of the planning enables the company to put the issues into perspective in relation to the plan in its entirety. Let's look at sample issues:

- Twenty-five percent of brands (units, etc.) are in decline phase of life cycle and 35 percent are projected to be in 36 months. Do we sell or rejuvenate?
- Top three leading brands/products not doing well against biggest newly emerging market.
- Competitors' new products taking major market share.
- "Under-penetrated" (not enough stores/outlets) in three major markets and "over-penetrated" (too many stores/outlets) in three other markets.
- Lack of presence in Mexican and Canadian markets.
- Antiquated technology system in distribution is hurting sales and customer relations.

Measurement and Results

In order to ensure success, all of the activities within a strategic plan need to be measurable. This can be achieved in two ways—either the expected results are specific and quantifiable or they are related to key dates, milestones, or timetables. Likewise, qualitative accomplishments can be measured within time parameters or using other established criteria, such as polls, image assessments, or opinion surveys. Specifying these expectations is critical in determining which goals are being achieved and, as a result, whether strategies need to be modified. Let's review some sample key measurements and results:

- Increase product/brand offerings by 20 percent during the planning period.
- Reverse the downward trend in the CSI and bring it back up to the 90 percent level by December 1.
- Have the new distribution system up and running (within budget) by June 1.
- Open the Mexico City, Toronto, and Vancouver sales centers by March 1.
- Consummate two cooperative product-branding agreements—one by March 1 and the second by April 1.
- Review brand awareness levels after the new advertising campaign has run 6 weeks to ascertain if the 15 percent increase has been achieved against the target markets segment.

Resources Plan

A key component of any plan is a resources plan, as it may often seem that there are never enough financial or human resources available for the execution of the plan. Although strategic plans may offer a means for measuring various targets, such as increasing the revenue by 15 percent per year, the achievement of these goals is contingent upon meeting base plan revenue goals and obtaining incremental external funding to achieve accelerated and new start objectives. Thus, it is first necessary to determine the plan's priorities and the costs associated with their execution. Then comes the balancing act—weighing what needs to be accomplished against what is affordable.

In a strategic context, numerous scenarios or options may be selected, and each can be interlinked with existing and new strategies. For example: "If we exceed our revenue growth goal of 15 percent in Year One, we will move on to Option Two, increase the budget, and accelerate the new product development."

In the strategic plan, the financial requirements and results should be prepared using a summation format. Any desired (significant) "special" program budget plans might also be delineated on a stand-alone basis. Other scenarios can be presented in the financial plan, such as the redeployment of sales proceeds from a disposition of an asset to an accelerated case objective or new starts goal such as a key acquisition. Unlike the operating budget, a strategic financial plan is more flexible and theoretical. In fact, in many instances it may be expressed in ranges versus hard dollar amounts. Table 16-1 presents an example of a financial plan summation from a strategic plan. Note that new starts are expressed as add-on revenues and profits. In some cases the new start may actually reduce profits in an acquisition year and accelerate revenue only. In later years, both revenues and profits are likely to show increases.

Alternate financial scenarios with related probabilities may also be presented in an appendix.

Appendixes

The final section of a strategic plan is the appendixes. Although appendixes are often included within the original document, we suggest that relevant statistical data and research findings be presented in an accompanying volume. This will ensure that the strategic plan remains an action document and is not

Table 16–1   Financial Plan Summation

	Year 1	Year 2	Year 3
Base Case:			
Revenues	$1.0 billion	$1.2 billion	$1.4 billion
Profits	$100 million	$120 million	$150 million
Accelerated Case:			
Revenues	$1.2–1.4 billion	$1.3–1.8 billion	$1.5–2.3 billion
Profits	$120–150 million	$135–175 million	$155–200 million
New Starts:			
Revenues	+$300–500 million	+$400–800 million	+$600 million–1.0 billion
Profits	+$30–50 million	+$45–85 million	+$65–100 million

Source: R. Haigh & R. Nykiel, "Future Shock and the Crossroads of Planning," a speech delivered to the Harvard Business Club, New York, NY (May 1970).

- Preface
- Executive Summary
- Competitive and Environmental Assessment
- Driving Forces
- Mission Statement
- Goals and Objectives
- Strategies and Tactics
- Program Plans

- Recommendations
- Vision Statement
- Slogan
- Issues
- Measurement and Results
- Resources Plan
- Appendixes

Figure 16–3   Key Elements in the Strategic Plan

weighted down with excessive numbers, data, and research findings. Examples of appendixes include the following:

- Optional financial plans at incremental and/or reduced levels with probabilities
- Business review chart—Historical trends
- Research findings that support or negate strategies
- List of potential acquisition candidates
- Detailed milestones/timetable
- Detailed current market trends/information
- Information on potential co-op and alliance partners
- Other data such as new logos, package designs, etc.

From preface to appendix, a strategic plan becomes the guide to navigate the hospitality corporation toward its ultimate goals. Fulfillment of its mission is supported by each section of the plan. Figure 16-3 summarizes the key elements in the strategic plan.

MANAGERIAL RESPONSIBILITIES

The CEO and senior management of a company are responsible for communicating and seeing that the objectives and strategies of the strategic plan are implemented. Senior management must motivate functional and operational personnel, exploit the corporate culture, and manage the business development process. With respect to the latter, the focus is on achieving the plan's goals and objectives while meeting the ROI and cash generation goals of both the annual operating plan and the longer-term strategic plan (see Figure 16-4). Senior management is responsible for managing and orchestrating the com-

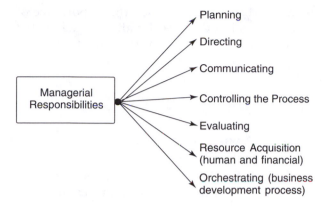

Figure 16–4   Focal Points of Management to Implement Strategic Plan

munications with employees, the owner, franchisees, the host community, the investment community, shareholders, and the public. Figure 16-5 delineates the strategic plan communications targets/audiences.

CHAPTER REVIEW

In this chapter we defined the strategic planning process within the context of hospitality industry organizations. We stated that it is a board and CEO level activity and that the timeframe has decreased from a 5- to 10-year planning period to a 3- to 5-year horizon. We delineated a number of approaches hospitality organizations utilize to conduct the strategic planning process. These include: board-level committees, formal officer-level function, team approach, and the inside/outside approach. We then provided a step-by-step walk-through of the actual components of a strategic plan, which include: the preface, executive summary, competitive and environmental assessment, driving forces, mission statement, goals and objectives, strategies and tactics, program plans, recommendations, vision statement, slogan, issues, measurement

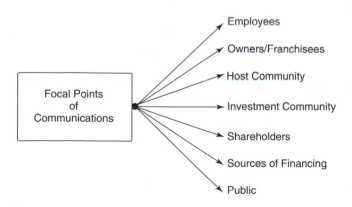

Figure 16–5   Focal Points of Strategic Plan Communications

and results, resources plan, and appendixes. We discussed the importance of communication of the strategy plan to all audiences. Finally, we delineated managerial responsibilities related to the strategic plan implementation and measurement/results.

KEY CONCEPTS/TERMS

Driving forces

Financial plan

Growth rate

Inside/outside approach

Milestones

Mission statement

Strategic planning

SWOT (strengths, weaknesses, opportunities, and threats)

DISCUSSION QUESTIONS

1. Why is a mission statement important to communicate to all audiences?
2. Select a hospitality organization and see if you can list two or three of its driving forces.
3. Why are the concepts of a "base case," "accelerated case," and "new starts" important in a strategic plan?
4. Why is it important to conduct a competitive and environmental assessment prior to the strategy formulation phase in the strategic planning process?
5. In today's environment, which approach do you think works best to actually develop a strategic plan: board committee, formal officer function, team approach, or inside/outside approach?
6. Why is it important to isolate issues for discussion at the end of the plan?
7. Linking objectives and strategies is the key to successful planning—why?

ENDNOTES

1. R. Nykiel, *Marketing Strategies* (New York: Cormar Business Press, 2002): 169.
2. Note: The tri-tiered concept of strategic planning was pioneered at the Xerox Education Group in the late 1960s and early 1970s.

3. B. Tregoe & J. Zimmerman, *Top Management Strategy* (New York: Simon & Schuster, 1980): 40–45. Note: This is a discussion on driving forces and another perspective.
4. E. Jascolt & R. Nykiel, *Marketing Your City, U.S.A.* (Binghamton, NY: Haworth Press, 1998): 59.

CASE 1

Continental Airlines—Leadership Goes Forward

In this chapter we pointed out that for a strategic plan to be successful it must be championed by the company leadership as well as extensively communicated to all constituencies. There is perhaps no better example of both than Continental Airlines' "Go Forward Plan." Briefly looking at the airline's history will help place the extraordinary success of this strategic plan into perspective.

History*

From its humble beginnings in the 1930s as Varney Speed Lines to the multi-billion-dollar corporation of today, Continental Airlines has had an interesting and somewhat volatile history.

Throughout its history, Continental has had its share of ups and downs. It has merged or consolidated with several airlines to become the third largest airline in the United States. The company has had to reorganize during Chapter 11 bankruptcies. It has gone from being one of the worst airlines to one of the best, and has won numerous awards for being the best in the industry. Continental has also supported war efforts by modifying military aircraft and transporting deploying U.S. servicepeople.

In the past decade, Continental Airlines has changed its CEO and its corporate culture. It has gone from a company where employees were embarrassed to be associated with the brand to a company that is considered one of the top 100 companies to work for.

This case study will focus on Continental Airlines' history, Gordon Bethune's Go Forward Plan, and how that strategic plan changed the airline.

Walter T. Varney and his partner Louis Mueller founded Varney Speed Lines, the precursor to Continental Airlines, over 60 years ago. On July 15, 1934, Varney Speed Lines flew its first flight, a 530-mile route from Pueblo, Colorado, to El Paso, Texas, with stops in Las Vegas, Santa Fe, and Albuquerque. That same year, Varney ceded control to Mueller. Two years later, Mueller sold 40 percent of the new company to Robert F. Six, who led the company for more than 40 years. On July 1, 1937, Six changed the company's name to Continental Airlines and moved its headquarters from El Paso to Denver.

During World War II, many U.S. companies found themselves focusing on government contracts and assisting in the war effort. At this time, Continental Airlines built the Denver Modification Center where it modified B-17 Flying Fortresses and B-29 Super Fortresses for the U.S. war effort.

In December 1953, Continental signed a merger agreement with Pioneer Airlines that added 16 new cities in Texas and New Mexico to its growing

*Information derived from www.continental.com/company/history/default.asp?SID =37D9BF5457C548D7BDE008F96763751B.

route map. And in 1959, Continental's first true jet flight (a Boeing 707-120) took place.

Continental moved its headquarters to Los Angeles in 1963. During the Vietnam War, Continental transported U.S. troops to the Orient. And Continental's Pacific experience during the war led to the formation of Air Micronesia. Its first flight covered more than 4,000 miles from Saipan to Honolulu. In 1969, the first Continental mainland–Hawaii service began.

Continental's route map underwent significant growth in the 1970s. In August 1976, the Civil Aviation Bureau awarded Air Micronesia with routes between Saipan and Japan. For Continental, the most significant expansion was President Carter's approval of a new route from Los Angeles to New Zealand and Australia in 1977.

In 1982, the airline merged with Texas International led by Frank Lorenzo (retaining the Continental name), offering service to four continents (North and South America, Asia, and Australia) with a fleet of 112 aircraft.

The 1978 airline industry deregulation turned the 1980s into a decade of turbulence for Continental. In 1983, Continental filed to reorganize under Chapter 11 of the Federal Bankruptcy Code. Rebuilding the company began immediately and by the end of 1984, Continental recorded a $50 million profit. In 1986, Continental emerged from Chapter 11, and then became the third largest U.S. airline with the consolidation of Frontier, People Express, and New York Air.

In 1987, the One Pass Frequent Flyer Program was created. And in 1988, Continental Airlines formed its first global alliance with Scandinavian Airline Systems.

The 1990s remained unstable as Frank Lorenzo's disassociation from Continental began when he sold most of his direct and indirect investments in the airline during the summer of 1990. In late 1990, rising fuel costs due to the Iraqi invasion of Kuwait led to Continental's second bankruptcy filing.

In February 1991, Continental unveiled its new blue and gray identity. It introduced a new logo and color scheme that symbolized the airline's real and growing potential to link the countries of the globe together. In 1992, Continental launched the award-winning Business First service on transoceanic flights. In November 1992, Air Partners/Air Canada invested $450 million in Continental, leading to Continental's second bankruptcy emergence in April 1993.

In early 1995, Continental's CEO Gordon Bethune unveiled his four-point strategic Go Forward Plan (see Figure 1) designed to improve Continental's operational performance and working environment for employees and achieve sustained profitability. During this year, Continental Airlines was recognized twice as being number one out of the 10 largest U.S. airlines for its domestic on-time performance.

In July 1995, Continental announced the largest quarterly profit in its history. At the end of this year, *Business Week Magazine* named Continental the Best NYSE Stock for the year. Continental's Class B common stock had risen from a low of $6.50 per share in early January to a high of $47.50 in December.

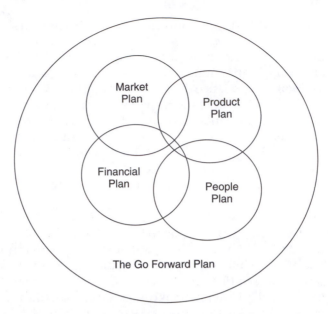

Figure 1 Continental Airlines—Components of the Go Forward Plan
Source: www.continental.com/company/history/1991-now.asp?SID=37D9BF5457
C548D7BDE008F96763751B.

Continental closed out 1995 with the largest annual profit in its 61-year history ($224 million).

In addition, during the fourth quarter of 1995, the airline ranked first in on-time performance and baggage handling and second in least complaints. In 1997, Continental became the first airline ever to receive back-to-back J.D. Power and Associates Awards for Best Airline on flights of 500 miles or more. The same year, it had a record annual profit of $640 million, and it announced a plan to consolidate its Houston headquarters into downtown Houston—Continental Center.

In late 1998, Continental Airlines and Northwest Airlines formally announced their alliance to enhance competition and improve consumer travel options. The alliance created a fourth major U.S. airline network competitive with "The Big Three" U.S.-based airlines.

In 1999, Continental launched daily nonstop service from Houston to Tokyo. This was the first nonstop flight from Houston to Asia. The same year, Gordon Bethune was named as one of the 50 best CEOs in America by *Worth* magazine. Continental Airlines and America West Airlines became the first two U.S. airlines to implement interline e-ticketing. And Continental implemented its Customer First program and fine-tuned customer service policies, established new functions, and provided training to thousands of staff.

In 2000, Continental Airlines was ranked as the nation's number one airline in customer satisfaction for both short-distance and long-distance flights in an independent study conducted by *Frequent Flyer* magazine in conjunction with J.D. Power and Associates. Continental won Best Short-Haul Executive/Business Class and Best Frequent Flyer Program. In September 2000, Continental Airlines ranked as the number one innovative user of information technology among all airlines, according to an *InformationWeek* 500 list.

On January 22, 2001, Continental Airlines celebrated its preeminence. In April, Continental Airlines' One Pass frequent-flyer program garnered four top Freddie Awards, including Program of the Year and Best Elite-Level Program, during *Inside Flyer*'s 13th annual Freddie Awards ceremony. The One Pass program also received the Best award in recognition of reduced miles from the United States to Latin America, as well as Best Web Site for 2000.*

Continental's Strategic Plan

In 1994, Continental was the worst airline among the 10 largest players in the airline industry, according to U.S. Department of Transportation statistics. From 1994 to 2001, Gordon Bethune, the CEO of the company, not only turned around the company but also established a culture by implementing the Go Forward Plan. This plan touched four key strategic elements of the business: market, finance, product, and people.

Market Strategy   Bethune and his team set up a goal for the Go Forward Plan, which is to make Continental "fly to win" by:

- Determining the target market
- Fitting the product to the market by an effective pricing and positioning strategy
- Making the product accessible to the customers

First, Continental eliminated 18 percent of the routes that did not generate a profit to the company and concentrated on its market strength. Then, it cut back flights between small cities and also its low-cost airline, Continental Lite. Meanwhile, the company increased flights out of the hubs including Houston, Cleveland, and Newark. Based on market research, promising routes such as a route between Raleigh-Durham and New York were created.

In order to market the product efficiently, Continental contracted the major travel agents because they brought nearly 80 percent of the business to the company, and it also reestablished commissions at a fair price to rebuild the relationship with those agents. The award-winning frequent-flyer program was restored to retain customers' loyalty, and e-ticket terminals were built in major airports around the country to make the product more accessible.**

*Information derived from www.continental.com/company/profile/awards.asp?SID =37D9BF5457C548D7BDE008F96763751B.

**Information derived from www.continental.com/company/history/1991-now.asp? SID=37D9BF5457C548D7BDE008F96763751B.

Financial Strategy   Before Bethune took the company, Continental's financial system could neither provide reliable information for its daily cost and revenue nor make a forecast on cash and revenue. This system was then replaced with an updated financial system. The new system was able not only to estimate cost based on the industry average and to forecast the number of flights landing each day according to the schedule, but also to measure the weight of each plane and the landing fees. The valuable information provided by the system created substantial profit to the company. For instance, Continental found out that an extraordinary amount of money was made on the European flights. After further analyzing those flights, Continental raised the price of the tickets to European destinations. This helped the company create an additional $10 million per year.*

The following financial strategies were implemented:

- Renegotiating some leases
- Postponing some payments
- Refinancing some of the large debt
- Adjusting the price structure

When the renegotiation with the creditors, including General Electric and Air Canada, and the renegotiation of leases and debt structure took place in 1995, Continental saved $25 million on long-term debt. When some unproductive flights such as A300s were removed from the fleet, Continental enhanced its ROI.

Product Strategy   In the 1980s, Continental was a heterogeneous mixture of several airlines: Continental, Frontier, People Express, and New York Air. Gordon Bethune and his management team recognized the damage of the mixed product to Continental's overall brand image and managed to eliminate some of the product. The management also enhanced the fleet by reducing the average age of the fleet. Thus, primary maintenance was significantly reduced. Meanwhile, Continental customized its product to meet the consumers' needs by:

- Cutting the flights and the cities the company flies to
- Flying where people want to go
- Providing desirable customer services

According to a survey conducted by the U.S. Department of Transportation, the quality of the airlines product is judged by on-time arrival percent-

---

*Information derived from Continental's Annual Reports 1991–2001, accessed online at www.continental.com/company/investor/reports.asp?SID=37D9BF5457C548D7BDE008F967637 51B.

age, lost baggage claims, complaints received, and the number of passengers denied upon boarding. The 1997 J.D. Power and Associates Airline Customer Satisfaction Study also indicated that on-time performance counted for 22 percent of a customer's overall satisfaction. Bethune wisely created an incentive program that rewarded every employee with a $65 bonus each month on the condition that the company was among the top five on-time carriers nationwide. Because his program was so successful, the company's on-time performance bounced from last place to first place within only 6 months.

People Strategy   Although the people plan is listed last in the Go Forward Plan, the first step taken by Bethune resulting in Continental's turnaround was related to his people plan. He demonstrated his open-door management style by opening the executive suite's door to every Continental employee, and he broke the barriers of communication from the top. Then, Bethune implemented the people plan step by step and recreated the Continental corporate culture, as follows:

- Casual dress on Friday
- Started managers' meeting on time, and make every flight on time
- Nonsmoking in Continental Airlines buildings and flights
- Burn the employee manual to enhance employees' creativity and capability
- Repaint every plane
- Reward cooperation

Thus, synergy was created when the market planning people and the operating people worked together to improve the schedule. A positive environment was facilitated when valuable people were brought into the company. The open-book policy allowed employees to see the true financial status of the company. Trust was built when Continental restored wage levels once the financial situation of the company was improved. A coherent relationship was established when Continental started treating travel agencies as its business partners. Customized service was provided when the frequent-flyer program was restored. In essence, Bethune turned the company around by creating a win-win-win situation among the customers, business partners, and Continental itself.

Terrorism Disrupts the Plan

The horrific events of September 11, 2001, affected millions of people worldwide. Here is a brief overview of important issues and an assessment of the factors, including financial implications, maintaining standards, and employee perspective.

Financial Implications Continental Airlines reported a fourth quarter 2001 loss of $149 million. The company's net loss for the full year was $95 million, despite a $174 million government grant to Continental for industry stabilization purposes. Revenue for the fourth quarter 2001 dropped 28.4 percent from the same period of 2000. Revenues decreased $2.43 billion from the previous year to $1.74 billion.

The company experienced a wide fluctuation in stock price during 2001. The stock price high for the year was $52.32 (July 2001). After the September 11 attacks, Continental stock dropped to a low of $12.35 per share. With over 10 million shares traded in one day in September, and almost that amount in days following, the company was reeling with the reaction of the nation—one can almost see the panic that followed.*

Maintaining Standards Throughout 2001, Continental led the major airlines in on-time performance and reliability. After the attacks, it maintained meal service, in-flight entertainment, blankets, pillows, and magazines. It decided to drop employees and flights rather than reduce quality. *Air Transport World* named Continental Airline of the Year for 2001.**

Employee Perspective For the third consecutive year, the company was named one of the "100 Best Companies to Work For" by *Forbes Magazine*, the only passenger airline among those companies named. This award is based on an evaluation of work environment, company culture, compensation and benefits, and other measures of job satisfaction. The company pared down flights after the attacks and reduced its workforce by 21 percent.

Continental reduced management compensation and did not pay employee profit-sharing amounts. Gordon Bethune, who made about $5.5 million in 2000, and President Larry Kellner, who made around $3.7 million in 2000, decided not to take compensation after September 26, 2001, in order to help decrease the amount of employees laid off.

Creating Strategy

Continental Airlines has infused its marketing messages with core values detailed in the four points of the Go Forward Plan for the past 7 years. This plan initiated a philosophy wherein four key strategic points are emphasized and subsequently manifested in its marketing presentations by way of clever and catchy phrases designed to both inform and entertain the customer. The key points are: "Fly to Win," "Fund the Future," "Make Reliability a Reality," and "Working Together." Within these points, the core values of dependable, on-time performance, safety and reliability, and award-winning service excellence have been emphasized as an advertising standard. These slogans encom-

---

*Ibid.

**Information derived from www.continental.com/company/news and G. Bethune and S. Huler, *From Worst to First* (New York: John Wiley & Sons, 1999): 294–295.

pass divergent yet essential business acumens ensuring the company's sustained presence and determination to enjoy further business success.

Continental does not advertise nationwide on network television or cable at all, considering this an inefficient use of its marketing dollars. It pinpoints those markets that constitute the greatest revenue-generating potential (those being Continental's route hub cities of New York, Cleveland, and Houston), advertising only as much as that particular market may return in sales. Continental does, however, advertise to a lesser degree in Miami, Washington, Boston, San Francisco, and Los Angeles. Continental's marketing strategies employ sports event sponsorship, magazine and newspaper print, billboards, network and cable television (in its target markets), and radio and internet mediums whose most valued target market is the high-yield male and female business traveler age 25 to 55. This group, who travel within 3 days of booking, generates more cumulative revenue than does the leisure traveler group despite the fact that it represents only 25 percent of all passengers accommodated. Continental considers the optimum mix to be 50–50, to which it is committed to achieve. With this objective, Continental directs virtually all advertising toward the business market, avoiding depiction of beautiful vacation scenes in any form whatsoever and devoting as much as 70 percent of its spending allowance in the New York metropolitan area alone.

Despite the downturn in air travel post–September 11, Continental remains steadfast in its commitment to delivery of uncompromised service. Cost-cutting changes in other carriers came in the form of reduced flights and airport lounge amenities, closed ticket offices, removal of ticket kiosks, and elimination of in-flight food, blankets, pillows, and complimentary reading material. Continental is unwilling to degrade its product in order to save money, realizing that the product itself is the selling point to which the customer responds and consciously chooses. And Continental continues to target the high-yield business traveler with incentive programs designed to stimulate sales activities by offering complimentary bonus programs through customer participation. MeetingWorks, Business*bonus*, RewardOne, and Miles of Thanks programs have been created to accrue points redeemable for upgrades, travel certificates, discounted fares, discount freight handling, and President's Club memberships. Media messages displayed most recently address the business traveler specifically, with copy focusing on Continental's added international destinations, new airplanes, and BusinessFirst service. Of course, all these efforts are intended to restore a financially viable, growing company. Time will ultimately tell with measurable results whether this steadfast strategy continues to work.

Case Discussion Questions

1. World events decimated the travel industry in the 2001–2003 timeframe. Some airlines filed for bankruptcy; others folded completely. Assuming that your airline went bankrupt and it continued to operate and eventually

emerged from bankruptcy, what would be the key objectives of your strategic plan during and post-bankruptcy?

2. In the Continental case, what do you believe were the strongest management strategies within the Go Forward Plan?

CASE 2

Holiday Inns, Inc.—Recognizing Change*

A key component to a successful strategic plan is to recognize macro trends and driving forces that will have an impact on your business strategy. As indicated in this chapter, if one does not recognize macro trends or driving forces with direct implications, the business strategy may be falsely premised and ultimately fail. In the case which follows, we will view the opposite—how one company paid attention to both internal and external driving forces and made very successful strategic managerial decisions.

The Mid-1970s

In the mid-1970s, Holiday Inns, Inc., was experiencing both internal and external driving forces that were pressuring its older senior management on multiple fronts. These driving forces included: an aging product; a new product (high-rise hotels) that did not fit or match up with the word "Inn," with resultant pressure from franchisees of the new product; court mandates to dispose of some manufacturing businesses that supplied products for the Holiday Inn system; competition in many markets; market saturation (too many Holiday Inns in a given market); and shifting interstate highway patterns, new airports, new suburbs, and decaying inner-city locations. From a positioning perspective due to its sheer size, market share, and franchising and royalty fee in-flow, Holiday Inn was a very profitable cash cow.

The Aging Problem   One major problem was the fact that many of the inns were becoming obsolete due to age and/or location deterioration. Facing the multitude of problems and threats, senior management decided upon some major strategic steps and initiatives. These included reviewing all existing businesses such as the bus company, steamship line, various manufacturing businesses, and lodging holdings and listening to franchisee pressure and bringing in select new management, including a new vice chairman of the board, new president of the then Inn Development Division, new executive vice president for inn development, new marketing officer, and new senior vice president for planning and development (responsible for strategic planning). Within a few months the new team completed the first formal competitive and environmental analysis and a comprehensive SWOT analysis, which focused on demand generators in each market (see Figure 1).

*The author was Vice President of Strategic Planning for Holiday Inn (1976–1978), and much of this case study is from personal experience in that position. Other sources include Holiday Inn Annual Reports; Promus Co. Annual Reports; www.USAToday.com/travel/vacations/destinations/2002/2002-05-24-holiday-inn.htm; and the Hospitality Industry Hall of Honor and Archives at Conrad N. Hilton College, University of Houston (TX).

Development Point Index		_____Points	Total_____Rank	
Indicator	Points	Bonus	Points Earned	
Airport Activity				
Convention Activity				
Corporate Activity				
Government Activity				
Feeder Market Significance				
Destination Market				
Population/Migration Trend				
Performance Factor				
Fair Market Share				
Other				
Total				

Figure 1   Summary of Demand Generators for Holiday Inns, Inc.

These analyses revealed that nearly 35 percent of the existing product would need replacement or be obsolete (due to the product itself and/or market location) within 120 months (see Figure 2). The analysis further revealed the need to immediately conduct some in-depth property-by-property financial analysis to determine how big this aging problem was, where it was (franchise system or parent company–owned inns), and when the impact on the "cash cow" would arrive.

AUSTIN, TX   **SMSA**

Development Timing	SMSA Recommended Product	Motel/Inn	Motor Hotel	Hotel
Immediate to 24 Months			A	
24 to 60 Months				C
60 to 120 Months		H		
Always				
Location Type:	Code			
Airport	A			
Suburban	S			
City	C			
Highway	H			
Resort/Destination	D			

Figure 2   Summary of Development Recommendation

In addition, a financial analysis model was created looking at everything from book values to dispositions. Given the fundamental questions about the health of the cash cow, the senior management proposed to the board that a comprehensive strategic planning effort be undertaken and funded immediately. The board agreed and suggested that an internal strategic planning team be assembled of those considered the key players and most qualified, and further, that this team move off site, away from their current duties, and devote full time to the effort. Also, the strategic planning team was to engage a reputable consulting firm to help provide objectivity and contribute to the process. The new position of vice president of strategic planning was created, the team was assembled, and the process was underway with the assistance of Temple, Barker and Sloane, a Boston area–based consulting firm.

The Strategic Plan Approach

The approach to the strategic planning effort was unique for its time and can be delineated as follows. First, the team studied all the recently completed competitive and environmental data, the analysis of the condition of the 1,200-plus inns in the system and their respective markets, and the financial analysis. A comprehensive matrix was developed which profiled the inns with respect to an "immediate to 10-year time frame" and also delineated the specific market with respect to growth, competition, obsolescence, and opportunity. This matrix was completed for all inns and the composite results analyzed for part one of the process—the condition and future of the Holiday Inn brand.

Second, based on the above, various financial scenarios were developed to look at options ranging from a selling/disposition strategy for existing parent company product to new inn concept development and room additions in growth markets.

Third, the strategic planning team and external consultant studied the company from a future profit and cashflow perspective, studied the industry to ascertain its business cycle, and studied all other industries to ascertain potential opportunities for entry, acquisitions, or development. A comprehensive business/industry cycle model was developed, which compared Holiday Inn's profit cycle to other industry sectors' and leaders' profit patterns. This was done to look for potential acquisitions that would support a desired consistent earnings flow and higher return on invested capital. All other existing businesses were reviewed with respect to their profit contributions and potential/market growth.

Fourth, a time/sequence strategy implementation model was developed. This model was premised on maintaining profit objectives and cash flow and raising various levels of incremental cash from the sales of identified assets, including parent company–owned inns and manufacturing and transportation businesses.

Fifth, new product concepts, brand segmentation, and incremental revenue generation all related to the lodging industry were explored.

And, finally a strategic plan was developed to communicate recommended business strategy changes, including strategies to overcome anticipated resistance by select board members and shareholders who might be opposed to any change or a particular change. This strategic communications plan would prove to be very valuable over the months ahead.

Plan Recommendations What were the direct and indirect results of this substantial undertaking? Before looking at significant events and their related timeline, here is a list of 10 of the strategy changes recommended as a result of the process:

1. Consider disposition of all manufacturing and transportation related to businesses.

2. Consider investment (either startup or acquisitions) in businesses that have profit/cashflow patterns that will support consistency in earnings at that time. (These were identified as the gaming industry and discount retail/drug stores.)

3. Sell off parent company inns that have no or low book values or fall within the "obsolete" market/product category within the next 60 months. Utilize the proceeds for the next concept development and acquisitions.

4. Make ownership investment in a Las Vegas casino on the strip.

5. Segment product by tiering—hotels, inns, etc.

6. Develop new brands.

7. Utilize the demographic and market analysis models to fit new product types to market segment demand/needs for future development.

8. In view of the aging of the Holiday Inn product and changes in the marketplace over the next 120 months, consider disposing of the Holiday Inn brand at maximum pricing.

9. Accelerate new businesses (e.g., gaming) and new lodging concepts to replace the Holiday Inn brand over the next 60 months and capitalize on companies' reservations/technical strengths, marketing, franchising, and development expertise for new businesses/brands.

10. Offer the existing franchise base new concepts/products to also accelerate growth, and build a new franchise system around each new brand.

Needless to say, these findings and recommendations were an extraordinary shock to many of those senior executives and board members. This was compounded by the fact that the Vice Chairman of the Board, the Corporate CEO and President, and the Executive Vice President were of strong religious beliefs that gaming was a sinful enterprise. In addition, the board's external directors had many among their ranks that sympathized with that antigaming position. The strategic planning team had anticipated this reaction and commissioned a survey of all shareholders (and lenders) to ascertain their perspective on this issue. With the models showing the numbers overwhelmingly in support of the strategy recommendations, over 80 percent of the shareholders surveyed supported entry into the gaming business. In fact, one mega-hotel/casino (defined as over 1,000 rooms with a large gaming area) would produce as much or more profit than the entire corporation was then generating in year two of its operation. In addition, the payback on the gaming investment was quite short (2 to 8 years) versus ongoing losses for many years for some of the manufacturing and transportation businesses.

Plan Results   All the recommendations were presented to the board, along with a specific opportunity in Las Vegas. The meeting ended after some heated discussions without approval. After considerable internal maneuvering and shareholder/franchisee pressure, a few months later the board was reconfigured. The Vice Chairman retired, the President and CEO and the Executive Vice President resigned, and the reconfigured senior management team (reduced in number) and the board of directors was in place. Most of the strategic plan recommendations were approved for implementation. While the specific Las Vegas deal was lost to other investors, the timeline/history that follows exemplifies a strategic planning process that really resulted in change.

Milestones

1952	First Holiday Inn is built by Kemmons Wilson and Wallace Johnson in Memphis, Tennessee.
1954—1974	Becomes vertically integrated, with products group distributing supplies, equipment, etc., to lodging, housing, healthcare, and foodservice markets.
1955	Sells franchises; Bill Walton hired to lead franchise expansion.
1957	Becomes public company to raise money to continue rapid expansion.
1968	Diversifies to maintain growth—acquires TCO Industries, holder of Continental Trailways Bus and Delta Steamship Lines.
Early 1970s	Growth slows.
1971—1979	Trailways profits decline.
1978	Expands overseas. Strategic decision is made to enter gaming.
1979	Kemmons Wilson resigns as chairman of the board; Roy Winegardner is appointed chairman; Lem Clymer resigns as president and director; Mike Rose is appointed

	president and CEO. Acquires Perkins' Cake and Steak and 40 percent of the River Boat Casino. Sells Continental Trailways. Enters into gaming industry.
1980	Purchases Harrah's (Harrah's Tahoe and Reno).
1981	Holds 99 percent ownership of Harrah's Marina, Atlantic City (purchases remaining 1 percent in 1983).
1982	Enters a joint project with Donald Trump for Harrah's Boardwalk (Atlantic City). Purchases the remaining 60 percent of the River Boat Casino. Forms two new chains—Hampton Inn and Embassy Suites. Sells Delta Steamship Lines.
1983	Opens the first Holiday Inn Crowne Plaza Hotel. Winegardner retires as chairman of the board; Rose is appointed chairman.
1984	Acquires Granada Royale and converts the property to Embassy Suites. Opens the first Embassy Suites and Hampton Inn.
1985	Name changed from Holiday Inns, Inc., to Holiday Corporation to project the multiple nature of the corporation. Enters a joint venture with Communications Satellite Corporation to turn Holiday's Hi-Net communications satellite network into the world's largest privately owned satellite communications system (in-room entertainment and teleconferencing). Transfers the Perkins' Restaurant chain to Tennessee Restaurant Co. in exchange for an initial 79 percent of the new company's stock, without voting control. Acquires 50 percent interest in Residence Inn.
1986	Sells its 50 percent interest in Trump's Boardwalk. Announces a major restructuring.
1987	Sells its interest in Residence Inn for $51.4 million (Residence Inn goes indirectly to Marriott). Lake Tahoe Casino opens. Implements a $2.6 billion recapitalization plan to enhance shareholder value. Closes the announced sale of 14 domestic and 140 international Holiday Inn hotels to Bass PLC (Holiday Inn and Crowne Plaza).
1988	Harrah's Del Rio casino/hotel in Laughlin, Nevada, opens. Reenters the extended-stay market through Homewood Suites.
1989	Announces its second restructuring: sells the Holiday Inn brand to Bass PLC for $1.98 billion and creates a new company.

As the milestones indicate, almost all of the 10 recommendations were fully implemented by the new management of the company over the next 120 months. The evolution/revolution initiated by Roy Winegardner and Mike Rose would ultimately culminate in the sale of Promus' lodging holdings to Hilton and result in Harrah's as the remaining entity encompassing the gaming/casino holdings.

What Holiday Inn management did so well was to not only recognize the internal and external forces of change, but also to identify the opportunities these same forces presented. In today's hospitality environment the pace of change and the impact of driving forces have accelerated. This has had a direct impact on shortening the strategic planning process to virtually an ongoing process.

Case Discussion Questions

1. Can you identify three or four macro trends or driving forces that are likely to impact the hospitality industry in the next 5 years?

2. Select one of the macro trends or driving forces and present your thoughts on how you would respond. What actions would you undertake? What changes would you implement?

Chapter 17

Organizational and Operational Concepts

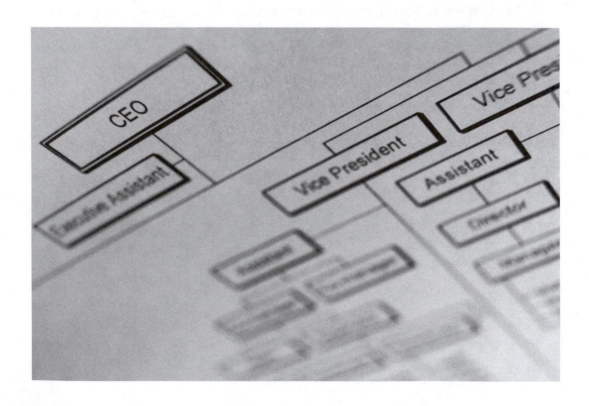

CHAPTER OBJECTIVES

- To discuss the concept of change and how it impacts organizational and operational approaches
- To describe various approaches to organization from a conceptual perspective within the hospitality industry
- To provide linkages between organizational concepts and desired outcomes from a managerial strategy perspective
- To look at various operational concepts currently deployed within the hospitality industry, including Six Sigma
- To discuss how outsourcing technology and other trends are influencing managerial strategies related to operations and organization

In an industry that has a dynamic (ever-changing) environment, organizational and operational approaches often require adjustment and modification. Change can be driven by a competitive situation, market behavior, human behavior, or the dynamics of the industry or company itself. Management is responsible for both monitoring change and selecting strategies to address change. In general, there are two types of change—unplanned and planned. Either one may require management to do things differently, adopt new ideas, or master/acquire new technologies. A simple example of the past decade was the retrofitting of millions of hotel and motel rooms to accommodate the need for computer/internet access. Both external and internal forces may cause organizational and operational change. Technology, the changing market, competition, the labor/workforce, and a crisis are examples of external forces that cause change. Internal forces include reinvention, reengineering, CQI, and an internal crisis (e.g., a major change in the financial condition of the company). Figure 17–1 summarizes external and internal forces of change.

SPONSORING CHANGE

Management can foster change or in essence use its authority, power, and influence to sponsor change. Management is responsible for being a change agent and when necessary acting to change priorities or targets. Managing the process of change can be modeled or subdivided into four phases.[1]

Phase 1:   *Planning for Change.* In this phase management recognizes the need for change and establishes a vision for change. Further, an assessment of the current status is undertaken and a plan is developed for changing.

Phase 2:   *Doing.* In this phase implementation is the objective. The vision is communicated and management exercises its authority/power to foster change. Progress is measured and successes are celebrated.

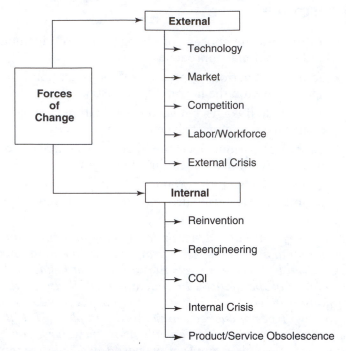

Figure 17–1   Forces of Change

Source: Adapted from R. Woods & J. King, *Quality Leadership and Management in the Hospitality Industry* (East Lansing, MI: Educational Institute of the American Hotel and Motel Association, 1996): 330–332.

Phase 3:   *Checking.* In this phase the change is monitored. This involves reevaluating the vision to see if it is still on target. The plan for change is assessed and evaluated.

Phase 4:   *Acting.* In this phase the focus is on continually improving. Looking for additional opportunity to improve is the ongoing goal. At this juncture, it is time to repeat the cycle or go through the four phases again. Figure 17–2 summarizes the change model and four phases.

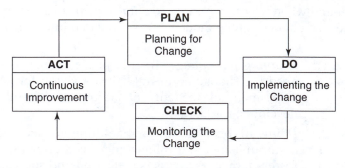

Figure 17–2   The Four-Phased Change Model

Organizational and operational change can be caused by external factors of a broad nature such as economic trends, technology, sociocultural events, and political occurrences (e.g., changes to the law). These types of change are sometimes referred to as remote (external to the company) and general (broad in nature). Think of what the last economic recession caused with respect to organizational and operational changes in hospitality industry firms. Think of the many new technologies that have caused operational changes in the hospitality industry work environment. Customers, suppliers, regulations, and competitors can also cause change. Think of how customers' tastes change and how that impacts foodservice establishments or how new competition forces a change in operations. These types of changes are sometimes referred to as "task oriented," as they require an action to be undertaken.

DIMENSIONS OF CHANGE

There are a number of dimensions to change, which provide constant challenges to organizations and operations. These dimensions include complexity, uncertainty, and illiberality. The dimension of complexity is defined as the range of activities occurring at any given time. Uncertainty refers to the dynamics and variability of change. Illiberality is defined as threats from external forces.

ORGANIZATIONAL CONCEPTS

How hospitality industry organizations are structured and how they function (operate) is the result of many factors. We often hear phrases such as "They are a very formal organization," or "They are loose." Formalization means the company has written and adhered-to rules, policies, and procedures. Informal or loose simply means the opposite in practice. There may or may not be rules, policies, or procedures, but in an informal organizational environment adherence and protocol are less important and less practiced. The structure of an organization often depends on the phase of development or life cycle of the company, the competitive environment, and the "climate" the leadership wants to have as the modus operandus.

ETHICS

Everything about a code of ethics—its tone, style, organization, and presentation—impact the success of its integration and the extent of its use. The code of ethics should be readily understood by everyone in the organization and frequently visited as a reference tool for managerial conduct of business.

At the very outset, an organization may be informal and focused on the technical skills (basic behaviors) to create the product or service offering. In fact, formality most likely would get in the way and slow the process down. As the firm begins to grow the organizational structure begins to form. The emphasis often begins to move from the basic technical skills toward the conceptual. Conceptual skills focus on the broader perspective as the firm moves from creation to transformation into a revenue and profit generating enterprise. Organizational concepts begin to get more functionally defined and the establishment of a hierarchy is normal as a firm enters a growth phase. Likewise, during the maturity, decline, and rejuvenation phases, organizations move toward new concepts, experimentation, and consolidation (in the decline phase).

CENTRALIZATION/DECENTRALIZATION

Historically, hospitality industry firms were organizations much like other service or manufacturing industry firms with entrepreneurs being the creators. Success resulted in a centralized model/concept with the founder (entrepreneur) at the top (as the CEO) and divisional and functional management reporting up the hierarchy of authority. Historic examples would include Holiday Inn under Kemmons Wilson, Carlson Companies under Curt Carlson, Marriott under J. Willard Marriott, and Wendy's under Dave Thomas, to name a few. As these organizations and the service sector grew and emerged as a major economic force, business firms began to recognize that centralization had some limitations when it came to operating businesses that were spread out geographically and were enjoying high-digit growth rates. Operating six units might allow for decisions to be centralized and made at the top, but operating six hundred called for a different organizational concept. To better serve the customer and frankly to expedite daily business, activity had to be delegated downward to the regional, district, zone, and ultimately unit level. This delegation of authority with a downward focus is decentralization. Examples include many upscale hotel brands such as Westin and Four Seasons, where the unit (property-level) general manager is "captain of the ship." Ultimately, decentralization and placing decision making as close to the customer interface as possible resulted in empowerment. Empowerment means providing defined authority at the employee level (e.g., front desk versus general manager). An example of this is Ritz-Carlton and its inverted pyramid organizational concept where empowerment of employees reinforces decentralized decision making closest to customer. The net result is a higher level of customer satisfaction and employee morale. Empowerment is not an organizational concept but rather an operational philosophy.

Other decentralized hybrids include the concept of "clusters." A cluster is defined as a concentration of units in a given geographic area (city, state, region, etc.). The cluster in essence is an organizational structure unto itself in the sense that it may share resources, have a cluster-level decision-making process/authority, and so on. A number of hospitality firms are using or have experimented with the cluster concept, including Hilton and Marriott International. Somewhat akin to the cluster idea is the concept (type of facility) organizational model. In the "concept" model, the physical property types are together under their own organizational entity. For example, resort properties, airport properties, and limited service may each be organized with all others of the same type within their category. Airlines, for example, often split and spin off their commuter service/short-haul operations from their major route carrier or hub operations.

Some companies employ a variety of team management concepts. These teams may be focused on product/service–level types of units (e.g., resorts, inns, etc.) or on special problems, opportunities, or situations. For example, there are "turn-around" teams focused on bringing units to profitability and "new opening" teams focused on getting major new units open and up and running smoothly. Teams may be used as specialists for everything from acquisitions to dispositions to quality control. Teams may also be used to actually run the total business enterprise. At the highest of levels is the "office of the president" concept, which may consist of a number of executives with different skills/strengths.

ETHICS

Every organizational structure should have an ethics program. The ten key components of an ethics program are:

1. Focus on ethical leadership
2. Vision statement
3. Values statement
4. Code of ethics and related monitoring system
5. Designated ethics official
6. Ethics task force or committee
7. Ethics communication strategy
8. Ethics training
9. Ethics help line
10. Ethical behavior—investigations, rewards, and sanctions

SIX SIGMA

A fairly recent development in organizational and operational concepts/philosophies is "Six Sigma." Motorola was the originator of Six Sigma. Motorola developed Six Sigma because it was being consistently beaten in the competitive marketplace by foreign firms that were able to produce higher quality products at a lower cost.

In the mid-1980s, Motorola's CEO, Bob Galvin, started the company on the quality path known as Six Sigma and became a business icon largely as a result of what he accomplished in quality at Motorola. Under Galvin, Motorola was known worldwide as a quality leader and a profit leader. After Motorola won the Malcolm Baldrige National Quality Award in 1988, the secret of its success became public knowledge and the Six Sigma revolution was on, as General Electric, Johnson & Johnson, and other major corporations adopted this Six Sigma concept. Today, it has spread to the hospitality industry where Starwood implemented the concept under the leadership of CEO Barry Sternlicht. Six Sigma is about helping the organization make more money. Six Sigma focuses on improving quality (i.e., reducing waste) by helping organizations produce products and services better, faster, and cheaper. In more traditional terms, Six Sigma focuses on defect prevention, cycle time reduction, and cost savings.

Six Sigma is a rigorous, focused, and highly effective implementation of proven quality principles and techniques. Incorporating elements from the work of many quality pioneers, Six Sigma aims for virtually error-free business performance. Sigma, σ, is a letter in the Greek alphabet used by statisticians to measure the variability in any process. A company's performance is measured by the sigma level of its business processes. Traditionally companies accepted three or four sigma performance levels as the norm, despite the fact that these processes created between 6,200 and 67,000 problems per million opportunities! The Six Sigma standard of 3.4 problems per million opportunities is a response to the increasing expectations of customers and the increased complexity of modern products and processes.[2]

Six Sigma's magic isn't merely statistical, nor is it high-tech. Six Sigma takes a handful of proven methods and trains a small cadre of in-house technical leaders, known as Six Sigma Black Belts, to a high level of proficiency in the application of these techniques. To be sure, some of the methods used by Black Belts are highly advanced, including the use of up-to-date computer technology. But the tools are applied within a simple performance improvement model known as DMAIC, or Define–Measure–Analyze–Improve–Control. DMAIC can be described as follows:

- **Define** the goals of the improvement activity. At the top level of goals will be the strategic objectives of the organization, such as a higher ROI or market share. At the operations level, a goal might be to increase the throughput of a production department. At the project level, goals might be to reduce the defect level and increase throughput. You should apply data mining methods to identify potential improvement opportunities.

- **Measure** the existing system. Establish valid and reliable metrics to help monitor progress toward the goal(s) defined at the previous step. Begin by determining the current baseline. Use exploratory and descriptive data analysis to help you understand the data.

- **Analyze** the system to identify ways to eliminate the gap between the current performance of the system or process and the desired goal. Apply statistical tools to guide the analysis.

- **Improve** the system. Be creative in finding new ways to do things better, cheaper, or faster. Use project management and other planning and management tools to implement the new approach. Use statistical methods to validate the improvement.

- **Control** the new system. Institutionalize the improved system by modifying compensation and incentive systems, policies, procedures, management responsibilities, budgets, operating instructions, and other management systems. You may wish to utilize systems such as ISO 9000 to ensure that documentation is correct.[3]

A very powerful feature of Six Sigma is the creation of an infrastructure to ensure that performance improvement activities have the necessary resources. Six Sigma makes improvement and change the full-time job of a small but critical percentage of the organization's personnel. These full-time change agents are the catalyst that institutionalizes change.

Leadership and Change Agents in Six Sigma

Six Sigma involves changing major business value streams that cut across organizational barriers. It is the measure by which the organization's strategic goals are to be achieved. This effort cannot be led by anyone other than the CEO, who is responsible for the performance of the organization as a whole. Six Sigma must be implemented from the top down.

Six Sigma "champions" are high-level individuals who understand Six Sigma and are committed to its success. In larger organizations Six Sigma will be led by a full-time, high-level champion, such as an executive vice-president. In all organizations, champions also include informal leaders who use Six Sigma in their day-to-day work and communicate the Six Sigma message at every opportunity. "Sponsors" are owners of processes and systems that help initiate and coordinate Six Sigma improvement activities in their areas of responsibilities.

Six Sigma "Master Black Belt" is the highest level of technical and organizational proficiency. Master Black Belts provide technical leadership of the Six Sigma program. Thus, they must know everything the Black Belts know, as well as understand the mathematical theory on which the statistical methods are based. Master Black Belts must be able to assist Black Belts in applying the methods correctly in unusual situations. Whenever possible, statistical training should be conducted only by Master Black Belts. Otherwise the familiar "propagation of error" phenomenon will occur, that is, Black Belts pass on errors to Green Belts, who pass on greater errors to team members. If it becomes necessary for Black Belts and Green Belts to provide training, they should do so only under the guidance of Master Black Belts. For example, Black Belts may be asked to provide assistance to the Master during class discussions and exercises. Because of the nature of the Master's duties, communications and teaching skills are as important as technical competence.

Candidates for Black Belt status are technically oriented individuals held in high regard by their peers. They should be actively involved in the process of organizational change and development. Candidates may come from a wide range of disciplines and need not be formally trained statisticians or engineers. However, because they are expected to master a wide variety of technical tools in a relatively short period of time, Black Belt candidates will probably possess a background in college-level mathematics, the basic tool of quantitative analysis. Coursework in statistical methods should be considered a strong plus or even a prerequisite. As part of their training, Black Belts receive 160 hours of classroom instruction, plus one-on-one project coaching from Master Black Belts or consultants.

Successful candidates will be comfortable with computers. At a minimum, they should understand one or more operating systems, spreadsheets, database managers, presentation programs, and word processors. As part of their training they will be required to become proficient in the use of one or more advanced statistical analysis software packages. Six Sigma Black Belts work to extract actionable knowledge from an organization's information warehouse. To ensure access to the needed information, Six Sigma activities should be closely integrated with the information systems of the organization. Obviously, the skills and training of Six Sigma Black Belts must be enabled by an investment in software and hardware. It makes no sense to hamstring these experts by saving a few dollars on computers or software.

Green Belts are Six Sigma project leaders capable of forming and facilitating Six Sigma teams and managing Six Sigma projects from concept to completion. Green Belt training consists of 5 days of classroom training and is conducted in conjunction with Six Sigma projects. Training covers project management, quality management tools, quality control tools, problem solving, and descriptive data analysis. Six Sigma champions should attend Green Belt training. Usually, Six Sigma Black Belts help Green Belts define their projects prior to the training, attend training with their Green Belts, and assist them with their projects after training. Figure 17–3 summarizes the change agents of Six Sigma.

Implementation and Results of Six Sigma

After over two decades of experience with quality improvement, there is now a solid body of scientific research regarding the experience of thousands of companies implementing major programs such as Six Sigma. Researchers have found that successful deployment of Six Sigma involves focusing on a small number of high-leverage items.

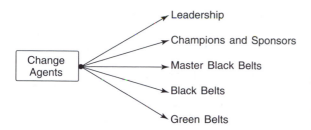

Figure 17–3   Change Agents of Six Sigma
Source: From http://mu.motorola.com/sigma.shtml.

The steps required to successfully implement Six Sigma are well documented. First, successful performance improvement must begin with senior leadership. Organizations should start by providing senior leadership with training in the principles and tools they need to prepare their organization for success. Using their newly acquired knowledge, senior leaders direct the development of a management infrastructure to support Six Sigma. Simultaneously, steps are taken to "soft-wire" the organization and to cultivate an environment for innovation and creativity. This involves reducing levels of organizational hierarchy, removing procedural barriers to experimentation and change, and a variety of other changes designed to make it easier to try new things without fear of reprisal.

Second, systems are developed for establishing close communication with customers, employees, and suppliers. This includes developing rigorous methods of obtaining and evaluating customer, employee, and supplier input. Baseline studies are conducted to determine the starting point and to identify cultural, policy, and procedural obstacles to success.

Third, training needs are rigorously assessed. Remedial basic skills education is provided to ensure that adequate levels of literacy and quantitative abilities and overall competency are possessed by all employees. Top-to-bottom training is conducted in systems improvement tools, techniques, and philosophies.

Fourth, a framework for continuous process improvement is developed, along with a system of indicators for monitoring progress and success. Six Sigma metrics focus on the organization's strategic goals, drivers, and key business processes.

Fifth, business processes to be improved are chosen by management and by people with intimate process knowledge at all levels of the organization. Six Sigma projects are conducted to improve business performance linked to measurable financial results. This requires knowledge of the organization's constraints. And sixth, Six Sigma projects are conducted by individual employees and teams led by Green Belts and assisted by Black Belts. Figure 17–4 recaps the six steps to Six Sigma success.

Although the approach is simple, it is by no means easy. But the results justify the effort expended. Research has shown that firms that successfully implement Six Sigma perform better in virtually every business category, including

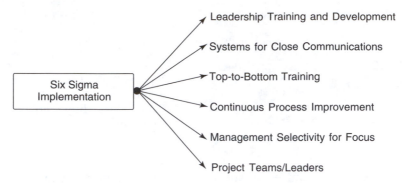

Figure 17–4   Steps to Six Sigma Success
Source: From www.qpronline.com/sixsigma/more_about_sixsigma.html.

return on sales, return on investment, growth, share price increase, and customer satisfaction. These key result areas are delineated in Figure 17–5.

OUTSOURCING, TECHNOLOGY, AND OTHER TRENDS

While we discussed outsourcing earlier in the text, it is important to point out that outsourcing is a driving force behind substantial organizational change now and perhaps well into the future. Hospitality industry firms, both in response to the economic downturn in 2000–2001 and in striving for profits, recognized that outsourcing and co-oping would both reduce costs and increase efficiencies. It is predicted that both trends will continue and help to decrease overhead and increase profits. Outsourcing and co-oping are changing purchasing, human resources, security, and even marketing. Major hospitality industry firms such as Cendant, Hyatt, Marriott, and Starwood, to name a few, have opted for a number of these options. Co-ops between service organizations and airlines are also proliferating.

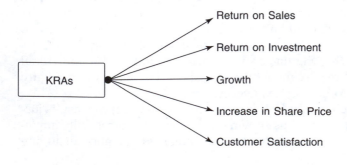

Figure 17–5   Six Sigma KRAs
(Key Result Areas)
Source: From
www.ge.com/commitment/
quality/whatis.htm.

TECHNOLOGY

Organizational and operational efficiencies have been and will continue to be driven by technology. Instantaneous data reporting systems, inventory systems, and distribution networks are all enhancing responsiveness and performance. Web-based marketing, more sophisticated databases, and online purchasing continue to add speed and convenience as well as result in greater returns and efficiencies.

Technology is also continuing to impact organizational and operational concepts. Technology that replaces the human resource and reduces cost or saves time is being embraced almost everywhere in the industry. For example, automated self-service technology is replacing humans in the check-in/check-out process, meal ordering, ticketing, and so on. Technology that enhances revenue management is also changing organizational structures. For example, more than a few organizations now have a "chief revenue management officer" or have designated this as a subtitle for their brand presidents/heads. "Chief technology officers" have also emerged as technology spending and its impact on the organization has grown. In fact, since 1995 technology expenditures have been increasing on average from 10 to 15 percent per year in the hospitality industry.

Finally, we are also seeing operations drawing more and more on seniors and imported labor to meet labor demands. This trend is likely to continue due to projected demand for employees and the need for multilingual and multicultural workforces.

CHAPTER REVIEW

We began this chapter looking at the concept of change, which is most apropos to the dynamic hospitality industry. We discussed the fact that both external and internal trends and events impact organizational and operational change. We reviewed the dimensions of change, including the concepts of uncertainty, complexity, and illiberality. We then reviewed a number of organizational concepts beginning with how companies move from entrepreneurial leadership/organization to a more formalized structure. We pointed out that formality and organizational skills are closely linked to the phases or stages of a company's life cycle. We looked at how skills evolve from entrepreneurial and technical in the early points of the life cycle to conceptual in the middle and later stages.

The organizational concepts of centralization and decentralization were presented along with hospitality industry examples. We discussed empowerment as well as the decentralized hybrid concept and other organizational approaches such as the cluster, "concept," and team management concepts.

We then took an in-depth look at the organizational philosophy of Six Sigma and its substructure of agents of change.

Finally, we looked at other concepts impacting organizational structure and operational environments. Included in this area were outsourcing, co-oping, technology, and the importation of labor.

KEY CONCEPTS/TERMS

Centralization	Formal structure
Clustering	Illiberality
Complexity	Labor importation
Decentralization	Outsourcing
Dynamic	Six Sigma
Empowerment	

DISCUSSION QUESTIONS

1. Why is it important to monitor change and its impact on a hospitality organization?

2. Discuss the advantages and disadvantages of a team management versus a centralized organizational approach.

3. How do desired outcomes (goals and objectives) affect organizational and operational concepts?

4. Select a hospitality industry segment (e.g., airlines, cruise lines, food service, lodging) and delineate how you believe technology will impact that segment from an operational and/or organizational perspective.

5. What advantages do you see in a decentralized organizational structure in a hospitality industry firm?

6. What are some reasons a hospitality industry company might change its organizational structure?

ENDNOTES

1. R. Woods & J. King, *Quality Leadership and Management in the Hospitality Industry* (East Lansing, MI: Educational Institute of the American Hotel and Motel Association, 1996): 330–332.
2. From www.sixsigma.com/library/content/ask-01.asp.
3. From www.qpronline.com/sixsigma/more_about_sixsigma.html.

CASE 1

Enterprise Rent-A-Car—Organizing around the Customer

Sometimes a simple, straightforward organizational or operational concept can impel a business to preeminence in its industry sector. In the car rental sector, Enterprise Rent-A-Car is an example of just that, using a concept that has worked so well that Enterprise has now surpassed Hertz as the largest car rental company in the United States in terms of fleet size and number of locations.

Enterprise's operating philosophy is very simple: "Put customers first, because if they are satisfied they will come back." Next come the employees: "Make sure they are happy, well informed (trained) and part of a team atmosphere."

Enterprise organized its business with another simple concept, bringing the product/service to the consumer. Enterprise picks up the customer at home, at work, at the repair shop, or wherever the customer desires. Highly competitive rental rates, bringing the product/service to the customer, and great employees have made Enterprise the fastest-growing large car rental firm in the world.

The employees who share in the privately held company's success welcome the exploding growth. All front-line supervisors and managers are paid the profits of their own operations.

Each of the nearly 4,000 offices operates as a small business, giving the employees the autonomy and the authority to meet the needs of the customers. Employees who went to college with plans to become professionals start by washing cars or servicing customers from behind the counter. However, they quickly move up the corporate ladder. In Enterprise's effort to hire the best, it has established a website that is dedicated to recruiting (www.erac.com/recruit/).

Enterprise's core business, renting cars in people's home cities, requires a very special kind of customer attention. It also requires low prices and convenient locations, so Enterprise can pick up customers stranded at repair shops and bring them to their rental cars. An Enterprise branch can be found within 15 minutes of 90 percent of the population in major metropolitan areas.*

The special home city rental market also requires advanced technology to keep costs low and customers happy. Enterprise has the world's largest investment in IBM AS/400 computers in one location. The company is hooked up to an AT&T satellite that allows all branches, from anywhere in the United States to Canada to the United Kingdom, to communicate with each other and headquarters instantly. The technology allows Enterprise to track information from when a customer's car should be ready at the repair shop to where each of its nearly 500,000 rental vehicles is located.

*Information derived from www.enterprise.com/about/press_0696.html.

Milestones*

1957	The company Executive Leasing is founded by Jack Taylor in St. Louis.
1961	Opens a second location. Growth pushes the number of lease units past 1,000.
1962	After 5 years in the leasing business, launches a car rental operation with 17 vehicles and starts a car sales division.
1967	Introduces the now-famous "e" logo that is still used today.
1969	Changes its name from Executive Leasing to Enterprise Leasing and expands outside of St. Louis with the opening of the Atlanta group. The total number of lease units surpasses 5,000. (The company was renamed in honor of the U.S.S. Enterprise aircraft carrier, on which Jack Taylor served in World War II.)
1970–1974	Expands into Orlando, Tampa, Houston, and Kansas City. Over 1,000 rental units are in service. In 1972, a branch manager in Orlando starts a new pick-up program that provides customers with a free ride to the rental office. The service quickly spreads to other Enterprise branches.
1975–1979	Opens branch offices in Colorado, Dallas, Indiana, southern Florida, and elsewhere. The number of rental units rises to 5,000. In 1976, begins offering fuel, maintenance, and insurance products (leading to the present-day Enterprise Fleet Services operation).
1980–1984	Rental units grow from 5,000 to 20,000 as expansion continues in southern California, San Francisco, Phoenix, New Orleans, Chicago, Texas, and Washington, D.C. Insurance replacement rentals become a bigger part of its business, due to legislation requiring insurance companies to provide their customers with replacement vehicles. In 1980, the National Reservation Center opens—customers can call a tollfree number to reserve Enterprise vehicles nationwide. By 1983, Enterprise has more than 100 offices.
1985–1989	By the end of the decade, several hundred locations across the country display the Enterprise logo. The number of rental units climbs from 25,000 to 75,000. In 1989, the company's name—Enterprise Leasing—

*Information derived from www.enterprise.com/about/history.html.

officially changes to Enterprise Rent-A-Car, to reflect the enormous growth of its rental car business.

1990–1992   Incredible growth continues in the United States as the company's fleet increases from 130,000 to 150,000 units with more than 1,000 branch offices open across the country. Because of a new national advertising campaign, the Enterprise "wrapped car" quickly becomes an icon.

1993–1995   Expands into Canada and the United Kingdom. Some 200,000 rental units and 1,500 locations in 1993 swell to more than 290,000 rental units and 2,500 locations in 1995—making Enterprise the largest car rental company in the United States. In 1993, the National Reservation Center goes to 24-hour-a-day operation.

1996–1998   Opens branch offices in Germany, while continuing to expand in the United Kingdom. The total number of vehicles in the fleet jumps from 350,000 to over 450,000 in just 2 years.

1999   Surpasses 500,000 vehicles in its rental and leasing fleet and has more than 4,000 locations worldwide.

2002   Becomes the largest rental car company in the world based on locations and fleet size.

The Enterprise Rent-A-Car case was selected as an example because it directly shows the results of an organizational and operational management strategy that was unique and that differentiated the firm from its competitors. Further, its success was due to understanding the customer's needs and addressing those needs effectively.

Case Discussion Questions

1. What risks do you see in the Enterprise Rent-A-Car strategy?
2. If you were an Enterprise manager, what would you do if a major competitor began to offer at-home or at-office delivery?

CASE 2

Four Seasons Hotels and Resorts—Keeping It Simple and Successful*

Organizational and operating philosophies sometimes evolve into the driving forces behind a corporation or a product/service offering. This case looks at the evolution of Four Seasons Hotels and Resorts from having a simple operating philosophy and a singleness positioning and product strategy to becoming the leading organization in the luxury hotel sector of the hospitality industry.

Four Seasons is synonymous with the luxury hotel. This company has chosen a singleness strategy that consists of offering one single product: all first-class hotels with ownership and management control. Unlike companies such as Hilton that offer a variety of brands and prices for different segments of the market, Four Seasons offers one product at a predetermined level of quality and service. It does not associate its name with any lower-price or lower-quality brand or product.

A Four Seasons hotel can be classified as a medium-sized facility, ranging from 200 to 500 rooms. The quality and personalized service that distinguish a Four Seasons property cannot be obtained in a convention hotel. The business traveler is the main customer, and Four Seasons' most common locations are the financial and business districts of large cities. Personalized attention to the guest's needs and comfort and an emphasis on quality food and beverage service are hallmarks of a Four Seasons hotel.

The result is an overall level of quality that guests perceive as an excellent value. The company's success in meeting customers' expectations is evidenced by the lack of price resistance that it finds in the market it serves.

The company is one of the leading managers of luxury hotels and resorts and manages only luxury hotel and resort properties. These properties are operated primarily under the Four Seasons and Regent brand names, in principal cities and resort destinations in 23 countries in North America, Europe, Asia, the Middle East, Australia, the Caribbean, and South America. The company earns 90 percent of its earnings before other operating expenses from management operations. Under its management agreements, Four Seasons generally supervises all aspects of a project's operations on behalf of its owner, including sales and marketing reservations, accounting, purchasing, budgeting, and the hiring, training, and supervising of staff. For providing these services, the company typically receives a base fee calculated as a percentage of gross revenues of the property operating performance.

---

*Information derived from www.fourseasons.com/about_us/company_information/ and www.fourseasons.com/about_us/investor_information/.

History

Isadore (Issy) Sharp founded the company in 1960 with the opening of the first Four Seasons hotel on Jarvis Street, Toronto, an area of once-exclusive residences that had declined into tenement housing. Sharp saw an opportunity, while others saw a difficult location because property values in the area were low and land was available at a reasonable price. He recognized that he had limited experience in hotel development and operation, and for this reason he hired a group of professionals including hotel architects, designers, consultants, and operating executives.

The first Four Seasons acquired a reputation for an impressive level of service and for distinctive food and beverage outlets. As the firm redefined its position in the market, the first property was sold, but the overall marketing strategy for the company had been developed. It took more than a decade of trial and refinement for the company to create a single vision that has made Four Seasons the leading operator in the world of mid-sized luxury hotels and resorts of exceptional quality.

Four Seasons' corporate singleness strategy is the result of many side steps, rather than big leaps. Sharp describes the growth of the strategy as an evolution of one idea upon the next. Four Seasons' success with this strategy can be attributed to:

- The decision to get into the hotel business and focus on operating medium-sized hotels of exceptional quality
- The determination that being the best means offering quality through exceptional service
- The decision to develop a culture of a dedicated and loyal workforce
- The determination to make a high-quality Four Seasons brand name perceived as more prestigious than its competitors

When the company set out to differentiate from its competition, it made the decision to become customer centered instead of product centered. The standard of quality is defined by highly personalized and anticipatory service. The principles behind the definition of quality are the same of those behind the company's operating philosophy. It is what Isadore Sharp called the "Golden Rule": simply treat others (partners, customers, coworkers) as you wish them to treat you.

The company's mission statement summarizes the main strategy, positioning, and how the objectives are to be attained:

> We have chosen to specialize within the hospitality industry, by offering only exceptional quality. Our objective is to be recognized as the company that manages the finest hotels, resorts, residence clubs, and other residential projects wherever we locate. We create properties of enduring

value using superior design *and finishes, and a deeply instilled ethic of personal service. Doing so allows Four Seasons to satisfy the needs and tastes of our discriminating customers, and to maintain our position as the luxury world's premier luxury hospitality company.*

Supporting Strategies

Four Seasons supports its operational philosophy and overall organizational image with multiple substrategies that include but are not limited to: positioning, pricing and status management, innovation, and publicity/public relations.

Positioning   Four Seasons has done an excellent job of positioning its brand as high-quality/luxury leader in the hotel and resort sector of the hospitality industry. Four Seasons developed a substantial base of knowledge and understanding regarding its customers, who they are, how they live, work, and spend their money. More importantly, Four Seasons knew how to translate the refinements and desired atmosphere of its customer base to its hotels and resorts. Moreover, it successfully conveyed this translation and concept in its marketing messages from the very beginning.

The company's first campaign included a series of advertisements in such business-oriented publications as *Forbes*, *The Wall Street Journal*, and *Business Week*. These ads were designed to create an image of Four Seasons hotels as tasteful, personalized, and service oriented.

The first advertisement campaign created awareness among its target market and helped define its position in the hotel sector. Further, in order to identify potential customers, Four Seasons identified those companies among the top 1,000 that generated significant amounts of business travel to existing or scheduled locations. The list developed was a highly select one, consisting of corporate travel managers, secretaries to top executives, and meeting planners. In concert with the increased awareness generated by the advertising campaign, the firm put its sales force to work. The emphasis was on persuading prospects from that list that Four Seasons offered a distinctive product they should try or patronage. While Four Seasons has significant competition such as The Ritz-Carlton, Mandarin, Rosewood, and Regent International, to name a few, it keeps its message consistent and focused on itself and its customer base.

The company has developed a unique service culture, positioning, perception, and management expertise that provide it an overall competitive advantage.

Pricing Strategies and Status Management   Pricing sends the first message about the position and status of a product or service. Four Seasons has done an excellent job of using rates and pricing to support positioning and enhance image. Even in down periods it will offer attractive packages instead of reduced-price promotions, which hurt the image. Status is a very powerful and strong motivator of Four Seasons' target market. Status is a matter of perception; a five-star hotel is perceived as "the place" one should stay if one seeks status. Again, the company's pricing strategy, often as one of the highest priced in the market, reinforces its image and positioning. Four Seasons' higher price actually contributes to its demand from the status-seeking segment. Four Seasons will not lower rates to gain occupancy because it knows it could damage its upscale image by offering discounts.

Four Seasons' status management strategy consists of not associating its name with any lower-rated or lower-priced brands. Prices stay high and discounting is minimized in order to protect the image and preserve the status.

Innovation   Many common practices in the hospitality industry today have been major Four Seasons innovations that have helped the company set itself apart as an innovator in the industry. Also, many of the attentive practices designated as "VIP" services at larger hotels are standard procedure at Four Seasons hotels. Guests with reservations are routinely preregistered and escorted to their rooms by a representative of management. Automatic checkout has been a Four Seasons standard feature since the 1970s, as have in-lobby amenities such as coffee, apples, and the like. Some important innovations that have become Four Seasons hallmarks include:

- **European-style concierge service**—Four Seasons was the first to employ concierge service company-wide in North America; in addition, the company made this a 24-hour service.
- **Private concierge service**—Complimentary concierge service is available to all clients, regardless of whether the traveler is staying in a Four Seasons property at the time.
- **Home-cooking program**—This features simple recipes that travelers would have at home, to offer a change of pace from the gourmet meals guests eat so often on the road. It was introduced in 1995 at selected properties and became a company-wide feature in 1997.
- **Exceptional restaurants**—The company dispelled the "hotel dining" stigma of high prices and inferior food by placing emphasis on quality food and beverage in its hotels.
- **Vegetarian dining**—The company introduced new menus with dishes that cater to the vegetarian in terms of the ingredients used.
- **Private reserve**—This program, introduced in 1990, provides custom-tailored service to frequent guests.
- **Executive suites**—Introduced in 1981, this creates an office away from home by offering accommodations that are almost 50 percent larger than the regular guest room. Sleeping accommodations are separated from a living area that is ideal for an informal business meeting.
- **Complimentary newspapers**—A common practice in the industry today, Four Seasons was the first hotel in North America to provide complimentary newspapers with room service breakfast delivery.
- **Twenty-four-hour business services**

- **Twenty-four-hour room service**
- **Digital display for the hearing impaired**
- **Complimentary early arrival/late departure**
- **Bathrooms with phones**

One of the newest innovations is the introduction of high-speed internet access. The Four Seasons Olympic Hotel in Seattle became the first hotel in the world to employ Guest-Tek's broadband internet access; this service makes connecting to the internet both quick and easy. Guests simply plug their laptops into the Global Suite or desk jacks, open their browsers, and they are automatically connected to log in for high-speed internet access.

Public Relations and the Community   Four Seasons is a small company that does not have the marketing and technology resources that companies such as Hilton and Marriott enjoy. Instead of using powerful loyalty programs, Four Seasons keeps customers loyal by giving them what is important to them—quality service, status, and satisfaction by meeting their personal needs.

Endorsements, awards, and other forms of recognition all add to status if publicized. More importantly, Four Seasons' target market likes to patronize award-winning, status-fulfilling establishments. Four Seasons' public relations remains consistently busy in view of the many awards received by the hotels and company. Here are just a few that enhance the company's positioning status:

- Four Seasons topped Mobil's Five Star awards list in the last 5 years and received more awards than any other hotel company in the world.
- The company figured prominently in *Condé Nast Traveler* magazine's list of the world's best places to stay. Forty-two properties were listed and several properties were noted in "best" lists including best food, location, rooms, and service.
- In the *Gallivan's Guide* 10th annual reader poll (2001), Four Seasons Hotels and Resorts was named number one in the Best Hotel Group Worldwide category. Among other awards given by this exclusive travel newsletter published in the United Kingdom are: Best Service Worldwide (Four Seasons Resort Bali and Four Seasons Resort Maldives at Kuda Huraa), Best Hotel Worldwide (Four Seasons Hotel Milan, Four Seasons Hotel George V Paris), and Best Hotel Cuisine Worldwide (Four Seasons Hotel George V Paris).
- Four Seasons properties received 20 of the 67 AAA Five Diamond awards for 2002; this was the 21st consecutive year Four Seasons has received more Five Diamond awards than any other hotel company.

Four Seasons understands the importance of the local market; the company believes that reputation in the local market reflects on its reputation worldwide. Four Seasons seeks to have the finest restaurants in the respective local communities in order to reinforce its image on a local level.

To approach and retain customers, the company takes a more cautious and personal style with the strategic use of public relations. The corporate awareness of the importance of positioning in the market extends to each hotel's relations with its community, and this is best demonstrated by Four Seasons' attention to detail when preparing to open a new property. The campaign to establish the position in the community starts before the construction of the property. The community's corporate meeting planners are polled, not just as a public relations gesture, but to establish their needs for facilities and services. Local corporate executives are interviewed and asked to identify their food preferences. The interviews permit the company's planners to understand the local tastes and design menus accordingly. Throughout the construction of the property, the local community is kept informed through news releases designed to describe the future hotel. After the opening, the company does not suspend its effort at being a good local citizen; a regular feature of Four Seasons hotels is the captain's table. These consist of gatherings of community and business leaders with the general manager. Members of the community are sometimes given a voice in the design of sleeping rooms and other property amenities. Most hotels also participate in cultural and philanthropic events that benefit the community. All managers are expected to be exemplary citizens in their respective communities.

Four Seasons does not perceive success as having the biggest market share or the largest revenues; being perceived as number one in its market segment constitutes the company's success. The success of the company has certainly been the result of a combination of many factors such as people, service, quality, and organizational and operational leadership.

As we delineated, the company has adopted several substrategies that support its organizational philosophy of uniqueness and differentiation in the luxury market. These operational and organizational strategies have provided:

- **Strong brand recognition**—Hotels are recognized for the exceptional quality of their guest services and facilities.

- **Superior operating results**—REVPAR and operating profit margins are above the average in the luxury segment of the lodging industry. Investors are attracted to the corporation as a result of its superior long-term financial performance, along with global presence and recognition.

- **Management team reputation**—Four Seasons' organizational philosophy attracts long-term management agreements. The company's executive management team consists of eight individuals who are responsible for the global strategic direction of the company and who have an average of over 20 years of experience with Four Seasons. This has helped to ensure consistency in service, operating culture, and work ethic.

- **Strong competitive position**—Four Seasons' strong competitive position enhances its ability to attract the best human resources and capital. In fact, Four Seasons' success in human resources management has been recognized by *Fortune* magazine, which included Four Seasons in the list of the 100 Best Companies to Work For in America for the fifth year in a row. Four Seasons ranked 61st among leading employers in the United States and was the only Canadian company to make the list in 2002.

Summarizing, Four Seasons' organizational and operational strategies have given the company a series of competitive advantages that have made it the leader in the hotel luxury segment. These strategies have given Four Seasons the ability to achieve higher rates and profitability and to attract financing, management, contracts, and outstanding personnel.

Case Discussion Questions

1. As indicated in this case study, innovations in operating strategy have resulted in brand success. What innovations of other firms' operations can you name that you believe have helped their brand?
2. Four Seasons' operational philosophy places substantial authority with the general manager. This represents a more decentralized approach. What do you see as the strengths and weaknesses of this approach versus centralization?

Chapter 18

Leadership Profiles

CHAPTER OBJECTIVES

- To delineate leadership skills in relation to lifecycle stages within the hospitality industry
- To profile a number of managerial approaches to leadership
- To define business acumen and outline the goals and focal points for managerial leadership strategies
- To discuss common traits of successful leaders within the hospitality industry

The hospitality industry provides a wealth of examples of leadership skills. Leadership expertise/skills are often tied to the actual situation or status of the organization. For example, a company with a current growth environment may look to a person and a structure that fosters business development activities. Here strategic leadership, vision, and deal-making skills form key criteria for a leader. In other circumstances, such as economic downturns and struggling performance, it may be more appropriate to have a financial/control leadership orientation. And still other circumstances such as a highly competitive environment might call for the leadership and organization to have a strong marketing orientation. The point is that often the life cycle of the brand/company and the market or economic environment influence the type of leadership required.

LEADERSHIP REQUIREMENTS

Embassy Suites provides an example of how the stage of the product life cycle and the market/economic climate influenced the leadership orientation during the launch and growth phase of the brand. Embassy's product concept was truly unique at the time of market introduction. Embassy also met and fulfilled a strong market demand in its design and operational concept. It filled a major void for product which offered in essence a bedroom and meeting/living room for the price of a single room. Embassy offered a complete complimentary breakfast and often a very attractive atrium interior. The product/service concept was very successful from a market acceptance and performance perspective. Then-CEO Hervey Feldman was the perfect match for the leadership orientation. Feldman was considered to be among the best development executives and creative deal-makers in the hospitality industry. When Feldman was asked what his management strategy was for Embassy Suites, he replied, "Build them as fast as we can and wherever we can." It was a very focused strategy that proved extraordinarily successful for the company and its leadership.

Another area that requires a good match between leadership and market climate is the financial area. The lodging sector historically has had a pattern of 8 to 10 years of an up-cycle followed by 1 to 3 years of a down-cycle. During the down-cycles there are some significant financial opportunities to acquire brands/chains. Also, on occasion a brand goes on the market for other reasons such as a company being over-extended or the ownership wanting to sell. A financial master at buying low and rejuvenating brands was Henry Silverman, CEO of Cendant. Silverman used his financial savvy to acquire lodging chains and other hospitality-related businesses at depressed prices. He was so successful that he built the largest collection of hospitality lodging brands in existence today. His acquisitions of such well-known brands as Days Inn, Howard Johnson, and Ramada (to name a few) demonstrated the perfect match of leadership acumen to market opportunity. Figure 18-1 delineates a variety of leadership strengths/approaches for different life cycles and market conditions.

The hospitality industry is replete with historical and current examples of leadership that match the needs of the company/brand. Examples include leaders such as Mike Rose whose strategic genius spun off nongrowth businesses and the "cash cow" Holiday Inn brand and reinvented the company, moving it, new name (Promus) and all, into gaming and the development of new brands such as Hampton Inn and Embassy Suites. Another example is Juergen Bartels, a master marketing and development strategist who can rekindle the fire of life on the deadest of brands. He segmented the Ramada brand, including conceiving the Renaissance concept; helped build a number of Carlson brands; and rejuvenated Westin and Le Meridien. Bartels is a leader by doing—high energy and highly motivated—just the right approach to rejuvenate a company/brand.

ETHICS

A true CEO (chief ethics officer) or moral manager is a person who maintains strong morals and values and possesses the ability to instill these ideals in others.

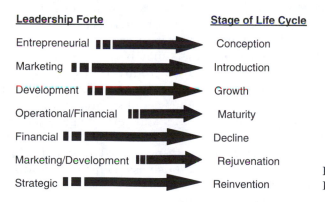

Leadership Forte	Stage of Life Cycle
Entrepreneurial	Conception
Marketing	Introduction
Development	Growth
Operational/Financial	Maturity
Financial	Decline
Marketing/Development	Rejuvenation
Strategic	Reinvention

Figure 18–1 Multidimensional Leadership Approaches

Other sectors of the hospitality industry provide more examples of leadership approach and brand success. In the airline sector, Herb Kellerher stands out as a people-oriented motivator who built Southwest Airlines to be the flyer's favorite. Steve Wynn, whose financial and creative approach ignited the casino business, helped bring Las Vegas into a new era. Mickey Arison's drive, ambition, and financial savvy led to the development of the world's largest cruise company at Carnival. In the foodservice sector we can readily see the marketing ability of Colonel Sanders, Dave Thomas, and Truett Cathy, to name a few. It should be pointed out that while an individual's strength may be in one discipline, most leaders have excellent skills in more than one area. Leaders also recognize their weaknesses and their organizations needs and acquire the talent to achieve their vision for the company.

BUSINESS ACUMEN

This is a good juncture to discuss the second topic of this chapter, business acumen and the focal points for managerial leadership success in the hospitality industry. While the hospitality industry is certainly people oriented, leadership success and failure are not measured by the popularity of a CEO with the employees. Certainly being a good "people person" has its benefits for a leader; however, the ultimate measurements of successful leadership have more to do with the leader's business acumen.

TECHNOLOGY

Communications, up-to-date management information, and sound decision making are all part of leadership, and technology is providing better and faster paths for each.

Leaders are supposed to make money and focus on achieving both strategic and financial goals and objectives. Leaders have to focus on cash generation, margin, inventory turnover (velocity), return on assets, growth, and customers.[1] Managing these six elements of a business usually results in positive results, and positive results are what is of most interest to shareholders. Figure 18-2 recaps the six key focal points for positive results.

In the hospitality industry return on assets may be viewed as return on assets owned (or return on investments—ROI) or return on assets managed (ROAM), for a management contract company. Return on assets has to be greater than the cost of using your own or other people's money (the cost of capital). Growth has its base in customer counts and revenue generated per customer (REVPAC). When both customer counts and REVPAC increase, the result is usually gains in market share and profit margins. Growth also has a psychological dimension in that it energizes a business, helps attract top talent, fosters fresh ideas, and creates new opportunities. Growth must also be profitable and sustainable for longer-term leadership success.

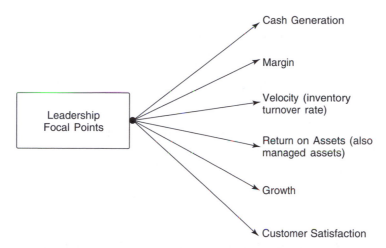

Figure 18–2   Leadership Focal Points for Positive Results
Source: Adapted from R. Charan, *What the CEO Wants You to Know* (New York: Crown Publishers, a div. of Random House, 2001): 29.

Leadership success often rests on asking the right questions, managing by prioritizing and communicating, and seeing that the organization has the skill sets in place to be successful. Let's look at each of these three areas. First, asking the right questions means being specific and getting down to what counts—asking about sales trends, growth, declines, or other significant patterns. Asking about profit margins—how they can increase, why they are declining, and so on. Asking for comparative analysis of the sales trends and margins against the industry and top five competitors. Asking about inventory velocity and return on assets ($R = M \times V$, where M = Margin). Asking about and discussing ways to increase cash generation or stem cashflow declines. Asking about market share trends and forecasts. And, always asking why?

To receive intelligent answers to these questions and to formulate action steps, leaders must possess (either themselves or within their organizational structure) skills in a variety of areas to be successful. Obviously, sales and revenue forecasting and inventory management skills are critical. Other skill sets include cash management, market and product mix analysis, operating margin management, pricing and advertising, and profit margin management. Feedback systems on customers, competitors, and operating environment trends are equally important.

Leaders ask the right questions, have in place the resources and systems to provide intelligent answers, and then manage, prioritize, and communicate desired actions. This involves reducing complexity and establishing three or four (no more than five) important priorities usually related to the leadership focal points delineated in Figure 18-2. Leaders who are successful know how to communicate goals clearly, and leaders continually seek to improve the fundamentals of the business.

Finally, leaders are masters at synchronization by putting the right people in the right jobs, by consistently delivering results, and by coaching and mentoring. A synchronized organization is like a championship rowing team pulling together with flawless timing and smoothly moving to victory. Synchronization expands the capacity of the whole organization. Great leaders employ synchronization techniques including social operating mechanisms (SOMs). SOMs involve meetings that are designed to filter out information, delineate priorities, and foster ideas. SOMs include conference calls focused on obtaining quick market intelligence and spotting trends (problems and opportunities) at the earliest possible moment. SOMs include using e-mail, voice-mail, and other technologies to expedite alerts, updates, and the like. Leaders utilize meetings to cut through complexities, provide focus, and most of all listen.

Leadership success involves not only knowing what to focus on, what skill sets are required, what questions to ask, and synchronizing, but also personal example. Personal example usually establishes the environment (climate), reinforces the vision and mission statement, and motivates others to succeed on a daily basis. Having observed hospitality industry leaders for many years as well as formally interviewed leaders and executive search firms, we have observed some common traits that have contributed to the success of great leaders.

LEADERSHIP TRAITS

Great leaders are categorically positively oriented people who think and convey success. Leaders are both goal and plan oriented. Successful leaders have goals (be they related to the business or personal) and have plans to achieve those goals. This means that successful leaders are organized. Leaders take action and are decisive individuals. This action orientation is focused on the goals and is a natural trait. Leaders are self-motivated action takers. Leaders are exceptionally great listeners and insatiable learners. Many of the top executive recruiters interviewed stated that these two traits (listening and learning) are among the top criteria in their decision process to recommend an individual for a leadership position. Successful leaders are extraordinarily persistent and demonstrate a hard-work ethic. Leaders are both fact collectors and risk takers. Leaders are analytical, detailed, and learn from both their analysis of facts and focal points as well as from their mistakes. Another trait of successful leaders is their ability to stay focused and keep others focused. Leaders focus by excellent time management and focus on what counts—money. Leaders do not get distracted from the vision and goals. They focus on their revenue and profit objectives. Leaders seldom follow others. Leaders distinguish themselves by innovation and being different. Leaders do not comprehend or tolerate mediocrity.

Successful leaders enjoy people, dealing with people, and communicating with all constituencies. Leaders enjoy learning from others as well as

Figure 18–3   Fourteen Traits of Successful Leaders

motivating others. Leaders are consistent, take responsibility, and are perceived by others as dependable and honest. Successful leaders are perceived as open and good listeners. Leaders are enthusiastic in nearly all aspects of their professional and personal lives. Leaders are high-energy individuals with great focus and communications skills. Finally, leaders have contacts and know how to gather critical information through their contacts. Leaders often are exceptional at networking to achieve their goals and objectives. Figure 18–3 delineates the traits of successful leaders.

ETHICS

Today a corporate leader must cease to exist solely as an executive and accept the responsibility as chief ethics officer.

CHAPTER REVIEW

In this chapter we looked at leadership skills in relation to the life cycle of a company or brand. We determined that matching skills to needs usually results in successful leadership. We looked at both leadership skills and approaches through the examples of select industry leaders, pointing out the relationship of leaders' managerial strengths to the point-in-time needs of the organization. We went on to define business acumen as being competent in the key skill areas and focal points of cash generation, margin, velocity, return on assets growth, and customers. We pointed out the importance of social operating mechanisms and the benefits of synchronization. Also, we looked at key traits of successful leaders and pointed out 14 of the most common for successful leadership.

KEY CONCEPTS/TERMS

Business acumen   Return on assets
Motivation

DISCUSSION QUESTIONS

1. What trait do you believe to be the most important for a leader to possess in the hospitality industry?
2. Why is business acumen important for leadership?
3. What type of organizational leadership approach would most or least motivate you?
4. Do you believe it is more important for a leader to focus on the present or future?
5. Why should a hospitality organization leader be at the helm of the strategic planning process?
6. How would you describe the ideal leader?
7. Which segments of the hospitably industry do you believe would benefit the most from the Six Sigma concept?

ENDNOTES

1. R. Charan, *What the CEO Wants You to Know* (New York: Crown Publishers, a div. of Random House, 2001): 29.

LEADERSHIP PROFILES

There are many extraordinary examples of entrepreneurial and executive leadership in the hospitality industry. The 10 leadership case profiles related herein are of individuals who exemplify one or more traits of leadership and whose accomplishments and contributions to the hospitality industry are more than deserving of recognition. Many of these case profiles are of individuals who have been inducted or are candidates for induction into the Hospitality Industry Hall of Honor. In this section their backgrounds, accomplishments, and leadership traits are delineated.

Leadership Profile 1
Curtis L. Carlson and Marilyn Carlson Nelson*

Curtis Leroy Carlson personified the leadership traits of a "goal" orientation, enjoying and motivating people (his employees), and caring for the community.

Selling newspapers was the first business venture for Curtis Carlson (1914–1999) as the 12-year-old son of a Minneapolis grocer. He became an entrepreneur when he recognized the profitability of managing additional paper routes. He organized a network of routes and employed his brothers to make those deliveries. After earning a BA in economics in 1937 from the University of Minnesota, Carlson began a promising career with Procter & Gamble, winning the Number One Salesman award for 1938. However, he also started the Gold Bond Stamp Company, an innovative company that introduced a trading stamp program for grocers to offer rewards to shoppers. The grocers that supplied Gold Bond stamps to their customers saw their business increase by 60 percent. By 1953, Gold Bond trading stamps had become a household word for Americans. Today's frequent-flyer and frequent-guest programs are extensions of the trading stamp concept and objective—to spur sales and command consumer loyalty.

Carlson's extraordinary success in the stamp business eventually enabled him to diversify his capital. In addition to real estate property, he purchased 50 percent interest in the downtown Minneapolis Radisson Hotel in 1960, acquired the remaining shares two years later, and then began adding new hotels. This is how Curt Carlson became an innkeeper.

Today, Curt Carlson's entrepreneurial and leadership skills are legendary and the names of his companies encompass the entire spectrum of the hospitality industry. They include Carlson Hospitality Worldwide with Regent International Hotels and Resorts, Radisson Hotels Worldwide, Radisson Seven Seas Cruises, and Country Inns & Suites by Carlson. These lodging operations

*Information derived from www.hrm.uh.edu/?PageID=205.

include over 470 locations in 42 countries and four cruise ships sailing worldwide. Carlson Marketing Group is a worldwide marketing services company. Friday's Hospitality Worldwide has more than 460 restaurants in 350 cities and 40 countries. Carlson has five different operations in the travel industry: Carlson Wagonlit Travel, A.T. Mays, Travel Agents International, Carlson Vacations, and Carlson Leisure Group with a total of 5,300 travel offices in 140 countries. Added to these companies are Carlson Hospitality Worldwide Procurement Group, Carlson Real Estate, and the newest company, Gold Points Plus.

The success of Carlson Companies, Inc., is remarkable, and Carlson proved he was the ultimate goal-driven entrepreneur. After nearly six decades, this privately held business comprises over 100 corporations with a worldwide work force of more than 145,000 who represent 125 different countries. At the end of 1996, the company generated system-wide revenues of more than $13.4 billion with 26 percent derived from businesses outside of the United States. Carlson Companies' brands had earned approximately $20 billion by 1997. It had become one of the largest privately held companies in the United States.

Curt Carlson was a firm believer in the free enterprise system. He considered profit to be an essential and honorable ingredient of a successful business. He gave immeasurably to his community through the economic growth of companies that provide jobs and good salaries with opportunities for advancement, education, and prosperity. His goals were not based on how much money each goal would bring. It is other things that make life important, he stated. "A company has a responsibility to move forward, or its employees will not move forward. . . . Every employee has ambitions for a better quality of life. I have a little philosophy. Every year, a person has to be better off today than a year ago. If that is so, the employee is satisfied and works hard. When this isn't so, you have problems with your employees." He also said that "you should reach as high as you can; if you miss getting to the stars, at least you reach the moon."*

A year prior to his death, Curtis Carlson passed the leadership on to his daughter, Marilyn Carlson Nelson. After she took over, the company increased its travel agency business by 200 percent. Carlson Companies by the year 2000 had gross sales of $31.4 billion and employed 188,000 people. Like her father, Marilyn places high importance on the employees of Carlson Companies. She is very proud of her initiative to create "A Great Place for Great People to Do Great Work." Her devotion to the employees can clearly be seen in the incredibly loyal employee base at the company. Under her leadership and that of her sons, Curtis Nelson (president and COO of Carlson Companies), the legacy of leadership of Curtis Leroy Carlson continues to push the Carlson Companies to hospitality industry preeminence.

*From www.hrm.uh.edu/?PageID=189.

Leadership Profile 2
Walter "Walt" Disney*

Walt Disney (1901–1966) personified the leadership traits of creativity, a detailed focus, and overcoming adversity.

Walt Disney was born on December 5, 1901, in Chicago, the fourth of five children. While none of the children finished school, Walt, a talented artist, attended the Kansas City Art Institute for one year. In 1918, he joined the Red Cross Ambulance Corps, and although he arrived in Europe just as World War I was ending, the time he spent in France made a lasting impression on him. Following his discharge Walt settled in Kansas City where he worked in a commercial art studio and later for a film ad company. Disney was a reserved and private man devoted to his family, wife Lillian Bounds Disney and daughters Sharon and Diane.

Unable to find satisfactory work in the film business, he and his brother Roy moved to Hollywood in 1923, forming Laugh-O-Gram Films, which made animated commercials shown in local movie theaters. They began making cartoon shorts in a relative's garage. By 1927, the brothers formed the Disney Brothers' Cartoon Studio. The following year the studio released "Steamboat Willie," starring Mickey Mouse in the first synchronized sound cartoon, and the Disney legend was born. Walt himself was the voice behind Mickey Mouse, whom he originally named Mortimer. However, Lillian, his new wife, said that Mortimer sounded too formal, and suggested Mickey. And so began the life of the world's best-loved and most well-known character.

The World War II years were difficult for the studio. It wasn't until the debut of the two television programs in 1955, "Disneyland" and "The Mickey Mouse Club," and the July 1955 opening of Walt's "brain child," Disneyland Theme Park, that Walt Disney Enterprises became financially successful. In 1955, however, nobody, especially the Disney board of directors, thought that the theme park would succeed. Walt Disney saw himself as an entertainer and a man with a creative vision. He was involved in every step of his studio's creative processes, and he was always willing to risk his personal fortune on the success of a project. His unique contributions to the world included a stable of family entertainment standards and a vision of the possibilities for the future.

During Walt Disney's lifetime he received 39 Oscars, 4 television Emmy Awards, and over 800 other awards. Disney paved the way in his industry by being the first to create the following:

- The first synchronized sound cartoon—"Steamboat Willie"
- The first full-color cartoon—"Flowers and Trees"
- The first animated feature—"Snow White"

*Information derived from www.hrm.uh.edu/?PageID=195.

- The first television series created by a major movie producer—"The Mickey Mouse Club"
- The first theme park—Disneyland

Before Walt's untimely death on December 15, 1966, from lung cancer, he purchased land in Orlando, Florida, for Walt Disney World (28,000 acres). While he did not live to see the completion of the park, he was instrumental in its planning. Walt Disney World quickly became one of the world's premier tourist vacation destinations. The various Disney theme parks set standards globally for theme parks and resort development with a variety of entertainment venues, hotels, restaurants, golf courses, campgrounds, and shopping villages.

Today, the Walt Disney Company has grown into a multifaceted, multibillion-dollar empire that includes not only the theme parks and motion picture and television studios, but also a television network, cable and radio stations, newspaper and book publishing companies, record companies, travel divisions, a cruise line, retail stores, special effects and engineering firms, new media companies, and much more. Walt Disney's accomplishments provide an extraordinary example of creativity, a detailed focus, and overcoming adversity.

Leadership Profile 3
Lord Charles Forte and Sir Rocco Forte

Lord Charles Forte personified the leadership traits of vision and action orientation. Forte was able to imagine the future and predict the impact of both the automobile and the airplane on the travel and tourism industry. He was one of the early pioneers of the hospitality industry in Europe.

Lord Charles Forte was born in 1908 in the village of Monforte Casalaticco, Italy. In 1913, he and his mother joined his father in Scotland where the family opened a successful restaurant and ice cream parlor. After completing his education in Scotland and Italy, Lord Forte managed a large family foodservice business at the age of 21. However, his vision was to have his own restaurant. Within 5 years he opened the Meadow Milk Bar at an exceptional location in central London. In spite of the economic conditions in Britain after World War II, the milk bar's success enabled Lord Forte to expand his company to include nine additional restaurants, as well as numerous government catering contracts and the entire airline catering contract for Heathrow Airport. He even received the contract to cater all of the food served at the 1951 Festival of Britain, an exhibition in London that had nearly 8.5 million visitors in 4 months.

Lord Forte purchased his first hotel, London's Waldorf, in 1958, and in 1962, his company entered the London Stock Exchange. His was the first company to recognize the importance of highway travelers by opening the first motorway service area in Britain. Three prestigious hotels in Paris made up the company's first major international hotel acquisition in 1968: the George V, the Plaza Athenee, and the Tremoille. Ahead of his time in recognizing the future importance of tourism, Lord Forte became "founder member" of the London Tourist Board. The 1970 merger with Trust Houses PLC and the 1973 purchase of the U.S.-based Travelodge properties helped to establish Forte PLC as a major force in the hotel and foodservice industry of Great Britain and around the world. In 1995, Forte PLC had 940 hotels with 97,000 rooms and more than 600 restaurants, including the original Meadow Milk Bar.

Lord Forte received his knighthood in 1970 and became a life peer in 1982. He is a Knight of the Grand Cross of the Italian Republic and was personally presented with a special Papal Medal by Pope Pius XII.

Lord Forte worked throughout his career to raise the status and establish the importance of the hospitality industry and tourism as a whole. As Margaret Thatcher once said, "Charles Forte is a man whose vision has never dimmed. . . . When he founded his business he was equipped with two vital strengths: a clear sense of right and wrong inherited from his parents and a sound education from his childhood in Scotland. By adding to these his own enterprise, determination and leadership, he has built a company which has provided billions of pounds in foreign earnings for our country and jobs for tens of thousands of people across the world."*

Like many families in the hospitality industry, characteristics and leadership traits are also found in the family members who follow in the footsteps of their entrepreneurial parent. In Forte's case, his son Sir Rocco Forte not only carried on his father's business but went on to establish his own legacy by developing a new hotel chain. Lord Charles Forte was a visionary who understood the impact of significant trends and events and acted to capitalize on each.

Leadership Profile 4
Conrad N. Hilton and Barron Hilton**

Conrad N. Hilton personified the leadership trait of persistence. He believed and stated that *faith* was the most significant word in the English language. As Hilton (1887–1979) built up the famous hotel chain that bears his name, two kinds of faith propelled him and give him the persistence he needed to ultimately succeed. Hilton expressed a deep faith in God and faith in others and himself. Both proved crucial in getting him through hard times.

His success was hardly instant. Born in rural New Mexico when it wasn't yet a state, Hilton was the son of a successful local businessman who put him to work from early childhood. His mother was a devout Catholic who taught him the importance of prayer—something Hilton believed in all his life.

Working for his father, Hilton learned a great deal about business. He mastered the art of bargaining, recalling proudly how he sold his first pair of

*From www.hrm.uh.edu/?PageID=192.
**Information derived from www.hrm.uh.edu/?PageID=183.

shoes to a Spanish matron. "The buyer is entitled to a bargain," he wrote in his autobiography, *Be My Guest*. "The seller is entitled to a profit. So there is a fine margin between a bargain and where 'the price is right.'" Years later, he would apply the same theory to million-dollar hotel deals.

Hilton learned from his father how not to treat employees. When Hilton was 21, his father delegated responsibility for the business to his son. But the older Hilton kept breathing down Conrad's neck.

"I learned at 21 how a man feels when he has been given a job but complete confidence has been withheld," he wrote. "Perhaps that is why, in later years, when I had carefully selected a man for a job, I left him completely alone, knowing I had either made the right selection or I had been wrong."

Like many children in the West at the time, Hilton shuttled between a number of regional schools. He admitted he wasn't a very good student, but at the New Mexico Military Institute he developed another important aspect of his faith. The cadets there enforced a strict code of truth telling, so that someone caught lying was treated as if he didn't exist. Hilton carried this code into adulthood, remarking, "I've never been able to deal with a liar."

Hilton tried his hand at a number of things before hitting his gold mine. He managed his sister's musical act, served a term in the New Mexico legislature, and, foreshadowing what was to come, persuaded a number of partners to join in buying a bank.

Although Hilton made the bank a success, a stint overseas in World War I showed him the world was bigger than New Mexico. On a friend's advice he set off for Texas, hoping to make a banking chain from the oil money that was then pouring in.

He couldn't find a bank to buy. But while in Cisco, Texas, he looked for a room at a hotel called the Mobley and found it overbooked. The owner was frantic. Sensing an opportunity, Hilton changed his plan and offered to take the Mobley off its owner's hands.

At the Mobley, Hilton saw that space could be made into money. He filled most of the former dining room area with bedrooms. He also turned an unused corner into a gift shop. Hilton called this "mining for gold."

Hilton realized the value of employee morale. He reminded his workers that he and his co-owner were "completely at their mercy once a guest got beyond the front desk. 'You're the only ones who can give smiling service. Ninety percent of the Mobley's reputation is in your hands.'"

After making the Mobley a success, Hilton branched out. His first additions were shaky hotels, which he bought cheap and refurbished.

By 1924, Hilton decided he was ready for the next challenge: building a new hotel in Dallas. This required raising far more money than he ever had.

It was tough. Several times he ran out of cash. But he made a point of being honest and upfront. Based on his reputation alone, friends and supporters lent him the money.

In 1925 the Dallas Hilton opened. Hilton was so jubilant he vowed to open a hotel a year. And he did—until the stock market crash of 1929.

Hilton had just committed to building a costly hotel in El Paso, Texas. He went ahead and opened it the next year, but the sudden drop in business from the Great Depression left him with crushing debts.

Hilton remained optimistic, however, and didn't give up faith. And just when all seemed lost, someone would come up with a loan. Amazingly, one day when Hilton was so broke he couldn't even find cab fare, a bellboy came up and gave him his life savings of $300—"just eating money," he said.

Hilton was so moved by this confidence in him that he refused to declare bankruptcy. "That would be having no faith," he told a friend. "Running out of hope. If I run out of that I'm dead and I know it."

All seemed lost when Hilton's hotels were repossessed over the next several years. But in 1933, seven Hilton loyalists put up $5,000 apiece to help him buy back his El Paso hotel. With keen investments over the next few years, Hilton managed to get back five of his eight hotels and repay all his debts—including to the bellboy.

By 1937, Hilton was ready to move beyond Texas. He bought the Sir Francis Drake in San Francisco and the Breakers in Long Beach, California. He built a new Hilton in Albuquerque, New Mexico. And then, after much negotiation, he won the palatial Stevens and the prestigious Palmer House in Chicago.

Hilton set his sights higher with each purchase. But when he bought the Roosevelt and Plaza Hotels in New York City, the Eastern establishment didn't look kindly on this Westerner invading their turf.

Hilton figured he could win their trust by filling a need—at the Plaza, a venerable establishment that had given way to a brokerage. With this gesture to tradition, Hilton was able to quietly refurbish the marble, tapestries, and plumbing and give the longtime residents a new place to relax. It worked.

Having thus made his name in New York, Hilton went for the big prize: the Waldorf-Astoria. The legendary hotel wasn't making money, but the owners were attached to it.

Loath to give up, Hilton spent the next 6 years lobbying and negotiating with the owners. He finally captured the prize in 1949 and soon had it in the black.

Yet he still wanted to raise the bar. In 1942 he opened his first foreign hotel in Puerto Rico, and after the Waldorf purchase he started moving into Europe.

For him, foreign hotels weren't just about business. A fervent internationalist and supporter of the United Nations, Hilton believed that American hotels abroad could foster goodwill and personal contact between nations.

With the expansion of his business in the international arena, he staunchly expressed his belief in world peace and global economic stability. He vigorously opposed the spread of communism and used corporate advertising to promote world peace through international trade and travel. Furthermore, his concern for the public was manifested by the formation of the Conrad N. Hilton Foundation in 1944.

The legacy of Conrad N. Hilton lives on via the Hilton Foundation, which maintains large building pledge agreements to various religious, educational, and medical nonprofit institutions. In 1972, the Hilton Foundation was instrumental in the construction of the Mayo Clinic. The Hilton Foundation's importance is further heightened by its tremendous contribution in grants to various entities. The foundation was instrumental in the construction of the Conrad N. Hilton College of Hotel and Restaurant Management at the University of Houston. The foundation has awarded grants in the following areas: blindness, domestic violence, homelessness, addiction and substance abuse, brain research, and water development in Africa.

It was because of Conrad N. Hilton's faith and persistence that at the time of his death in 1979 he controlled the world's largest hotel organization. And, like other families in the hospitality industry, his son Barron succeeded him and further developed the Hilton legacy.

In 1954, Barron Hilton joined Hilton Hotels Corporation as vice president, and in 1966, he assumed the responsibility as president and CEO. In February 1979, he assumed the additional responsibility of chairman of the board. He is credited with expanding Hilton Hotels' credit card operation into the universal Carte Blanche system and was also responsible for developing the Hilton Inn franchise program.

Barron Hilton expanded his company into Nevada gaming with the purchase of the Las Vegas Hilton and the Flamingo Hilton in 1970. These two hotel/casinos accounted for roughly half of the company's total operating income and made Hilton Hotels Corporation the first Fortune 500 and New York Stock Exchange company to enter the gaming business. In 1982, Hilton Hotels reentered the international market by introducing the Conrad International Hotels brand name.

Leadership Profile 5
Howard D. Johnson

Howard Dearing Johnson (1896–1972) personified the leadership traits of acting fast, innovation, and passion for a quality and consistent product. He also expressed drive, a set of values, and high creativity.

Howard Johnson was one of those rare human beings who see their destiny and have the drive, the talent, and the imagination to seize it. He set out to make a name for himself—and didn't rest until that name had become one of the world's great brands and one of the best-known landmarks in travel.

He not only built one of the first great restaurant chains and one of the first midprice hotel chains, but he pioneered many of the most successful foodservice and hospitality innovations. The franchisee ownership concept, the turnpike restaurant concept, the super-premium ice cream concept, the theme restaurant concept, the commissary food distribution concept, the "America's Menu" concept, the quality motor lodge concept, the "Kids-Go-Free" family travel concept—all are classic examples of the business and marketing genius of Howard Johnson. He set a standard of consistent quality, honest value, fun, clean environments, and caring customer service that would change family travel—and the hospitality world—forever.

As with any great enterprise, there were bumps in the road. But Howard Johnson—the proud brand name, the standard of service, and the solid values—not only survived, but grew stronger than ever as the baton was passed when Cendant Corporation acquired the brand. Howard Johnson had already earned its place as one of the world's best-known families of hotels—the hotels that "make you feel at home."

In 1925, Howard Johnson borrowed $2,000 to buy a small corner drugstore in Wollaston, Massachusetts. It sold candy, newspapers, and patent medicine—but Howard quickly noticed that the real action was at his old marble soda fountain. He figured that if he could invent a better-tasting ice cream cone, the world (or at least Wollaston) would beat a path to the Howard Johnson store. He came up with a "secret formula" for vanilla and chocolate ice cream. The secret was, in fact, based on his mother's recipe for ice cream—with all-natural ingredients and twice the normal butterfat content. It was an immediate sensation, so he quickly added other flavors. He had invented a super-premium ice cream. When summer came, he opened a beachfront ice cream stand, and that first summer he sold $60,000 worth of ice cream cones—at a nickel a cone. By 1928 he was selling $240,000 worth of ice cream cones. He kept adding flavors until he reached 28 varieties. "I thought I had every flavor in the world," Howard remarked. "The 28 flavors became my trademark." He advertised it, truthfully, as "New England's Best Ice Cream," and his success reinforced what became the guiding principle of his business life: "Quality sells."

Over the next few summers he added more beachfront stands, and decided to do for the lowly hot dog what he had done for the ice cream cone. Instead of using the normal hot dog stand method of slapping them on a greasy grill, then wrapping them in stale buns, he invented the idea of clipping the frankfurters at both ends, notching them lengthwise, and then cooking them in pure creamery butter that would infuse into the meat. He used only the highest-quality meats (unheard of in those days) and lightly toasted, buttered fresh rolls. He had elevated the hot dog to connoisseur status, and it was to become one of the unforgettable joys of visiting Howard Johnson's restaurants for generations. Again, that extra drive for quality would pay enormous dividends in the years to come.

His success was beginning to be noticed by others, and thus he was able to convince some skeptical bankers to lend him enough money to open a restaurant in Quincy, Massachusetts. It was located in Quincy's first "skyscraper"—a 10-story granite art deco building that still looks magnificent today. This first Howard Johnson's restaurant featured fried clams, baked beans, chicken pies, those elegant frankfurters, and, of course, the now locally famous Howard Johnson ice cream. He was restless to expand—but the stock market crashed, the Depression began, and the banks weren't lending money.

Then Howard had a remarkable idea, one that would change the course of American business enterprise. In 1935, he persuaded an acquaintance to open another Howard Johnson's restaurant in Orleans on Cape Cod under a franchise. Howard Johnson would design the space, create the menu, set the standards, and deliver the food and ice cream. The franchisee, under a license, would own the property and receive the bulk of the revenues. Howard, always a stickler for quality, demanded that the restaurant be run by his quality standards, or the contract was void and the franchisee would have to remove the Howard Johnson sign.

Seemingly overnight, out of the depths of the Depression, a phenomenal business success was born. By the following summer there were 17 Howard Johnson's restaurants. All were successful beyond anyone's wildest expectations. Paul Herbert, for instance, opened a 70-seat restaurant in Cambridge, Massachusetts, putting up $10,000 as one-third of the cost, the remainder to be financed over 3 years. Herbert hoped he would gross $60,000 a year, but he actually grossed $200,000 during the first 12 months. It was something of an understatement when he declared, "You're in a good business when you own a Howard Johnson franchise." That sentiment was to be repeated by many hundreds of happy and wealthy franchisees. By the end of 1936 there were 39 more franchised restaurants.

Howard Johnson moved with lightning speed, for he had seen that the growing popularity of the automobile was sending millions of hungry Americans out on the road, and there were no decent eating places to satisfy their needs. He created the highway landmark concept, featuring the bright orange roof and the Simple Simon and the Pie Man road sign. By 1939 there were 107 Howard Johnson's restaurants along East Coast highways generating revenues of $10.5 million.

All were run according to the "Howard Johnson Bible"—a set of strict standards of cleanliness, service, recipes, menu items, and quality (as well as interior and exterior design) that were developed and rigidly enforced by Howard Johnson himself. It was quite a voluminous bible, and it left nothing to chance. The author meticulously wrote every instruction on anything and everything that had to do with the running of his restaurants. He would allow no variation from one restaurant to the other. One chapter was devoted to "Howard Johnson Waitresses—Your Appearance from Head to Toe." An entire page covered the subject of being courteous, including instructions on how to "assist customers with their wraps."

As the vast American highway system began to span the continent, millions of travelers, in their Ford "woody" station wagons and Chevy coupes, eagerly searched for the familiar orange roof and the big Howard Johnson sign with Simple Simon and the Pie Man on top. They searched, for they knew exactly what they would find inside—the best fried clams anywhere, hot dogs grilled in butter and served on toasted rolls, old-fashioned chicken potpie, generous turkey dinners with mashed potatoes, moist rich brownies, games and puzzles for the kids, high chairs for the tots, and 28 flavors of the world's best ice cream. All served family style, by smiling waitresses in their prim, starched blue and orange dresses, all to be enjoyed in spanking clean, colorful surroundings.

Here was the nation's "Host of the Highway," where everyone invariably found a warm welcome, a familiar experience, and a special feeling that became part of growing up in America. In less than 14 years, the dreamer who aspired to create a better ice cream cone now directed a mammoth franchise network of over 10,000 employees, with 170 restaurants, many serving a million and a half people a year.

The Pennsylvania, Ohio, and New Jersey turnpikes were built, and Howard Johnson bid and won exclusive rights to serve the hungry turnpike multitudes. There were 200 Howard Johnson's restaurants on the morning that America woke up to three huge black letters on the front page: "WAR!" With World War II came gas rationing, food stamps, and the end of pleasure trips. One by one, the restaurants were forced to close. By the summer of 1944 only 12 remained in business. Howard Johnson managed to stay barely afloat by serving commissary food to war workers and army recruits. But by the time America was celebrating V-J Day, Howard was working late into the nights getting ready for the travel boom and the highway expansion that he knew had to be coming.

Howard Johnson was about to make one of the biggest comebacks in business history. After the war, this country turned its incredible energy to building houses in a new world called "suburbia," building big, powerful cars that seemingly everyone could afford, and building the endless interstate highway system that connected our cities and our people, coast to coast. It was a world custom-made for our "pioneer of the highways" Howard Johnson. And he didn't waste a minute. By 1947, construction was underway or about to begin on 200 new Howard Johnson's restaurants that would stretch across the Southeast and Midwest. These were slightly smaller buildings than the prewar originals, but Howard Johnson still provided over 700 items, including his famous fried clams, saltwater taffy, and 28 flavors of ice cream. By 1951 Howard Johnson sales totaled $115 million. By 1954 there were 400 Howard Johnson's restaurants in 32 states. About 10 percent were company-owned turnpike restaurants that were extremely profitable. The orange roof just kept spreading until it rivaled Coca-Cola's trademark as the most familiar icon in America at that time.

In 1959, the company founder, who still made his headquarters in Wollaston, Massachusetts, decided it was time to turn the reins over to his son, 26-year-old Howard Brennon Johnson, who succeeded him as president. Young Howard, a graduate of Andover and Yale, told a reporter, "I knew from the age of five that I wanted to join the company. It was all we talked about at home. And my father was the kind of person you almost couldn't let down." The senior Howard Johnson remained as chairman and treasurer.

Howard Johnson, through his leadership traits of moving fast, being creative and innovative, and insisting on quality and consistency, gave the world an extraordinary leadership example and even more. He gave the hospitality industry the engine for its growth into one of the largest industries on earth—he gave it franchising, the concept of a themed business, and the distribution concept of commissary food.

Leadership Profile 6
Ray Kroc*

Ray Kroc personified the leadership trait of drive once he decided on his dreams and goals. Kroc (1902–1984) believed a person always should keep growing and acquiring knowledge. Kroc was already 52 years old when he got the franchise rights to a small hamburger stand from Dick and Mac McDonald in San Bernardino, California. He had been running a successful business selling milkshake mixes.

"Yet I was alert to other opportunities," Kroc wrote (with Robert Anderson) in *Grinding It Out: The Making of McDonald's*. "I have a saying that goes, 'As long as you're green you're growing. As soon as you're ripe you start to rot.'"

Kroc pursued growth with a vengeance. He turned that franchise agreement into the largest fast-food chain in the world.

Growing up, Kroc wasn't an avid student. Instead, he spent his time daydreaming about his future and his future success. "I'd imagine all kinds of situations and how I would handle them," Kroc wrote. But they weren't idle fantasies he conjured.

"I never considered my dreams wasted energy; they were invariably linked to some form of action," Kroc wrote. "When I dreamed about having a lemonade stand, for example, it wasn't long before I set up a lemonade stand."

That lemonade stand was the first in a long series of jobs. Kroc took a lesson from almost every one. For example, working behind the lunch counter at his uncle's drugstore soda fountain, he discovered the importance of a positive attitude in sales. "That's where I learned you could influence people with a smile and enthusiasm and sell them a sundae when what they'd come for was a cup of coffee," he said.

It was at a job selling ribbon novelties that Kroc discovered the art of tailoring his spiel to the needs of his customers. "I'd have a sample room set up in whatever hotel I was staying in, and I'd learn what each buyer's taste was and sell to it. No self-respecting pitcher throws the same way to every batter, and no self-respecting salesman makes the same pitch to every client."

While selling paper goods for the Lilly Cup Co., he saw that customers appreciated a straightforward, brief approach. "They would buy if I made my pitch and asked for their order without a lot of beating around the bush," he said. "The key to closing a sale is to know when to stop selling. Too many

*Information derived from www.hrm.uh.edu/?PageID=196.

salesmen, I found, would make a good presentation and convince the client, but they couldn't recognize that critical moment when they should have stopped talking."

Good salespeople also need integrity, Kroc insisted. Take the time Lilly Cup issued an across-the-board 10 percent salary cut for all its personnel during the Depression. Because Kroc was then the company's top salesman, he was excused from the cut. Kroc thought that unfair and asked to be included. When the company refused to change its policy, he handed in his notice.

There were few other jobs around, but Kroc stood his ground. When his boss asked if he could afford to be so independent, Kroc said he'd muddle through.

In 1938 he signed a deal to be the exclusive sales agent for the Multi-Mixer, a milkshake mixer that could handle five shakes at once. It meant giving up a steady income, but Kroc believed he could make it work. He told a group of graduate students at Dartmouth College that you can achieve anything if you set your mind to it and have the drive inside.

"You're not going to get it free, and you have to take risks. I don't mean daredevil risks. But you have to take risks, and in some case you must go for broke," he said. "If you believe in something, you've got to be in it to the end of your toes. Taking reasonable risk is part of the challenge."

It wasn't easy. He had to take an unwanted partner to get the business started, and buying out the partner later put a severe strain on the company's resources. Rather than get irritated about it, Kroc chose to look on the upside. "Perhaps without that adversity I might not have been able to persevere later on when my financial burdens were redoubled," he said. "I learned then how to keep problems from crushing me."

Kroc opened his first McDonald's in Des Plaines, Illinois, in 1955. After he ironed out early problems, the concept caught on. As he increased the number of franchises, Kroc had to add staff. He had specific qualifications in mind when he looked.

He never looked for "yes men." He wanted people willing to disagree. "I believe that if two executives think the same, one of them is superfluous," he said.

Once hired, a Kroc employee was delegated authority to do his or her job. One early executive, Harry Sonneborn, came up with an unusual lease-to-purchase deal to acquire future store sites. Kroc thought the idea was crazy.

"But I let Harry plunge ahead without interference," Kroc said. "I believe if you hire a man to do a job, you ought to get out of the way and let him do it. If you doubt his ability, you shouldn't have hired him in the first place."

Similarly, when Sonneborn hired an expensive consultant, others in the office were certain Kroc would be angry. "But that was the farthest thing from my mind," he wrote. "I know that you have to spend money to make money, and as far as I was concerned, Harry was simply doing the job I'd hired him to do."

In 1967, all the economists were predicting a recession, so most businesses planned cutbacks in construction. Not Kroc. He ordered expansion to proceed.

"Hell's bells, when times are bad is when you want to build," Kroc said. "Why wait for things to pick up so everything will cost you more? If a location is good enough to buy, we want to build on it right away and be in there before the competition."

As the company became more successful, it required larger stores with seating. Some on the executive team urged caution. Kroc, however, was thinking big. "I believe that if you think small, you'll stay small," Kroc said.

Over the course of his career, Kroc had to spend major cash to steer his company where he wanted it to go. He bought out the McDonald brothers' share of the business.

"I don't stew about what the other guy is making in a deal like this," he said. "I'm concerned about whether it's going to be a good thing for McDonald's."

When Kroc retired from the chairmanship of McDonald's in 1977, his drive had taken a one-store hamburger stand into the world's largest fast-food chain.

Leadership Profile 7
J. Willard Marriott, Alice S. Marriott, and J. W. "Bill" Marriott, Jr.*

J. W. "Bill" Marriott, Jr., carries on the leadership traits that were ingrained in the family by his parents J. Willard and Alice S. Marriott. These traits include determination, listening, principles-driven, and an extraordinary dedication to the business exemplified by a hard-work ethic second to none.

J. Willard Marriott successfully launched a restaurant business with the opening of the first Hot Shoppes/A&W Root Beer stand in 1927. This prosperous venture stemmed from Marriott's notion of providing inexpensive quality food and services. The Depression years fueled a tremendous ingenuity in Willard. He recognized the success of low-cost restaurants and the failure of luxury restaurants.

Consequently, J. Willard expanded his business opportunities by entering the airline and hotel industry. Specifically, in 1957, J. Willard opened his first hotel, the Twin Bridges Marriott in Washington, D.C. Following thereafter, Marriott hotels were launched in Dallas, Philadelphia, and Atlanta. As a result, the Marriott company earned $84 million in revenue with 9,600 employees by 1964. In the late 1960s, J. Willard acquired the Big Boy restaurant chain and the Roy Rogers fast-food restaurant division. However, J. Willard's business ventures did not stop with the hotel industry. A decade later in 1976, he entered the entertainment industry with the creation of the Marriott Great America Theme Parks that aimed to provide wholesome family entertainment. Additionally, the Marriott standard of quality and wonderful service sailed the high seas with the company's acquisition of three luxury Sun Line cruise ships that sailed to the Caribbean and the Aegean/Mediterranean areas.

*Information derived from www.hrm.uh.edu/?PageID=194.

In the mid-1980s, the Marriott company earned $4.5 billion in revenue with 200,000 employees, and by 1989, the company opened its 500th hotel in Warsaw, Poland. A decade later in 1994, Marriott doubled its revenues by acquiring approximately $8.4 billion in revenue. The Marriott Corporation today is one of the leading hospitality companies, with annual sales of over $2 billion. The success of the Marriott company stemmed from a belief in community. M. O. "Bus" Ryan, a senior vice president of Marriott Hotels, described his relationship with J. Willard Marriott as one of a father and son.*

Alice was born on October 19, 1907, in Salt Lake City, Utah. At the age of 19 she received a B.A. in Spanish from the University of Utah. Two days after graduation she married J. Willard Marriott and they moved to Washington, D.C., where Willard had opened the A&W Root Beer stand. Alice was the bookkeeper for the business. With root beer sales slowing down as fall approached, Alice came away from the Mexican embassy with the recipes for chili con carne and hot tamales. These items were added to the menu, and the root beer stand became The Hot Shoppe, a popular family restaurant.**

Having learned leadership traits from the example set by his parents, Bill Marriott succeeded his father as CEO in 1972. The company continued to grow through acquisitions and by developing new lodging brands. Courtyards by Marriott was introduced in 1983 as the company's second lodging brand. Marriott entered the vacation timeshare business the following year. In 1985, he assumed the role of chairman of the corporation, after his father's death. Marriott Corporation restructured to sharpen its focus on lodging, senior living and contract services, and selling its fast-food and family restaurants.

In 1993, Marriott split into two separate companies, Marriott International, a lodging and services management company, and Host Marriott Corporation, which focused on real estate and airport concessions. Marriott's lodging brands continued to grow with the acquisition of The Ritz-Carlton Hotel Company. In 1996, Host Marriott Services Corporation was formed when Host Marriott Corporation divided to separate its real estate and airport concessions. Richard Marriott, Bill's brother, serves as chairman and CEO of Host Marriott.

As of December 30, 2003, Marriott International employed approximately 144,000 people and nearly 2,600 operating units in the United States and 68 other countries and territories. Major brands and businesses include: Marriott, The Ritz-Carlton, Courtyards, Residence Inn, Fairfield Inn, TownePlace Suites, Renaissance, and Ramada International brands; vacation club (timeshare) resorts, and executive apartments.

Like his father, Bill is extraordinarily dedicated, extremely hard-working, principles-driven, and a good listener. He faithfully follows a set of simple business principles developed by his father. "Take care of your employees and they'll take good care of your customers." "Provide customers with good

*From www.hrm.uh.edu/?PageID=185.
**From www.hrm.uh.edu/?PageID=204.

service and a quality product at a fair price." "Stay in close touch with your business and always strive for success and never be satisfied."

Leadership Profile 8
William Patterson*

William A. "Pat" Patterson personified the leadership traits of innovation and a willingness to be different. He believed the true value of a company was in its people.

In 1933, Patterson was running Boeing Air Transport, a precursor of United Airlines. It had recently purchased a competitor, Varney Air Lines, and someone handed him a list of the many Varney employees to be dismissed.

"Wait a minute," Patterson said, according to an article that appeared in a special issue of *Shield*, the United employee publication. "The personnel are three quarters of an airline's assets. These people must be worth something, or they wouldn't have built Varney up to be worth the $2 million we paid for it."

At Patterson's behest, jobs were found for virtually all of the Varney crew—including a few who went on to become respected 40-year veterans of United.

Patterson himself spent 37 years with the airline, from its infancy to 1966, the dawn of the jumbo jets. During his career, he built United into one of the country's biggest and most successful airlines.

A career in the airline business was an unlikely choice for Patterson, who was born in Waipahou, Hawaii, where his father managed a sugar plantation. His father died when Billy—as he was called then—was just 8 years old. The family moved to San Francisco when Patterson was 14. To help out his mother and siblings, he left school to take a job the next year as an office boy at the Wells Fargo bank.

There he took to studying one of the bank's most successful officers, E. I. Raymond. Raymond ingrained in Patterson the value of education and got him to go back to school. "It was the best help I could have had," Patterson told *U.S. News & World Report*. "Mr. Raymond showed me how to help myself."

By 1927, Patterson had worked himself up to junior officer. "I had the authority to make loans of up to $15,000 between noon and 1:30, while my vice-president-boss was at lunch," Patterson said.

It was during those hours that he met Vernon Gorst, who ran Pacific Air Transport. Pacific Air had just won a government contract to carry mail between Los Angeles and Seattle. But Gorst needed $5,000 to get his planes off the ground.

Forget the conventional wisdom that airplanes couldn't fly north of San Francisco because of the mountainous terrain. Patterson believed in Gorst

*Information derived from C. Schleir, "He Left United's Sky Friendlier," *Investors Business Daily* (Jan. 18, 2002): A3.

and made the loan—despite the misgivings of his superiors when they returned from lunch.

"Patterson told (his superiors) that one way to get new business started was to start new businesses," according to *Shield*.

Back then there wasn't much passenger airline business. The airlines flew two passenger planes, usually only during daylight hours, and could comfortably operate just 3 hours flying at 120 mph.

But the business fascinated Patterson. So when he saw an opportunity to join Boeing Co., he did so. His passion and willingness to take a risk won him notice. Soon, he was named to run the four airlines that Boeing owned under the name United, the nation's first transcontinental airline.

When Patterson believed in an idea, he went forward with it. In the 1930s, flying was an emotionally fraught experience. One of his associates, San Francisco sales manager Steve Stimpson, had what he called "a passing thought." He suggested having young women as regular crew members, contending it would have a positive psychological effect. Many in the company thought it was a bad idea, including one executive who wired Patterson: "If Boeing Air Transport is going to set up a circus performance, consider this my resignation."

Patterson wired back: "Your resignation is accepted."

Combined with performance, Patterson was concerned with safety. "I am convinced that air transportation will progress only in proportion to its safety record," he said. So he looked for innovative ways to make the airlines safer. For example, he ended the industry practice of paying pilots by the miles they flew. Instead, he guaranteed them a monthly minimum and offered a bonus to those pilots who canceled flights in hazardous weather conditions. "It has the effect of removing monetary incentive to fly when marginal weather conditions might make a borderline case," Patterson said.

He was prepared to pay more for safety. Before 1952, all airlines provided only one-class service. That year, the government allowed the carriers to charge a lower fare for what it called "high-density seating." Coach service was born.

Patterson, however, conducted tests that indicated that not all 66 passengers in the high-density configuration of the DC-4 could be safely evacuated in 60 seconds. He personally ripped out one line of seats so seating was five abreast instead of six, limiting to 54 the number of passengers the plane would hold.

Patterson willingly pioneered "new ideas to get riders on his planes," *Time* magazine said in a cover story on Patterson. He knew that some businessmen were reluctant to fly because their wives were concerned about safety. He examined the problem and decided the best way to silence the objections was to get the wives on board. For a while, he let wives of men on business trips fly free to get them over their fear of their husbands' flying.

Patterson took risks, but he retained his caution. He preferred to spend time studying a situation before rushing in. For example, shortly after the end of World War II, many of the larger previously all-domestic airlines rushed to provide international service. But Patterson had his staff study the prospects of the international market. As a result, Patterson concluded that the timing wasn't right; the market wasn't there. Other airlines incurred substantial losses.

In the early 1950s, airlines were looking to the next generation of aircraft. Some opted for hybrid turboprops (a jet engine driving a propeller) that would be available immediately. The turboprops were faster than prop planes and would provide quicker service until jets could be introduced commercially. Patterson opted to take the long-range view and wait for the development of true jets.

"This speed advantage will last for two, possibly three years," he told *Forbes* magazine. "But when we get our jets, we'll cruise at around 550 mph—or 125 mph faster than any turboprop. On long, cross-country hauls, the turboprop will be an obsolete airplane, and before it's half depreciated at that. We've got to look further ahead."

Patterson knew when to hold 'em and when to fold 'em. In 1966, after 37 years with the airline, he decided to step down as chairman "even though the position would be something of an honorary one."

He recognized that "you can't be a part-time leader." He didn't want to hang around so that the young blood running the airline would feel constrained by his presence.

"Those who are charged with responsibility in the future will be free to use their own initiative and wisdom in the policies they establish," he said. "They should have no inhibitions concerning the past. And my continued presence on the board could create such inhibitions."

As a result of his innovation and daring to be different, William Patterson built United Airlines into the world's largest carrier at the time of his retirement in 1966.

Leadership Profile 9
C. R. Smith*

C. R. Smith personified the leadership traits of observing details, being analytical, and acting upon the findings. For Smith no detail was too small. For example, while driving to Detroit's Metropolitan Airport one afternoon he passed a road sign promoting his company, American Airlines. What he saw disturbed him: The hands of the stewardess on the billboard struck him as too large. He had it changed fast.

Besides paying attention to little things, Smith believed in acting quickly. *Time* magazine wrote in a 1958 cover story: "In a corporate world often dom-

*Information derived from C. Schlier, "He Kept Carrier Flying High," *Investors Business Daily* (July 9, 2002): A4.

inated by slow-moving boards and committees, C. R. Smith acts with bewildering speed."

Cyrus Rowlett Smith (1899–1990) was born and raised in Texas. He had a difficult childhood. His father left the family when C. R. was 9 years old. C. R., the oldest of seven children, immediately became the "man of the house." He held various jobs, mostly as a bookkeeper. From an early age, he recognized his worth.

As *The Saturday Evening Post* recalled in a profile of Smith, during World War I he was a bookkeeper at a cotton mill that lost most of its older employees to the war. So he was working 15 hours a day. He suggested a Christmas bonus was in order. "The boss agreed and gave him a box of 25 10-cent cigars," wrote the *Post*. "Smith quit."

He set his sights on college—a remarkable goal for someone who never completed grade school. Based on his real-world experience, Smith received special permission to enter the business school at the University of Texas, where he received a bachelor's degree in business in 1924.

He continued to show his trademark initiative in college. He formed C. R. Smith & Co., a firm that specialized in mailing lists. He copied the names of stockholders from the records on file in the state capital and sold the lists to companies in New York City and Chicago. He later began providing the names of new parents to the publishers of parenting magazines and others who wanted to reach that market.

He was soon earning $300 a month from this and other part-time entrepreneurial efforts. He had to take a pay cut when he graduated from college and took a full-time position as a junior accountant at Peat Marwick, where he earned only $150 monthly.

From his first days on the job, Smith was confident nothing was beyond his grasp. He was assigned to audit an insurance company, though he knew nothing about the business. With the audit 5 days away, he secreted himself in the state library in Austin and read "everything he could find on the subject of insurance," *The Saturday Evening Post* wrote. "While making the audit, he completed his book-learning education in his hotel room at night, and he came through successfully."

His next position was as an assistant treasurer for Texas-Louisiana Power Co. When TLPC purchased a small airmail carrier, Southern Air Transport, Smith was put in charge. When Southern Air was purchased by a larger holding company, a subsidiary of American Airways, Smith was put in charge first of the subsidiary and, in 1934, the entire carrier, renamed American Airlines.

The company was awash in red ink when he took over. Quick action was needed. So he examined the problems and set about fixing them. For one, each of the smaller airlines that merged to make up American brought its own equipment to the company. That created an expensive, complicated, and potentially dangerous maintenance situation.

Instead of carrying spare parts for and training mechanics in the intricacies of eight different aircraft, Smith mandated that American standardize on an all-Douglas fleet. Early on, Smith realized that the future of the business was in passengers, not mail, and that safety was the paramount concern of potential fliers. In memoranda to employees, he wrote, "You wash out safety, you wash out American Airlines."

He understood that slogans alone wouldn't suffice, and that he needed to deliver the safety message in person. "Smith flew around the country bucking up pilot morale and driving home the message of vigilance among his maintenance crews," *The Saturday Evening Post* wrote.

Smith was willing to defy convention to get his message across. Airline safety was a taboo subject when it came to customers—until Smith okayed an ad that read "Afraid to fly?" and went on to discuss American Airlines' safety record.

Smith was always willing to try something to encourage customers. He was one of the first to install sleeper seats. He offered frequent-flyer discounts and promoted flying by using celebrity endorsements.

As noted by *BusinessWeek,* "Smith's key point of business philosophy is that the airplane is a tool and must be replaced when a more efficient tool turns up." When no new and needed tools were on the horizon, he'd design them. Working with company engineers, Smith came up with numerous modifications he wanted to the DC-2—an aircraft he didn't like.

He spoke with Donald Douglas about American's needs. Douglas wasn't interested. But when Smith wanted something, there was no stopping him. So he made Douglas an offer he couldn't refuse. He committed for 20 of the new aircraft at $100,000 each "with an option for 20 more even though a complete design did not exist on paper."

Often, Smith's willingness to commit early to a new aircraft meant he got the planes at a discount. "He placed the first order for 25 of Douglas's big, fast DC-7s, which he got for some $700,000 less than later buyers," wrote *Time* magazine.

Smith knew you didn't always have to be the "firstest with the mostest." When jet aircraft came on the market, he held back until it became clear that two companies—Boeing and Douglas—would be competing for orders.

"He shrewdly figured this would increase his bargaining power—as it did," *Time* wrote. "To land American's order, Boeing agreed to enlarge the 707 fuselage (and) sell the planes for $500,000 less apiece than the DC-8."

Smith was willing to think outside the box. In 1945, when airlines were selling tickets to movie stars and big-business executives, Smith authored an article for *The Saturday Evening Post* calling for lower fares as a spur to mass travel.

C. R. Smith's ability to observe details, analyze, and act decisively helped to create what was at one point the largest and most profitable airline in the United States. These traits also led to his selection as deputy commander of the Air Transport Command (1942–1945) and as commerce secretary in 1968.

Leadership Profile 10
Kemmons Wilson*

Kemmons Wilson personified the leadership traits of entrepreneurship, enjoying people, enthusiasm, high energy, and striving for excellence.

Wilson entered the hotel industry business by opening his first Holiday Inn on August 1, 1952, in Memphis, Tennessee. He revolutionized the industry by allowing children to stay for free and providing swimming pools, air conditioning, free cribs, telephones, television, ice, and free parking. Wilson brought comfortable accommodations to the middle class at prices they could afford. Eleven Holiday Inns opened by the end of 1954. Five years later, the 100th Holiday Inn opened in Tallahassee-Apalachee, Florida, in September, 1959.

The following year, the Holiday Innkeeping School, predecessor of the Holiday Inn University, was created to teach new innkeepers the "Holiday Inn Way." The Holiday Inn company expanded outside the United States in 1960 with the opening of Holiday Inn-Chateaubriand in Montreal, Canada. Additionally, in 1967 the Institutional Mart of America (IMA) opened in Memphis, Tennessee, at Holiday City, providing the industry with its first year-round hotel supplies and equipment showplace.

In 1968, the 1,000th Holiday Inn opened in San Antonio, Texas, and the first European Holiday Inn opened in Leiden, Holland. With the expansion of Holiday Inn hotels abroad, the corporate name was changed the following year from Holiday Inns of America, Inc., to Holiday Inns, Inc. Furthermore, the familiar slogan "The Nation's Innkeeper" was revised to "The World's Innkeeper."

The "World's Innkeeper" had an interesting philosophy. To Wilson, success meant never having to settle for anything less than excellent. He expressed that "in this country, you don't have to settle for being average . . . you can dare to do better . . . and I challenge you to do this. Whatever your career choice, make your work count."

By 1971, the worldwide Holiday Inn system became the first food and lodging chain in history to have facilities in operation in all 50 states. Most importantly, the company reached the 200,000-room mark in December 1971, duplicating in less than 5 years growth that had originally taken 15 years. This didn't move Wilson to retire; instead he began a new venture by launching a new lodging company called Wilson World in 1982. He also developed a major timeshare resort just 4 miles from Disney World in Orlando and a state-of-the-art executive aviation service business in Memphis, his home. In August 1989, the acquisition of Holiday Inns, Inc., by Bass PLC, now Six Continents Hotels, was completed.

Kemmons Wilson is the personification of a warm, friendly leader who motivates others with his enthusiasm and example. Most people who have met

*Information derived from www.hrm.uh.edu/?PageID=188.

Wilson feel his warmth and immediately like the man. Kemmons Wilson was a natural-born leader.

There are many more industry leaders we could comment upon in this section. We suggest that studying the accomplishments and leadership characteristics and traits of some of the past and present hospitality industry leaders listed below will enhance your understanding of leadership.

More Hospitality Industry Leaders

Ted and Mickey Arison	Herb Kellerher
Stuart Bainum	Kirk Kerkorian
Juergen Bartels	Sol Kerzner
Gordon Bethune	Mike Leven
Ed Carlson	Thomas Monaghan
Jan Carlson	William Norman
Truett Cathy	Chris Pappas
Robert Crandall	Jay Pritzker
Bill Darden	Mike Rose
Cecil Day	William Rosenburg
Robert Dedman	Horst Schulze
Paul Dubrule and	Isadore Sharp
Gerard Pelisson	Henry Silverman
Gabriel Escarrer Julia	Ellsworth Statler
Bob Evans	Dave Thomas
Ruth Fertel	Jonathan Tisch
Jennie Grossinger and	Lawrence and Preston Tisch
Elaine Grossinger Etess	Donald Trump
John Q. Hammons	Roy Winegardner
Robert Hazzard	Steve Wynn
Ernest Henderson	
Ed and Lynn Hogan	
Ron Jackson	

Many other leadership examples are referenced within the text. During my 30-year-plus career in the hospitality industry, I had the good fortune to work for some of these leaders and to meet many others. From each I learned something about hospitality management strategies and leadership—you will too as you pursue your career in the hospitality industry.

Leadership Profile Discussion Questions

1. Select one leader from the Leadership Profiles presented in this chapter and list what you believe are their top three positive traits.
2. Which leader presented in the Leadership Profiles do you think displayed the most traits of leadership (see Figure 18-3, Fourteen Traits of Successful Leaders)?

Glossary

Accountability   Means of ensuring that the actions of an individual or an institution may be traced uniquely to that individual or institution.

Acquisition   The taking over or buying of a business to add to existing businesses.

ADIs (areas of dominant influence)   The areas that television broadcasts reach in a given market.

Alliance   An association to further the common interests of the members. A formal arrangement with a separate company for purposes of development and involving exchange of information, hardware, intellectual property, or enabling technology. Alliances involve shared risk and reward (e.g., codevelopment projects).

Ambience   A feeling or mood associated with a particular place, person, or thing.

Amortization   The period of time over which a mortgage or loan is paid off.

Analytical tools   Means of turning raw data into usable information.

Asset   An item of ownership convertible into cash; the total resources of a person or business, such as cash, notes and accounts receivable, securities, inventory, goodwill, fixtures, machinery, and real estate. (Opposed to liability.)

Automation   The computerization of manual functions.

Benchmark   A control source against which you compare the area you're studying.

Booking pace   The rate at which reservations are made.

Brainstorming   A group technique of solving specific problems, amassing information, stimulating creative thinking, developing new ideas, etc., by unrestrained and spontaneous participation in discussion.

Brand assets   All of the positive elements linked to a brand.

Brand associations   Any characteristics that are mentally linked to a brand.

Brand awareness   The aided or unaided ability to name or recall a brand.

Brand collector   An entity that collects manufactured brands or trademarks.

Brand equity   The net result of all the positive and negative characteristics linked to a brand.

Brand extension   Extension of the use of a brand name to other products or services.

Branding   Carrying the brand or trademark of a manufacturer, hotel, or service.

Brand loyalty   The core of brand equity as related to the loyalty of the customer.

Brand strategy   Management of all of the components of a brand in an orchestrated and planned process.

Break-even analysis   An analysis of the level of sales at which a project would make zero profit and zero loss.

Buddy system   A training process where a new employee is paired up with a seasoned employee for training purposes.

Business acumen   The insight, judgment, and skills required to successfully manage a business.

Centralization   The placing of power and authority in a center or central organization.

Chain   A group of enterprises or institutions of the same kind of function usually under a single ownership, management, or control.

City pair   The origin and destination points of a flight segment.

Closing   The final part of a sales transaction, often defined as obtaining the customer's signature on a contract.

Cluster management   Provision of a single point of control for management of similar brands or multiple units of a brand within a given area.

Cold call   A sales call made without an appointment and/or the pre-qualification of a potential customer.

Commission   A percentage or dollar amount paid as a form of compensation for closing a sales transaction.

Complexity   The range of activities occurring at any given time in an organization.

Concentration   The percent within a given demographic target market segment that purchases the product (i.e., "Of all the 18–24-year-olds, 80 percent are purchasers of the product.").

Concept development   Opportunity identification, opportunity analysis, idea generation and enrichment, idea selection, and concept definition.

Conflict resolution   The process of resolving a dispute or a conflict permanently by providing for each side's needs and adequately addressing their interests so that they are satisfied with the outcome.

Connectivity   The condition of being connected or linked to the electronic channels of distribution.

Consortium   A group (as of companies) formed to undertake an enterprise beyond the resources of any one member.

Consultative selling   A method of selling, popularized in the 1960s and 1970s, in which the sales representative consults with the potential customer and then modifies the product or service based on the customer's needs.

Cooperative agreement   An agreement between two or more businesses providing funding for marketing or other mutually advantageous objectives.

Core competencies   The capabilities of a company that exceed those of other companies, which provides it with a distinctive competitive advantage and contributes to acquiring and retaining customers.

Cost controls   The lowering of costs to increase profit; critically important for the mature business where total demand for the product or service is not growing.

CQI (continuous quality improvement)   The ongoing efforts within a company to meet the needs and exceed the expectations of customers by changing the way work is performed so that products and services are delivered better, faster, and at less cost than in the past.

CPA   In marketing, a customer perceptions audit; in accounting, a certified public accountant.

Creative   Managed so as to get around legal or conventional limits.

Crisis   Any situation that, if it left unchecked, jeopardizes the ability of an organization to function.

Crisis management   The coordinated efforts to handle the effects of an unexpected, unfavorable event.

Cross-selling   The strategy of using an existing customer base for one product as the prospective customers for another product.

CSI (customer service index)   An index (usually 100 points) used to measure customer satisfaction levels.

Customization selling   Tailoring a product or service to the customer's specifications.

Database   In marketing, an electronic file of names, addresses, and often key information about customers and potential customers.

Decentralization   The delegation of power from a central authority to regional and local authorities.

Delivery package   In public relations, the package of information provided to the media on any particular topic.

Demand   The customer side of a commercial relationship (demand and supply).

Demographics   The description of the vital statistics or objectives and quantifiable characteristics of an audience or population.

Deregulation   The act or process of removing restrictions and regulations.

Draw   In sales, a method of compensation usually involving a commission with a draw or guaranteed salary plus bonus.

Driving forces   The organization's vision, mission, values, and core competencies that provide the motivation to the business and employees.

Dynamic   An ever-changing situation or business environment.

EBITDA (earnings before interest, taxes, depreciation, and amortization)   A financial measure defined as revenues less cost of goods sold and selling, general, and administrative expenses.

Egocentrism   Limited in outlook or concern to one's own activities or needs.

Electronic marketing   Marketing through electronic channels such as the internet, e-mail, fax, or telephone.

Empowerment   Provision of official authority or legal power to a subordinate to promote self-actualization or influence.

End-user   The person or entity to finally consume a product or service.

E-procurement   Online purchasing.

Equity   The money value of a property or of an interest in a property in excess of claims or liens against it; a risk interest or ownership right in property; the net investment of owners or stockholders in a business.

ESOP (Employee Shared Ownership Position)   A method of compensating employees with shares of a company's stock.

Esprit d'corps   Promotion of team spirit to build harmony and unity within the organization.

Expatriate   An individual who leaves one's native country to work and live elsewhere and then returns to the home country after one's assignment.

Expense-plus approach   In budgeting, estimating the sales levels required to cover expenses and make a profit.

Exposure   The number of times a message or photo is viewed by the public across all media.

Extended stay   A hotel stay of seven or more nights.

Feasibility study   The methods and techniques used to examine technical and cost data to determine the economic potential and the practicality of a project application.

Feeder market   The geographic locations that "feed" their business to a business entity.

Flat organization   A firm with several subordinates reporting to one supervisor.

Focus group   A qualitative market research technique in which a group of participants of common demographics, attitudes, or purchase patterns are led through a discussion of a particular topic by a trained moderator.

Formal structure   An organization governed by written and enforced rules, policies, and procedures.

Four As   In communications strategy, awareness, attitude influence, action-causing behavior, and action resulting in consumption.

Four Cs   Consumer wants and needs, costs to satisfy needs, convenience to buy, and communications.

Four Ps   Product, price, place, and promotion.

Franchise   A continuing relationship in which the franchisor provides a licensed privilege to the franchisee(s) to do business, and offers assistance in organizing, training, merchandising, marketing, and managing in return for a consideration. A form of business by which the owner (franchisor) of a product, service, or method obtains distribution through affiliated dealers (franchisees).

Front loading   An attempt to provide adequate budgets for short-term projects at the expense of long-term projects which will be under-funded. It is an attempt to delay the acknowledgment of a potential cost overrun. It is often the result of inadequate or unrealistic negotiated contract target costs.

GAP analysis   The difference between projected outcomes and desired outcomes. In product development, the gap is frequently measured as the difference between expected and desired revenues or profits from currently planned new products if the corporation is to meet its objectives. Also, the difference in total funding needed for a proposal and the amount of funding already made available.

GDS (global distribution system)   A computerized reservation network through which users, travel agents, airline employees, or travelers view data on a wide range of travel services.

Globalization   The move toward a world market, a worldwide investment environment, and the integration of national capital markets.

Grid concept   A tool that views the present market, future markets, and competitive conditions and allows the user to gain a perspective on products and services through the evaluation process.

Heavy user   A frequent purchaser or repetitive user of a product or service.

Hierarchy   The highest to lowest rank of the body of persons in authority usually beginning with the CEO and board of directors in a corporate entity.

Horizontal integration   The acquisition or ownership of other operators at the same producer or processing level in the supply chain.

Hub and spoke   The model created by travelers that use one location as a home or hub, then venture to other destinations for one-day trips to tour other areas.

Illiberality   Threats to an organization from external forces.

Image   A popular conception (as of a person, institution, or nation) projected especially through the mass media.

Incentives   Rewards to customers to stimulate purchases. Also, rewards for sales personnel who reach predetermined sales objectives.

Independent   One who is not bound by or definitively committed to a particular brand or company.

Inside micro approach   A budgeting method that utilizes the sales history and projects a three-year trend line.

Intermediary   An individual or entity that goes between a product or service and the customer; for example, a travel agent.

Inverted pyramid   An organizational concept that inverts the traditional organization chart by placing the customer and/or customer contact personnel at the top and the CEO and board of directors at the bottom of the hierarchy.

Itinerary   The route of a journey or tour or the proposed outline of one.

Joint venture   A company established for the cooperation of two or more companies in accomplishing a specific task.

Labor importation   The introduction into one country of employees from other countries.

Labor relations   The organizational function whose role is to work with and negotiate with unions.

Laddering   A probing technique, used in one-on-one sessions and focus groups, designed to delve into the real reasons for participants' attitudes and behavior toward a topic.

Lease buy-back   A transaction that involves the sale of some property, and an agreement by the seller to lease the property back from the buyer after the sale.

Leverage   The use of debt financing or of the rise or fall of an investment at a proportionally greater amount than comparable investments.

Liability   A financial obligation, or the cash outlay that must be made at a specific time to satisfy the contractual terms of such an obligation.

Limited partnership   A partnership that includes one or more partners who have limited liability.

Linkages   Referrals and connections to other sites on the internet.

Load factor   The number of seats occupied as a percentage of total seats/capacity in an airline vehicle.

Management company   A company that manages hotels for owners, typically in return for a combination of fees and a share of the revenues.

Management contract   A written agreement between an owner and an operator of a hotel by which the owner employs the operator as an agent who assumes full responsibility for operating the hotel.

Managerial style   The motivational techniques and personalities of a manager defined by the manager's daily actions with employees and peers.

Mapping   Utilizing multidimensional models based on quantitative and qualitative research to position products/brands/attributes against competitors in the marketplace.

Market assessment   An evaluation of a market to establish its viability for business entry or other actions.

Marketing mix   The mix of the various marketing weapons or disciplines, such as price or promotions.

Media relations   The relationship generated with the print and broadcast media by an organization and its spokespersons.

Milestone   A key date, occurrence, or goal that is vital to a strategic plan as well as measurable.

Mission statement   The business philosophy; the organization's purpose with reference to its customers, products/services, markets, philosophy, and technology.

Morpho box   A matrix tool that breaks a product down by needs met and technology components, allowing for targeted analysis and idea creation.

Multinational   A firm that operates in more than one country.

Negative lease   A situation in which the leasee is not generating a profit due to the terms of the lease in relationship to the performance of the asset.

Niche positioning   Establishing as a goal to target and serve a small segment of the market.

No-show   A participant who registers and is confirmed, but does not come. (Facilities compensate for no-shows by overbooking.)

Outside macro approach   A sales budgeting method that establishes a quantifiable sales target percentage increase based on the total market/category trend for the next three years.

Outsourcing   Purchasing a significant percentage of intermediate components from outside suppliers.

Partnership selling   A sales method popular in the 1990s in which the sales representative views the customer as a partner in defining product or service needs and delivery thereof.

PCDs   Personal communications devices.

Penetration   The degree of the market share held by a given firm or product.

Per diem   The daily amount allowed for travel-related expenses (hotels, meals, etc.) by organizations.

Perception   A mental image.

Perks   Items received for purchase or rental of a product or service.

PIMS (profit impact of marketing strategy)   Research that confirms the thesis that perceived quality improves market share and profitability for brands.

Platform   The item-by-item list of things that directly support an ad proposition.

Points of encounter   All instances of interface with the customer or potential customer.

Policy   A high-level overall plan embracing the general goals and acceptable procedures of an organization.

POP (point of purchase)   The location at which collateral materials such as tabletop cards and posters are purchased in stores, hotel rooms, restaurants, and the like.

POS (point of sale)   The point at which the customer transaction is consummated. Also, the point at which data about the customer and transaction are collected for analytical purposes and management information.

Positioning   The relationship of your product or service offering in relationship to all others.

Price points   Specific levels of pricing at which sales may be stimulated to increase or the points at which price increases begin to impact sales negatively.

Pricing   Setting the price for a product or service, which may include analysis of costs, competing products, channels of distribution, the aspirations of the market, and how the company wants to position its product in the minds of customers.

Prioritization   In database marketing, the ranking of targets that are most likely to purchase.

Proactive selling   The seller initiates contact with a prospective customer.

Product attributes   The positive elements related to a product, for example, durability.

Product branding   The name given to a product.

Product hybrid   A variation on a base product.

Product life cycle   The stages a product goes through, from starting out as a new product, to perhaps being adopted only by innovators, to increased adoption and acceptance by more customers, to maturity, to sales decline. The four stages of the life cycle are: introduction, growth, maturity, and decline.

Product tiering   The availability of additional product of different price or service levels, for example, hotels or inns under the same brand.

Proposition   The strongest factual statement one can make on behalf of one's product/service.

Psychographic   Relating to the differences between people in terms of lifestyle, social class, and personality; especially important in determining a target market and for pursuing a marketing plan.

Publicity   One facet of public relations, consisting of brand mentions in the media, positive or negative.

Public relations   The marketing communications weapon that reaches a target audience with created messages.

Pyramiding   Offering a variety of prices from which consumers may select their choice; may include the opportunity to sell up or sell down.

Quality   The collection of attributes which when present in a product means the product has conformed to or exceeded customer expectations.

Ratio analysis   A tool for expressing relationships between a firm's accounting numbers and their trends over time that analysts use to establish values and evaluate risks.

Reactive selling   The buyer initiates the contact and the seller responds.

REIT (real estate investment trust)   Investment in real estate or loans secured by real estate and issue shares in such investments. REITs are not subject to income taxes but must pay out 95 percent of income in the form of dividends to shareholders.

Rep agreement   An agreement to purchase from one particular representative in return for positive service from that representative.

Repeat factor   The measurement of brand loyalty as indicated by the percentage of customers who are repeat purchasers.

Retention   The ability to retain customers for future business.

Revenue management   A business practice that can basically be described as a way for a business to maximize revenue, and thereby profits, by selling its products to the right customer at the right price at the right time.

REVPAC (revenue per available customer)   Revenue per available customer; an integral component of measuring long-term customer value.

REVPAR (revenue per available room)   Revenue per available room; used in evaluating the performance of a lodging firm.

RFI   Request for information.

RFP   Request for proposal.

ROAM (return on assets managed)   The return on assets managed, a concept utilized by companies that manage others' assets under a contract.

ROI (return on investment)   "Payback time"—the amount of time it takes to get one's money back after investing it in a project.

ROIC (return on invested capital)   A measure of financial performance and a financial performance forecasting tool.

Royalty fee   A fee paid (usually a percentage of sales) by a franchisee to a franchisor for use of the brand and all elements associated with that brand.

Saturation   The supplying of a market with as much of a product as it will absorb.

Segmentation   The process of dividing the consuming market into manageable segments with common characteristics.

Service   A product, such as an airline flight or an insurance policy, that is intangible or at least substantially so. If totally intangible, it is exchanged directly from producer to user, cannot be transported or stored, and is instantly perishable. Service delivery usually involves customer participation in some important way. Services cannot be sold in the sense of ownership transfer, and they have no title of ownership.

Simultaneous input/inventory control   The net result of a reservation's impact on inventory through global networks that operate in microseconds to adjust inventory data.

Six Sigma   An organizational and operational concept based on rigorous and focused goals and strategies, including proven quality principles and techniques.

Slippage   (1) The factor of those people who purchase a product with the intent of claiming a promotion reward for such purchase (e.g., sending for a refund, receiving a premium, or redeeming a coupon) who fail to fulfill this intent; (2) the ratio between such purchases and purchases by those people who claim such a reward; usually stated as a percentage of total purchases.

Stakeholders   People who have some interest in a business.

Strategic planning   Of or relating to the vision, mission, values, objectives, goals, and strategies of the organization's future state.

SWOT   Strengths, weaknesses, opportunities, and threats.

SWOT analysis   An analysis for the purpose of aligning one's internal strengths with external opportunities and conversely identifying important threats and ensuring that these external threats are not focused on one's weaknesses in such a way that one will fail commercially.

Symbols   Letters or pictures used to identify companies and their brands.

Target market   The most likely purchasers of one's product.

Team management   Several managers working together for a common task.

Time management   The skill of being able to organize and allocate time to activities, situations, or tasks so as to use time effectively and achieve the required results without wasting time or being waylaid.

TMS (travel management system)   A system to arrange travel services for individuals or companies, including reservation of accommodations. A TMS could be a travel management center, commercial ticket office, electronic travel management system, or other commercial method of arranging travel.

TQM (total quality management)   A business improvement philosophy that comprehensively and continuously involves all of an organization's functions in improvement activities.

Transnational   A corporate business that has transcended its national roots and identity and become multinational with facilities in many countries and no overriding feeling of obligation or loyalty to any one of them. Such companies typically move their production facilities from nation to nation in response to labor costs and tax advantages. As a result, they are generally independent and beyond the control of any one national political system. Transnational corporations have had a major impact on previously isolated indigenous societies.

Turnover   The amount of time it takes to fill a newly vacated room or table.

Value   Any principle to which a person or company adheres with some degree of emotion. It is one of the elements that enter into formulating a strategy.

Vertical integration   The acquisition or ownership of operations at different and usually sequential levels of the supply chain, anywhere from raw materials to end customers.

Vision   An act of imagining, guided by both foresight and informed discernment, that reveals the possibilities as well as the practical limits of new product development. It depicts the most desirable future state of a product or organization.

Visual training   A method of training using video, diagrams, and/or visual displays, utilized for employees who cannot read and understand the language in use.

Volume   A measure of units sold expressed within a given time frame (hourly, daily, monthly, etc.).

Bibliography

Aaker, David A. (1996). *Building Strong Brands*. New York: Free Press.
——— (1991). *Managing Brand Equity*. New York: Free Press.
Arnold, David (1992). *The Handbook of Brand Management*. Reading, MA: Addison Wesley.
Berrigan, John, & Finkbeiner, Carl (1992). *Segmentation Marketing: New Methods for Capturing Business Markets*. New York: HarperBusiness.
Berry, Leonard L., & Parasuraman, A. (1991). *Marketing Services: Computing through Quality*. New York: Free Press.
Block, Tamara B., & Robinson, William A. (1994). *Sales Promotion Handbook*, 8th ed. Chicago: Dartnell.
Bogart, Leo (1967). *Strategy in Advertising*. New York: Harcourt, Brace and World.
Chase, Cochrane, & Barash, Kenneth L. *Marketing Problem Solver*. Radnor, PA: Chilton.
Clancy, Kevin J., & Shulman, Robert S. (1991). *The Marketing Revolution: A Radical Manifesto for Dominating the Marketplace*. New York: HarperBusiness.
Cravens, David W. (1987). *Strategic Marketing*, 2nd ed. Homewood, IL: Richard D. Irwin.
Drucker, Peter (1974). *Management—Tasks, Responsibilities, Practices*. New York: Heineman.
Feig, Barry (1993). *The New Products Workshop: Hands-On Tools for Developing Winners*. New York: McGraw-Hill.
Gottschalk, Jack A. (1993). *Crisis Response*. Detroit: Visible Ink Press.
Hayden, Catherine (1986). *The Handbook of Strategic Expertise*. New York: Free Press.
Holloway, Robert, & Hancock, Robert (eds.) (1969). *The Environment of Marketing Behavior*, 2nd ed. Lincolnwood, IL: NTC Business Books.
Kotler, Philip (1999). *Kotler on Marketing*. Upper Saddle River, NJ: Prentice Hall.
——— (1972). *Marketing Management*. Upper Saddle River, NJ: Prentice Hall.
Lele, Miland M. (1992) *Creating Strategic Leverage*. New York: Wiley.
Levitt, Theodore (1986). *The Marketing Imagination*. New York: Free Press.

Magrath, Allen J. (1992). *The 6 Imperatives of Marketing: Lessons from the World's Best Companies*. New York: AMACOM.

Manning, Gerald L., & Reece, Barry L. (1998). *Selling Today*. Upper Saddle River, NJ: Prentice Hall.

McKay, Edward S. (1993). *The Marketing Mystique*, rev. ed. New York: AMACOM.

McNeill, Daniel, & Freiberger, Paul (1993). *Fuzzy Logic: The Discovery of a Revolutionary Computer Technology and How It Is Changing Our World*. New York: Simon & Schuster.

Michalko, Michael (1991). *Tinkertoys: A Handbook of Business Creativity for the '90's*. Berkeley, CA: Ten Speed Press.

Myers, James H., & Tauber, Edward (1997). *Market Structure Analysis*. Chicago: American Marketing Association.

Nykiel, Ronald A. (1998). *Marketing Your City: U.S.A.* Binghamton, NY: Haworth Hospitality.

——— (1998). *Points of Encounter*. Kingston, NY: Amarcor.

——— (1997). *Marketing in the Hospitality Industry*, 3rd ed. East Lansing, MI: Educational Institute of the American Hotel and Motel Association.

——— (1994). *You Can't Lose if the Customer Wins*. New York: Berkeley.

——— (1992). *Keeping Customers in Good Times and Bad*. Stamford, CT: Longmeadow Press.

Parmerlee, David (1992). *Developing Successful Marketing Strategies*. Lincolnwood, IL: NTC Business Books.

Posch, Robert J., Jr. (1988). *Marketing and the Law*. Upper Saddle River, NJ: Prentice Hall.

Rapp, Stand, & Collins, Tom (1988). *MaxiMarketing: The New Direction in Advertising, Promotion and Marketing Strategy*. New York: New American Library.

Ray, Michael, & Myers, Rochelle (1986). *Creativity in Business*. Garden City, NJ: Doubleday.

——— (1993). *The 22 Immutable Laws of Marketing: Violate Them at Your Own Risk!* New York: HarperBusiness.

——— (1981). *Positioning: The Battle for Your Mind*. New York: McGraw-Hill.

Reis, Al, & Trout, Jack (1986). *Marketing Warfare*. New York: McGraw-Hill.

Richey, Terry (1994). *The Marketer's Visual Tool Kit*. New York: AMACOM.

Schwartz, Peter (1991). *The Art of the Long View: Planning for the Future in an Uncertain World*. New York: Doubleday Currency.

Sherlock, Paul (1991). *Rethinking Business-to-Business Marketing*. New York: Free Press.

Summer, J. R. (1985). *Improve Your Marketing Techniques: A Guide for Hotel Managers and Caterers*. London: Northwood Books.

Tregoe, Benjamin B., & Zimmerman, John W. (1980). *Management Strategy*. New York: Simon & Schuster.

U.S. Government Printing Office (1995). *Directory of National Trade Associations of Businessmen*. Washington, DC: GPO.

Vavra, Terry G. (1992). *Aftermarketing: How to Keep Customers for Life through Relationship Marketing.* Homewood, IL: Business One Irwin.

Wilson, Aubrey (1992). *New Directions in Marketing: Business-to-Business Strategies for the 1990's.* Lincolnwood, IL: NTC Business Books.

Yesawich, Peter (2000). Remarks at UCLA Investment Conference, Los Angeles.

Index